T0375649

# Authentic Christianity

## Studies in 1 John

Richard W. Tow

WESTBOW
PRESS®
A DIVISION OF THOMAS NELSON
& ZONDERVAN

WestBow Press books may be ordered through booksellers or by contacting:

WestBow Press
A Division of Thomas Nelson & Zondervan
1663 Liberty Drive
Bloomington, IN 47403
www.westbowpress.com
1 (866) 928-1240

ISBN: 978-1-9736-4595-5 (sc)
ISBN: 978-1-9736-4596-2 (hc)
ISBN: 978-1-9736-4594-8 (e)

Library of Congress Control Number: 2018913773

Print information available on the last page.

WestBow Press rev. date: 12/15/2018

In a time when biblical literacy is waning and values are less than absolute, *Authentic Christianity* is a helpful and needful book for today's church members—and attenders. Consisting of thirty chapters, a conclusion, and bibliography, it moves through the 1st Epistle of John segment by segment, mining biblical guidelines and blessings at every corner. A Scripture index also is provided making it even more useful. As the author states in the conclusion: "The purpose of this book is to call us, the church, back to the biblical criteria for assurance of salvation, as taught by the Apostle John in this epistle."

*Ben Aker, PhD*
*Professor Emeritus of NT and Exegesis*
*Assemblies of God Theological Seminary*

I want this book in the hands of every one of my students and ministry leaders. The church is at a crossroads wherein we are teetering along a slippery slope that has ensnared a generation with a gospel unlike that preached by Christ and His disciples. This book exposes the single greatest obstacle that we have faced in our thirty years of evangelistic ministry to the unbeliever, and that is the under-believer! An unbelieving world finds it nearly impossible to embrace a faith that leaves the convert in much of the same condition that they were before coming to Jesus. Thank you for putting such a work into the hands of the church.

*Pastor Troy D. Bohn*
*Director – Raven Ministries International Training Center*

I highly recommend Dr. Richard Tow's *Authentic Christianity* for pastors, Christian leaders, Bible students and anyone serious about studying I John in a deeper way. Dr. Tow presents practical ideas and lessons for how 21st Century Christians can protect our hearts and minds against modern day false teachings, how to sincerely and biblically live our lives with love and a clear conscience. Tow's research expounds John's message for the assurance of salvation through the witness of the Holy Spirit, a transformed life, love for our fellow Christians, and a solid belief in Christ as the Son of God. Pastors will find this work an important contribution to their preaching library.

*Dr. Donald W. Eubank*
*Chaplain, Lieutenant Colonel (retired), U.S. Army*
*Endorsing Agent, Military-VA Chaplains, Foursquare Gospel Church*

This book should be required reading for anyone in ministry, from the Sunday school teacher, home group leader, youth pastor, Christian counselor, and the senior pastor. The Church is slowly apostatizing due to its ignorance of what constitutes a genuine biblical believer. We live in a day when rock stars, movie stars and sport celebrities, to name a few, claim to be "born again." John's epistle more than any other New Testament book differentiates between the true child of God and those who are merely claiming to be one. John no doubt vividly recalled Jesus words, "Not everyone who says unto Me, 'Lord, Lord', will enter the kingdom of heaven. . ." John's bottom line is "These things I have written . . . in order that you may know that you have eternal life." Find out what John means by "know." It's a matter of life or death.

*David Ravenhill, Author and Itinerant Teacher.*
*Siloam Springs, Arkansas.*

*This book is dedicated to*

*my faithful wife and ministry partner, Jeanie Tow,*
*my local congregation which supported me throughout the process,*
*and the friends, family, and professionals who made this publication possible.*
*Through their wise counsel significant improvements were made.*

*These things I have written to you who believe in the name of the Son of God, that you may know that you have eternal life, and that you may continue to believe in the name of the Son of God.*

*—1 John 5:13 (NKJV)*

*This is what the LORD says, "Stand at the crossroads and look, ask for the ancient paths, ask where the good way is, and walk in it, and you will find rest for your souls. . . ."*

*—Jeremiah 6:16 (NIV)*

# Contents

# Foreword by Ben Aker

In a time when biblical literacy is waning, and values are less than absolute, *Authentic Christianity* is a helpful and needful book for today's church members—and attenders. Consisting of thirty chapters, a conclusion, and bibliography, it moves through the 1st Epistle of John segment by segment, mining biblical guidelines and blessings at every corner. A Scripture index also is provided making it even more useful. As the author states in the conclusion: "The purpose of this book is to call us, the church, back to the biblical criteria for assurance of salvation, as taught by the Apostle John in this epistle."

This book arises out of a pastoral-congregation context—it was taught and refined through Bible study, providing both interpretation and application. As John's first epistle is packed with fruitful and excellent advice and encouragement, so is this exposition of it. Every verse is included in discussions and comment, the easy verses/topics as well as the difficult ones. For example, "a sin unto death and a sin not unto death." There is a chapter on "Fatherly Affirmations" (Ch. 7), "The Power of a New Nature" (Ch. 14), and one on Idolatry (Ch. 30).

This book can serve any combination of ways. It can be used as a commentary, as a model of preaching through a book, a textbook for a Bible class, and as a source for further research (to name a few).

These are just some reasons I recommend this book.

Ben Aker, PhD
Professor Emeritus of NT and Exegesis
Assemblies of God Theological Seminary

# Preface

*Authentic Christianity* provides a theologically sound exposition of 1 John with relevant, practical application. While careful exegesis has been exercised in the preparation, the goal is pastoral equipping of God's people. Above all else, people need to have eternal life and the assurance of genuine salvation. John's objective in writing this letter is stated in 5:13: "These things I have written to you who believe in the name of the Son of God, that you may know that you have eternal life, and that you may continue to believe in the name of the Son of God" (NKJV).

In this exposition, I have sought to express John's message afresh to today's church. In doing so, I hope to inspire other pastors, teachers, and leaders to do likewise through their giftings. John's epistle invites people into genuine relationship with God that is affirmed by the way they live their lives. Throughout church history millions have professed salvation who were never born again. It's hard to imagine anything more tragic. John's message in this letter answers that problem.

John provides reliable criteria for knowing we have eternal life and helping those we lead to know that as well. *Authentic Christianity* is written to bring those truths alive in the hearts of the readers. Ultimately, only the Holy Spirit can make this happen. My prayer is that God would graciously open our hearts to what the Holy Spirit has inspired John to convey in this epistle. John was dealing with deception in his day, and we deal with it today. In fact, the Bible warns of an exceptional onslaught of deception in the last days (2 Tim. 3:13). The knowledge of what the Apostle John teaches in this letter is a powerful protection against these deceptions.

There are some excellent commentaries that deal with technical issues in 1 John. Those resources are listed in the bibliography and have been carefully examined. I am indebted to those authors and other men and women of God who have enhanced my understanding of the word of God. Sometimes I support my message with their insights. Sometimes I disagree on specific points. I always seek to do that with humility and respect for their wisdom and consecration to the Lord. Even when we don't fully agree, we can learn from one another by rethinking our understanding at a greater depth.

## ASSUMPTIONS

As a conservative Christian, I have written with certain assumptions that I don't take time to defend in this book. The Bible is the inspired word of God, inerrant in the original text. It is God's revelation of the way of redemption and authoritative in its instruction for daily life. Textual criticism is a valid discipline and is at times addressed. However, this analysis does not concern itself with higher criticism, a discipline that often undermines confidence in the authority of Scripture because of its false, naturalistic pre-assumptions.[1] First John was written by the Apostle John who also wrote the Gospel of John, most likely before he wrote this epistle. I also assume John wrote 2 John, 3 John, and Revelation. The discussion of authorship is a valid debate, but it is beyond the scope of this book. The bibliography provides some excellent resources for processing issues of authorship and other matters that are assumed in this work. The date John wrote this letter is probably in the last decade of the first century.[2] John is writing to professed Christians in an orthodox community, and he enjoys deep relationship with those people. John often refers to them lovingly as "little children." The apostle would have been elderly at that time, and he was probably writing from Ephesus.

## STRUCTURE

I have structured this book for easy reading. Each chapter has three sections:

1. the text being examined
2. an expository message adapted from sermons preached to my congregation and
3. chapter endnotes.

Most of the technical issues are addressed in the endnotes so that a consistent flow can be maintained in the expository narrative. As a teacher, I find this information essential, even though I seldom communicate it to my congregation. I want to inform my readers on the exegetical analysis and research behind the exposition. One thing is paramount in this process: fidelity to what the Bible actually says. We need to understand what the Holy Spirit has inspired John to communicate to the church. For the sake of readers who may not be familiar with the Greek language, I have used the transliterated form for these words.

In the endnotes, I often cite other scriptures that come to mind on a subject. These can inspire additional thoughts that a pastor might want to express to his or her congregation. The Holy Spirit leads us to communicate truth that a specific congregation needs at that particular time. As we listen and rely on Him, He brings the exact message needed at that hour. I have also provided a subject and scripture index in this work so that the book can be easily used as a reference resource.

Internal evidence in the epistle suggests that John is fortifying his readers against emerging Gnostic error, especially a denial of the incarnation and doctrines of antinomianism.[3] These warnings are highly relevant today. There are misunderstandings of the grace of God that need to be addressed. There are growing influences of cults like Jehovah's Witness and Christian Science that are fundamentally Gnostic in their heresy. John's epistle provides doctrinal teaching that fortifies believers against such error. Rather than addressing the historical setting of Gnosticism upfront in this book, I deal with it as needed in my exposition of passages. Chapters five, fourteen, and twenty-five provide background information on Gnosticism.

It is common practice to supply an outline of 1 John prior to expounding the text. I chose to discuss that where it most naturally fit in John's teaching. Therefore, a discussion of the structure of 1 John can be found in chapter twenty-three.

## ABBREVIATIONS

My objective is to enlighten the reader in what the Bible teaches. Therefore, I quote and re-quote Scripture often. That is our authority for believing what we believe. The following abbreviations have been used to reference translations of Scripture:

KJV: King James Version
NASB: New American Standard Bible
NIV: New International Version
NKJV: New King James Version
NRSV: New Revised Standard Version.
May God bless your study of His word.

# Endnotes: Preface

1  Robertson McQuilkin, *Understanding and Applying the Bible* (Chicago, IL: Moody Press, 1992), 30–32. Cf. David A. Black and David S. Dockery, eds., *New Testament Criticism & Interpretation* (Grand Rapids: Zondervan, 1991). s. v. "The New Testament, History, and the Historical-Critical Method," by D. A. Hagner, 77–83.

2  Donald Guthrie, *New Testament Introduction,* rev. ed. (Downers Grove, IL: InterVarsity Press, 1990) 879.

3  The word antinomian is from the Greek word *anti* (meaning against) combined with the Greek word *nomos* (meaning law). It is "the view that the gospel renders obedience to the law (*nomos*) unnecessary and even damaging to one hope of salvation." Alan Richardson, ed., *A Dictionary of Christian Theology* (Philadelphia, PA: Westminster Press, 1969) s. v. "Antinomianism," by P. S. Watson, 11.

Chapter 1

# Finding Relational Fulfillment
# 1:1–4

That which was from the beginning, which we have heard, which we have seen with our eyes, which we have looked upon, and our hands have handled, concerning the Word of life — the life was manifested, and we have seen, and bear witness, and declare to you that eternal life which was with the Father and was manifested to us — that which we have seen and heard we declare to you, that you also may have fellowship with us; and truly our fellowship is with the Father and with His Son Jesus Christ. And these things we write to you that your joy may be full.

1 John 1:1-4, NKJV[1]

Expository Message

Are you relationally deprived? How often do you feel isolated and alone? I'm not just talking about when you are literally alone, but even when you're in a crowd. Do you have many acquaintances, yet very few friends? A lot of Christians struggle with loneliness and the depression that often accompanies that loneliness.

The common cure is often self-defeating. People go to social media for relief. They accumulate hundreds of friends on Facebook. Then they see pictures of all the fun those friends are having. Then they wonder even more why their lives are so empty.

Over many years of pastoring, the most common complaint I heard from Christians was, "I have no friends." They weren't saying they didn't know anyone. They were saying, "I don't have people I can open my heart to and receive support. I don't have people I feel free with. I don't have people who know me and affirm me as esteemed and valuable." Research has shown that the more a person uses social media to find relational satisfaction, the less satisfied that person feels in the long run.[2] The relationships in that venue are usually very superficial.

We all know the church should be the answer to this problem. We also know the church, as it is today, is often not the answer. The German philosopher Schopenhauer compared the human race to a bunch of porcupines, huddling together on a cold winter's night. He said,

> The colder it gets outside, the more we huddle together for warmth; but the closer we get to one another, the more we hurt one another with our sharp quills. And in the lonely night of winter eventually we begin to drift apart and wander out on our own and freeze to death in our loneliness.[3]

We know by experience what he's talking about? We have been poked by a few sharp quills, even in church? And we have poked others as well, even if it is often unintentional. So, we need solutions that work. And the Bible offers solutions that work.

## JOHN'S INVITATION TO THE COMMON LIFE

John opens his letter with an invitation: "That which we have seen and heard we declare to you, that you also may have fellowship with us" (1:3). The word translated "fellowship" has a stronger meaning than is generally understood by that English term. The Greek word, *koinōnia*, means to share, participate, or to have in common.[4] Paul used the word when he talked about believers partnering with him in the work of the ministry.[5] He used the word in reference to people sharing material goods with those in need.[6] It includes social activity, but goes deeper than that. It's about the relationship we have with one another in Christ. The New English Bible translates verse 3 as, "What we have seen and heard we declare to you, so that you and we together may share in a common life, that life which we share with the Father and his Son Jesus Christ." John is inviting people to come into the "common life" we have with the Father through Jesus Christ. When people are truly experiencing the common life that John is talking about, the loneliness and isolation we talked about earlier are resolved.

But what is this common life that John is inviting people to experience? Is it the superficial pew-sitting of the American church? Is it the audience/performance that prevails in modern Christianity? I think it's something much different than that. I think that's why the current church experience leaves people lonely and unsatisfied in their relationships.[7]

To understand the common life John is talking about, we go all the way back into the distant eternity. There we find three persons living in perfect harmony and perfect satisfaction: The Father, Son, and Holy Spirit. Each relates to the other in perfect love. The Trinity abides in a perfect love relationship. The Trinity exists in one common life, a life so united by love that there is only one God, yet three persons. To understand the common life John is referring to, we must first understand it as the life that the Trinity abides in. Salvation is an invitation to come into that life through Christ. In the new birth we become partakers of the divine nature.[8] We become a part of the family of God.[9]

Notice in verse 1 how this common life is centered on Jesus: "That which was from the beginning, which we have heard, which we have seen with our eyes, which we have looked upon, and our hands have handled, concerning the Word [*Logos*] of life." Who is the Logos (Word) in Scripture? It's Jesus, isn't it?[10] He was with the Father in eternity. He was active in creation. John makes the divinity of Jesus very clear in the opening of his gospel. John 1:1–3 declares, "In the beginning was the Word, and the Word was with God, and *the Word was God*. The same was in the beginning with God. All things were made by him; and without him was not any thing made that was made" (emphasis mine, KJV). If we are to enter into life, we must embrace Jesus for who He really is. He is more than a teacher. He is more than a prophet. He is God manifested in the flesh.[11] Now in John 1:4 we're told that the life—the common life we are invited to enjoy—comes to us through Christ. "In him was life; and the life was the light of men" (KJV). For mankind, there is only one source of eternal life: Jesus. His life brings light to our darkness. His life is the salvation we need.

Jesus is the centerpiece of our common life. In Colossian 1:16–18 Paul wrote, "For by him were all things created, that are in heaven, and that are in earth, visible and invisible, whether they be thrones, or dominions, or principalities, or powers: all things were created by him, and for him: And he is before all things, and by him all things consist. And he is the head of the body, the church: who is the beginning, the firstborn from the dead; that in all things he might have the preeminence" (KJV). In all things, He must be given the preeminence. Any group of people who won't give Jesus the preeminence will not enjoy the abundant life God has provided for them. It's not just a matter of doctrine, although that's essential; as a practical matter, our love, adoration, and purpose must center on Christ. He is the head of the body, the church. Every crown falls at His feet. He is the Alpha and Omega. He is the Beginning and the End.[12] I am my Beloved's and He is mine. There is salvation in no other name. There is life in no other name.[13]

The globalists present noble objectives. They say they want to make the world a better place to live. They want to end poverty. They want to end wars and bring peace to mankind. But when it comes to Jesus, they also say, "We will not have this man to reign over us."[14] Their rebellion is an affront to God. Their pursuit of peace is futile without the Prince of Peace. It is an antichrist system doomed to failure.

The error we must avoid is even more subtle than that of the globalists. It's the error the nation of Israel fell into. They kept a form of godliness. They kept their religious services. But their lives were not really devoted to God. They lived in pursuit of their own desires and ambitions. They drew near to God with their lips, but their hearts were far from Him.[15] To give Jesus the preeminence, we live to please Him.[16] We come together to love and adore Him. We worship from the heart. We enter into His gates with thanksgiving and into His courts with praise. We acknowledge Jesus as King of Kings and Lord of Lords. The common life John is talking about begins with Jesus and our relationship with Him. He is the source of the life we're talking about.

So, John says in verse 3 of our text, "And truly our fellowship [our common life] is with the Father and with His Son Jesus Christ." Make no mistake about it; this is first and foremost a fellowship with the Father and His Son Jesus Christ. It's not purely horizontal. It's not a humanistic club. It starts and ends with God. Are you interested in that?

John gives this invitation on the basis of his own experience. He's not talking in the abstract. He has been with the Lord Jesus. He knows what he's talking about. "That which was from the beginning, which we have heard, which we have seen with our eyes, which we have looked upon, and our hands have handled, concerning the Word of life." God was manifested in the flesh. We talked with Him. We touched Him and hugged Him. We heard Him speak. We saw Jesus in the flesh with our own eyes. Verses 2–3: "The life [the eternal life of God, the life of highest quality, not just existence, but life lived in the love of God, the common life we're being invited into] was manifested, and we have seen, and bear witness, and declare to you that eternal life which was with the Father and was manifested to us — that which we have seen and heard we declare to you."

Evangelism is about inviting people to participate in the life of God. It is about getting your sins forgiven. It is about a legal acquittal and declaration of right standing with God.[17] But if we stop there, we have stopped short of what this great salvation is all about. It is also about participating in the common life of God and His people. A core weakness in the American church is the limited understanding of what salvation is. Salvation is much more than a ticket to heaven. It is much more than avoiding hell. It is certainly more than using God to get the things you want. It is coming into the mutuality of life with God and His people.

John is speaking from experience. He invites people into something he is personally enjoying. That's a key to evangelism. We must experience first what we're inviting others to come into. John says in verse 3, "That which we have seen and heard we declare to you." When you're talking to unbelievers, talk with them about what you have seen and heard. Share with them your personal testimony. Tell them about God's goodness and mercy in your life. Then invite them into the common life.

There is a joy in participating in the common life of God. John even says that he declares these things and makes this invitation so that others may enjoy what he is enjoying. First John 1:4: "And these things we write to you that your joy may be full."

## EARLY CHURH'S EXPERIENCE IN THE COMMON LIFE

I want to show you in the Bible a picture of people living experientially in this common life. Acts 2:1 begins with this phrase: "And when the day of Pentecost was fully come, they were all with one accord in one place" (KJV). The 120 were at peace with one another and in unity with one another. That statement would not be surprising to me, if it were made after they were filled with the Holy Spirit. I have had times, and you most likely have as well, when the love of God was so poured out in my heart, that I just loved everybody. It was a fruit of the Spirit just flowing out of me. It came as a result of a fresh infilling of the Holy Spirit. I know that this common life is possible when we are filled with the Holy Spirit. And this is a prerequisite for living experientially in the joy of Christian koinōnia, the common life in the Spirit. Ephesians 5:18 tells us to be continually filled with the Spirit.[18] There is no doubt in my mind that after the Spirit fell on the 120, they were in one accord. But Acts 2:1 says they were in that state before the outpouring of the Spirit. Perhaps there is an indication there of something needing to happen in preparation for revival. Perhaps getting things completely right with brothers and sisters in Christ prepares us to receive an outpouring of the Spirit.

But the question on my mind is how they got in that attitude of heart, prior to the Holy Spirit falling on them. Maybe it was their interaction with Jesus during the forty days after His resurrection. At least five things happened during that time. (1) They all got focused on the Lord. They were all looking to Jesus, the author and finisher of our faith. Keeping Jesus as the center is one key to Christian unity. (2) His resurrection filled them with hope and expectation. When Christians become discouraged, they tend to fight with each other more. Maybe they're trying to figure out why things are as they are and are tempted to blame one another. Vision and hope are powerful influences toward unity. (3) Jesus gave them a common cause when He gave the Great Commission. They had been given a common purpose and command. (4) Jesus had been teaching them during that forty days, and the subject of love was surely addressed. (5) They had been praying together for ten days straight. Nothing unites Christians like praying together. It can't be superficial; but when Christians spend time praying with and for one another, they naturally unite. Maybe somewhere in all this is an explanation of how they got to that state of unity; and maybe there is something there for how we, as God's people, live in unity with one another.

At its core, our unity is a simple reality that is not dependent on how we behave. When you received the Lord, your spirit was joined to the Holy Spirit. When I received the Lord, my spirit was joined to the Holy Spirit. We are ontologically united with all believers whether we act like it or not. First Corinthians 6:17 says, "But he that is joined unto the Lord is one spirit" (KJV). Our union with one another is very real because of our union with the Holy Spirit. Ephesians 4:4–6 says, "There is one body, and one Spirit, even as ye are called in one hope of your calling; One Lord, one faith, one baptism, one God and Father of all, who is above all, and through all, and in you all" (KJV). However, living in that experientially, on a daily basis, is another story. We have an adversary whose key strategy is to divide and conquer. We have to walk in the Spirit and not in the flesh, if we are to keep this unity functioning in our relationships with each other. In Ephesians 4:1–3 Paul wrote, "I, therefore, the prisoner of the Lord, beseech you to walk worthy of the calling with which you were called, with all lowliness and gentleness, with longsuffering, bearing with one another in love, endeavoring to keep the unity of the Spirit in the bond of peace" (NKJV). Are you endeavoring to keep the unity of the Spirit in the bond of peace? Are you a cuddly bear or are you a porcupine? Do you have sharp quills that make it hard for people to get close to you? These are practical issues we all have to deal with.

Now, look with me at a group of people who are living in this common life in all its richness. These people in Acts 2:1 are in one accord. They are filled with the Spirit of love. Others are evangelized and joined to their group. And at the end of Acts 2 we see what their lives looked like. Acts 2:41–42: "So then, those who had received his word were baptized; and that day there were added about three thousand souls. They were continually devoting themselves to the apostles' teaching and to fellowship, to the breaking of bread and to prayer" (KJV).

Luke lists four activities that characterized their lives. They continued steadfastly in these activities. It defined the common life they were experiencing together. (1) The apostles' teaching: The word of God was primary in their gatherings. (2) Fellowship: This is the same word we dealt with in 1 John—koinōnia—the intimacy and caring for one another. (3) The breaking of bread: Their fellowship included meals together and the Lord's Table.[19] As evangelicals, we don't place the emphasis on the Communion Table that the Scripture gives it. That ordinance keeps us ever mindful of the essentials: the Lord's death, resurrection, and second coming. It also reminds us of the common life we share in Christ.[20] That's why it is to be a time of introspection in which we make sure our relationships with others are right. (4) Prayer: "My house," Jesus said, "shall be called a house of prayer." Not an entertainment center, not a social center, but a house of prayer![21] No prayer means no power to live this common life! Living the common life is characterized by these four activities.[22] These are the four pillars of a healthy church. When these are neglected, the life of the church suffers.

"And fear came upon every soul: and many wonders and signs were done by the apostles. And all that believed were together, and had all things common; And sold their possessions and goods, and parted them to all men, as every man had need" (Act 2:43-45, KJV). All that generosity was purely voluntary; it flowed out of the love the Holy Spirit put in their hearts.[23] It wasn't communism where people are made to do this. What this reflects is the love and care they had for one another as they lived this common life. Verses 46–47 says, "And they, continuing daily with one accord in the temple, and breaking bread from house to house, did eat their meat with gladness and singleness of heart, Praising God, and having favour with all the people. And the Lord added to the church daily such as should be saved" (KJV). I don't think those people were suffering from the loneliness and isolation that is so common in the church today. They lived life together in a healthy, fulfilling way because of the love that was shed abroad in their hearts by the Holy Spirit.[24]

My struggle is this: Why don't we experience something more like that today? What is robbing us of fully enjoying this common life given to us in Christ? I don't think you can orchestrate it through human means. God has to shed His love abroad in our hearts to make it work. The vertical relationship with God is absolutely essential for it to happen. When it is happening, we feel connected and loved. We enjoy being with our brothers and sisters in the Lord. The problems we talked about at the beginning of this chapter are resolved. But maintaining that is not as easy as it sounds. What can we do to at least move in that direction?

1. We can pray. We can ask God to fill us with His Spirit. We can ask God to shed His love abroad in our hearts. We can ask God to enable us to love our neighbors as ourselves.
2. We can pray *for* one another and we can pray *with* one another. Prayer was one of the key activities in Acts 2:42 associated with this kind of common life.
3. We can be givers, rather than takers. The greatest hindrance to a community of love is selfishness. James 3:16: "For where envying and strife is, there is confusion and every evil work" (KJV). There is a dying to self that is necessary (Matt. 16:24–25) for Christians to enjoy all these benefits.
4. We can endeavor to keep the unity of the Spirit in the bond of peace. We can be good forgivers. We can walk in the Spirit. We can be peacemakers.
5. We can devote ourselves to "the apostles' teaching and to fellowship, to the breaking of bread and to prayer."

Even if we're not getting all the answers today, maybe the Lord would give each of us something that helps us move in the right direction. What would the Lord have you to do? Is there an attitude issue in your heart that needs to be addressed? Is there a person who needs to be forgiven? Is there a prayer that needs to be prayed?

# Endnotes: Chapter 1

1    In this book, once a verse is quoted, any subsequent quotes of that verse in the chapter are being quoted in the same version unless indicated otherwise.

2    Maria Konnikova, "How Facebook Makes Us Unhappy," *The New Yorker,* September 10, 2013. Retrieved Aug. 4, 2017 at http://www.newyorker.com/tech/elements/how-facebook-makes-us-unhappy.

3    Amit Chowdhry, "Research Links Heavy Facebook And Social Media Usage To Depression," *Forbes,* April 30, 2016. Retrieved August 4, 2017 at https://www.forbes.com/sites/amitchowdhry/2016/04/30/study-links-heavy-facebook-and-social-media-usage-to-depression/#7c02ecc44b53.

4    Arthur Schopenhauer, as quoted, in Edward Rowell, ed., *Fresh Illustrations for Preaching & Teaching from Leadership Journal* (Grand Rapids: Baker Books, 2000), s. v. "Loneliness," by Wayne Brouwer, 135.

5    Joseph Thayer, *Thayer's Greek Lexicon,* 1896, s. v. "NT:2842." Accessed in Electronic Database: Biblesoft 2000.

6    Gal. 2:9. Luke 5:10 uses a form of the word in reference to the fishing partnership of Peter, James, and John. 9 2 Cor. 9:13.

7    I thank God for the good that is being done in the American church across denominational lines. With the decline of Christianity in America, we must, however, acknowledge that something more is needed.

8    2 Pet. 1:4.

9    John's chief concern in writing this letter is that his readers would be born of the Spirit and live in koinōnia with God and his people. In 1 John 5:13 he restates his purpose for writing this letter.

10   Spiros Zodhiates writes, "The word Logos in John 1:1, 14; 1 John 1:1 stands for the preincarnate Christ. . . ." Spiros Zodhiates, *The Complete Word Study Dictionary: New Testament,* 1992 (Iowa Falls, IA: World Bible Publishers, Inc., 1994) 925.

11   In these opening verses, John is not only emphasizing the divinity of Jesus, but also His full humanity. Gnostic error was already beginning to emerge, denying the incarnation. Heresies against sound Christology were taking root, and John is confronting the problem with his personal knowledge of Christ. It would be appropriate to deal with the incarnation more fully in this first chapter. However, I have chosen to deal with it later in this book, especially in chapters 18 and 25.

12   Cf. Eph. 5:23; Col. 2:19; Rev. 1:8, 11; 4:10; 21:6; 22:13.

13   Cf. 1 John 5:12; Acts 4:12.

14   Cf. Luke 19:14, KJV.

15   Cf. Isa. 29:13; Cf. Isa. 1:10–17; Amos 5:21–24.

16   Cf. 2 Cor. 5:9.

17  Cf. Rom. 3:24–28; 5:1; 8:1; Gal. 2:16. Luther's revelation of justification by faith has asserted a powerful and positive impact on the Protestant Church. These truths must be proclaimed, but not to the exclusion of other biblical truths about salvation.

18  In Eph. 5:18, *plērousthe* (be filled) is in the present tense, indicating habitual, continual action.

19  We have a clearer separation of these today, probably in response to Paul's teaching in 1 Cor. 11.

20  The word translated communion in 1 Cor. 10:16 is koinōnia as a reference to the Lord's table. Second Cor. 13:14 refers to the communion (koinōnia) of the Holy Spirit.

21  Matt. 21:13, KJV.

22  For a fuller teaching on Acts 2:42, see my message entitled, "Life-styles of the Revived & Fervent in Spirit," available at https://www.sermoncentral.com/sermons/life-styles-of-the-revived-fervent-in-spirit-richard-tow-sermon-on-love-83200.

23  Peter's comment to Ananias in Acts 5:4 makes this abundantly clear.

24  Cf. Rom. 5:5, KJV.

# CHAPTER 2

# Fatal Error
# 1:5–7

This is the message which we have heard from Him and declare to you, that God is light and in Him is no darkness at all. If we say that we have fellowship with Him, and walk in darkness, we lie and do not practice the truth. But if we walk in the light as He is in the light, we have fellowship with one another, and the blood of Jesus Christ His Son cleanses us from all sin.

1 John 1:5-7, NKJV

Expository Message

In this passage, the Apostle John confronts a fatal error; one that is widespread in our churches today. The error essentially says, "You can have your cake and eat it too." It is popular because it appeals to the flesh. It avoids the crucified life. It side-steps denying oneself and taking up a cross.[1] It is a discipleship that lets me go my own way, yet soothes my conscience with a little dose of religion every Sunday morning.[2] First John 1:6 confronts the error, "If we say that we have fellowship with Him, and walk in darkness, we lie and do not practice the truth." As stated in the previous chapter, the Greek word translated "fellowship" is koinōnia; it refers to the life we share with God and with fellow-believers. It is the common life that we have in Christ. Clearly, this verse is talking about people who claim to be Christians: "If we say we have fellowship with Him." It's not talking about people who live in sin and make no claim to be Christian. It's people who say they know God and are on their way to heaven.

John wrote, "If we say," making a strong distinction between saying and doing. Saying is not enough. Your actions speak louder than your words, as far as God is concerned. James makes the same distinction in his epistle:

> Therefore, get rid of all moral filth and the evil that is so prevalent and humbly accept the word planted in you, which can save you. Do not merely listen to the word, and so deceive yourselves. Do what it says. Anyone who listens to the word but does not do what it says is like someone who looks at his face in a mirror and, after looking at himself, goes away and immediately forgets what he looks like. But whoever looks intently into the perfect law that gives freedom, and continues in it—not forgetting what they have heard, but doing it—they will be blessed in what they do (James 1:21–25, NIV).

The blessing always comes in the doing! When we hear the word, but don't do it, we are in danger of deceiving ourselves. When we claim to be living the life, but really are not living it, we are in a process of deceiving ourselves.

## THE FOUNDATION OF JOHN'S MESSAGE: A REVELATION OF GOD

The foundation for John's message begins with a revelation of God. First John 1:5 says, "This is the message which we have heard from Him and declare to you, that God is light and in Him is no darkness at all." Truth is grounded in who God is. That's why it is absolute. God does not change.[3] His character does not change. He is the Eternal One. Truth is not something relative to the culture. Truth is not one thing in the 19th

Century and something else in the 21st Century. Fashions and fads may come and go, but truth proceeds from who God is, and that never changes.

John's message here begins with the nature of God: God is light. In this epistle John makes two fundamental statements about the nature of God.[4] We find the first one in our text ("God is light"), and the second one is given in 1 John 4:16: "God is love" (NKJV). This second statement is wholeheartedly embraced by people all over the world. They put their own definition of love into that verse. They distort the true meaning of John's statement. But people like the idea that God is love. For most of them it means He is tolerant and indulgent. Biblically, that is not what it means. But they attach that meaning and run with it. The revelation that "God is light" is not so popular, especially when its meaning is rightly explained. God does not compromise His moral excellence.[5] He lives in moral purity because that is who He is. He calls us to moral purity because that is who He is.[6] Walking in darkness is unacceptable because "God is light and in Him is no darkness at all." He has no fellowship with darkness. It's contrary to His nature.

I once had a parishioner come to me with a question. He had apparently been watching too many Star Wars movies. He inquired, "Is there a dark side of God?" The errors of pantheism and of dualism were around long before Star Wars came out. But I'm pretty sure that's where he got the question. I answered him with this verse. "God is light and in Him is no darkness at all" (1:5). Darkness was never in the heart of God. It was birthed in the prideful heart of Lucifer.

The world's concept of God is twisted and distorted for two reasons. First, they have drawn their information from unreliable sources. Their understanding of God has come through secular movies and TV shows. Their gurus are people like Oprah Winfrey and the hosts of Good Morning America. There is revelation available that would clear matters up considerably. The Bible reveals God for who He really is. But you have to read it to get that insight. Secondly, they have not experienced Him for themselves.[7] They have not come to Him in humility and asked to know Him. They have assumed they already know. The world feeds on distorted views of God. That is no surprise, since "the whole world is under the control of the evil one" (1 John 5:19, NIV).

What is more disturbing is the deception in the church. Even in the first century, the Apostle John is dealing with error. "If we say that we have fellowship with Him, and walk in darkness, we lie and do not practice the truth." John is addressing the problem, even as we must address the same problem today.

What has opened the church up to so much error in our day? Relativism is a factor: the abandonment of absolutes. Closely associated with that is pragmatism. We, evangelicals, have filled our pulpits with pragmatists. If it works, it must be right. We begin with the world's measure of success: size and popularity. It's the wrong beginning point! Then denominations turn to methods and techniques for growth. Pastoral conventions should be about seeking God, knowing God, and hearing God; but the agenda often turns to church growth techniques. What can we do to get more numbers? So, we learn about marketing. We hire consultants to give us techniques for raising more funds. We shape the service and the sermon to the tastes of the audience.[8] And we get what we're shooting for. We get people in the building. We get a whole lot of people who are saying they have fellowship with God, but their lifestyles are contrary to His nature. Some are living in sexual immorality. Some lie and cheat on the job. Many are consumed with covetous desires for the things of this world. Somehow these people think they can walk in darkness and have fellowship with God at the same time. How do they come to this conclusion? Too often, pastors avoid the issue and fail to confront the error; even worse, some pastors tell them they can continue in sin that grace may abound.[9]

Often the justification for all this is in the name of staying up with the times. It's no longer politically correct to condemn homosexuality, so maybe we should not say anything about that or just accept it as a personal preference. If we tell the young couples who are living in heterosexual sin to either get married or move out of the house, they might leave the church. I ask the question: what are they getting in the church? Are they being deceived into thinking it's alright? Does that really help them? Are they being led to believe you can walk in that kind of darkness and still enjoy fellowship with God? Is the fellowship you have at your church really biblical koinōnia or is it just a big humanistic club with a religious veneer? John's not pulling any punches. And remember, this is the man known as the Apostle of Love.

"God is light and in Him is no darkness at all." That is John's beginning point. We must begin with who God is. We must begin with a true concept of His nature and will. We don't begin with popular opinion. We don't begin with what the world calls success. We begin with God! God is *light*. That is the standard for our behavior. Light is moral purity and truth. Light is holiness. Some people don't like that word, holiness. They equate it with legalism.[10] Some people say it's an Old Testament concept. No, it is communicated in John's statement, "God is light." Peter says it this way, "But as He who called you is holy, you also be holy in all your conduct, because it is written, 'Be holy, for I am holy'" (1 Pet. 1:15–16, NKJV). Notice how Peter does the same thing as John is doing in our text. He bases his assertion on the nature and character of God. From the platform of God's nature in verse 5, John issues his warning in verse 6.

## THE ERROR: CLAIMING FELLOWSHIP WITH GOD WHILE LIVING IN SIN

The error John confronts is a claim to be in fellowship with God while living an unholy life. It is a common error in our churches today. It is a well-packaged lie that has enough truth in it to make it difficult to untangle. It says I can keep my wicked ways and still inherit eternal life. I can walk in darkness, yet have the common life that God offers in this great salvation. It celebrates the glory of man and gives the creature what he wants. It does this with a distorted message of grace.[11]

Nothing is more precious than the true message of grace. Nothing is so necessary as the grace of God. Paul said, "By the grace of God I am what I am" (1 Cor. 15:10, KJV). Have you experienced the grace of God? Oh, how I love and cherish grace. "Amazing grace how sweet the sound that saved a wretch like me."[12] We will sing of it throughout eternity. "For by grace you have been saved through faith and that not of yourselves, it is the gift of God" (Eph. 2:8, NKJV). Without the grace of God, we get nowhere in the kingdom of God. Without the grace of God, we are doomed to live in our corruption forever. Only by the grace of God do we receive forgiveness of sin. Only by the grace of God are we accepted into the family of God.

Grace, grace, God's grace, grace that will pardon and cleanse within.

16

Grace, grace, God's grace, grace that is greater than all
our sin.[13]

One of the most wonderful words in the Bible is "grace." Out of a
glorious conversion, John Newton wrote:

'Twas grace that taught my heart to fear,
And grace my fears relieved.
How precious did that grace appear
The hour I first believed.[14]

Do you remember the day you first experienced the amazing grace of
God? I am a grace preacher! But the grace we preach must be the grace
revealed in the Bible.

False grace, distorted grace, says I can walk in darkness and enjoy
fellowship with God at the same time. But John has written, "If we say
that we have fellowship with Him, and walk in darkness, we lie and do
not practice the truth." The popular message of grace is one that excuses
our sin because of what Jesus did on the cross. Yes, grace is ours because of
what Jesus did on the cross. But grace does not *excuse* sin. Grace does not
overlook sin. Grace cleanses and conquers sin. First John 1:7: "But if we
walk in the light as He is in the light, we have fellowship with one another,
and the blood of Jesus Christ His Son *cleanses* us from all sin" (emphasis
mine). It does not say grace excuses our sin. It says it cleanses us from it.
Grace does not leave us wallowing in sin like an unclean sow. It takes us
out of the pig pen and puts us on solid ground. It *cleanses* us from all sin.

Any message of grace that makes it feel easier to sin is not biblical grace.
Biblical grace teaches just the opposite of indulgence. Titus 2:11–12 begins,
"For the grace of God that brings salvation." There are some popular
versions of grace that don't bring salvation. Paul is talking here about the
grace of God that brings salvation! That biblical grace "has appeared to all
men, teaching us that, denying ungodliness and worldly lusts, we should
live soberly, righteously, and godly in the present age" (NKJV). What does
biblical grace teach? It teaches us "that, denying ungodliness and worldly
lusts, we should live soberly, righteously, and godly in the present age."
A grace message that teaches us that we don't have to deny ungodliness

and worldly lusts is a false grace. A grace message that minimizes the consequence of sin is a cheap, imitation grace. It is running rampant through the church. It is attractive to the carnal mind. It is one of the most destructive devices Satan has going for him today. And people are flocking to hear the message. They don't analyze it against Scripture. They just like what they hear and keep coming back. Biblical grace will always teach you to "live soberly, righteously, and godly in the present age."

Distorted grace sounds something like this: "You surely will not die.[15] I know the legalist told you that you would surely die in your disobedience. But we're way past all that. We have inside knowledge[16] that tells us we can cross the line without such judgments. The God we serve is a God of love. He would understand. We are standing up against legalism. We are free. The beauty of God's grace is that we're free from the Law." And I say, yes, we are free from the legalistic system of salvation under the Jewish Law, but we are never free to live in disobedience to God.[17] The grace of God teaches us something altogether different than that. "So, if the Son makes you free, you will be free indeed" (John 8:36, NASB). Jesus is not saying that He makes us free to sin without consequence. He is saying, "I'll free you from the bondage of sin." How do I know that? He had just said, "Everyone who commits sin is the slave of sin" (John 8:34. NASB). It's not freedom *to* sin; it's freedom *from* sin!

Distorted, corrupted concepts of grace minimize the consequences of sin. They echo Satan's suggestion: "You surely will not die." They give the false assurance, "God's grace has you covered. Go ahead; it will be fine. You can always just ask forgiveness afterwards." But the word of the Lord was clear. If you eat of that tree, you *will* die. That was the word of the Lord to Adam and Eve. The Serpent questioned such a "harsh," legalistic boundary. Maybe you can cross the line. You may even get some things you really want. He had some "inside knowledge" for her. Here are the Serpent's words in Genesis 3:5: "For God knows that in the day you eat from it your eyes will be opened, and you will be like God, knowing good and evil" (NASB). Crossing God's boundaries didn't seem bad at all once she bought that lie. Eve looked at that tree and saw how attractive it was. She was convinced that it would be pleasant to eat of it. And so, she did. We all know what she got was very different from what the Serpent promised. It's always that way.

Peter talks about false teachers who promise liberty yet are under all kinds of bondage themselves. Second Peter 2:18–19 says, "For when they speak great swelling words of vanity, they allure through the lusts of the flesh, through much wantonness, those that were clean escaped from them who live in error. While they promise them liberty, they themselves are the servants of corruption" (NASB). The promise of the false grace teachers is liberty, freedom from the commandments of God. Using their brand of grace, they tell people they're free to do as they please. But living in corruption brings bondage to that corruption. Nobody outmaneuvers God. "If we say that we have fellowship with Him, and walk in darkness, we lie and do not practice the truth" (1 John 1:6).

Light is a metaphor for truth and moral purity. Darkness is the opposite of that. Darkness is a metaphor for moral corruption. "This is the judgment, that the Light has come into the world, and men loved the darkness rather than the Light, for their deeds were evil. For everyone who does evil hates the Light, and does not come to the Light for fear that his deeds will be exposed. But he who practices the truth comes to the Light, so that his deeds may be manifested as having been wrought in God" (John 3:19-21, NASB). Darkness is equated with practicing evil. Walking in darkness is living a lifestyle contrary to God's character and commandments. Paul provides specific examples of darkness in Ephesians 5:3–12.

But immorality or any impurity or greed must not even be named among you, as is proper among saints; and *there must be no* filthiness and silly talk, or coarse jesting, which are not fitting, but rather giving of thanks. For this you know with certainty, that no immoral or impure person or covetous man, who is an idolater, has an inheritance in the kingdom of Christ and God. Let no one deceive you with empty words, [This is the warning I am giving in this chapter. Don't let false teachers deceive you with empty or vain words.] for because of these things the wrath of God comes upon the sons of disobedience. Therefore do not be partakers with them; for you were formerly darkness, but now you are Light in the Lord; walk as children of

Light (for the fruit of the Light *consists* in all goodness and righteousness and truth), trying to learn what is pleasing to the Lord. Do not participate in the unfruitful deeds of darkness, but instead even expose them; for it is disgraceful even to speak of the things which are done by them in secret (NASB).

As pastors, we are to expose and reprove "the unfruitful deeds of darkness." It's tempting to simply avoid these subjects—to not upset people in the audience. It might reduce the crowd; some of the congregation may not like it and leave. The most common temptation we face is to just stay away from negative subjects—just talk about upbeat things—keep the people happy and keep them coming back. When success is measured by how many we have in attendance, then there is pressure to keep them coming back. There is pressure to maintain an image and keep the budget balanced. But we must not side-step these issues, hoping they will just work themselves out. Paul puts the responsibility on us to expose the unfruitful works of darkness. Call people out of darkness into light.

I am shocked at the way some churches glory in their so-called "liberty."[18] It's all done in the name of combating legalism. Yet it comes down to authorizing people to "walk in darkness," while claiming to have fellowship with God. They get just as close to sin as they can in the public setting. Some open their small groups with a bottle of beer. Some proclaim a gospel of fun. And many people run after that message. Paul told Timothy, "Preach the word; be ready in season *and* out of season; reprove, rebuke, exhort, with great patience and instruction. For the time will come when they will not endure sound doctrine; but *wanting* to have their ears tickled, they will accumulate for themselves teachers in accordance to their own desires, and will turn away their ears from the truth and will turn aside to myths" (2 Tim. 4:2–4, NASB). Is that happening today? Is that happening in America? It's one sign of the last days. "If we say that we have fellowship with Him, and walk in darkness, we lie and do not practice the truth." That's the error John says we must avoid.

# THE ALTERNATIVE: LIVING IN OBEDIENCE TO GOD

The alternative is walking in the light, living in the realm of transparency and obedience to God. That comes with wonderful benefits. First John 1:7: "But if we walk in the light as He is in the light, we have fellowship with one another, and the blood of Jesus Christ His Son cleanses us from all sin." Look at this first benefit in the light of the last chapter: "We have fellowship [koinōnia] with one another." We enjoy the common life with one another, including all the relational satisfaction, peace, and joy. People will try to have this while walking in darkness. It won't work. It will be a mess. The prerequisite for this koinōnia (this common life) is walking in the light. Walking in the light means I live in obedience to the commandments of God. Jesus said, "If you keep My commandments, you will abide in My love; just as I have kept My Father's commandments and abide in His love" (John 15:10, NASB). Abiding in God's love is living in the common life. It is having fellowship with God and with His dear children. It's only possible as we walk in the light. I will deal more with verse 7 in the next chapter.

The fatal error John is warning of is claiming to be a Christian while walking in darkness. Are you walking in darkness? Are you walking in the light? Are you living in the realm of God's commandments? Is your behavior characterized by light? Or are you living in deception? Has someone told you that you can have it both ways? Don't let anyone deceive you into thinking you can live a lifestyle of sin and enjoy relationship with God at the same time. Darkness and light are simply not compatible. If you're living in sin, God has an answer for the problem. Jesus's blood can cleanse you. God can deliver you from the bondage. The solution is simple. Make a decision today to turn from the darkness. Step into the light; acknowledge the sin and renounce it. You will find much mercy and love in His light. You will find Him there with arms open wide. "If we confess our sins, He is faithful and just to forgive us our sins and cleanse us from all unrighteousness."

# Endnotes: Chapter 2

1   Cf. Luke 9:23–24; Gal. 5:24.

2   Cf. Jer. 6:14.

3   Cf. Mal. 3:6; Heb. 13:8.

4   Although John writes this epistle in a more impassioned and erratic style than we moderns might prefer, the letter could be divided using these two key revelations with part one focused on God revealed as light (chapter 1:1–3:10) and the second focused on God revealed as love (chapter 3:11–5:21). Cf. Raymond Brown, *The Epistles of John*, The Anchor Bible, Vol. 30 (Garden City, NY: Doubleday & Co., 1982) 124.

5   "In Him there is no darkness at all" (1 John 1:5, NASB).

6   Cf. 1 Pet. 1:14-16; 2:9; 2 Pet. 3:11; 1 John 3:7.

7   Cf. Psalm 34:8, "O taste and see that the Lord is good" (KJV).

8   The Church Growth Movement has helped the churches be more effective in its techniques and methods. That is consistent with what we see in Acts 6 when the apostles made the wise choice to delegate to chosen deacons. However, my concern in this message is the compromises made by the modern church in its efforts to increase attendance and facilitate growth. Charles Colson's observations seem even more evident today than when he voiced them in his book, *The Body*. Colson writes, "When compared with previous generations of believers, we seem among the most thoroughly at peace with our culture, the least adept at transforming society, and the most desperate for meaningful faith. . . . Rather than offend, however, the church has gradually, almost imperceptibly, slipped into accommodating the culture. It begins with a small step, something almost unconscious. Like the pastor who never quite gets around to teaching about sin and repentance, or the one who simply smooths the edges off some of the hard sayings of the gospel." Charles Colson with Ellen Santilli Vaughn, *The Body: Being Light in Darkness* (Dallas, TX: Word Publishing, 1992) 31, 234. When we prioritize the world's standards of success over fidelity to God and His word, the end result will be disappointing. The deception lies in the fact that there may be temporary signs of success before the long-term consequences become evident.

9   Cf. Rom. 6:1; Jer. 6:14.

10  This is understandable since prominent legalistic groups used the word, holiness, to describe themselves. Nevertheless, holiness and legalism are not the same thing. Believers need a biblical understanding of holiness. May a revival of biblical holiness come to America!

11  Dietrich Bonhoeffer, *The Cost of Discipleship*, trans. R.H. Fuller, rev. ed. (New York: Macmillan, 1960), 30. Bonhoeffer distinguishes between the "costly grace" taught in Scripture, in contrast to "cheap grace" that does not result in biblical discipleship.

12  Fettke, Tom, ed., *The Hymnal for Worship & Celebration* (Waco, TX: Word Music, 1986) s. v. "Amazing Grace," by John Newton, 202.

13  Ibid., s. v "Grace Greater Than Our Sin," by Julia H. Johnston, 201.

14  Ibid.

15  Cf. Gen. 3:4, NASB.

16  The Gnostics John is confronting boasted of inside knowledge. For many of them it led to the antinomianism John condemns in this epistle. Cf. Burdick, 59, 62.

17  From Adam in Genesis, all the way through the book of Revelation into heaven, the creature (man) is to obey the Creator. That never changes! Jesus said, "If you love Me, keep My commandments" (John 14:15).

18  Of course, there is liberty in our relationship with God—not liberty to continue in sin (Rom. 6:1–2), but freedom from its dominion (Rom. 6:14–16). The error on the other side of what I'm teaching in this chapter is legalism as confronted by Paul in Galatians. When people are not taught biblical reliance on the provision of Christ's sacrifice and the empowering grace of the Holy Spirit, they can fall into legalistic, self-effort. John balances his statement in 1 John 1:6 with statements in 1:7–2:2 and in other verses in this epistle. These are expounded in later chapters of this book.

# CHAPTER 3

## Walking in the Light
## 1:7–10

But if we walk in the light as He is in the light, we have fellowship with one another, and the blood of Jesus Christ His Son cleanses us from all sin. If we say that we have no sin, we deceive ourselves, and the truth is not in us. If we confess our sins, He is faithful and just to forgive us our sins and to cleanse us from all unrighteousness. If we say that we have not sinned, we make Him a liar, and His word is not in us.

1 John 1:7-10, NKJV

### Expository Message

In the previous chapter, we focused on a common problem in the church today. It's described in 1 John 1:6: "If we say that we have fellowship with Him, and walk in darkness, we lie and do not practice the truth (NKJV). How many people in church today fit that description? They claim to be Christians; they say they are in fellowship with God, yet they are living in sin. Their lifestyle is characterized by darkness and disobedience to God. God says they are living a lie. They are not genuine. They are deceiving themselves. Being in church does not make you a Christian. Saying you're in fellowship with God does not make it so. Walking the walk is the real evidence of your relationship with God.

"If we say that we have fellowship with Him, and walk in darkness, we lie." John is using the metaphor of walking to indicate a person's lifestyle, the direction and steps a person typically makes in his daily life. You're either living in the environment of God's light or you're living in darkness. The Greek word translated *walk* in verse 6 and in verse 7 is in the present tense. That tense indicates continuous action. John is talking about a person's habitual manner of life.[1] God is light; in Him is no darkness at all. If we are to be in fellowship with Him, we must live in the light. He does not fellowship with darkness.[2] He does not compromise His integrity and moral purity.[3] It is impossible to live a life of sin and be in fellowship with God at the same time.

But there is a path we can choose that not only brings us into fellowship with God, but also empowers fellowship with other believers as well. That is the path we want to discuss in this chapter.[4] First John 1:7: "But if we walk in the light as He is in the light, we have fellowship with one another, and the blood of Jesus Christ His Son cleanses us from all sin" (NKJV). What a wonderful possibility!

We only appreciate how magnificent that statement is when we realize the brilliance of His light. "God is light and in Him is no darkness *at all*" (emphasis mine).[5] There is no element of darkness in His light. When the nation of Israel encountered that light at Mount Sinai, they were terrified. They trembled and shook in fear.[6] That light blinded the eyes of Saul of Tarsus.[7] Paul calls it an *unapproachable* light.[8] No man can walk in that light without the grace of God. Our God is a consuming fire.[9] You don't just walk in the light because you decided to. You walk in the light because God called you out of darkness into His marvelous light.[10] Without the blood of Jesus, the holy light of God would consume us instantly. But Jesus is the propitiation for our sins.[11] Jesus is the sacrifice that makes it possible to walk in His light.

Before we proceed in our exploration of walking in the light, let us praise God that it is even possible. "Therefore, brethren," Hebrews 10:19–22, "since we have confidence to enter the holy place by the blood of Jesus, by a new and living way which He inaugurated for us through the veil, that is, His flesh, and since *we have* a great priest over the house of God, let us draw near with a sincere heart in full assurance of faith" (NASB). Living in the light is only possible because of Jesus's sacrifice on the cross. We could never step into that light without Him. The wonderful news I have for you is this: By this new and living way, *you* can walk in the light! You can live in fellowship with Almighty God. You can know Him and commune with Him. In fact, He invites each and every one of us to walk with Him in the light. "Can two walk together, except they be agreed?"[12] Fellowship (koinōnia) requires agreement. Jesus has brought us into agreement with the Father. Jesus has reconciled us to the Father.[13] Jesus has brought us into the light. Fallen man loves darkness. But a change has come over us. We now love the light and hate the darkness!

## MEANING OF WALKING IN THE LIGHT

What does walking in the light involve? It involves living in obedience to the commandments of God. Is your life characterized by obedience to the Lord? Jesus said, "*If you keep My commandments* [that's a conditional clause] you will abide in My love; just as I have kept My Father's commandments and abide in His love" (emphasis mine, John 15:10, NASB). Don't overlook that little word, *if,* in 1 John 2:3–4. "By this we know that we have come to know Him, *if we keep His commandments.* The one who says, 'I have come to know Him,' and does not *keep His commandments,* is a liar, and the truth is not in him" (emphasis mine, NASB). In his concluding remarks, in Revelation 22:14, John writes, "Blessed are those who do His commandments, that they may have the right to the tree of life, and may enter through the gates into the city" (NKJV).

From the first commandment that God gave Adam and Eve[14] to that closing statement in the book of Revelation, obedience to God by His creatures is always and will forevermore be the rule of life. Any doctrine that excuses disobedience to God is from the pits of hell. Never, never, under the Old Covenant or New Covenant, is it okay to disobey God. When all the theological twists and turns have been made, the final word must be obedience! That is the proper relationship of a creature to the Creator. The New Covenant was not instituted to do away with obedience; it was enacted by God to empower obedience.[15] "For this is the covenant that I will make with the house of Israel after those days, saith the Lord; I will put my laws into their mind, and write them in their hearts: and I will be to them a God, and they shall be to me a people" (Heb. 8:10, KJV).[16]

Hebrews 5:9 says that Jesus "became the author of eternal salvation unto all them that *obey* him" (emphasis mine, KJV). What does walking in the light include? It includes living in obedience to the commandments of God: respecting the boundaries on behavior that He establishes.

Walking in the light also means following the example of Jesus.[17] First John 2:6: "The one who says he abides in Him ought himself to walk *in the same manner as He walked*" (emphasis mine, NASB). We do not experience salvation by merely following the example of Jesus. We are saved by His sacrifice and resurrection.[18] But once saved, we are to walk like He walked.[19] We are to live the kind of unselfish life He lived. "Let this mind be in you," Philippians 2:5, "which was also in Christ Jesus" (KJV). We no longer pursue the things the world pursues. We no longer think like the world thinks. Our motivations are different. Our way of thinking is different and, therefore, our way of life is different.[20] We have in America a lukewarm church that's told people to make a few concessions to Jesus, go to church on Sunday morning, put some money in the basket, serve turkey at the mission on Thanksgiving; then the rest of your time is your own. Don't do anything too bad but pursue the American dream with a little token religion to go with it. When we examine Scripture, that line of thought sounds very lukewarm. When we hear Jesus talk about following Him, Christianity sounds much more radical than most people understand it to be.

Here is the way Jesus described walking in the light in Luke 14:26–27: "If anyone comes to Me and does not hate his father and mother, wife and children, brothers and sisters, yes, *and his own life also*, he cannot be My disciple. And whoever does not bear his cross and come after Me cannot be My disciple" (emphasis mine, NKJV). He summarizes the point in verse 33: "So likewise, whoever of you does not forsake all that he has cannot be My disciple" (NKJV). That's radical commitment, not just for a dedicated few, but for all the followers of Jesus. Christianity is not just a belief in God that leaves you living the same kind of life you would have lived without God. It transforms your whole orientation toward life. Biblical Christianity is revolutionary. It's like stepping out of black darkness into a brilliant light. If your encounter with Jesus has not changed the purpose and direction of your life, come back to the cross and consecrate yourself to be a disciple, a true disciple, of Jesus. Walking in the light is to walk as Jesus walked.

Walking in the light includes honest confession of our sins, transparency before God. Walking in the light does not mean sinless perfection; it means sincere progression. It means a sincere desire to always please the Lord. It means laying aside every weight and sin that so easily besets us and running this race with perseverance.[21] But we all come short of the perfect glory of God, even with our best efforts. Romans 3:23 says, "For all have sinned, and come short of the glory of God" (KJV). The tense of the Greek verbs in that verse are interesting. "For all have sinned" is in the aorist tense; we sinned in the past. "And fall short" is in the present tense: continuous action.[22] We are continuously falling short of the glory of God. We shoot the arrow at the bullseye, but we don't always hit a bullseye. We do fall short of perfection, even though we aim for absolute, complete obedience to our Lord. Walking in the light does not mean sinless perfection. Otherwise we would not need the blood of Jesus to cleanse us of sin. The verses that follow in 1 John 1:8-10 bring further clarity. "If we say that we have no sin, we deceive ourselves, and the truth is not in us. If we confess our sins, He is faithful and just to forgive us our sins and to cleanse us from all unrighteousness. If we say that we have not sinned, we make Him a liar, and His word is not in us" (NKJV).

How do people say they have *no sin*? Some deny the very existence of sin. The secular psychologist may call it a neurosis due to excessive feelings of guilt. The Christian Scientist may explain it as a figment of the imagination. The humanist insists man is basically good and there is no such thing as original sin.[23] Just give the man a better environment, and all will be well.

One of the ways the devil has undermined the gospel is to simply deny the need for the gospel. If there is no such thing as sin, then there is no need for a Savior who would deliver us from our sins.[24] If they can turn the discussion toward better self-esteem and more positive thinking, they can avoid the need for repentance and salvation. The horror of this denial is that it makes God out to be a liar. God has said that "all have sinned and come short of the glory of God." Who is right, God or high-minded man? "Let God be true but every man a liar."[25] It is blasphemy to make God out to be the liar by denying the existence of sin. Look closely at 1 John 1:10: "If we say that we have not sinned, we make Him a liar, and His word is not in us." Some do that by denying the very existence of sin.

Some deny their sin by redefining the standard. First John 3:4 defines sin as transgression of the law. God gave the law to show us what sin is. Paul said in Romans 7:7, "I would not have known sin except through the law. For I would not have known covetousness unless the law had said, 'You shall not covet'" (NKJV). The law teaches us moral boundaries. The law is designed to convict us of crossing those boundaries. The law is our schoolmaster to bring us to our knees at the foot of the cross.[26]

Now who has the right to set the boundaries on our behavior? May I suggest, it is the One who created us in the first place? The moral law of God issues forth out of His eternal character. God is light. God has designed us to reflect that light. God sets the boundaries on our behavior and reveals those boundaries in His word. The rebel throws off the authority of God and claims the right to set his own boundaries. He may even get others to agree with him. He may even take it to the nation's Supreme Court and get them to agree with him.[27] So hand joins with hand to tell God that the boundaries He has established in His word are no longer applicable; in effect telling God, "You may have restricted sexual behavior to the marriage covenant between a man and a woman, but we're re-writing the rules. In fact, anyone who insists on Your rules is a religious prude and a bigot." So, in that, they have turned the law of God upside down and inside out, so much so that they now call good evil and evil good. Little do they know that God has already pronounced judgment on such insanity. Isaiah 5:20–21 says,

> Woe to those who call evil good, and good evil; Who substitute darkness for light and light for darkness; Who substitute bitter for sweet and sweet for bitter! Woe to those who are wise in their own eyes And clever in their own sight!" (NASB).

Some people deny their sin by simply changing the rules to suit their behavior.[28]

Some people justify themselves by comparing themselves to others.[29] They are extremely good at identifying faults and failures of others. By using this false standard, they feel pretty good about themselves.[30] A Pharisee went to the temple to pray. Luke 18:11–12 records his prayer.

"God, I thank You that I am not like other people: swindlers, unjust, adulterers, or even like this tax collector. I fast twice a week; I pay tithes of all that I get" (NASB). He can see the sins of others very clearly: extortion, adultery, and other degenerate behavior. But he has this big beam in his own eye called self-righteousness. It is rooted in the sin of pride, the mother of all sins. And he is blind to his own sin. Jesus contrasted this man's prayer with that of the tax-collector.

> But the tax collector, standing some distance away, was even unwilling to lift up his eyes to heaven, but was beating his breast, saying, 'God, be merciful to me, the sinner!' I tell you, this man went to his house justified rather than the other; for everyone who exalts himself will be humbled, but he who humbles himself will be exalted" (Luke 18:13–14, NASB).

Notice how Jesus puts His finger on the underlying issue: pride. The tax-collector humbled himself and acknowledged his transgression. The Pharisee justified himself using a few good deeds that he had done. Good deeds, no matter how religious, do not make up for disobedience in other areas. God's standard is perfection! We all come short of it in thought, word, and deed every day.[31] That's why Jesus taught us to pray daily in the Lord's Prayer, "forgive us our sins." It's because we need that forgiveness on a daily basis. We also pray, "lead us not into temptation; but deliver us from evil" (Luke 11:4, KJV). We pray that because we know our own vulnerability to temptation. We know our dependence upon the grace of God to live a holy life.

Some people minimize, rationalize, and ignore their sin. That, for all practical purposes, is denying the sin they have. They never confess sin. If they are angry, it was really someone else who made them angry. If they are offended, it is because someone else did something wrong. They can't see the wrong in holding the grudge. They are too focused on what the other person did. They are obsessed with the speck in the other person's eye and don't see the beam of unforgiveness in their own eye. If they have a nasty habit or addiction, it is because their childhood was really bad. "Daddy bawled me out and even threatened to spank me. It was traumatic. I never got over it. That's why I do these things. It's not my fault." The point I'm making is this: The sins of others never justify your own sin. Those people will give an account to God for what they did. You will give an account for what you did or even how you reacted to their actions.

First John 1:9 says, "If we confess our sins, He is faithful and just to forgive us our sins and to cleanse us from all unrighteousness." This is crucial to walking in the light. How are we to confess our sins? This obviously begins with acknowledging the transgression. The Greek word John uses here is *homologeō*. It literally means "to say the same thing."[32] *Homoios* means "same," and *legō* means "to say." The confession John is looking for is to say the same thing about the behavior as God says about it. Not only do we admit that we did it, but we also agree with God about its seriousness. We humble ourselves before God without giving excuse for the behavior.

We come into the light of God's countenance and we open our soul to His scrutiny. We say with David, "Search me, O God, and know my heart: try me, and know my thoughts: And see if there be any wicked way in me, and lead me in the way everlasting" (Ps. 139:23–24, KJV). We stay under that light awhile.[33] We allow God to bring to our remembrance things that we may have dismissed as insignificant. Our tendency is to be very sensitive to the violations we receive from others; we remember even the small slights.[34] But we're not always so sensitive about the wrongs we have done. We may need the Holy Spirit to point those out to us. We may need Him to show us when we are making prideful, self-serving statements. One prayer God is faithful to answer is this one: "Search me, O God, and know my heart: try me, and know my thoughts: And see if there be any wicked way in me." The heart is deceitful above all things, and desperately wicked: who can know it?[35] We can't know the depths of our transgressions without the help of the Holy Spirit.

The closer we walk with God, the more aware we are of our sins.[36] The closer to the light we live, the clearer we see, even the smaller transgressions. Get close to the light and you will find good reason to repent. But you will find much mercy and forgiveness as well.

When I was a child, our family rented a house. I remember Mom feeling along the wall searching for the light switch as we walked into that place for the first time. Everything seemed fine until the light was turned on. Then we saw hundreds of cockroaches scurrying throughout the room. They were everywhere. We only saw them when we got into the light. This is why the light is so essential. A man walking in the darkness may have all kinds of creepy sins without even realizing it. My mother was a great housekeeper. She killed those roaches with DDT, and we scooped them up with broom and dust pan. After a while we were rid of those pests. But the process began with stepping into the light and seeing the problem.

The most common failure to confessing sin comes as people shrug their trespasses off as insignificant. They simply overlook their own sins and assume God has done the same.[37] They have operated in that behavior so long, they don't necessarily see it as wrong. They justify themselves saying, "That's just the way I am." Then they simply ignore the matter. But walking in the light involves facing our sins and resolving the offenses we have committed against God and against others. If we ignore the sin, it loads us down like a full backpack. We carry around the weight of our guilt. We live at a distance from God and from fellow believers. The sin does not go away with time. It has to be confessed and cleansed.

The confession of sin required in 1 John 1:9 deals with each act of disobedience.[38] It is not sufficient to make a general confession without the details. It's the details that we must turn from. It's the specific acts of disobedience that must be repented of. A broad confession that says, "God I'm sorry for the wrongs I did today," is ineffective. What sins? Is there anyone that was affected by these sins? Do you need to confess the wrong to that person? How will you turn from that in the future? Effectual confession takes its time to deal with the matter thoroughly. A general confession of being a sinner implies little culpability. It's often little more than a confession of being human. Do you want the slate clean? Then confess the specific transgressions to the Lord. You may have heard the old song that says, "Count your blessings, name them one by one."[39] That is excellent advice. But in addition to that, you may need to "Count your transgressions, name them one by one." Are you willing to do that, as well?

In some cases, confession to the Lord alone is not sufficient. We may need to confess that sin to someone we have offended (Matt. 5:23–24). We may need to make restitution (Exod. 22:1; Luke 19:8). James 5:16 tells us to confess our faults one to another, that we may be healed. I wonder how much healing would take place in our lives if we did these things right.

Those who help people recover from addictions have discovered the healing power of confession. Steps four through ten in a twelve-step program revolve around the need to honestly face the wrongs we have done and make it right with the people we have wronged. It is a significant part of the recovery program.[40] But we take it all too lightly. We skim the surface and carry on without really doing biblical confession. Our relationship with God suffers. Our relationships with others suffer. And we fail to make the spiritual progress that could be made. *Walking in the light* includes confession of sin according to the biblical pattern.

## BENEFITS OF WALKING IN THE LIGHT

What does walking in the light provide for us? It provides cleansing from sin. "But if we walk in the light as He is in the light, we have fellowship with one another, and the blood of Jesus Christ His Son cleanses us from all sin." It's not just that He forgives us and removes the legal debt we owe. He also cleanses us from the *defilement* of the sin. Sin contaminates and creates dysfunction. Those who work with mechanical equipment know how important it is to keep the moving parts clean. Otherwise, they will not continue to functioning effectively. If sin is not dealt with on a daily basis, we will not function well either. Our thinking gets distorted. We lose our peace and joy. I wonder how much needless junk we have in our lives simply because we do not confess our sins in a biblical way and keep short accounts with God. "Do not let the sun go down on your anger."[41]

Our culture is opposed to anything that makes us feel bad. But sometimes we have to feel bad (experience conviction of sin) before we can really feel good. Daily cleansing by the blood of Jesus is important maintenance. How's your maintenance program working? The failure to deal with sin may explain the lack of joy and peace and contentment in our lives. When is the last time you asked someone to forgive you? At times that is necessary. Cleansing is ours if we come under God's light and address the issues biblically.

Notice the assurance we are given in 1 John 1:9: "If we confess our sins, He is faithful and just to forgive us our sins and to cleanse us from all unrighteousness." If we will do our part, God will do His. He is faithful and just to forgive us. Because of who He is; because He is faithful to do what He says He will do; because he is righteous to keep His word, we will be forgiven and we will be cleansed—from *all* unrighteousness. The blood of Jesus is sufficient to deal with any and all failings and transgressions. The question that rings in my heart is this: Are we availing ourselves of this great privilege by coming to God on a daily basis and dealing with specific sins? Or are we just carrying that stuff around and tolerating it? There may be more available to us than we're living in. Most of us shortcut the confession process way too much.

If we walk in the light, we're also assured of fellowship with one another. The cleansing from sin and the fellowship go hand in hand. Fellowship with God is implied. But fellowship with one another is explicitly stated. When I deal with my sins and selfishness, I open the way for sweet fellowship with other believers. When I live in the light and love of God, I am conditioned to interact successfully with others. Fellowship (koinōnia) with one another is something we can then enjoy. I'm talking about something more than a picnic at the park. I'm talking about New Testament living the shared life with each other in its fullness.[42]

Fellowship with other believers is also an indication that I am walking in the light. If I can't get along with fellow believers, that may be alerting me to something in me that needs to be dealt with. Is it really everybody else's fault? Am I just a victim of everyone's insensitivity? Or is there something in me that is sabotaging the fellowship? Is there pride or selfishness or irritability or something I need to address, so that I can enjoy fellowship with other believers. Those who walk in darkness are not promised this fellowship. It comes as we walk in the light.

There is wonderful joy and peace available to every believer who will live under the light of God's standard and keep short accounts with him. Bruce Fogarty seemed to know the beauty of that when he penned this poem. It's entitled "The Morning Hour."

. . . . . . . . . . . . . . . . . . . . . . . . . . . . .

Alone with God, my sins confess'd
He speaks in mercy, I am blest.
I know the kiss of pardon free,
I talk to God, He talks to me.

. . . . . . . . . . . . . . . . . . . . . . . . . . . . .

34

Alone with God no sin between
His lovely face so plainly seen;
My guilt all gone, my heart at rest
With Christ, my Lord, my soul is blest.[43]

That's a good way to live!

# Endnotes: Chapter 3

1   Cleon L. Rogers, Jr. and Cleon L. Rogers III, *The New Linguistic and Exegetical Key to the Greek New Testament* (Grand Rapids: Zondervan Publishing House, 1998) 592.

2   Cf. 2 Cor. 6:14, "For what fellowship hath righteousness with unrighteousness? and what communion (koinōnia) hath light with darkness?" (KJV).

3   The Son of God has already come into this dark world and made atonement for sin. Now He calls us to respond to that by coming into His light, acknowledging the sin that light exposes, and turning from sin to obedience.

4   Full text in New International Version: "This is the message we have heard from him and declare to you: God is light; in him there is no darkness at all. If we claim to have fellowship with him yet walk in the darkness, we lie and do not live by the truth. But if we walk in the light, as he is in the light, we have fellowship with one another, and the blood of Jesus, his Son, purifies us from all sin. If we claim to be without sin, we deceive ourselves and the truth is not in us. If we confess our sins, he is faithful and just and will forgive us our sins and purify us from all unrighteousness. If we claim we have not sinned, we make him out to be a liar and his word has no place in our lives" (1 John 1:5–10).

5   1 John 1:5, NKJV.

6   Cf. Heb. 12:21; Exod. 19.

7   Cf. Acts 22:11.

8   1 Tim. 6:16, NASB.

9   Heb. 12:29, KJV. Cf. Deut. 4:24.

10   Cf. 1 Pet. 2:9–10; John 15:16; John 6:44.

11   1 John 2:2, KJV.

12   Amos 3:3, KJV.

13   Cf. Col.1:21–22; 2 Cor. 5:18.

14   Cf. Gen. 2:16–17.

15   Cf. Rom. 8:3–4. While John uses the terminology of walking in the light or abiding in Christ, Paul emphasizes the Spirit by telling believers to walk in the Spirit.

16   Cf. Jer. 31:33; Heb. 10:16.

17   Jesus said in John 8:12 "I am the Light of the world; he who follows Me will not walk in the darkness, but will have the Light of life" (NASB).

18   Cf. Rom. 10:9-10; 1 Pet. 1:18–21.

19   Cf. Eph. 5:8; 3 John 4.

20   Cf. Eph. 4:17–19.

21   Cf. 2 Cor. 5:9; Col. 1:10; Heb. 12:1–2.

22   Rogers and Rogers, 322. Cf. Daniel B. Wallace, *Greek Grammar Beyond the Basics: An Exegetical Syntax of the New Testament* (Grand Rapids: Zondervan,

1996) 503. Our full experience of glory comes at the resurrection (Rom. 8:23-24). In the mean time we continue to press into God (Phil. 3:12-14) in anticipation of that day.

23  1 John 1:8 teaches that we must not deny the existence of our sin nature, and we must not deny the fruit of that nature, sinful acts. Scholars disagree as to which one is being addressed in verse 8 and verse 9. However, there is general agreement among conservative theologians that our sinful nature (Rom. 5:15–19) must be acknowledged, and our sinful acts must be confessed.

24  Cf. Matt. 1:21.

25  Rom. 3:4, KJV.

26  Cf. Gal. 3:24.

27  This, in fact, happened on June 26. 2015 with the Supreme Court ruling on same-sex marriage (Obergefell v Hodges).

28  The relativism in our society is often viewed as simply another way of perceiving reality. However, the insistence of the individual on creating his or her own morality (rather than submitting to that which is revealed by God in His word) is very close to what Satan offered Eve when he said in Genesis 3:5, "when you eat of it your eyes will be opened, and you will be like God, knowing good and evil" (NIV). Like God, you can be your own source of defining good versus evil.

29  Cf. 2 Cor. 10:12.

30  In John 9 the Pharisees argued with Jesus, rather than receiving correction from Him. They defended themselves and attacked Jesus rather than confessing their sin. In verse 41 Jesus said to them, "If you were blind, you would have no sin; but since you say, 'We see,' your sin remains" (NASB). The sin is only cleansed when we confess it.

31  However, preachers of the Word must lift up that standard (Matt. 5:48). We are not authorized to lower the standard.

32  Rogers and Rogers, 592.

33  The Lord's Prayer provides guidance on how to pray. The process of praying "forgive us our sins" may take an hour. It's not just a matter of quoting the phrase.

34  Of course, this should not be (1 Pet. 4:8).

35  Jer. 17:9–10, KJV.

36  I am referring here to the ability to see specific transgression through the conviction of the Holy Spirit and process them biblically. There is a nagging sin-consciousness that the Accuser (Rev. 12:10) will put on a believer that is very debilitating. It is typically a general sense of guilt that leaves the believer feeling he is simply not good enough. It does not lead the Christian through the process of repenting of *specific* transgressions and receiving forgiveness. Instead it leaves him under a cloud of inadequacy. The conviction of the Holy Spirit is very different from this general sense of condemnation brought on by Satan.

When the Holy Spirit convicts, He leads us to repentance and cleansing from the sin.

37  Even if they momentarily recognize the wrong, they quickly forgive themselves and assume God has done the same. They give little thought to the significance of what they have done.

38  Burdick, 126: "The verb *homologōmen* is an iterative present depicting the practice of confessing after each act of sin."

39  Fettke. Tom, ed., s. v. "Count Your Blessings," by Johnson Oatman, Jr., 563.

40  *Twelve Steps and Twelve Traditions,* 1952 (New York: Alcoholics Anonymous World Service, Ind., 1988) 42–95.

41  Eph. 4:26, NASB.

42  Dallas Willard wrote, "Confession alone make *deep* fellowship possible, and the lack of it explains much of the superficial quality so commonly found in our church associations. What, though, makes confession bearable? Fellowship. There is an essential reciprocity between the two disciplines." Dallas Willard, *The Spirit of the Disciplines: Understanding How God Changes Lives* (San Francisco: HarperSanFrancisco, 1988) 188.

43  Knight, ed., s. v. "The Morning Hour," by Bruce Fogarty, 93. This is the second and fourth stanza of the poem.

# CHAPTER 4

# Wrestling with Sin
## 2:1–2

My little children, these things I write to you, so that you
may not sin. And if anyone sins, we have an Advocate with
the Father, Jesus Christ the righteous. And He Himself
is the propitiation for our sins, and not for ours only but
also for the whole world.

1 John 2:1–2, NKJV

### Expository Message

The famous evangelist, Billy Sunday, expressed an attitude toward sin that
I want to replicate in my own life. He said, "I'm against sin. I'll kick it as
long as I've got a foot, and I'll fight it as long as I've got a fist. I'll butt it
as long as I've got a head. I'll bite it as long as I've got a tooth. And when
I'm old and fistless and footless and toothless, I'll gum it till I go home to
Glory and it goes home to perdition!"[1]

If you struggle with sin, you're not alone. Paul described his battle in
Romans 7:21. "When I want to do good," Paul writes, "evil is right there
with me" (NIV). Have you found that to be true in your life? It's not just
an issue with the external influences of the world and the devil. It is closer
to us than even that. It is a principle in our flesh that wants its own way in
opposition to the will of the Father. "When I want to do good." Do you
want to do good? I know you do, if His righteous seed is in you. But there

is "another law at work in the members of my body, *waging war*" (emphasis mine), Paul says in Romans 7:23. One part of me wants to please God in every way I possibly can. Another part of me rises up and sabotages my best intentions. It is a frustrating experience all Christians encounter. How can I walk this out successfully?

In our text, the Apostle John gives insight on how that is done. It's something every one of us needs to know. It's something you and I may need to understand at a greater depth. On the one hand, what John says is not new to many of us. On the other hand, if we knew it as thoroughly as John knew it, we would probably be living in greater victory than we're currently experiencing. So, let's read 1 John 2:1–2 again and hear what the Spirit might say to us through this aged apostle. "My little children, these things I write to you, so that you may not sin. And if anyone sins, we have an Advocate with the Father, Jesus Christ the righteous. And He Himself is the propitiation for our sins, and not for ours only but also for the whole world." I find in that passage, first a word of counsel: "These things I write to you, so that you may not sin." That is immediately followed by this wonderful word of comfort: "If anyone sins, we have an Advocate." Those two statements provide a balance for walking in the light.

## WORD OF COUNSEL

Look with me first at John's word of counsel in verse one. "My little children, these things I write to you, so that you may not sin." This fatherly apostle is gently saying, "Do not sin!" It's never better to sin than to not sin. "The wages of sin is death."[2] Sin does not produce good things in our lives. Sin robs us of God's best. Through Jesus we can receive forgiveness of sin. But even when we receive that forgiveness, there will still be consequences for the behavior. God may forgive a Christian for robbing a bank, but the courts may still sentence him to ten years in prison for what he has done. The addicted gambler may receive forgiveness from the Lord for the stupid thing he did with the family's grocery money. But the bookie will keep his money anyway. His losses will not be returned to him. He will have to work that out. Consequences follow sin.[3] John says, "Don't do it. Don't cross the line. Don't disobey God." Do you hear the father's heart in his words, "My little children, these things I write to you, so that you may not sin"?

John has just given some assurances of God's grace in chapter one. "But if we walk in the light as He is in the light, we have fellowship with one another, and the blood of Jesus Christ His Son cleanses us from all sin" (NKJV). The blood of Jesus has the power to cleanse you from all sin. God does not reject the child who stumbles and falls. He picks him up and cleanses his defilement and heals his wounds. John has even said in the following verses that we all sin. We all need the provision of the cross on a daily basis. "If we say that we have no sin, we deceive ourselves, and the truth is not in us" (1 John 1:8, NKJV). Then comes this wonderful assurance in 1 John 1:9, "If we confess our sins, He is faithful and just to forgive us our sins and to cleanse us from all unrighteousness" (NKJV).

That is the solution for the believer. It sounds so simple that there is a danger we would take on a cavalier attitude toward sin. If God's solution is that easy, then why discipline myself to walk the straight and narrow. Why not "go with the flow?" Why not enjoy myself like the world does, and simply ask God to forgive me? Knowing the possibility of that kind of response, John clarifies his intentions in 2:1: "I write to you, so that you may not sin." "My purpose in telling you these things is to help you *not* sin. Far from this being a license to sin, I'm calling you to holiness. I'm telling you to not indulge the flesh. My counsel to you is to not sin! Don't take the matter lightly. It is of upmost importance." Sin is of the devil. First John 3:8 says, "He who sins is of the devil" (NKJV). Jesus did not come to support you in your sin. He came to deliver you from it! "You shall call His name Jesus," the Lord told Joseph, "for He will save His people from their sins" (Matt. 1:21, NASB). That is God's primary goal for you: to save you *from* your *sins*. Yes, as a consequence of that, He saves you from hell. But you must be saved from your sins to be saved from hell. Until the church gets this understanding of salvation, she will be weak, anemic, and lukewarm.

It is good news that in Jesus we are saved from the penalty of sin. Penalty is not good. No one wants penalty. Even the unrepentant murderer on death row does not want penalty. Yes, Jesus saves us from the penalty of sin. But salvation is more than that. He also saves us from the *power* of sin. Romans 6:14: "For sin shall not be master over you, for you are not under law but under grace" (NASB). If you do not want to be saved from the power of sin, I have to wonder whether you're saved at all. I have to wonder whether His righteous seed abides in you. Do you delight in the law of God your inner being?[4] In your heart, do you want to do the will of the Father all the time, every time? If so, you are being saved from the power of sin, even if there are sins and failures along the way.

The Greek tense of the verb *to sin* in 1 John 2:1 is aorist subjunctive.[5] It's talking about an act of sin. John used the present tense in chapter one when he talked about walking in darkness or walking in the light. Present tense was used to indicate continuous action. There he was talking about lifestyle.[6] But here John is talking about an act of sin, not a lifestyle of sin. "These things I write to you, so that you may not sin"—so that you may not commit any act of sin.[7] John distinguishes a lifestyle of sin in contrast to an act of sin by the way he uses the Greek in this epistle. Here he is saying, "I don't want you to commit even one act of sin."

The goal is perfection.[8] Jesus said, "Be perfect, therefore, as your heavenly Father is perfect" (Matt. 5:48, NIV). Do not lower the standard.[9] Keep that standard before you at all times. John is writing his epistle with that goal in mind: so that you may not commit any act of sin. Will we fall short of that standard? Yes, we will. But we make a grave error when we lower the standard to where we are. "Be perfect, therefore, as your heavenly Father is perfect" (Matt. 5:48, NIV). That's the bullseye. That's the standard that John is presenting to his readers. Paul said in 2 Corinthians 5:9, "So we make it our goal to please him, whether we are at home in the body or away from it" (NIV). Is it the goal of your life to never sin? You will come short of that, but it should be your goal. Is it your aim in everything you do to please Him?[10] That is John's goal for us in the text.

Did you hear about the backwoodsman who went to church for the first time? He had told his friends that he was going to check it out. When he got back with his buddies, they ask him what the sermon was about. The backwoodsman simply replied, "Sin." Wanting to know more, they inquired, "And what did he say about it?" The backwoodsman answered, "He was again' it!"

John wants his readers to know, when it comes to sin, he is against it and God is against it. It is not to be tolerated or excused. It is to be avoided and resisted with all diligence. Do not take the gracious provisions of God as a green light for sin.[11] "My little children, these things I write to you, so that you may not sin." This is one of John's primary reasons for writing this epistle: "So that you may not sin."

Notice again the affection with which John writes, "My little children." This is language of endearment. Although the line is drawn firmly for them to avoid sin, it is drawn with a father's love. "I don't want you to sin, because I know the damage it will do to you. I know the price you will pay. Don't sin! Avoid it like the plague, because it is even more deadly." If we are to be successful in our walk with God, this has to be our attitude toward sin. "What fellowship hath righteousness with unrighteousness? And what communion hath light with darkness?" (2 Cor. 6:14, KJV). "For you were once darkness," Paul wrote, "but now you are light in the Lord. Live as children of light" (Eph. 5:8, NIV). John has given us his clear counsel on the matter of sin. But he does not leave us there.

## WORD OF COMFORT

He follows up with a word of comfort. In 1 John 2:1 he writes, "And if anyone sins, we have an Advocate with the Father, Jesus Christ the righteous." On the surface, John may seem to contradict himself. Don't sin, but if you sin, God has made provision for that in Jesus Christ. The two statements complement one another; they insure balance. Don't fool yourself into thinking you can walk in darkness and all will be well. On the other hand, don't despair when you stumble along the way.

John often links the name, Jesus, with the title, Christ. He is confronting Gnostics who have distorted the revelation of our Lord. Because of their flawed concept of the world, some Gnostics separated Jesus from the Christ, the Anointed One. Some taught that Christ came upon Jesus, the man, at His water baptism and left Him before His sufferings at the cross.[12] John makes sure his readers understand Jesus is the Christ, the Son of God. You can be wrong about a lot of things, and still make it to heaven. But what you cannot afford to be wrong about who Jesus really is. There is salvation in no other name.[13] Paul warned the Corinthians about those who would preach "another Jesus,"[14] those who would distort the revelation of Jesus to their own destruction. In Galatians 1:8 Paul pronounced a curse on those who would pervert the gospel of Jesus Christ. He wrote, "But though we, or an angel from heaven, preach any other gospel unto you than that which we have preached unto you, let him be accursed" (KJV).

Recently, I woke up with these words ringing in my ear: "There is coming an avalanche of deception and false teaching." I had heard Steve Hill prophesy that before his death.[15] But this time the Lord was speaking it to me. Maybe this is one reason God is having us examine 1 John so closely. There is a lot of deception already happening. In chapter two, I addressed some of the current distortions of the message of grace. There I warned of the dangers that accompany that error; and I will continue to declare that warning. If the trend continues, there will be shipwrecked lives everywhere. But that may only be the beginning.

In America we are experiencing notable chaos in the political arena. While we are focusing on that, Satan is undermining the one hope for America, the church. Everything depends upon what the church does! We're dealing with a spiritual problem first, and secondarily a political problem. The church is the head, and the politicians are the tail. Don't think the tail wags the head. No, the head wags the tail. The destiny of America rests with the church of America.[16] In 2016 the church received a reprieve from the increasing governmental oppression against Christian liberty.[17] During this reprieve, God is giving *the church* additional opportunity to repent. God is giving His people some time, according to 2 Chronicles 7:14, to humble ourselves, pray, seek His face, and turn from our wicked ways. If we seize the opportunity and do that, all will be well. But if we continue on an apathetic, lukewarm path, it will be disaster like we have not imagined. This is our space for repentance. God calls the terms. Once that opportunity is passed, the judgment is set. It will not be reversed by last minute apologies to God. Jesus is walking among the candlesticks of the American church and calling His people to repentance.[18] The world will be the world. They will sin because it is their nature to sin. But God holds the church to a higher standard. What are God's people supposed to be doing right now? Second Chronicles 7:14 gives us the answer: "If My people who are called by My name will humble themselves, and pray and seek My face, and turn from their wicked ways, then I will hear from heaven, and will forgive their sin and heal their land" (NKJV). No substitutes; make sure you're doing that!

John is using familial language in our text. He is talking to the church.

He is talking to Christians. "If anyone sins, we have an Advocate with the Father." He begins verse one with, "My little children." This message is not to the world. He is talking to born-again believers. Notice the Advocate is not spoken of as with *the Judge*. That is what we might expect. God is the Judge of all the earth. But John says it's with the *Father*. There is double assurance here: An Advocate who is for you and a Father who is for you. Is He your Father? Then this message of comfort is for you! This word of comfort is not for unbelievers. "My little children, these things I write to you, so that you may not sin. And if anyone sins, we have an Advocate with the Father, Jesus Christ the righteous."

What is an Advocate? It is one who speaks in our defense: "One who pleads the cause of another before a judge."[19] The term was used in reference to a defense attorney. But John uses the term in the context of the family. "We have an Advocate *with the Father*." (emphasis mine). Jesus is sure to win the case in your behalf because the Father is the one who sent Him to be your Advocate. You do have an adversary, the devil. When you fail, he is quick to accuse you before God and in your own heart and mind.[20] If you don't know about your Advocate, you can easily become despondent and depressed. This is why John is telling us these things. So that we won't lose hope when we fail.: "And if anyone sins." You don't need an advocate if there is no case against you. No one hires a defense attorney unless he is charged with a crime. John does not say, "And if anyone *sins not*, we have an Advocate." It is when you fail that you need Jesus to be your Advocate. And it is when you fail that He is your Advocate!

The Greek word translated Advocate is *paraklētos*, one who is called to come to one's side as a helper.[21] John is the only New Testament writer to use the term. He used it in reference to the Holy Spirit in John 14 when Jesus was in the upper room with His disciples. Jesus promised to not leave His followers as orphans, but to send the Holy Spirit. In John 14:16 He said, "And I will pray the Father, and He will give you another Helper, [The King James Version translates it Comforter; it is the same word that is translated Advocate in our text.] that He may abide with you forever" (NKJV). So, we have the Holy Spirit as our advocate here on earth, and we have Jesus as our advocate in heaven. And we have every reason to take comfort in that.

John punctuates the effectiveness of Jesus's advocacy when he says our

Advocate with the Father is "Jesus Christ *the righteous*" (emphasis mine). Not only is He the Christ, appointed by the Father to be our Advocate, High Priest, but He is *righteous* before the Father. If you are going to have someone stand up in your defense, you want that person to be in good standing before the court. Jesus is one with the Father. He is the Second Person of the Trinity. He will represent you well. He will present your case in the integrity of who He is. He will not excuse your sin. He will not dismiss its significance. It is a violation of the law and deserves punishment. But the punishment has already taken place 2000 years ago. He "Himself bore our sins in His own body on the cross."[22] Isaiah 53:5-6: "But he was wounded for our transgressions, he was bruised for our iniquities: the chastisement of our peace was upon him" (KJV). The punishment for that sin was placed upon Him. He bore it in our behalf. And the Father would not unjustly require that penalty to be paid a second time. Our Advocate pleads His own sacrifice in our defense.

Verse 2 of our text explains how He represents us. "And He Himself is the propitiation for our sins." He is our Advocate, our representative, our intercessor, our great High Priest. He brings before the Father His eternal sacrifice of Calvary. It is more than sufficient for you and me. We do not have to add penance or self-flagellation to it. That would only detract from the glory of the sacrifice. That actually dishonors the sacrifice and the One who provided it. The sacrifice of the cross is more than enough to win your case.

> Just as I am, without one plea,
> But that thy blood was shed for me'
> And that Thou bidd'st me come to Thee,
> O Lamb of God I come, I come![23]

That is the way we initially come to God. And that is the way we continually come to God as faltering Christians. Our only plea is that His "blood was shed for me." "He Himself is the propitiation for our sins."

Propitiation is an important theological term. Since John is addressing the concept, we would do well to understand its meaning. In simple terms, it means atoning sacrifice. In fact, that is the way the New International Version translates it. It is foreshadowed by the Old Testament animal sacrifices. "Without shedding of blood there is no remission of sin."[24] Remission of sin is forgiveness of sin.[25] Propitiation includes the forgiveness of sin, expiation, and the removal of guilt.[26] But it means more than that. The Greek word here is *hilasmos*. It is an appeasing of the wrath of God. [27] Liberal theologians don't like that because it implies that God is angry. They have decided on their own that God cannot be a God of wrath, since He is a God of love. They can't reconcile the two complimentary realities, so they dismiss the revelation of God's wrath against sin. But Romans 1:18 says, "The wrath of God is revealed from heaven against all ungodliness and unrighteousness of men" (NASB). And according to Revelation 6:16–17, men will one day be saying to the mountains and rocks, "Fall on us and hide us from the presence of Him who sits on the throne, and from the wrath of the Lamb; for the great day of their wrath has come, and who is able to stand?" (NASB). I would not be too quick to dismiss the wrath of God as non-existent.

We learned in 1 John 1 that God is light. His holiness and divine justice demand punishment of sin. Wrath is His righteous response to rebellion. It is not arbitrary. It flows out of His moral character. But we see that in perspective when we remember John 3:16. "For God so loved" that He provided in Christ the propitiation that reconciles us to Himself.[28] Divine justice demanded punishment of sin. Divine love provided the Lamb that takes away the sin of the world. Robert Law wrote, "Propitiation is no device for inducing a reluctant deity to forgive; it is the way by which the Father in heaven restores His sinning children to Himself."[29]

When we think of Jesus as our Advocate and our propitiation, we must never think of the Father as our adversary, or even being reluctant. Our adversary is the devil, the accuser of the brethren. God, the Father, is so *for us* that He sent His only begotten Son to make a way of salvation for all who will receive it. Jesus wins our case; and the Father delights in pronouncing the verdict.

"And He Himself is the propitiation for our sins, *and not for ours only but also for the whole world*" (emphasis mine). The atonement is provided for *all* who will receive it. It is for us who have received it. It is for anyone who will receive it. "For God so loved the world, that He gave His only begotten Son, that whoever believes in Him shall not perish, but have eternal life."[30] There is one condition in that sentence: "Whoever believes in Him." The provision is there, "not for ours only but also for the whole world."

Faith must be exercised to receive the things of God. God gave the land of Canaan to the first generation of Israelites who came out of Egypt. It was provided for them; it was theirs for the taking. But they did not receive it! They failed to enter in. Why? Because of their unbelief![31]

There is a popular doctrine in the church today that emphasizes grace in the following way. It says something like this. "When Jesus died on the cross He paid for all your sins, past, present, and future. Did you know that your sins past, present, and future are already forgiven?" There is some truth to the statement. On the cross, Jesus did pay for our sins: past, present, and future. The propitiation for all the sins of the world for all generations was made at Calvary. But we must each receive that by faith. Hebrews 4:2 says, "For unto us was the gospel preached, as well as unto them: but the word preached did not profit them, not being mixed with faith in them that heard it" (KJV). There is something completely inconsistent and even inconceivable that I would exercise faith and repentance today for sins I plan to commit tomorrow. No, we will deal with tomorrow's sins tomorrow. It is our plan to have no sins tomorrow, although we may fall short of that goal. The problem with this popular doctrine is the implication that we need not concern ourselves much with our sins, because they were all already taken care of at the cross. On God's part, the atonement for all sin was finished at the cross. But the New Testament requires us to deal with our sins, to confess our sins as discussed in chapter three. We don't just chalk it up as nothing to worry about. Just because the provision for forgiveness has been made, does not mean I have automatically received it.

Universalists take this text and twist it to their own destruction. They say the sacrifice has been made for the sins of the world and all the world will therefore be saved. Some even say the devil and his demons will ultimately be saved. It is all based upon a misunderstanding of the love of God. It is a damnable heresy that comforts the wicked in their sin. But read Revelation 19 and 20. Look at the Great White Throne judgment. Let the words of Revelation 20:15 instruct you: "And whosoever was not found written in the book of life was cast into the lake of fire" (KJV).

The comfort John is giving in our text is to the believer. We wrestle with sin because we want to please the Lord in everything we do, yet we often fall short of that goal. It grieves us severely when we fail the One who loved us and gave Himself for us. We do not take our sins lightly. But we do not despair either. For Jesus Christ is our Advocate. As our High Priest, He ever lives to make intercession for us.[32] God has made a way for us to resolve those issues. "If we confess our sins He is faithful and just to forgive us our sins and to cleanse us from all unrighteousness" (1 John 1:9). We would never abuse such a loving provision of grace. But when we fail, we fall on that provision and receive the help we need.[33]

Are you in need of that provision? Is there anything clouding your relationship with God? He invites you to come now and receive forgiveness and restoration. You have an Advocate in Jesus.

# Endnotes: Chapter 4

1   Billy Sunday, "25 Christian Quotes About Sin," *What Christians Want to Know*. Retrieved Aug. 27, 2018 at https://www.whatchristianswanttoknow. com/25-christian-quotes-about-sin/.

2   Rom. 6:23, KJV. Sin has a corrupting, defiling effect on the soul. It not only needs to be forgiven; it needs to be cleansed as well.

3   Cf. Gal. 6:7–8.

4   Cf. Rom. 7:22.

5   John does not make this statement as a direct command. That would have been done with the imperative mood, rather than subjunctive. But his statement communicates the desire of his heart for them as a spiritual father; and it should be embraced by the hearing ear as a directive.

6   Rogers, and Rogers, 592.

7   Spiros Zodhiates, *The Epistles of John: An Exegetical Commentary* (Chattanooga, TN: AMG Publishers, 1994) 46.

8   Burdick, 129–130.

9   When the standard is lowered, even with good intentions, we hinder the Holy Spirit's work of conviction and repentance. Conviction comes when people are awakened to the difference between the standard and their behavior.

10  Cf. Col. 1:10; 2 Cor. 13:11 (NIV); Heb. 12:1.

11  Cf. Rom. 6:1–2.

12  Cerinthus taught this. Alan Richardson, ed., *A Dictionary of Christian Theology*, s. v. "Gnosticism," by A. R. C. Leaney, 136.

13  Cf. Acts 4:12.

14  2 Cor. 11:4, KJV.

15  Steve Hill is the evangelist who led the Brownsville Revival in Pensacola, Florida from 1995 to 2000. Over two million people attended the meetings which impacted the whole nation and beyond. Hill died March 9, 2014.

16  Research in the beliefs of the emerging generation indicate increasing departure from commitment to biblical standards. The sheer demographics of those trends will move the nation away from godly principles if the church fails to reach sinners with the gospel. While Christians should exercise their influence in the political arena, a grass-roots revival is what is needed in the long run. For the demographic trends, see George Barna and David Barton, *U Turn* (Lake Mary, FL: FrontLine, 2014) 39-40.

17  An example of the oppression that was mounting can be seen in ObamaCare v. Hobby Lobby and the legal battles fought by Catholic dioceses during that period to preserve their religious freedom.

18  Cf. Rev. 1:12–13.

19  Zodhiates, *The Epistles of John*, 46–47.

20  Cf. Rev. 12:10; Zech. 3.

21  Burdick, 130.

22  1 Pet. 2:24, NASB.

23  Fettke, Tom, ed., s. v. "Just as I Am," by Charlotte Elliott, 342.

24  Heb. 9:22, KJV. .

25  Cf. Heb. 9:22, NIV.

26  Burdick, 131–132: ". . . *hilasmos* is here followed by *peri ton hamartiōn, concerning sins*, rather than the objective genitive case as would be expected if the passage were speaking of expiation *of* sins. It is God who is propitiated with regard to sins; it is not sins that are expiated." Burdick also refers the reader to Leon Morris, *The Apostolic Preaching of the Cross*, pp. 205–207, in regard to the meaning of *hilasmos* in this passage.

27  Thayer, s. v. "NT:2434."

28  Cf. 2 Cor. 5:19, "That God was in Christ, reconciling the world unto himself" (KJV).

29  Robert Law, *Tests of Life: A study of the First Epistle of St. John*, 3rd. ed. (Edinburgh: T & T. Clark, 1909) 3rd ed. reprint, Grand Rapids: Baker Book House, 1968, 162.

30  John 3:16, NASB.

31  Cf. Heb. 3:19.

32  Cf. Heb. 7:25.

33  Cf. Heb. 4:16.

# CHAPTER 5

# Combating Gnostic Error
## 2:3–6

Now by this we know that we know Him, if we keep His commandments. He who says, "I know Him," and does not keep His commandments, is a liar, and the truth is not in him. But whoever keeps His word, truly the love of God is perfected in him. By this we know that we are in Him. He who says he abides in Him ought himself also to walk just as He walked.

1 John 2:3-6, NKJV.

## Expository Message

How can a person know that he knows God? That is the question John is answering in our text. He begins in 2:3, "Now by this we know that we know Him." John is addressing an extremely important issue, perhaps the most important issue anyone will ever face. Do you really know the Lord? How do you know that you know Him? When other people tell us they know the Lord, how can we know whether their profession is true or false? The born-again experience is a profoundly personal event. It occurs internally, deep inside the person. No one can see it happen. God sees it. The individual experiences it. Hopefully, out of that experience the new convert makes a public profession of faith and is baptized in water. People can observe the person's commitment to water baptism. But no one can see into his inner-man and see the new birth. We must rely on external evidence in order to discern the truth of his profession of faith.[1]

In our text, John gives us an objective test. What is the test? The internal change is demonstrated in the external behavior: "If we keep His commandments." This is not about what a person feels. It is not about spiritual lingo. Here is how we know: "Now by this we know that we know Him, if we keep His commandments" (2:3).

We must first apply that test to our own lives before we use it on others. Am I living in obedience to God's word? Am I keeping His commandments? Our first order of business is to make sure there is no beam in our own eye obstructing our view. This moral test also informs our discernment concerning the profession of others. For in the next verse John says, "He who says, 'I know Him,' and does not keep His commandments, is a liar, and the truth is not in him." That is strong, confrontive language coming from the Apostle of Love, but the stakes are too high for beating around the bush. The statement must be so clear that it cannot possibly be misunderstood. Eternal destinies are at stake! A person's lifestyle reveals the inner condition of the soul. There is a connection between what a person does and what a person is.

This test of practical morality runs through John's epistle. The word translated commandment, *entolē*, occurs more times in this little epistle than in any other book in the New Testament. John uses it fourteen times in 1 John and four times in 2 John.[2] The commandments of God provide an objective measurement of reality: by this—if we keep His commandments.

We must not reverse the relationship John gives between knowing God and keeping His commandments. Genuinely knowing God is what causes us to walk in truth. It is what causes us to live according to His commandments. Keeping the commandments does not cause a person to know God. The connection cannot be established in that direction. Paul makes that clear in Romans 3:20 where he writes, "By the deeds of the law no flesh will be justified in His sight" (KJV). Obedience to the commandments is empowered by the Spirit. The one who is truly born of the Spirit demonstrates that reality by a lifestyle of obedience to God.

"He who says, 'I know Him,' and does not keep His commandments, is a liar and the truth is not in him." We heard John say something similar to this in chapter 1, verse 6. "If we say that we have fellowship with Him, and walk in darkness, we lie and do not practice the truth" (NKJV). In both verses, what the person is saying turns out to be untrue. Walking in darkness and not keeping His commandments stand parallel with one another. Look how this theme continues throughout the letter.

> 2:5–6: "But whoever keeps His word, truly the love of God is perfected in him. By this we know that we are in Him. He who says he abides in Him ought himself also to walk just as He walked." How did Jesus walk? He always did the things that please the Father (John 8:29). He said in John 15:10, "If you keep My commandments, you will abide in My love; just as I have kept My Father's commandments and abide in His love" (NASB). He gave the example of walking in obedience to the Father's commandments and calls us to the same kind of walk.

> 2:29: "If you know that He is righteous, you know that everyone who practices righteousness is born of Him" (NKJV).

> 3:10: "In this the children of God and the children of the devil are manifest: Whoever does not practice righteousness is not of God, nor is he who does not love his brother."

> 5:2: "By this we know that we love the children of God, when we love God and keep His commandments" (NKJV).

Why is this theme so important to John? It was a truth being challenged by false teachers in his day. The errors propagated by these false teachers later became prominent in a movement known as Gnosticism. Although a thorough discussion of that movement is beyond the scope of this book, it will be helpful to address a few errors that were already affecting the church in John's day.

## HISTORICAL BACKGROUND: EARLY GNOSTIC ERROR

John is combating Gnostic error that is threatening the wellbeing of the church.[3] Gnosticism was in its early stages in John's day. It never became an organized, structured institution. The movement was named after its emphasis on "*gnōsis*" as the pathway to spiritual redemption. *Gnōsis* is the Greek word meaning "knowledge" or "insight."[4] The verb form used in our text is *ginōskō*, to know. The Gnostics had their own opinion as to how a person can know that he knows God. It was at variance with the true gospel message. So John writes, "Now by this we know [*ginōskomen*] that we know [*egnōkamen*] Him." This issue of how we know that we know God is a major contention between John and these false teachers.

Gnosticism was a diverse movement much like the New Age Movement of today. It is difficult to define because of the complexity and disparate teachings in the various branches of the movement.[5] Webster's Dictionary defines Gnosticism as, "The thought and practice esp. of various cults of late pre-Christian and early Christian centuries distinguished by the conviction that matter is evil and that emancipation comes through gnōsis."[6] Much of our understanding of the Gnostics comes through the writings of early church fathers like Irenaeus who lived in the second and third centuries.

It would require a whole book to deal with Gnosticism in any depth. But some knowledge of their typical heresies provides helpful background for understanding John's polemic statements in this letter. For example, John is confronting error when he writes in our text, "He who says, 'I know Him,' and does not keep His commandments, is a liar, and the truth is not in him" (2:4). Therefore, consider the following Gnostic concepts.

### Dualistic View of the World

Creation myths among gnostic systems vary in their detail. But a common theme is that "angelic powers," including the God of the Old Testament, "were in rebellion against the supreme power" when they created the material world.[7] . Gnostics believed that God "had no intention of creating a material world, only a spiritual one." The supreme being generated a number of spiritual beings. One [or more] of these beings, far removed from God Himself, "fell into error, and created the material world."[8] The Gnostic Gospel of Phillip teaches that "the world came into being through a mistake or a transgression."[9]

With this cosmogony, Gnostics viewed the material world as evil and insisted on a separation between the worlds of the material and the spiritual. They distanced God from the creation of the material world; they embraced an extreme dualism that viewed all matter as evil and opposed to that which is good and spiritual. Of course, this significantly influenced their understanding of Christology and soteriology.

## Gnostic Christology

With that erroneous foundation of extreme dualism, Gnostics produced various heresies concerning the nature of Christ. Most relevant to 1 John is their rejection of the incarnation. John opened this epistle with a strong affirmation of Christ's incarnation. He is combating their errors. He did the same thing in his gospel. "And the Word was made flesh and dwelt among us (and we beheld His glory)" (John 1:14, KJV). The Gnostic would say no to that. He would say God could not dwell in a flesh-and-blood, material body. One form of Gnosticism taught Christ only appeared to be in a human body (Docetism).[10] Gnosticism rejects the biblical testimony of who Jesus is. And that is a fatal error!

Because of their view that all matter is evil, Gnostics rejected the idea of a bodily resurrection as well. They distorted it into a purely spiritual event that takes place upon "the acquisition of true gnosis during life on earth."[11] Paul was confronting that in 1 Corinthians 15. John's defense of Jesus's full humanity and His full deity as Son of God is a major theme in this epistle.

## Gnostic Anthropology

One false concept common in Gnosticism is that a person's soul existed with God before later falling into a physical body. Unfortunately, some Christians today embrace this Gnostic error. Some cults teach a preexistence fallacy as well.[12] Plato believed that "a soul lives *after* the death of the body, but also it already existed *before* life in the present body." He even believed that a soul can have "belonged to another body" and can be reincarnated. For Plato, the goal for every human is to regain knowledge (gnōsis) of where he came from (in the heavenly realm) and where he is going (back to its origin with the supreme God in the spiritual realm). The person is to recall the knowledge he had before being trapped in a human body.[13] Plato's philosophy had a profound impact on the Gnostic movement. In Colossians 2:8 Paul warned Christians to not be spoiled "through philosophy and vain deceit, after the tradition of men" (KJV). It was happening, and it was to be avoided.[14]

## Gnostic Redemption

The Gnostic concept of redemption was based on revelation of mysteries and passwords, rather than the sacrificial death of Jesus.[15] For them the physical death of Jesus was discounted and beneath spiritual realities. It was material and therefore could not be redemptive. So, they essentially rejected the way of salvation through the propitiation of Christ. For them salvation was a personal quest of knowledge. The knowledge that brought redemption for the Gnostic was not an intellectual, rational type of knowledge that someone might learn at a university. It was mystical, intuitive revelation.[16] It focused on personal, spiritual experiences. Gnostics saw Christ as a teacher and revealer of knowledge, not the Lamb that takes away the sin of the world.[17]

So we see John, in his epistle, emphasizing the blood of Jesus and the sacrifice of Calvary. We see him using phrases like "the blood of Jesus His Son cleanses from all sin" (1:7); and "He Himself is the propitiation for our sins" (2:2); and "This is the One who came by water and blood, Jesus Christ; not with the water only, but with the water and with the blood" (5:6).[18]

## Gnostic Thought Concerning the Commandments of God

As already mentioned, most Gnostics did not equate the God of the Old Testament with the supreme God. Instead many believed the Old Testament God to be angels who enslaved people with arbitrary rules and commandments.[19] The Gnostic Marcion taught "there was an infinite distance between the cruel God of the Old Testament and the unknown highest God of perfect love."[20] In contrast to the Old Testament God, the supreme God of love (according to Marcion) "requires nothing of us, but rather gives everything freely, including salvation. This God does not seek to be obeyed, but [simply] to be loved . . . at the end, there will be no judgment, since the Supreme God is absolutely loving, and will simply forgive us."[21] Can you see any current trends in that direction? Some of today's popular notions of love are not anything new. Marcion was preaching it in the second century.

History tells us that Simon the Sorcerer in Acts 8 became a major Gnostic leader. Remember when he wanted to give Peter and John money for the power of the Holy Spirit, and Peter told him he was "poisoned by bitterness and bound by iniquity" (Acts 8:23, NKJV). Simon did not repent; instead, he promoted himself "as the manifestation of the highest God," and drew a huge following.[22] His brand of Gnosticism, the Simonians, said the Old Testament prophets had not been inspired by the most high God, but by the angels who created the world. These angels, they insisted, led humankind into slavery with all kinds of arbitrary commandments. Notice their hostile attitude toward the commandments of God? "The Simonians thought that people could not be redeemed by doing 'righteous works', but only by Simon's grace."[23] Of course, we cannot be saved by doing "righteous works," but salvation does not come through "Simon's grace." It comes through biblical grace that teaches us that "we should live soberly, righteously, and godly in the present age" (Titus 2:12). These Gnostics preached their own brand of grace, and it did not produce a godly lifestyle. They had enough truth mixed with their error to make it sound right to the uninformed.

These Gnostic attitudes toward the commandments of God provide interesting background for our text. John's test of whether a person knows God stands in clear contrast to their rejection of those commandment. Notice John's emphasis on keeping the commandments. "Now by this we know that we know Him, *if we keep His commandments*" (emphasis mine, 2:4).

## Gnostic Asceticism and Antinomianism

Their inordinate separation between the material and the spiritual led to extreme doctrines concerning the physical body. Since the body was material and of no eternal value, some Gnostics used ascetic practices to keep it under control. Irenaeus made this statement concerning the followers of Saturnilus (Saturninus): "Marriage and procreation, they maintain, are of Satan. Many of his followers abstain from animated things (i.e. animal food), and through this feigned continence they lead many astray."[24] Paul dealt with the problem of asceticism in Colossians 2 and 1 Timothy 4.

Other Gnostics took the opposite position. They reasoned that it did not matter what was done in the physical body, as long as one had gnōsis.[25] For them behavior done in the material realm could not affect the pneumatics to which they had attained.[26] Their error was antinomianism. For example, the Simonians believed that "those who had set their hope on Simon and [his companion], Helen, would also be free to do what they wanted."[27] Observe the libertine position. If you put your hope in Simon and Helen, you would be able to do whatever you wanted to do. Since these Gnostics believed the true self was separate and above the physical cosmos, there was no reason their followers should obey the moral rules of purity in their physical behavior.

John is confronting the antinomian heresy in our text. The following words of a modern-day Gnostic reveals the gravity of the heresy. Stephan Hoeller regards his individual human *pneuma* as superior to and possessing a sovereignty over the primitive law of "Thou shalt" and "Thou shalt not" promulgated by the demiurge. By demiurge, he is referring to the lesser God of the Old Testament. Then he writes, "To imagine that one's pure, divine spirit could be even affected, and even less lost because of transgressing against the petty laws of a cosmic tyrant appeared laughable to the Gnostics. Threats of demiurge retribution cannot frighten the Gnostic, for the rules of the lower world has no dominion over the *pneuma* which originates within and is destined to return to the realm superior to his own." He then goes on to talk about the value of cultivating freedom from external laws and commandments.[28]

The basic Gnostic idea is this: "I had a spiritual (*pneuma*) experience that has brought me into a higher realm. It no longer matters what I do. I am destined to enter a superior realm." I don't often hear it stated in such blasphemous tones, but I hear an echo of this thinking in some Christian circles. A person says the sinner's prayer, has an experience with God, but like the Gnostic, says to himself, "I have redemption; now I can do whatever I want to, and, in the end, I will go to heaven." It is a false peace that should be examined carefully. That person's eternal destiny rests on whether he is right or whether he is wrong. In our text, John says we should apply an objective test to be sure. "Now by this we know that we know Him, if we keep His commandments. He who says, 'I know Him,' and does not keep His commandments, is a liar, and the truth is not in him."

## APPLICATION TODAY

Now we will examine the significance of John's statement for us today. In our text, John clarifies what it means to know God. That is our greatest goal in life. Knowing or not knowing God determines one's eternal destiny. In John 17:3 Jesus equated it to eternal life. "This is eternal life [What is eternal life?] that they may know You, the only true God, and Jesus Christ whom You have sent" (NASB). Do you know God? No one can know "the only true God" except through Jesus.[29]

John is talking about our relationship with God. In chapter one he used the Greek word koinōnia in a discussion of that subject. Here in our text he uses the Greek word *ginōskō* (to know): "Now by this we know [*ginōskomen*]." That is in the Greek present tense: we continually know. "That we know [*egnōkamen*] Him." That is in the Greek *perfect* tense which means at a definite time in the past we came to know Him and we continue to know Him.[30] In fact, we perceive more and more clearly that our knowing Him is genuine through its results: a growing willingness to obey.[31] The relationship had a definite beginning, the day you were born again. But the depth of it continues to grow. Paul set it as the goal of his life. He said that he counts everything loss for the excellence of the knowledge of Christ. In Philippians 3:10 he wrote, "That I may know him, and the power of his resurrection, and the fellowship of his sufferings, being made conformable unto his death; If by any means I might attain unto the resurrection of the dead" (KJV). Paul's life was marked by continual growth in his knowledge of God—not his knowledge *about* God, but his personal, intimate knowing God in his daily experience.

The Gnostic focused on knowing *himself,* his origin and destination. Paul and John focused on knowing *God*. Secular Psychology is about self-identity and self-esteem. God is pretty much left out of the picture. It's a subtle trap. Keep looking inward to find *yourself.* It caters to the ego. There must be something in me really great. I just need an epiphany of self-realization. But Paul had a different orientation: "That I may know *Him*" (emphasis mine). It is in knowing *Him* that we discover who *we* are "in Christ." Our peace is found in Him. Our identity is found in Him. There is a big difference between the Gnostic inward, self-centered orientation and Paul's God-ward orientation. This quote from the second century Gnostic, Monoimus, demonstrates the Gnostic focus on knowing self.

> Abandon the search for God and the creation and other matters of a similar sort. Look for him by taking *yourself* as the starting point. Learn who it is who *within you* makes everything his own and says, "*My* god, *my* mind, *my* thought, *my* soul, *my* body." Learn the sources of sorrow, joy, love, hate. Learn how it happens that one watches without willing, rests without willing, becomes angry without willing, loves without willing. If you carefully investigate these matters you will find him *in yourself.*[32]

Those words sound strangely similar to much of the false teaching that is being promoted today. It appeals to people's sense of self-importance. Robert Grant sees this as "the first and most important point in defining Gnosticism." He writes, "It is a religion of saving knowledge, and the knowledge is essentially self-knowledge, recognition of the divine element which constitutes the true self.[33]

Gnostic ideas and concepts are often communicated in today's society through psychology. Carl Jung was an avid reader and proponent of Gnostic literature.[34] In fact, that's where he got many of his ideas. Of course, he was also steeped in spiritism, astrology, and the occult.[35] Freud did the same.[36] Our culture is far more influenced by Gnostic thought than most of us would imagine. It is mostly packaged as psychology. Let me give you some Gnostic thinking that you may be familiar with. "Whatever is right for you, is right. You just do what *you* feel is right." It's a highly individualized morality, not based on the commandments of God, but on one's own personal insights. One modern Gnostic said, "Each human being is in truth his or her own absolute lawgiver."[37] When you consider how prevalent thinking like that is in our society, it is rather alarming. But it's more alarming when you realize many Christians think that way, and some pulpits proclaim a message very close to that. The warped emphasis on love without moral accountability is a setup for what is to come in the way of Gnostic error.

An event occurred in December 1945 that is having an impact on us today. An Egyptian peasant was exploring some caves when he came upon an entire collection of Gnostic codices. His discovery is known as the Nag Hammadi find. The literature was slow to see the light of day. But one man was very influential in getting it published, Carl Jung.[38] Now Gnostic ideas hidden away for hundreds of years are being read. It is particularly disconcerting when you think about the mentality of multitudes in the emerging generation who reject institutionalized Christianity, but instead seek spirituality without unwanted moral restraints.[39] The modern Gnostic, Stephan Hoeller wrote, ". . . Jung's insights need to be considered as one of the latest and greatest manifestations of the stream of alternate spirituality which descends from the Gnostics."[40] The best defense against this is an active proclamation and teaching of biblical truth, joined with genuine born-again experiences.[41]

Knowing God is a very personal, spiritual experience based on biblical truth. Do you remember the day you were born of the Spirit? The inner witness began then and continues today. Romans 8:16 says, "The Spirit Himself bears witness with our spirit that we are children of God" (NKJV). John declares the same thing: "By this we know that we abide in Him, and He in us, because He has given us of His Spirit" (1 John 4:13, NKJV). There is an inner witness of the Spirit that tells us we are His children. It is a subjective proof. But John teaches us to test that heart-felt reality with some objective evidence as well. "Now by this we know that we know Him, if we keep His commandments."[42]

Knowing God cultivates love for God which produces obedience to God. If we love Him, if we know Him, we will keep His commandments. We do not keep those commandments purely out of external duty. Instead, our hearts are changed. What we once loved, we now hate. What we once hated, we now love. The law of God is written, not on tables of stone, but on our hearts. It becomes our delight to do the will of the Father. We keep the commandments because we want to; we want to please the Lord in everything we do. The promise of that is recorded in Jeremiah 31:33. "But this shall be the covenant that I will make with the house of Israel; After those days, saith the Lord, I will put my law in their inward parts, and write it in their hearts; and will be their God, and they shall be my people" (KJV). God puts His law in our hearts. The obedience flows out of that. The internal change of heart is manifested in the external behavior. Verse 34 says, "And they shall teach no more every man his neighbour, and every man his brother, saying, Know the Lord: for they shall all know me, from the least of them unto the greatest of them" (KJV). This is available to each and every one of us.

In verse 5 of our text, John makes an additional statement about knowing God. "But whoever keeps His word, truly the love of God is perfected in him. By this we know that we are in Him." To know God is to be *in Him* or as Paul would put it *in Christ*.[43] We come into union with the Lord. We dwell in His fellowship. He talks with us, and we talk with Him. In our communion, we come to know Him better and better. It is the real purpose of life! It's sad that so many people miss it. They are very busy about many things, and sadly they miss the one thing that really, really matters.[44]

Many people don't know God, because they ignore Him. Many are in a storm, yet they are ignoring God—trying to solve the problem without Him. They look to other people for the solution. Some look to the government for answers. But the big failure is a failure to look up. Psalm 121:1–2 says, "I will lift up my eyes to the mountains; From where shall my help come? My help *comes* from the Lord, Who made heaven and earth" (NASB). Are you looking up? Are you looking to the Lord for your answers? Jeremiah wrote, "Thus says the Lord, 'Cursed is the man who trusts in mankind And makes flesh his strength, And whose heart turns away from the Lord'" (17:5, NASB). That's the kind of thing that breaks God's heart. Jeremiah draws this contrast: "Blessed is the man who trusts in the Lord And whose trust is the Lord" (17:7, NASB).

To ignore is "to refuse to take notice of."[45] The root meaning of "gno" in "ignore" is "to know." It hypothetically goes back to our Greek word gnōsis.[46] We don't want to ever ignore God. We want to keep our minds stayed on Him and live in communion with Him. Rather than ignore God we want to look to Him continually. He is a very present help in time of need.[47]

John focuses on the word of the Lord in verse 5: "Whoever keeps His word." The Psalmist wrote, "Your word I have hidden in my heart, That

I might not sin against You" (Ps. 119:11, NKJV). Keeping God's word in our heart is closely linked with keeping His commandments. John is expanding the scope some because the word includes the commandments, but it includes more. It includes the promises of God, the plans of God, the ways of God, etc. Are you embracing God's word and living in its strength? The Psalmist wrote, "I will delight myself in Your statutes; I will not forget Your word" (119:16, NKJV). Being true to God's word begins in the heart, but it also manifests in the actions. John says, "But whoever keeps His word, truly the love of God is perfected in him. By this we know that we are in Him." What does it mean, "The love of God is perfected in him"? It means God's love has fulfilled its goal in him.[48] The purpose of God's love in his heart is realized in the person's behavior.

The point John is making is reiterated in 1 John 2:6. "He who says he abides in Him ought himself also to walk just as He walked." The lifestyle of the person who knows God should be like the lifestyle of his Master. When Jesus washed the disciples' feet, he said to them, "If I then, the Lord and the Teacher, washed your feet, you also ought to wash one another's feet. For I gave you an example that you also should do as I did to you" (John 13:14–15, NASB). John has made his point three ways in our text. A person who really knows God will:

1. Keep God's commandments (2:3-4)
2. Keep or live by His word (2:5)
3. Walk or live the way Jesus lived (2:6).

The important thing is that we honestly apply the test that John proposes here. Am I keeping God's commandments? Does my lifestyle really demonstrate the authenticity of my faith? "Now by this we know that we know Him, if we keep His commandments."

# Endnotes: Chapter 5

1   Cf. Jas. 2:17–18.

2   Zodhiates, *The Epistles of John,* 56.

3   Gnosticism was in its early stages of development when John wrote this epistle. It reached its peak in the middle of the second century and persisted into the third century. The errors in my discussion just give a quick overview of a few significant heresies in the movement. In this book I use the term Gnostic to refer to the false teachers John is confronting. But that term was developed much later in history. Although these teachers emphasized gnōsis in their false concept of redemption, it is highly unlikely they would have referred to themselves as Gnostics and unlikely John would either. Later in chapter two John refers to them as antichrists. Cf. Earle Cairns, *Christianity Through the Centuries,* 1954 (Grand Rapids: Academic Books Zondervan, 1981) 98; Burdick, 54–64.

4   Riemer Roukema, *Gnosis and Faith in Early Christianity* (Harrisburg, PA: Trinity Press, 1999) 3.

5   The New Age Movement includes Spiritualism, Satanism, Unification Church, Native American Shamans, and various other cults and occultism. The diversity is significant. For an extensive discussion see Russell Chandler, *Understanding the New Age* (Dallas, TX: Word Publishing, 1988).

6   *Merriam Webster's Collegiate Dictionary,* 10 ed., s. v. "Gnosticism," 499.

7   R. M. Grant, *Gnosticism and Early Christianity,* 1959, 2nd. ed. (New York: Columbia University Press, 1066) 16.

8   Justo L. Gonzalez, *The Story of Christianity,* Vol. 1 (New York: HarperCollins Publishers, 1984) 59.

9   Roukema, 142.

10  Ibid., 163; Gonzalez, vol. 1, 60.

11  Cairns, p. 99; Roukema, p. 143, 160.

12  Cf. Carson's comments on the Mormon teaching That "Jeremiah actually existed as a 'spirit child,' as an 'intelligence,' before he was conceived." D. A. Carson, *Exegetical Fallacies,* 2nd ed. (Grand Rapids: Baker Books, 1996) 115.

13  Ibid., 76–77.

14  Gnosticism combined Jewish and Christian thought with Platonic philosophy, Eastern religions, and other cultic ideas. Philo of Alexandria was a Jew who tried to express the Jewish religion in terms which were current in his Hellenistic world (Roukema, 87). His writing fed into the Gnostic movement. Maybe he just wanted to make it more user-friendly to his readers. Maybe he just wanted his religion to be more relevant to the culture. Does any of that sound familiar? What he actually did was propagate error.

15　*The Second Book of Jeu* contains 14 passwords. According to Platonic thought the soul returning to its origin would need secret passwords at each planet for the angels to let them pass. Cf. Roukema, 49–50, 112.

16　Eduard Lohse, *The New Testament Environment*, trans. John Steely, (Gottingen, Germany: Vandenhoeck & Ruprecht, 1971, 11th reprint, Nashville, TN: Abingdon Press, 1989) 255–256.

17　Roukema, 112–113, 164.

18　All three of these quotes are from the NASB.

19　Roukema, 16.

20　Ibid., 136.

21　Gonzalez, vol.1, 61.

22　Roukema, 16.

23　Ibid. As with Simon, much of the erroneous grace teaching today emphasizes freedom from the laws of God. That can be appealing to the carnal mind. It is often prefaced by true statements as to the inefficacy of the Law as a means of salvation. That is then followed up with the offer of an unbiblical form of grace. Genuine regeneration through biblical grace produces the fruit of righteous works.

24　Irenaeus, *Adv. Haer. I 24, 2* as quoted by Kurt Rudolph, *Gnosis: The Nature & History of Gnosticism*, 1977, trans. by R. M. Wilson (San Francisco: Harper & Row, Publishers, 1984) 257. Cf. Roukema, 34.

25　Colin Brown, ed, *The New International Dictionary of New Testament Theology*, Vol. 2, 1967 (Grand Rapids: Zondervan, 1986) s. v. "Knowledge," by E. D. Schmitz, 394. Cf. Raymond E. Brown, 80.

26　Irenaeus, *Adv. Haer. 1.1.11* (Valentinians) as quoted by Rudolf Schnackenburg, *The Johannine Epistles: Introduction and Commentary: Introduction and Commentary*, Translated by Reginald and Ilse Fuller (New York: Crossroad Publishers, 1992) 80.

27　Roukema, 16–17. Helen was the "First Thought," and "the Mother of all" reincarnated in Helen of Troy according to the Gnostic system. Roukema, 15.

28　Stephan A. Hoeller, *The Gnostic Jung and the Seven Sermons to the Dead* (Wheaton, IL: The Theosophical Publishing House, 1982) 41–42.

29　John 14:6; Acts 4:10-12; 1 Tim. 2:5. Paul prayed for the Christians at Ephesus that they would "know the love of Christ" (Eph. 3:19, KJV). You only know His love by knowing Him.

30　Zodhiates, *The Epistles of John*, 55.

31　Rogers and Rogers, 593.

32　Hippolytus, Ref. VIII.15.1-2 as quoted by R. M. Grant, *Gnosticism and Early Christianity*, 9. Italics are by supplied by R. M. Grant.

33　R. M. Grant, *Gnosticism and Early Christianity*, 10.

34　Hoeller, 16–26.

35  Ibid., xxi, 3.

36  Ibid., 5. The study of human behavior is certainly a valid discipline. Unfortunately, much in the field of psychology has been tainted by Gnostic and occultic concepts.

37  Ibid., 42.

38  Ibid., 18–19.

39  Of course, this tendency is not confined to the emerging generation, fallen mankind of any age is susceptible to such an appeal. It should also be said that the positive side of Nag Hammadi find is much more original information on what the Gnostics actually taught.

40  Hoeller, 32.

41  The trend in many Christian churches to minimize the importance of doctrinal teaching weakens the churches resistance to these emerging errors. Our best defense against error is to teach the truth (1 Tim. 4:13, 16; 2 Tim. 4:2–3).

42  Gnostics place considerable emphasis on spiritual experiences as well. They serve as a counterfeit to the new birth taught in the Bible. To distinguish the authentic from the counterfeit we need to use biblical tests like the one the Apostle John gives in our text.

43  Cf. Rom. 8:1; 12:5; Gal. 3:28; 6:15; Eph. 1:3; 2:6, 10, 13; 3:6; Col. 1:2, etc.

44  Cf. Luke 10:41–42.

45  *Merriam Webster's Collegiate Dictionary,* 10th ed., s. v. "Ignore," pp. 576–577.

46  Douglas Harper, "Ignore," *The Online Etymology Dictionary.* Retrieved Sept. 5, 2017 at http://etymonline.com/index.php?allowed_in_frame=0&search=ignore.

47  Cf. Ps. 46:1; Heb. 12:1–2.

48  Law, 212–213. Cf. Donald Burdick, 138. See chapter 19, "Why We Love," in this book for a fuller discussion of this concept.

# CHAPTER 6

# Love and Hate
# 2:7–11

Dear friends, I am not writing you a new command but an old one, which you have had since the beginning. This old command is the message you have heard. Yet I am writing you a new command; its truth is seen in him and in you, because the darkness is passing and the true light is already shining. Anyone who claims to be in the light but hates a brother or sister is still in the darkness. Anyone who loves their brother and sister lives in the light, and there is nothing in them to make them stumble. But anyone who hates a brother or sister is in the darkness and walks around in the darkness. They do not know where they are going, because the darkness has blinded them.

1 John 2:7–11, NIV

## Expository Message

How do we know that we're really saved? This is a key question being answered in this epistle. In 1 John 2:3 the apostle gives this test: "Now by this we know that we know Him, if we keep His commandments" (NKJV). The saved person lives a life of obedience to the commandments of God. We explored that test in chapter five.

In our current text, John zeroes in on one particular command: "You shall love your neighbor as yourself."[1] Next to loving God with all our hearts, this is the greatest of all the commandments. John is introducing a major theme in this epistle: loving one another. This chapter will revolve around that theme.

John bases this letter on two great revelations of God. First John 1:5 says "God is light," and 1 John 4:16 says "God is love."[2] Our understanding of God must be based on both revelations. A train cannot run on only one track. Both tracks must be in place for the train to run properly. The church can only function on both revelations. If it only preaches a God of light without love, it will become harsh, judgmental, and uncaring. If it only preaches a God of love without light (which is the more common problem today), it will become soft, indulgent, and undisciplined. God is both light and love. The illustration I just gave is imperfect because the light and love of God are not separate the way train tracks are. God does not manifest Himself as light on the one hand and love on the other hand. His nature is characterized by both at the same time in everything He does. The light of God is characterized by love. The love of God is characterized by light (moral purity). God showed me this in an open vision. It is difficult to put in words something you see in the Spirit, but I will put it this way: emanating from God are glorious rays with the quality of both light and love.[3] One does not exclude the other. Both qualities can radiate in unity as an expression of a person's nature. John does not want us to pit love against light, or vice versa. God's character is love and light all at the same time.

Based on this nature of God, John provides a series of tests which demonstrate whether a person is truly a Christian or not. These tests give objective evidence of the internal condition of a soul. First and foremost, we apply these tests to ourselves. They tell us whether we're really in the faith or not. Paul said to the Corinthians, "Examine yourselves to see whether you are in the faith; test yourselves. Do you not realize that Christ Jesus is in you—unless, of course, you fail the test? (2 Cor. 13:5, NIV). Coming under the piercing light of God can be an uncomfortable experience. Light exposes darkness. Light exposes flaws. If I look into a mirror in the dark, I may not see that I have egg on my face.[4] I may think all is well, when it really is not. But if I am in the light, and look into that mirror, I will see the problem, and can then address it. Paul told those professing Christianity at Corinth to examine themselves as to whether they were in the faith or not. It is similar to what John is telling us to do in this epistle. Don't just assume you're fine. Your eternity is at stake. When a person is about to take a long road trip, it is wise to examine the condition of your car before you go. You want the brakes to be in good condition. You will check the tires for air pressure and adequate tread. You may even get a mechanic to assist you with the process. The trip we are taking is an eternal one. We want to make sure all is well.

Here are a few tests we have seen is this letter so far. They are tests that let us know whether we're in the faith or not. In 1:6 John writes, "If we claim to have fellowship with him and yet walk in the darkness, we lie and do not live out the truth" (NIV). Our walk or lifestyle is either characterized by light (moral uprightness) or darkness (sin and disobedience). Saying we're in fellowship with God is not enough; we must actually live in that fellowship. Of course, the Greek word translated fellowship is koinōnia. Its core meaning is sharing, having in common, or joint participation.[5] What is being shared is communicated by the context. John introduces this letter by saying, "We proclaim to you what we have seen and heard, so that you also may have fellowship [koinōnia] with us. And our fellowship [koinōnia] is with the Father and with his Son, Jesus Christ" (1:3, NIV). He is talking about sharing the life of God, the spiritual union of Christ and the believer.[6]

Some people emphasize a distinction between union with God and fellowship with God—as if there were three categories: unbelievers, Christians in fellowship with God, and Christians out of fellowship with God. I don't see John making that distinction. He is contrasting true believers with unbelievers. He is particularly addressing unbelievers who profess Christianity but are really not in Christ. John has two categories: those in the light and those in darkness. I realize, there is a difference between a man like Lot who was saved by the skin of his teeth, so as by fire[7] and Abraham who became the Father of Faith.[8] There is a difference between a Christian who is walking with God (as exemplified by Enoch, Abraham, and Paul) versus one like Jonah who is running from God and needs the chastening of the Father to get him back in line.[9] I'm not saying there is no distinction between a mature Christian and an immature Christian. We can see that distinction in Paul's epistles; and

John differentiates between children, young men, and fathers. But the distinction between a Christian in fellowship and a Christian out of fellowship does not seem to fit the mindset of John in this epistle. John is distinguishing between those in koinōnia with God, participating in the common life of the Trinity, versus those who are outside that covenant of grace. For John, you're either in the light or in darkness; you either know Him or you don't. John contrasts the genuine Christian versus the empty professor of Christianity. "If we claim to have fellowship with him and yet walk in the darkness, we lie and do not live out the truth."

John gives another test in 1:8, "If we claim to be without sin, we deceive ourselves and the truth is not in us" (NIV). The person living in the light sees his problem with sin; he honestly confesses it and lives in reliance on the blood of Jesus to cleanse him of those acts of disobedience. He knows his continual dependence on Jesus's sacrifice at Calvary.

In 2:3 John states the test of obedience this way: "Now by this we know that we know Him, [That phrase is equivalent to saying we have fellowship (koinōnia) with Him] if we keep His commandments." We have the assurance that we do indeed have eternal life *if* we keep His commandments. We do not earn eternal life by keeping His commandments. The eternal life that God puts in us produces a lifestyle of obedience to God. "Now by this we know that we know Him, if we keep His commandments." We talked about that test in the last chapter.

Now our text in 2:7–11 gives the test of love. The reality of our new birth is also demonstrated in our relationships with other believers, and in the way we treat our brothers and sisters in Christ. First John 2:7–11: "Dear friends, I am not writing you a new command but an old one, which you have had since the beginning. This old command is the message you have heard. Yet I am writing you a new command; its truth is seen in him and in you, because the darkness is passing and the true light is already shining. Anyone who claims to be in the light but hates a brother or sister is still in the darkness. Anyone who loves their brother and sister lives in the light, and there is nothing in them to make them stumble. But anyone who hates a brother or sister is in the darkness and walks around in the darkness. They do not know where they are going, because the darkness has blinded them."

## COMMANDMENT TO LOVE

The commandment to love serves as the basis of this test. On the surface, John seems to contradict himself. This is the kind of verse skeptics read at a superficial level and then say, "The Bible is full of contradictions." But John is not contradicting himself.[10] He is first anchoring the commandment to love in that which is already revealed and authoritative. Then he brings them to a higher level of realization of this truth, much like Jesus did in the Sermon on the Mount. In Matthew 5:21–22 Jesus said, "You have heard that it was said to the people long ago, 'You shall not murder, and anyone who murders will be subject to judgment.' But I tell you that anyone who is angry with a brother or sister will be subject to judgment. Again, anyone who says to a brother or sister, 'Raca,' is answerable to the court. And anyone who says, 'You fool!' will be in danger of the fire of hell" (NIV). Jesus is taking the old commandment to not kill to a higher level of understanding and application. Look at verses 27–28, "You have heard that it was said, 'You shall not commit adultery.' But I tell you that anyone who looks at a woman lustfully has already committed adultery with her in his heart" (NIV). Here is both the old and the new. The Old Testament commandment is not put away.[11] It is fulfilled at a deeper level in keeping with its original intent: that even in the heart, the seed of that sin would have no place.

First John 2:7: "Dear friends, I am not writing you a new command but an old one, which you have had since the beginning. This old command is the message you have heard." What I am about to tell you is not some new novelty I have come up with. It is rooted and grounded in the revelation you already have. Remember, the early church's Bible was the Old Testament. All that the apostles taught was built upon the Old Testament and the teachings of Jesus. Leviticus 19:18 commanded, "Do not seek revenge or bear a grudge against anyone among your people, but love your neighbor as yourself. I am the Lord" (NIV). The old command was there in their scriptures.

Are you familiar with the term progressive revelation? Progressive revelation is the concept that more current revelation flows out of previous revelation and is always consistent with it.[12] This is why, on the Road to Emmaus, Jesus used the Old Testament scriptures to teach these disciples

72

what was happening through Him (Luke 24:27). He could have just told them, but he grounded current truth in the previous Old Testament revelation concerning Him. New truth does not reverse old truth. It clarifies and expands it. Remember the test Isaiah taught: "To the law and to the testimony: if they speak not according to this word, it is because there is no light in them" (8:20, KJV). John is being true to that principle. He grounds His teaching in the light that has already been given in the Old Testament and by Jesus Himself.[13]

Remember Jesus's answer when asked what the greatest commandment is? "'Love the Lord your God with all your heart and with all your soul and with all your mind.' This is the first and greatest commandment. And the second is like it: 'Love your neighbor as yourself.' All the Law and the Prophets hang on these two commandments" (Matt. 22:37-40, NIV). All the commandments of God are wrapped up in this word *love*. Paul taught that concept in Romans 13:8–10: "Let no debt remain outstanding, except the continuing debt to love one another, for whoever loves others has fulfilled the law. The commandments, 'You shall not commit adultery,' 'You shall not murder,' 'You shall not steal,' 'You shall not covet,' and whatever other command there may be, are summed up in this one command: 'Love your neighbor as yourself.' Love does no harm to a neighbor. Therefore love is the fulfillment of the law" (NIV). So, it is no wonder that the Apostle John would focus on this one commandment of loving one's neighbor as oneself.

Why doesn't John use the first great commandment, rather than the second, to develop this test of authentic Christianity? Probably because the second is more observable. The way I treat others is something other people can see with their eyes. It provides an objective test.

Do you love your neighbor as yourself? Doing that and living accordingly is more challenging than it might sound. On the one hand, we are to hate sin.[14] God's love is not indulgent and tolerant toward sin. Jude 23 talks about pulling people out of the fire, "hating even the garment spotted by the flesh" (KJV). Jesus loved righteousness and hated iniquity (Heb. 1:9). We are to hate the sin. But we are to love the sinner. How do we hate sin, but love the sinner? C. S. Lewis struggled with that for a good while until one day it occurred to him that there was one man to whom he had been doing that all his life—namely himself. He wrote, "However much I might dislike my own cowardice or conceit or greed, I went on loving myself. There had never been the slightest difficulty about it. In fact the very reason why I hated the things was that I loved the man."[15] To obey this second great commandment, all we have to do is to apply that same mindset toward other people.

So, John begins with the authority of the old commandment to love your neighbor as yourself. But this commandment is also fresh and new because Jesus enlarged on it. Remember when He was in the upper room preparing the disciples for His departure? What He shared with them at this time is of upmost importance. There He talked to them about loving one another. In John 13:34–35 He said, "A new command I give you: Love one another. As I have loved you, so you must love one another. By this everyone will know that you are my disciples, if you love one another" (NIV). In our text John uses the same exact Greek words translated here as, "A new command."[16] First John 2:8 says, "Yet I am writing you *a new command*" (emphasis mine).

In what way is the commandment new? It is new in its level of realization and the fulfillment of its original intent. Beyond loving one another as we love ourselves, Jesus raised the standard. Now He says to love one another, "As I have loved you." The way Christ has loved us goes beyond the way we love ourselves. He loved us more than He loved Himself. He loved us so much that He sacrificed Himself for us. His love for the disciples was not altered when they forsook Him and denied Him. He continued to love unconditionally regardless of their faltering response. The old command to love others is taken to a richer, fuller level. In that respect, it is new. "Yet I am writing you a new command; its truth is seen in him and in you, because the darkness is passing and the true light is already shining." Notice the phrase, "Its truth is seen in him and in you." We have seen that this love is true in Him. His death on the cross fully demonstrated that. But can it really be true in you and me?[17] Is it really possible that we could love one another as He loved us, in like manner? Yes, because "the darkness is passing and the true light is already shining." That's a good translation because it expresses the progression of light and revelation that is happening in us. The Greek tense is expressing something that is in the process of happening, not something that has already happened. Some translations use the past tense and say, "The darkness is past."[18] But we still contend with darkness, both in our struggle with our own flesh and in our struggle with the world around us. However, the kingdom of God is advancing according to plan, and we are personally coming into more and more light as we mature in Christ. Loving in this way is possible because the Christ who loves that way is now in you through the Holy Spirit. You and I can love each other as the Holy Spirit sheds that love abroad in our hearts (Rom. 5:5). Because this new capacity to love is available to us, we are responsible to walk in it.

Why is loving one another in this way a good measurement of genuine Christianity? It cannot be done without the new nature. It is impossible to love like that through sheer willpower. That kind of love comes from only one source, the Holy Spirit. God must impart it through His influence.

So, it's a new commandment rooted in past revelation. John comes with that authority behind his instruction. It is new because it has been elevated to a new, higher level in the New Covenant.

## TEST OF LOVE

With that understanding, John shares his test of love: "Anyone who claims to be in the light but hates a brother or sister is still in the darkness" (1 John 2:9). John is talking to people who profess Christianity; they say they're in the light; they claim to be Christians. But if the person is not loving in his actions toward other Christians, he is in darkness, not light. He is not a Christian. Jesus said, "If then the light within you is darkness, how great is that darkness!" (Matt. 6:23, NIV). If what you're calling light is really darkness, then you're in deep deception and the darkness is very great.[19] If a person says he's okay, claims he's in the light, yet hates his brother, he has failed this test. He is in darkness. In our text, John is talking about loving our brothers and sisters in Christ. He is dealing with the family. He is not addressing our attitude toward unbelievers in these passages.[20] We know we are to love the unbelievers, as well, just like God does according to John 3:16. We are to even love our enemies. But that is not John's subject here. He's talking about relationships between Christians.

What does it mean to hate one's brother? John is contrasting it with love here in our text. So, it is the opposite of that. It is not loving one's brother. First Corinthians 13:4–7 describes how love *behaves*. "Love is patient, love is kind. It does not envy, it does not boast, it is not proud. It does not dishonor others, it is not self-seeking, it is not easily angered, it keeps no record of wrongs. Love does not delight in evil but rejoices with the truth. It always protects, always trusts, always hopes, always perseveres" (NIV). So, any behavior contrary to that might be considered hateful.

Hate can range all the way from murderous antipathy to disinterested apathy. John illustrates the less aggressive side of hate in 3:17: "But whoever has this world's goods, and sees his brother in need, and shuts up his heart from him, how does the love of God abide in him?" (NKJV). So, if I am just self-centered, uncaring, and passive, I have failed the love test. That is an expression of hate that we sometimes overlook.

Hate often begins with jealousy and envy. Joseph's brothers hated Joseph because they were jealous of the favor Jacob was giving him. Genesis 37:4 not only says they hated him, but it also says they "could not speak peaceably unto him" (KJV). The jealousy and hatred in their hearts caused them to be contentious and argumentative. No matter what Joseph said, they took it wrong. Have you ever dealt with someone like that? You guard your words carefully because you know they're just looking for something to get upset over. Jesus encountered it in His interaction with the scribes and Pharisees. They were jealous of the anointing on His life. They envied the favor He had with the people. They looked for ways to discredit him. They were always laying a trap for Him.[21] It was hateful behavior.

In 3:12 of this letter, John uses Cain as an example of hate. When he saw God accept Abel's sacrifice and reject his, instead of repenting, he lashed out at Abel and killed him. The ultimate desire of hate is to eliminate the other person. Sometimes that is expressed in a physical murder, as in the case of Cain. Sometimes it gets close to that as in the case of Joseph's brothers. But often the seed desire is expressed in more subtle ways like destroying the person's reputation or speaking evil of the person to others. Paul lists some manifestations of hate in Ephesians 4:31, "Get rid of all bitterness, rage and anger, brawling and slander, along with every form of malice" (NIV). Hate often produces division and contention among people. It sows seeds of discord.[22] It is inconsistent with the koinōnia John is calling people to. The next verse in Ephesians 4:32 gives a contrast that helps us see what Paul is talking about. "Be kind and compassionate to one another, forgiving each other, just as in Christ God forgave you" (NIV).

The root of hate is often an unresolved offense. An unwillingness to forgive and let it go can fester into hate and bitterness. When Absalom heard how Amnon raped and mistreated his sister, Tamar, 2 Samuel 13 says Absalom hated Amnon and eventually murdered him. The murder proceeded from the unresolved offense. We might not go so far as to physically murder a person, but carrying hate and resentment in the heart is very common. Wishing harm to another, speaking evil of the person, or not being able to speak peaceable to the person is something that people who profess to be Christians often do. It's no small matter in God's eyes. John deals with the subject further in 3:14–15. "We know that we have passed from death to life, because we love each other. Anyone who does not love remains in death. Anyone who hates a brother or sister is a murderer, and you know that no murderer has eternal life residing in him" (NIV). Some expositors say hate and unforgiveness cause you to lose fellowship with the Lord, but you're still saved. But John does not say that. John says, "Anyone who does not love *remains in death*" (emphasis mine). John's assessment is much worse than disruption of fellowship.

Notice how *not loving* one's brother or sister in 3:14 is stated in parallel with *hating* one's brother or sister in 3:15. For John, a failure to love one's brother is an expression of hate. "Anyone who does not love remains in death. Anyone who hates a brother or sister is a murderer, and you know that no murderer has eternal life residing in him." John says two things about the person who hates his brother. (1) He remains in death. (2) He does not have eternal life residing in him. John is not saying this person's fellowship with God is hindered. He says this person is a murderer at heart and does not have "eternal life residing in him." It is evidence the person is not even saved!

John deals with the negative side of this in verses 9 and 11 of our text. Verse 11 says, "But anyone who hates a brother or sister is in the darkness and walks around in the darkness. They do not know where they are going, because the darkness has blinded them." John says three things about the person who *hates a brother or sister*. (1) He "is in darkness." In 3:14 John says he "remains in death." That is his sphere of existence. He does not have eternal life. (2) He "walks around in darkness." He lives in the absence of light. He is not receiving the wisdom and counsel of God. The darkness in him also surrounds him and characterizes his life. (3) "They do not know where they are going." Their journey through life is aimless. They have not discovered the real purpose and meaning of life. A person in that condition just stumbles along over one offense after another. He is mad at God; he is mad at the world; and he is mad at the followers of Christ. He is angry and blind. It's hard to image a worse condition than the one John describes here. I don't know why some people minimize the problem by saying he has lost his fellowship with the Lord, but he's still saved. John is not creating a second category of believers. He is exposing the death and darkness in the professor who is not a true believer.

On a more positive note, John affirms the believer who loves the brethren. In 1 John 2:10 he writes, "Anyone who loves their brother and sister lives in the light, and there is nothing in them to make them stumble." The person who loves his brother has the affirmation and assurance that he is indeed the real thing, he is indeed abiding or living in the light. Then John adds this one clause, "And there is nothing in them to make them stumble." Is John talking about that person stumbling or is he talking about him causing someone else to stumble? He is primarily saying that person would not stumble because he is in the light. In contrast to those who are walking in darkness—those blind, and not knowing where they are going (as described in the next verse)— the person living in the light will not get tripped up by anything. He will deal with offenses in a biblical way, and they will not turn into a root of bitterness. He will deal with envy and jealousy and not let it have dominion over him. The Greek word translated stumble is *skandalon*. We get our English word "scandal" from it.[23] The person will not be scandalized. The Greek word can be translated offense.[24] The person who loves will not be offended.[25] Additionally, he will not cause offense to others.[26] He will not be a stumbling block. He will not cause others to stumble. "Dear friends," John writes in the fourth chapter, "let us love one another, for love comes from God. Everyone who loves has been born of God and knows God. Whoever does not love does not know God, because God is love" (4:7–8, NIV). John will have a lot more to say about the love of God later in this epistle.

Let me share a story that illustrates the love we are to have for one another. The story takes place in the part of Brooklyn, New York that was identified as "the neighborhood where a person is most likely to get shot." Bill Wilson was the pastor of Metro Ministries in the area. He has been stabbed twice, beaten, and had buildings burned down. He shares the following testimony:

> One Puerto Rican lady, after getting saved in our church, came to me with an urgent request. She didn't speak a word of English, so she told me through an interpreter, "I want to do something for God, please." "I don't know what you can do," I answered. "Please let me do something," she said in Spanish. "OK. I'll put you on a bus. Ride a different bus every week and just love the kids."
>
> So every week she rode a different bus—we have 50 of them—and loved the children. She would find the worst looking kid on the bus, put him on her lap, whisper over and over the only words she had learned in English: "I love you, Jesus loves you."
>
> After several months, she became attached to one little boy in particular. "I don't want to change buses anymore, I want to stay on this one bus," she said.
>
> The boy didn't speak. He came to Sunday school each week with his sister and sat on the woman's lap, but he never made a sound. And each week she would tell him all the way to Sunday school and all the way home, "I love you, Jesus loves you."
>
> After a few weeks before Christmas, the bus pulled up to his stop, and he got in, "I love you, Jesus loves you," the lady said.
>
> To her amazement, the little boy turned around and stammered, "I—I—love you, too." Then he put his arms around her and gave her a big hug.

That was 2:30 on a Sunday afternoon. At 6:30 that night, the boy was found dead in a garbage bag under a fire escape. His mother had beaten him to death and thrown his body in the trash.

"I love you, Jesus loves you." Those were some of the last words he heard in his short life—from the lips of a Puerto Rican woman who could barely speak English.[27] Love is active. Love finds a way to serve. Love reaches out to others. "By this everyone will know that you are my disciples, if you love one another."

# Endnotes: Chapter 6

1   Mark 12:31, NASB.

2   King James Version used for both verses.

3   John describes something similar in Revelation 1:16 when he writes, "His countenance was like the sun shining in its strength."

4   Cf. Jas. 1:23–25.

5   Burdick, p. 104. Also see Thayer, s. v. "NT:2842."

6   Barker, Kenneth L., ed., *The NIV Study Bible,* 1985 (Grand Rapids: Zondervan, 1995) s. v. "1 John 1:3, fellowship with us" by Donald Burdick, 1907.

7   Cf. 1 Cor. 3:15; 2 Peter 2:7.

8   Rom. 4:11.

9   Cf. Heb. 12:11–13.

10  John is using a literary style with paradox which graphically leads an audience to think through the meaning of one's words. This method was employed in antiquity to engage the audience's attention. Craig S. Keener, *The IVP Bible Background Commentary: New Testament* (Downers Grove, IL: InterVarsity Press, 1993) 738.

11  Cf. Matt. 5:17.

12  Lewis S. Chafer wrote, "The Scriptures unfold many highways of truth with unbroken development as true in the case of 'the blade, then the ear, after that the full corn in the ear." Lewis S. Chafer, *Systematic Theology,* Vol. IV, 1947 (Dallas, TX: Dallas Seminary Press, 1974) 203. Cf. Rudy Gray, "What Is Progressive Revelation?" *The Courier Informing and Inspiring South Carolina Baptists.* Retrieved Sept. 14, 2017 at https://baptistcourier.com/2016/01/what-is-progressive-revelation/.

13  John's reference in 2:7 to an old commandment which they had already heard from the beginning takes them back to earlier teaching which would have been grounded in Old Testament scriptures as well as the words of Jesus. Ultimately this commandment proceeds from the eternal nature of God, for God is love. H. A. Ironside understands John to be referring to the beginning of the Christian era, although these distinctions do not change the thrust of John's instruction. H. A. Ironside, *Address on the Epistles of John and an Exposition of the Epistle of Jude* (Neptune, NJ: Loizeaux Brothers, 1931), 17th printing, 1979, 15.

14  Cf. Ps. 97:10; Amos 5:15.

15  C. S. Lewis, *Mere Christianity* (London: C. S. Lewis Pre. Ltd., 1952) revised and amplified, New York: HarperCollins Publishers, 2001, 117.

16  Cf. Burdick, 141.

17  John is giving assurance to those "in Christ" that what was true of Him is also true of them.

18  For example, the King James Version and the 1599 Geneva Bible.

19 Charles H. Spurgeon, *The Gospel of the Kingdom: A Popular Exposition* (Pasadena, TX: Pilgrim Publications, 1974) 37–38.

20 C. H. Dodd, *The Johannine Epistles* (London: Hodder and Stoughton, 1946) p. xlvi.

21 Cf. Matt. 22:15–46.

22 Cf. Prov. 6:16-19.

23 *Merriam Webster's Collegiate Dictionary*, 10th ed., s. v. "Scandal," 1042.

24 The root meaning of *skandalon* is the trigger on a trap. Timothy Friberg, Barbara Friberg, and Neva F. Miller, *Analytical Greek Lexicon to the New Testament*, Baker Greek New Testament Library (Grand Rapids: Baker Books, 2000). Accessed in electronic data base: Bibleworks, version 6.0, 2003.

25 Cf. 1 Pet. 4:8.

26 Cf. Matt. 18:6; Rom. 14:13, 21.

27 Bill Wilson, "Why I Chose to Live in Hell," *Charisma*, Oct. 1996, 55-62.

CHAPTER 7

# Fatherly Affirmations
# 2:12–14

> I am writing to you, dear children, because your sins
> have been forgiven on account of his name. I am writing
> to you, fathers, because you know him who is from the
> beginning. I am writing to you, young men, because you
> have overcome the evil one. I write to you, dear children,
> because you know the Father. I write to you, fathers,
> because you know him who is from the beginning. I write
> to you, young men, because you are strong, and the word
> of God lives in you, and you have overcome the evil one.
>
> 1 John 2:12–14, NIV

## Expository Message

We understand this passage best when we put it in the context of what John
has already written in this epistle. John opens his letter with a passionate
statement concerning the incarnation of Christ. That doctrine had been
under attack by the Gnostics.[1] The honor of Christ was at stake, and the
true way of salvation was being challenged by Gnostic error concerning
the nature of Christ. John immediately gives personal affirmation of the
genuine humanity of the Redeemer. He has skipped the formality of the
traditional greeting and promptly launched into a defense of His Savior
and the apostolic doctrine of incarnation.[2]

Shortly thereafter, he confronted the antinomianism (the lawlessness) of these false teachers in 1:6: "If we claim to have fellowship with him and yet walk in the darkness, we lie and do not live out the truth" (NIV). John does not want believers deceived by that deadly error. His concern for them burns like fire in his bones. Like an alarmed parent seeing his child in danger, he responds quickly and passionately. He writes out of a fatherly concern for the safety and wellbeing of this church. He is speaking from his heart to his spiritual children.

Immediately before our text John declares two key tests for authentic faith. In 2:3-4 he states the test of holiness: "Now by this we know that we know Him, if we keep His commandments. He who says, 'I know Him,' and does not keep His commandments, is a liar, and the truth is not in him." That is certainly an in-your-face statement. The test of love that immediately follows is equally demanding and confrontive. First John 2:9-11: "He who says he is in the light, and hates his brother, is in darkness until now. He who loves his brother abides in the light, and there is no cause for stumbling in him. But he who hates his brother is in darkness and walks in darkness, and does not know where he is going, because the darkness has blinded his eyes." Those are strong words that could be difficult to hear.

Thus, we have the context for our passage in this chapter. John's words have been intense and at times confrontive. The standards John has set forth have been high and challenging. It could feel overwhelming, if his readers do not know where he is coming from, as a spiritual parent. So, he pauses to make sure they don't misunderstand his intentions. Does he think they have forsaken the faith and become apostates themselves? No, John would never want them to think that. He would never want them to take these exhortations as a rejection. Remember all the strong warnings and exhortations in the book of Hebrews? Hebrews 6:4– 8 is a terrifying warning against apostasy. It talks about people who once knew the truth and turned from it. It says they are like thorns and thistles that are useless, and just need to be burned. It describes the worst condition a person could ever be in. Then the writer of Hebrews offers this word of assurance in Hebrews 6: 9: "Even though we speak like this, dear friends, we are convinced of better things in your case—the things that have to do with salvation" (NIV). John is doing something similar to that here.

## FATHERLY ASSURANCE

Now John pauses to give a word of affirmation. He states his fatherly confidence in them. "I am writing to you, dear children, because your sins have been forgiven on account of his name. I am writing to you, fathers, because you know him who is from the beginning. I am writing to you, young men, because you have overcome the evil one. I write to you, dear children, because you know the Father. I write to you, fathers, because you know him who is from the beginning. I write to you, young men, because you are strong, and the word of God lives in you, and you have overcome the evil one" (1 John 2:12-14).

The style of this letter is very different from the way Paul wrote his letter to the Romans. There Paul is organized and methodical. He carefully lays out his argument step by step. We westerners love Romans because it fits our way of doing things. We love the logic Paul demonstrates in that book. But John is not so methodical. His background is different. He was a fisherman; Paul was an educated, trained Pharisee. John speaks as a father to his children. He speaks from the heart and is spontaneous in his style. Both styles are valid. Both are equally inspired by the Holy Spirit. In both cases, the Holy Spirit is using the personality of the writer and the circumstances of the letter.

Hear the heart of this aged father in the faith, as I paraphrase the message. In the early part of this letter he warns his spiritual children. "People who say they are in fellowship with God but are living in sin are liars and are not practicing the truth. People who say they have no sin are deceiving themselves and the truth is not in them. Here is how we know whether we really know the Lord or not, if we keep His commandments. And loving one another is a big part of that. He who says he's a Christian ought to be living the same kind of unselfish life the Lord lived. He who says he's a Christian and still holds unforgiveness in his heart toward his brother is in darkness." All that could be a bit overwhelming to hear. How well do you keep all the commandments of God? How well did you do in the last chapter with the test of love? Can you say, "I got an A+ on that test?" I finished that test realizing I've got a lot of growing to do in this area of love. John sets a very high standard for us. It is the standard God sets. But it can generate some concern in the heart. John is not condemning his readers. He is alerting them to the dangers that surround them. He is calling them to higher ground. He does not want them to misinterpret his message. So, he takes time to make sure they know the assumptions that guide his thinking.

His assumption is that they do know the Lord, both old and young alike.[3] His assumption is that they are overcomers and that they are not being overcome by the evil one. He is about to warn them to not love the world or the things in the world. But that is not to say that he thinks they have been overcome by the spirit of the world. A pastor must speak plainly to his congregation. He must give them the unadulterated truth. He must warn them of the dangers of sin and deception. But all that must be balanced with words of love and affirmation.[4] In our text, we will see how kindly John affirms these people in the progress they have made in the Lord.

There is debate as to whether John is identifying three groups in this passage or one with two subsections. Since John often refers to the whole congregation as *dear children* in this letter, some believe the words in verses 12 and 14 are to everyone. Then he divides that group into the fathers and young men. Others see three groups here: children, young men, and fathers. It really doesn't matter much which position you take. The message is essentially the same either way. What John says specifically to each group has an application to the others at some level as well. The children's sins have been forgiven; but the young men and the fathers have also been forgiven. The young men have overcome, but so have the fathers. And the children will be entering into the battle very soon. The children know the Lord, but at their own level, so do the young men and fathers. What John does with each group is focus on the most important aspect of their particular stage of development. It seems more likely that John is addressing three groups in the congregation: children, young men, and fathers.

John is not leaving the women out. He is addressing the whole congregation, men and women alike. He is simply writing in the language of his culture.[5] It would have been distracting to vary from it. So, when he says young men, he means young women as well. When he speaks to the fathers, he is also talking to the mothers. Additionally, John is not identifying these categories based on physical age. He is speaking metaphorically. He is talking about levels of spiritual development.

In this passage, we can identify "dear children" as those new in the faith. In verse 14 John uses a different Greek word for dear children than he did in verse 12. The words are synonyms.[6] Both are talking about the very young. These are new converts, novices. The young men are those who have been through some trials and battles and have grown in the grace and knowledge of the Lord Jesus Christ.[7] Those called fathers are people who have some deep experience with the Lord and are seasoned in the grace of God. John will give a word of encouragement to each group.

When I first read this passage, verse 14 seemed to be purely repetitious. Why would John say virtually the same thing twice? John does use a lot of repetition in this epistle. Some things bear repeating. John often repeats the importance of a godly lifestyle. This is so crucial to their wellbeing that they must not miss that message. John talks often about the dignity, divinity, and humanity of Jesus Christ. This was under attack, and it must be defended. So, he talks about the incarnation of Christ. He talks about Jesus as the one who was from the beginning. He insists "Whoever has the Son has life; whoever does not have the Son of God does not have life" (5:12, NIV). That theme runs through the letter. For emphasis, John is using some repetition in our text.

But more than that, he is making an important point. The tense of the Greek verb *graphō* (to write) changes in verse 14. Our text uses the Greek present tense in verses 12 and 13. That is translated, "I am writing to you" and refers to this epistle (1 John). But in verse 14 the Greek tense changes to aorist which typically is used for past tense. In verse 14 he is referring to messages he has previously written to them, perhaps in his gospel or some other letter. What John is saying now is consistent with what he has been saying to them all along. The importance of forgiveness of sin, overcoming the evil one, and knowing the Father is not something new that he is springing on them. These have always been central to his message. The New International Version does not bring this out very well because it considers the Greek in verse 14 as an epistolary aorist. Therefore, it translates the verb, "I write."[8] However, the New King James Version, International Standard Version, and others translate it, "I have written to you."

The Gnostics offered new, novel revelations: things that would appeal to the pride and curiosity of the average person. When Satan is operating as an angel of light, he often presents new, mysterious, novel information and revelation. "We know something nobody else knows. It sets us just a little above all the rest. And you can know it too."[9] That sense of superiority was in the Gnostics and is a dangerous lure.

The internet can be used for good or bad. It can be a vehicle for truth, but it can also be a vehicle for error. In the last few years, I have dealt with people who found strange doctrines on the internet and were quite proud of their new knowledge. The problem was it was not new knowledge; it was old error packaged in new wrappings. John does not want these people tossed about by every wind of doctrine.[10] He wants them established in eternal truth: tried and true truths. John's message was not built on shifting sand, but on the rock with Jesus Christ as the chief cornerstone. Like Paul, John was determined to know nothing among them but Jesus Christ and Him crucified.[11] His message has not changed, and he does not want his readers to turn from it to another gospel.[12] We must not be enticed by novelty. We must not be fooled by new, mysterious revelations that pander to curiosity and pride. We must put our roots down in biblical truth and stay true to the word of God. John has written these things to them before, but he is not ashamed to give them the same message again.

## SPECIFIC AFFIRMATIONS

John provides a specific word of affirmation for each category of believers. To the new converts he says in verse 12, "I am writing to you, dear children, because your sins have been forgiven on account of his name." He is saying to them, "I rejoice with you in this: your sins are forgiven!" Nothing could be more important. Without that, everything else is futile. If there were no remission or forgiveness of sin, there would be no hope of salvation, no hope of relationship with God, no hope of heaven. The forgiveness of sin is essential to Christian life. In the past, we were dead in trespasses and sins.[13] The wages of sin is death and separation from God.[14] There must be forgiveness of sins before a person can participate in the life of God. Sharing in the koinōnia of the Trinity requires that our sins must first be forgiven.[15]

There is only one way this forgiveness is possible for us. Notice how John adds the phrase, "On account of his name." Because of Jesus, you can be forgiven. Because of what Jesus has done in your behalf, your sins are forgiven. Your sins were not forgiven because you had great potential. Your sins were not forgiven because you were very sorry for your sins. Your sins were not forgiven just because God is love.[16] There is some truth in that; but it is not enough. Your sins are forgiven because Jesus died on the cross in your behalf. He paid the penalty for your transgression. He died and rose again for your justification.[17] As John said it, a few verses earlier, "We have an advocate with the Father—Jesus Christ, the Righteous One. He is the atoning sacrifice for our sins" (1 John 2:1–2, NIV). If you take that out of the equation, there is no forgiveness available: "Without the shedding of blood there is no forgiveness." (Heb. 9:22, NIV). But praise God, "the blood of Jesus, his Son, purifies us from all sin" (1 John 1:7, NIV). So, dear little children, don't rejoice that the spirits are subject unto you, but rejoice that your names are written in heaven.[18] Rejoice that your sins are forgiven.

John embellishes his message to the children a bit in verse 14. There he celebrates their condition as those who "know the Father." The Greek word translated know is in the perfect tense.[19] In the past, they came to know the Father, and they continue to know Him. Notice, it doesn't say they know *God*. That would be a true statement. But they know God *as Father*. The Spirit has come into them, whereby they cry, "Abba Father."[20] They have been born of the incorruptible seed through the message of the cross.[21] Their knowing is personal and experiential. They don't just know *about* the Lord, they know Him like a child knows his mother or father.

John is encouraging very young Christians here. They have a lot to learn. They are not yet tried and true like the young men and fathers. They are just now putting on their sword for battle, whereas, the young men and fathers have fought and won some battles. But they know the Father and their sins are forgiven. "O happy day, when Jesus washed my sins away."[22] They can sing with the saintly song writer, Fanny Crosby,

> Blessed assurance, Jesus is mine.
> O what a foretaste of glory divine.
> Heir of salvation, purchase of God,
> Born of His spirit, washed in His blood.[23]

John commends them in their progress. It is all that is expected of them, as newborns. They are as much in the family as the fathers and young men. So that is John's affirmation for the little ones.

Then he affirms the fathers. I don't know why he chooses that order. I would have expected him to go to the young men next. But the fathers have this in common with the children. They both know the Lord. The knowing of these seasoned believers is richer and deeper than that of the children. It is no more real, but it is more informed and ingrained. When my oldest daughter was three years old, she knew my wife, Jeanie. She knew her as Mommy. She did not know Jeanie the way I knew her as my wife. My knowledge of Jeanie was more complete. These fathers' knowledge of God in our text is more complete than that of the children or the young men. When you have walked with someone for many years, you progressively know that person better and better. That was what Paul was wanting in Philippians 3 when he talked about pressing forward that he might *know* Him and the power of His resurrection and the fellowship of His sufferings. That was the primary goal of his life, to know God. The primary excellence of the fathers is that they *know* God. Out of that flows stability and confidence. They know how to go to God for answers. They know His ways as well as His acts.[24] They are a source of wisdom and counsel because they know Him well. John repeats the same commendation to the fathers in verse 14 as he gave in verse 13.

In both verses, he adds the phrase, "Who is from the beginning." That is a reference to the eternal existence of Christ. Remember how John opened this epistle referring to "that which was from the beginning" (NIV). He immediately talked about Christ, the Word who became flesh. John did the same thing in His gospel. He says in John 1:1–3, "In the beginning was the Word, and the Word was with God, and the Word was God. He was with God in the beginning. Through him all things were made; without him nothing was made that has been made" (NIV). The Gnostics were denying all that. They saw Jesus as only a created being. The same error exists today with Jehovah's Witnesses and other cults. Many groups are willing to give some recognition to Jesus as a prophet, as a good man, as a significant religious leader. But there is no compromise on this point. You either accept Him for who He is or you have rejected His offer of salvation. He is God the Son, Creator with the Father and the Spirit.

His capacity to save you is based on who He is as well as what He has done. So, John says, "I write to you, fathers, because you know him who is from the beginning." He had commended them for that in the past, and he continues to affirm them in that.

Finally, John comes to the young men. They have not been in this as long as the fathers. They're seasoned, but not as seasoned as the fathers. They know God more fully than the children, but not as fully as the fathers. Wisdom is the mark of the fathers. Courage and vigor characterize these young men. They are not afraid of the battle. They have fought a good fight and are willing to fight more, in order to advance the cause of Christ. Like David they can say, "He trains my hands for battle; my arms can bend a bow of bronze (Ps. 18:34, NIV). By their God, they can "run through a troop" and leap over a wall.[25] Their strength is in the Lord. They are strong in the Lord and the power of His might. They know how to put on the whole armor of God and do battle with the enemy.[26]

First John 2:13: "I am writing to you, young men, because you have overcome the evil one." It's a refreshing word after hearing the high standard John has raised for believers. I do need to grow in my capacity to love the unlovely. I do need to be more consistent in keeping the commandments of my Lord. I have not already attained. But my spiritual father, John, has strengthened my heart with this affirmation. He has written to me because I have done some overcoming. I am progressing in my journey. The enemy has thrust hard at me. There were times when my faith was sorely tried. But God has not allowed my adversary to triumph over me. Today, I can look up to the Lord and say with the Psalmist, "I know that you are pleased with me, for my enemy does not triumph over me. Because of my integrity you uphold me and set me in your presence forever" (Ps. 41:11–12, NIV). My feet almost slipped at times, but God cleared the way for me to stand and win over my adversary.[27] We have known the heat of the battle. The enemy has told us many times that we would not make it. But by the grace of God, here we are! And I hear the Lord saying to some of you, "I am writing to you, young men, because you have overcome the evil one." We never get to a place where there is no more temptation, no more battles. But we can overcome the evil one by the power of Jesus's might.

In verse 14 John addresses the young men again. There he gives the secret of their strength. "I write to you, young men, because you are strong, and the word of God lives in you, and you have overcome the evil one." The *evil one* is the devil. It's not just talking about evil as a principle. It's the evil person (Satan) and his host. "For we wrestle not against flesh and blood, but against principalities, against powers, against the rulers of the darkness of this world, against spiritual wickedness in high places."[28] The battle is very real; but so are the victories. The greater the battle, the greater the victory. David learned that when he brought down Goliath. He became a young man in the Lord at an early age.[29]

What is the key to this strength? "The word of God lives in you." The word translated *lives* is in the present tense and means it is dwelling in them continually.[30] It has become a part of who they are. The word has become flesh in them.

Remember when Jesus faced the devil in Luke 4? He answered every temptation with the word hidden in His heart. "It is written: 'Man shall not live on bread alone'" (Luke 4:4, NIV). He was quoting Deuteronomy 8:3, "Man does not live on bread alone but on every word that comes from the mouth of the Lord" (NIV). "It is written: 'Worship the Lord your God and serve him only'" (Luke 4:8, NIV). Again, in verse 12, "Jesus answered, 'It is said: 'Do not put the Lord your God to the test'" (NIV). All three times Jesus used the sword of the Spirit to defeat the enemy.[31] Luke tells us two things followed that victory: (1) the devil retreated, and (2) Jesus returned to Galilee "in the power of the Spirit" (Luke 4:14, NIV).

Please make the personal application of John's message. If you are a follower of Jesus, John is commending *you*. John has spoken forthrightly about the necessity of obedience and holiness. He has insisted that we love one another as Christ loved us. Those exhortations were stated with uncompromising clarity. But with equal clarity John is commending sincere disciples of Jesus, regardless of their spiritual maturity level. You can take courage in these realities: that your sins are forgiven, and you know the Father (you also know Him who is from the beginning—the Son), and you have overcome the evil one. Be encouraged in what God has already done in your life. Let it stir faith for more!

# Endnotes: Chapter 7

1   Cf. Chapter 5 of this book, "Combating Gnostic Error."

2   The text for this chapter serves as a delayed greeting for the letter. Normally that comes at the beginning. But the urgency of his message compelled John to launch right into the issues. In this "de facto greeting," John personally addresses his readers, "not by name but by age group." Robert Yarbrough, *1–3 John: Baker Exegetical Commentary in the New Testament* (Grand Rapids: Baker Publishing, 2008) 114. Stephen Smalley says this pericope is written in a "quasi-poetic arrangement," perhaps, according to O'Neill, from an original Jewish pattern, now appearing as verse 14." Stephen Smalley, *1, 2, 3 John*, Word Biblical Commentary, Vol. 51, David Hubbard, gen. ed. (Waco, TX: Word Books, 1984), 66–67.

3   What John says in this text/greeting is directed at the genuine, orthodox Christians. It is obvious from the rest of the epistle these statements are not true of the false professors who only claim to know the Lord, but do not pass the tests John provides. Cf. Smalley 67.

4   Cf. Eph. 4:15, KJV: "speaking the truth in love."

5   Keener, 738. Cf. Burdick, 174.

6   Smalley, 68, 78. Both are terms of endearment. Westcott thinks that *teknia* emphasizes "the idea of subordination and *paidia* implies "kinsmanship." Brooke Foss Westcott, *The Epistles of St. John: The Greek Text with Notes*, 1883 (Grand Rapids: Eerdmans, 1974) 60–61.

7   Cf. 2 Pet. 3:18.

8   Cf. Rogers, and Rogers, 594; Smalley, 76–78. Zodhiates, *The Epistles of John*, 93, Donald Burdick (p. 175) and some others think John is using an epistolary aorist in verse 14 which simply looks at the current letter from the viewpoint of the reader, whereas the present tense views it from the standpoint of the writer. Although that is possible, I personally think John was being more purposeful than that in his change of tense.

9   The Serpent's temptation to Eve offered knowledge that would make her like God (Gen. 3:4–5). Cf. 2 Cor. 11:3.

10   Cf. Eph. 4:14.

11   Cf. 1 Cor. 2:2.

12   It has become popular to substitute a social gospel that calls people to kind acts toward others without repentance from personal sin. The Bible does call Christians to contend for social justice (Isa. 58) and tangible, concrete expressions of love (1 John 3:18). But to think these behaviors will prevail in people whose hearts are not transformed by the new birth and commitment to live according to the commandments of God is a fool's dream. Transformation of a society happens as people are delivered from their fallen selfishness one

person at a time. It is a works gospel that substitutes social activity for personal relationship and obedience to a holy God. The social justice flows out of intimate communion with God, not instead of that.

13  Cf. Eph. 2:1.

14  Cf. Rom. 6:23; Isa. 59:2.

15  This epistle is an invitation to share in the koinōnia of the Trinity (1 John 1:3). Considering the context, translating koinōnia as fellowship can be misleading. *The Bible in Basic English* says, "So that you can be united with us; and we are united with the Father and with His Son Jesus Christ." Burdick correctly describes koinōnia in this context as ". . . the spiritual union of the believer with Christ—as described in the figures of the vine and branches (Jn 15:1–5) and the body and head (1 Co 12:12; Col. 1:18—as well as communion with the Father and with fellow believers." Barker, ed., *The NIV Study Bible*, s. v. "1 John 1:3, fellowship with us" by Donald Burdick, p. 1907. Is that the connotation most people get from the word "fellowship"?

16  Sadly, many people expect to be saved because of their concept of God's love, a kind of indulgent attitude that is tolerant of just about anything. But faith in Christ and His sacrifice is absolutely essential for any forgiveness of sin and any realistic hope of salvation.

17  Cf. Rom. 4:25.

18  Cf. Luke 10:20, KJV.

19  Perfect tense indicates past action with continued effect. Some translations say *have known* the Father. See Young's Literal Translation, NKJV, International Standard Version, etc.

20  Rom. 8:15 (KJV); Gal. 4:6 (KJV).

21  Cf. 1 Pet. 1:23.

22  Fettke, ed., s. v. "O Happy Day" by Philip Doddridge, 532

23  Ibid., s. v. "Blessed Assurance" by Fanny J. Crosby, 345

24  Cf. Ps. 103:7.

25  Ps. 18:29, KJV.

26  Cf. Eph. 6:10–18.

27  Cf. Ps. 73:2; Ps. 18:36 (*The Message).*

28  Cf. Eph. 6:12 (KJV).

29  We also see this young-man strength in Jesus at 12 years old (Luke 2:46–50, 52).

30  Burdick, 176.

31  Cf. Eph. 6:17.

# CHAPTER 8

# Avoiding a Worldly Heart
# 2:15–17

Don't love the world's ways. Don't love the world's goods. Love of the world squeezes out love for the Father. Practically everything that goes on in the world — wanting your own way, wanting everything for yourself, wanting to appear important — has nothing to do with the Father. It just isolates you from him. The world and all its wanting, wanting, wanting is on the way out — but whoever does what God wants is set for eternity.[1]

1 John 2:15–17, *The Message*

Expository Message

In the preceding verses, John has commended the believers on their relationship with God. Their sins are forgiven; they have overcome the evil one, and they know the Lord. He has affirmed them and encouraged them.

## COMMAND TO NOT LOVE THE WORLD

Now he hits them with this command: "Do not love the world or anything in the world" (NIV). The Greek strongly implies that was happening to some extent.[2] You belong to the Lord. You know Him. But watch out! Remember when Jesus was speaking to the church at Ephesus in Revelation. 2? He commends them for their work, their labor, their perseverance, their discernment, and their rejection of evil. Those are wonderful affirmations coming from the Lord Himself. Then in Revelation 2:4 He corrects something that needs to be addressed: "Yet I hold this against you: You have forsaken the love you had at first" (NIV). God always deals with both sides of the truth. He does that forthrightly and honestly. You are doing very well in some areas, "Yet." I wonder what the Lord would put after that word in His conversation with us. I wonder what He would commend us for. And I wonder what He would say after the word, "Yet." My desire is that He would not have to add a "Yet" concerning my life. He would only do it to protect me. He would only do it to help me along in my journey. He only adds the correction because He loves us and wants the best for us. But He adds it where it is needed. John is saying to these believers, "You've got some wonderful things going for you. Hold onto those. Nevertheless, watch out for this one thing: worldliness. It can sneak up on you and subtly lead you astray."

The Greek word translated "world" is *kosmos*. It occurs six times in these three verses. We will encounter this word twenty-three times in this epistle. So, it's important that we understand what it means. What does John mean in our text by *the world*? The root meaning of the word kosmos is "order or adornment."[3] We get our word "cosmetic" from it. Peter uses it that way when he talks about the way Christian women should adorn themselves. [4] But that usage is rare in the New Testament. We also get our word "cosmic" from this term. With the foundational connotation of "order," there are three other ways kosmos is used in the New Testament.

Sometimes it is used in reference to the created universe, the heavens and the earth. "The earth is the Lord's, and everything in it, [David wrote] the world, and all who live in it" (Ps. 24:1, NIV). God created the heavens and the earth; it all belongs to Him. In some contexts that is the way kosmos is used.

In other passages it is simply referring to humanity as a whole. That's what *the world* means in John 3:16. "For God so loved the world, that he gave his only begotten Son" (KJV). God loves mankind and offers forgiveness and salvation to all who will receive it.

The most common way kosmos is used in the New Testament is as the evil system of unregenerate men and fallen angels, controlled by

Satan, operating in opposition to God. This is the way John uses the term here in our text. In 1 John 5:19 he writes, "We know that we are children of God, and that the whole world is under the control of the evil one" (NIV). Jesus referred to Satan as "the prince of this world."[5] So the world John is referring to here in our text includes the activity of unsaved people, evil spirits, and all the desires that they pursue. Paul wrote in Ephesians 6:12, "For we wrestle not against flesh and blood, but against principalities, against powers, against the rulers of the darkness of this world, against spiritual wickedness in high places" (KJV). The problem is not just ungodly people, although they are a part of the world system. But the problem includes Satan and all his host. Typically, they do not present themselves as diabolical beings dressed in red suits with a tail. They present themselves as angels of light offering fame, fortune, and pleasure.[6] *The world* is the whole, organized operation of men and fallen angels opposing the purposes of God. It began with the fall of Lucifer and then the fall of Adam. It is driven by selfish desire and rebellion against God. We see it at the Tower of Babel in Genesis, and we see it fall in Revelation 18. It includes both religious and secular expressions of animosity toward God. The animosity culminated in the crucifixion of Jesus. In John 15:18–19, Jesus tells His followers, "If the world hates you, keep in mind that it hated me first. If you belonged to the world, it would love you as its own. As it is, you do not belong to the world, but I have chosen you out of the world. That is why the world hates you" (NIV).

We know what the world is because we were once part of it. Paul told the Ephesian Christians, "As for you, you were dead in your transgressions and sins, in which you used to live when you followed the ways of this world and of the ruler of the kingdom of the air, the spirit who is now at work in those who are disobedient. All of us also lived among them at one time, gratifying the cravings of our flesh and following its desires and thoughts. Like the rest, we were by nature deserving of wrath" (NIV).

John says we are not to love the world or "anything in the world." That includes a love for material things. But it is not just talking about that. John explains what he means by the things in the world in verse 16 of our text. "For everything in the world—the lust of the flesh, the lust of the eyes, and the pride of life—comes not from the Father but from the world" (NIV).[7] The world is characterized by selfish desire. The kingdom of God is characterized by unselfish love. The world is driven by these three desires.[8] Anytime we're motivated by one of these desires, we are most certainly off course. We are operating according to the ungodly course of this world. Sometimes it takes the form of the baser sins of greed and hate and sexual immorality. But often it functions at a more subtle, refined level. To just live a self-centered life of any kind is operating according to the course of this world. Un-godliness can simply be leaving God out. It's ignoring God and living life as you please. That may appear rather harmless on the surface. The good old boy works a job and enjoys his beer on Saturday night, then sleeps in Sunday morning. What's so bad about that? It violates the first and greatest commandment! "Love the Lord your God with all your heart and with all your soul and with all your mind" (Matt. 22:37, NIV). Worldliness is all around you in many shapes and forms.

When we try to define worldliness with a list of specifics, we tend to fall into legalism: don't smoke, don't play cards, don't watch movies, don't wear jewelry. John defines it as a heart issue. What are you loving? One person might be able to play cards, and there be absolutely nothing wrong with it. Another person may need to set that aside because it is capturing too much of his affections and attention. I have known musicians who have laid aside their music for a season because it became the love of their life. There is nothing wrong with music. But if you love it more than God, then it becomes an idol. Anything that captures the desire and focus of our life more than God is an idol. And the last thing John says in this epistle is "Dear children, keep yourselves from idols" (NIV). Exactly what are these desires that characterize the world?

The lust of the flesh is a pursuit of sensual gratification. It includes sexual sins; but the scope of what John is talking about is broader than that. Gluttony is a sin of the flesh. Some people interpret the flesh as the physical body. But John is not condemning the physical body. Your body is the temple of the Holy Spirit. Your body belongs to the Lord.[9] Romans 12 tells us to offer up our bodies in service to the Lord. But within our body and soul is a fallen nature that is not subject to God and gives us a whole lot of trouble.[10] It plays off of perfectly legitimate, natural desires. The desire to eat is a God-given motivation for self-preservation. But when that is misdirected into excesses and gluttony it is a sin. Sexual desire is given for procreation and bonding in the marriage covenant. But when those boundaries are violated, it is transgression and becomes destructive. The flesh is never satisfied.[11] If we follow the carnal nature, we will go further and further into excesses, and those excesses lead to death.[12] The subtler lusts of the flesh tend to be more of a problem for the Christian, for example, the love of entertainment and excitement.[13] Legitimate things can become illegitimate when they capture our hearts and become the focus of our lives. "Do not love the world or anything in the world." What is it that you would rather do than anything else? Where do you spend your time and money? What do you passionately want to have. The answers to those questions help us understand which areas in our own lives must be kept in its proper place. Maintaining our appearance is appropriate. Being obsessed with our appearance is not. Properly enjoying a hobby can be refreshing and legitimate. Putting that before your walk with God is not okay. We should always be willing to lay it down the moment the Lord tells us to do so. In fact, it is sometimes a good idea to fast from something like that, just to make sure you're not too attached to it.

In 1 Corinthians 7:31 Paul talked about using the world, but not abusing it. You can use hobbies and entertainment and food, but always seek first the kingdom of God. God gives us things in this life to enjoy, and He resources us with what we need to do His will.[14] But life must not become a pursuit of those things. We must use those things in pursuit of one thing, the will of the Father.

The lust of the eyes is the inordinate attraction to things seen through the eye gate. The eyes are the gateway to the soul. So, in the Sermon on the Mount, Jesus says, "Anyone who looks at a woman lustfully has already committed adultery with her in his heart" (Matt. 5:28, NIV). Nothing physical has occurred. But through the imagination of the heart, sin has occurred.[15] David was enticed into sin when he saw Bathsheba bathing.[16] Achan fell into coveting when he saw the Babylonian garments, and the silver, and the gold.[17] I hear the world using a new phrase, eye candy. They use it in reference to clothes or furniture or anything pleasing to look at. Beware when the devil offers eye candy; it is an enticement into his web.

It's interesting how these three desires were what the devil used on Eve in the Garden, and what he used on Jesus in the wilderness. Genesis 3:6: "When the woman saw that the fruit of the tree was good for food [lust of the flesh] and pleasing to the eye [lust of the eyes], and also desirable for gaining wisdom [pride of life], she took some and ate it. She also gave some to her husband, who was with her, and he ate it" (NIV). Jesus encountered the same three temptations in Luke 4, but He overcame each temptation using the sword of the Spirit. I don't care who you are, the devil will come at you with these three temptations. John is telling us what to watch out for. If it appeals to one of these three desires, it is not from the Father.

The pride of life is about those things that people use to exalt themselves, to feed the ego. It may be social status; it may be physical appearance; it may be performance on the ball field; it could be success in a career. It very often revolves around personal possessions and other success symbols.[18] The possessions themselves is not the problem. The wrong attitude toward them is. The open or secret pride in what one has or has attained to is a slippery slope. When David numbered the people, he was operating in the pride of life; it brought judgment on his kingdom (1 Chron. 21). When Nebuchadnezzar was in his palace bragging about the great kingdom he built, he was operating in the pride of life. While the words were still in his mouth, God's judgment fell and he lost his sanity (Dan. 4:30–31). We tend to understand God's displeasure with the baser sins like lying and cheating and adultery. But the worst sin in God's eyes is pride![19] That sin separates us from God more than any other. Some people manage their pride in subtle ways so that it is not immediately discernable. But if it's there, it's a problem regardless of whether other people pick up on it or not.

What makes the world go around? These three basic motivations: lust of the flesh, lust of the eyes, and pride of life. Effective marketing capitalizes on these desires. What motivates people to buy the cars they buy? The need for transportation is a factor. But it is certainly not the only factor. People also choose cars for the image it gives them. The BMW sends an image of success. The liberal professor buys the small electric car because he wants people to view him as environmentally sensitive. The young cowboy gets a four-wheel-drive pick-up and puts his rifle in the rear window because he has an image to project. The balding man in the convertible sportscar wants you to view him as still with it. Image, image, image! We have to be careful that we're not living for image. We are to live to please God and fulfill His will for our lives. You can save a chunk of money if you do that.[20]

That is John's description of the world and the things in it. It is something every one of us has to deal with. We can't run from it; we have to overcome it. Throughout the centuries there have been Christian groups whose response to the world has been one of retreat. But that is not what Christ told us to do. We have to go out into the world to earn our daily bread and to be light and salt.

John's command is: "Do not love the world or anything in the world." It is not a command to physically withdraw from the world. It is a command to guard your heart with all diligence. It is a command to set your affections on things above and keep them there.[21] In John 17:15 Jesus specifically said that He was not asking the Father to take us out of the world, but that He (the Father) would protect them from the evil one. Then He prays in verse 18, "As you sent me into the world, I have sent them into the world" (NIV). Jesus has commissioned us to, "Go into all the world and preach the gospel."[22] So physically we're out there in the world mixing with unbelievers and telling them the good news of Jesus Christ. But while we're doing that, we maintain a distance from the things they love. Our values are different. We don't allow these three motivations to dominate our thoughts and goals: "The lust of the flesh, the lust of the eyes, and the pride of life."

A ship never sinks because of the water around it. It sinks because of the water that gets in it. And it doesn't matter if that water comes in through a huge tsunami wave during a storm or slowly seeps in through cracks in the hull. The more common problem is that it slowly seeps in through cracks and compromises in our lifestyle. The church in America is taking on water! The methods and philosophies of the world are getting in. We are in danger of sinking because the water is coming in the ship itself. We're supposed to be light and salt that is changing the world around us. Instead we are going to the world for methods and ways to build our congregations.

We are adopting the marketing techniques of the world, and they work! They don't work for building the kingdom of God. That requires transformation of the heart, and the world has no methods for that. But they do work for building large religious organizations. As I said earlier, effective marketing plays off these three desires. The lust of the flesh is the desire for sensual stimulation. Since we don't have the Spirit of God moving in the service, we excite the people with sound and lighting. We give them an experience that excites sensual gratification. We bombard their senses and they enjoy the show. The lust of the eyes is expressed in Christian eye candy: beautiful buildings, great graphics, and beautiful people on the stage. Everything is well-orchestrated and pleasant to watch. I'm not talking about doing things with excellence. I'm talking about appealing to the flesh. Most of all the pride of life is a powerful motivator. "We are the biggest and best! Look what we have done." Of course, we say we're boasting in the Lord. But God knows our hearts. He knows whether we are walking in pride or not.[23] The church at Laodicea was very proud of its accomplishments. They were saying, "I am rich; I have acquired wealth and do not need a thing."[24] And by all appearance it was true. But Jesus sees the true condition of every church and every individual. His evaluation was this. You "do not realize that you are wretched, pitiful, poor, blind and naked" (Rev. 3:17, NIV). Spiritually, you're in a pitiful condition. You're boasting about your success. But here's what I see! Someone summed up what I'm saying quite well when he said, "When the church feels it must become like the world to reach the world, we have not won the world, the world has won us.[25]

The church needs to set the standard and the direction, not the other way around. The more we compromise with the world, the more degenerate they become. We cannot afford to follow the world's trends in America. The wickedness is getting worse and worse. Let me give you a few facts to back that up. Since 1976 there has been a dramatic drop in marriage for young adults. In 1976, 93% of women between 25 and 29 years old were married. That number in 2014 was only 46%, 47% less than it was back then. In 1976, 90% of the men that age were married. In 2014, it dropped to 32%, 58% less than it was.[26] Now if you think those unmarried people between the ages of 25 and 29 are not having sex, you are very naïve. No wonder there is a steep rise in STD's. And the world's solution for that is not about people going back to traditional values and abstaining from sex outside of marriage. The world's solution is more government funds and more sex education in the schools. [27] The sex education our young kids need is simple: no sex outside of marriage. The Supreme Court is going down the same destructive path. On June 26, 2015 our Supreme Court declared God's definition of marriage invalid, making same-sex marriage legal in all 50 states.[28] And the White House lit up with rainbow colors celebrating the abomination.

The world around us is on a downward slide and we have to go the other direction. There is no compromise on issues like that. James said to the church in his epistle, "Don't you know that friendship with the world means enmity against God? Therefore, anyone who chooses to be a friend of the world becomes an enemy of God. Or do you think Scripture says without reason that he jealously longs for the spirit he has caused to dwell in us?" (4:4–6, NIV).

"Do not love the world or anything in the world." Why does John give this command in our text? When I would tell my teenagers to do something, they usually wanted to know why. As a parent, I don't have to tell them why. The command should be sufficient. They should do it simply because I told them to do it. But, as a parent, I also want them to understand what is behind my directive. So, I tell them why. John does this without them even asking.

## REASONS FOR THE COMMAND

John gives two reasons for the command to not love the world. First, it is impossible to love God and love the world at the same time. The two are mutually exclusive. The two kingdoms are headed in opposite directions. You cannot go north and south at the same time. Jesus said, "No one can serve two masters. Either you will hate the one and love the other, or you will be devoted to the one and despise the other. You cannot serve both God and money" (Matt. 6:24, NIV).

The most prevalent motivator in the world is the love of money. Money gives people power to get what they want. It gives them status and esteem. It feeds the pride of life. With it people can buy luxury, comfort, and pleasure for the flesh. In essence, to love money is to love the world. There are a lot of decisions in life that come down to the will of God or money so that I can pursue my own will. Your attitude toward money is a strong indicator of your love for the world. I'm not saying people who have money love the world. You can be flat broke and your heart be filled with greed and covetousness. You can have money, and as long as it doesn't have you, it's not a problem. But 1 Timothy 6:9 tells us, "Those who want to get rich fall into temptation and a trap and into many foolish and harmful desires that plunge people into ruin and destruction" (NIV). The Greek translated desires in this Timothy passage is *epithumia*. It is the same word translated lust in our 1 John text: "The lust of the flesh, the lust of the eyes." The desire for money is a snare. Having money is not necessarily a snare. But once your heart has turned toward the money, you're in trouble. Paul adds in verse 10, "For the love of money is a root of all kinds of evil. Some people, eager for money, have wandered from the faith and pierced themselves with many griefs" (NIV).

Look closely at the second half of 1 John 2:15. "If anyone loves the world, love for the Father is not in them." John has been giving us tests that indicate whether we are really following God or not. "If we claim to have fellowship with him and yet walk in the darkness, we lie and do not live out the truth." (1:6, NIV). "Whoever says, 'I know him,' but does not do what he commands is a liar, and the truth is not in that person" (2:4, NIV). "Anyone who claims to be in the light but hates a brother or sister is still in the darkness" (2:9, NIV). Now in 2:15 he writes, "If anyone loves the world, love for the Father is not in them." That constitutes a test of our sincerity.

Our tendency is to try to have it both ways: Two dollars' worth of God on Sunday and the rest of the week reserved for other pursuits. But John is not proposing a gray area where you can have some of God and some of the world. Why? Because one master or the other will win out! One love or the other will take control. "No one can serve two masters. Either you will hate the one and love the other, or you will be devoted to the one and despise the other." It will eventually go one way or the other.[29] One love will prevail over the other and dominate the life.

Jesus never calls followers to half-hearted, lukewarm Christianity. Listen to what He says in Matt. 16:24–26. "Whoever wants to be my disciple must deny themselves and take up their cross and follow me. For whoever wants to save their life will lose it, but whoever loses their life for me will find it. What good will it be for someone to gain the whole world, yet forfeit their soul? Or what can anyone give in exchange for their soul?" (NIV). He's not proposing some neutral, demilitarized zone. He's calling His followers to all-out commitment. A double-minded approach to God and the world will not lead to victory.[30] In Galatians 6:14 Paul declares his attitude toward world. "But God forbid that I should glory, save in the cross of our Lord Jesus Christ, by whom the world is crucified unto me, and I unto the world" (KJV). He's saying, "I am dead to everything world has to offer. I have no appetite for its dainties." After contrasting works of flesh with the fruit of Spirit, Paul said, "And they that are Christ's have crucified the flesh with the affections and lusts" (Gal. 5:24, KJV). What are we to do with the lust of flesh, the lust of eyes, and the pride of life? Die to it entirely; give it no place; refuse to cater to its demands. "Put to death, therefore, whatever belongs to your earthly nature: sexual immorality, impurity, lust, evil desires and greed, which is idolatry" (Col. 3:5, NIV). John's first reason for the command is that the two loves are mutually exclusive.

John's second reason is the temporary nature of the world and the things in it. The world and all that is in it is passing away. It will not last.[31] It will ultimately prove worthless. It is a bubble that will burst. "The world and its desires pass away, but whoever does the will of God lives forever" (1 John 2:17). Ultimately none of it will prove to be of any enduring value. "Vanity of vanities, all is vanity."[32] That was Solomon's estimation of the world and the things in the world. He tried them all, and it ended in frustration.

I heard the story of a man's wake in Ireland. Most of us are not familiar with a wake. It's a vigil and showing of the body of someone who has just passed away. I think it is more common in the Catholic tradition. In Ireland the body is brought to a home and all the friends gather in honor of the person who has passed away. In this particular case, the man who died loved refurbishing old cars. It was the love of his life. So, at the wake they took his body and placed it behind the steering wheel of a corvette that he had refurbished. Can you imagine coming to the event and seeing that? Their intention was to honor the man, no doubt. But for me, it was a vivid picture of the futility of this man's life. The central investment of your life was old cars?[33] A million years from now in eternity, what will they be? They will rust, deteriorate, and one day be consumed in a ball of fire in the final judgment. Moses prayed in Psalm 90:12, "Teach us to number our days, that we may apply our hearts unto wisdom" (KJV). Is it wisdom to give your days and weeks and months to something with no eternal value? That is John's point in our text One old gospel song put it this way:

This world is not my home I'm just passing through.
My treasure is laid up somewhere beyond the blue.[34]

Where is your treasure? Where are you investing your life? Are you investing it in eternal things? Have you laid up your treasure in heaven "where neither moth nor rust destroys, and where thieves do not break in or steal?"[35] Jesus said, "Where your treasure is, there your heart will be also" (Matt. 6:21, NASB). Invest in the kingdom of God. Nurture your love for God and it will grow. Remember the rich man who kept building bigger barns? God said to him "You fool! This very night your life will be demanded from you" (Luke 12:20, NIV). None of the things he had spent his life acquiring would do him one bit of good in eternity. There are a lot of people who live their lives as if there were no eternity. It is the most foolish thing anybody can do. Live with an eye toward heaven. Live with an eternal perspective and eternal purpose.

In contrast to living for the world and the things in the world, John concludes verse 17 of our text by saying, "But whoever does the will of God lives forever." Our purpose in life is not to make ourselves more comfortable or to impress other people with our possessions and attainments. Our purpose in life is to do the will of the Father. That's the way Jesus lived.[36] And that's the way we are to live. Loving the Father and doing the will of the Father are irrevocably tied to one another. The man in verse 17 who does the will of God is also the man in verse 15 who loves the Father. Let me show you that in John 14:21. Jesus said, "Whoever has my commands and keeps them is the one who loves me. The one who loves me will be loved by my Father, and I too will love them and show myself to them" (NIV). Then in verses 23–24 he continues, "Anyone who loves me will obey my teaching. My Father will love them, and we will come to them and make our home with them. Anyone who does not love me will not obey my teaching. These words you hear are not my own; they belong to the Father who sent me" (NIV). Do you see the connection between loving God and doing His will in those verses?

So, John began in verse 15 with the command, "Do not love the world or anything in the world." He gives two reasons for doing that. One is that you can't have it both ways. You either love the world or you love the Father. One desire or the other will prevail. Secondly, the things in this world are passing away. They have no eternal value. Don't invest your life in them. Use them as needed in order to do the will of God. But don't love the world or the things in the world. May God empower all of us to live that way.

# Endnotes: Chapter 8

1   Eugene H. Peterson, *The Message: The New Testament in Contemporary Language* (Colorado Springs, CO: Navpress, 1993) 591.

2   Burdick, 176.

3   G. Kittel, *Theological Dictionary of the New Testament, vol. III* (Grand Rapids: Eerdmans, 1965) s.v. *"kosmos,"* by G. Hermann Sassein, 867, 883–896.

4   Cf. 1 Peter 3:3.

5   Cf. John 12:31; 14:30; 16:11 (KJV). In Matthew 4:8–10 Satan offered to Jesus dominion over this kingdom if He would submit Himself to him (Satan) in worship. It was a bona fide temptation which Jesus overcame.

6   Cf. 2 Cor. 11:13–15; 2 Tim. 3:6–8.

7   Within this verse is another reason Christians should not love the world. These three desires do not come from the Father. They originated in Lucifer's prideful heart. They are from a polluted source. The Father gives natural desires that are wholesome (Gen. 1:27, 31). In his comments about the phrase, "Comes not from the Father but from the world" at the end of verse 16, Donald Burdick (p. 180) says "John's preposition *ek* with the ablative case obviously has reference to source. The attitudes described…come from the world system that Satan has set up in opposition to God."

8   The Greek word translated lust, *epithumia*, is morally neutral as a term. However, this context clearly indicates an evil connotation which is the way the word is usually used in the New Testament. Cf. Burdick, 178.

9   Cf. 1 Cor. 6:15, 19; 1 Thess. 5:23.

10  Cf. Rom. 8:7; 7:20–25.

11  Cf. Prov. 27:20; Eccl. 1:8; 4:8; 5:10.

12  Cf. Rom. 6:23; Gal. 6:8.

13  As stated earlier, the lust of the flesh is not just sexual. It includes any inordinate pursuit of sensual gratification.

14  Cf. 2 Pet. 1:3; 1Tim. 6:17; Eccl. 3:13; 5:18–19; Matt. 6:31–34.

15  Cf. Job 31:1; Ps. 101:3; 119:37.

16  2 Sam. 11:2. Here the lust of the eyes led to sins of the flesh and murder.

17  Josh. 7:20–21. Also note the lust of the eyes in Lot (Gen. 13:10–11).

18  The Greek word here, translated "life," is *bios*. It is clearly used in reference to possessions in 1 John 3:17. Burdick (p. 180) understood the pride of life as ". . . either a boasting of life-style or a boasting about wealth and possessions. . . ."

19  Lewis, *Mere Christianity*, 122: "Unchastity, anger, greed, drunkenness, and all that, are mere fleabites in comparison: it was through Pride that the devil became the devil: Pride leads to every other vice: it is the complete anti-God state of mind."

20  Cf. Isa. 55:2; Eccl. 5:10.

21  Cf. Prov. 4:23; Col. 2:3–6.

22  Mark 16:15, NASB.

23  The concern being expressed here is not about churches having nice buildings, quality technology, and talented people. Hopefully, we do have those things. The concern is the substitution of worldly grandeur in place of the operations and manifestations of the Holy Spirit. The concern is that organizations might build momentum based on the three motivations described in 1 John 2:16, rather than the influence of the Holy Spirit on people's hearts.

24  Rev. 3:17, NIV.

25  Franklin L. Kirksey, "The Woeful Story of the World System," *Pastor Life.* Retrieved Sept. 30, 2017 at http://www.pastorlife.com/members/sermon. asp?fm=whatnew&USERID=&SERMON_ID=6716. Franklin also offers this very relevant quote from A. W. Tozer. "Christianity is so entangled with the world that millions never guess how radically they have missed the New Testament pattern. Compromise is everywhere. The world is whitewashed just enough to pass inspection by blind men posing as believers, and those same believers are everlastingly seeking to gain acceptance with the world. By mutual concessions men who call themselves Christians manage to get on with men who have for the things of God nothing but quiet contempt." (*The Divine Conquest,* 111). Tozer was speaking to a much less compromised church than we have today in America.

26  Stephanie Coontz, "How unmarried Americans are changing everything," *CNN* (Sept. 22, 2017). Retrieved Sept. 30, 2017 at http://www.cnn.com/2017/09/21/ opinions/how-unmarried-americans-are-changing-the-game-coontz/index. html.

27  Maggie Fox, "CDC Sees 'Alarming' Increase in Sexually Transmitted Diseases," *NBC News* (Nov. 17, 2015). Retrieved Sept. 29, 2017 at https://www.nbcnews. com/health/sexual-health/cdc-sees-alarming-increase-sexually-transmitted-diseases-n465071; Mary Bowerman, "CDC: 'Alarming' increase in STDs," *USA Today Network,* Nov. 18, 2015. Retrieved Sept. 29, 2017 at https://www.usatoday. com/story/news/nation-now/2015/11/18/cdc-alarming-increase-stds/75978596/.

28  OBERGEFELL ET AL. v. HODGES, Supreme Court of the United States, October Term 2014. Retrieved Sept. 30, 2017 at https://www.supremecourt. gov/opinions/14pdf/14–556_3204.pdf.

29  Cf. Matt. 6:24; Gal. 5:9.

30  Cf. Jas. 1:6–8; 4:8; 1 John 5:4.

31  Cf. 1 Cor. 7:31; 2 Pet. 3:12; Matt. 7:24–27.

32  Eccl. 1:2, KJV.

33  This story was told as a factual event by a pastor in his sermon. Unfortunately, I cannot remember the source.

34  The Statler Brothers, "This World Is Not My Home," *Songlyrics*. Retrieved Sept. 29, 2017 at http://www.songlyrics.com/the-statler-brothers/this-world-is-not-my-home-lyrics/.

35  Matt. 6:20, NASB.

36  Cf. John 5:30, 36; 6:38.

CHAPTER 9

# Antichrist Deceptions
## 2:18–19

Dear children, this is the last hour; and as you have heard that the antichrist is coming, even now many antichrists have come. This is how we know it is the last hour. They went out from us, but they did not really belong to us. For if they had belonged to us, they would have remained with us; but their going showed that none of them belonged to us.

1 John 2:18–19, NIV.

Expository Message

In the verses prior to this, John has warned Christians about the seductions of the world. "Do not love the world or anything in the world."[1] The things in the world include the lust of the flesh, the lust of the eyes, and the pride of life. Satan uses those desires to turn our affections away from the Father. It is a very real danger for every one of us. So, John tells us to be on guard against it. Watch out for the influence of the world system.

111

## REMINDER OF PREVIOUS TEACHING CONCERNING THE ANTICHRIST

Now in our text John narrows down his warning to the deceptive spirit of antichrist. First, he reminds his readers of what they have already been taught about *the antichrist* who will come into the world.[2] "Dear children, this is the last hour; and as you have heard that the antichrist is coming." Here he is talking about a specific person who will rise up in power during the years shortly before Christ's second coming. He will have all the wisdom and deception that Satan can muster. He will be unique in his scope of influence. Revelation 13:3 says that the whole world will marvel at what he does and will follow him. Never in the history of mankind has there been leader with the kind of power and control this man will have. His ability to deceive will be unlike anything this world has ever seen.

In Daniel 7 God gave Daniel a vision of four kingdoms. The first was the Babylonian kingdom. Its capital was located in what is now Iraq. Nebuchadnezzar was the most prominent king in that empire. Belshazzar was the last king of Babylon. He was defeated by Darius, ruler of the Mede-Persian Empire.[3] Persia is now known as Iran. Cyrus was its most famous king. The Greeks, led by Alexander the Great, defeated the Mede-Persian Empire. Then the fourth kingdom was the Roman Empire. In this vision, the Roman Empire had ten horns on its head. These ten horns represent ten kings that will rise to prominence in the last of the last days. Then Daniel saw something that deeply disturbed him. He saw a little horn that had eyes, symbolic of his insight and intelligence. Daniel 8:23 says he "understands sinister schemes" (NKJV). And he has a mouth that spoke proud, boastful things. This man will lead with amazing confidence and charisma. We know from Revelation 13:6 that he speaks blasphemy against God. Three of the ten kings fell before this little horn. That may mean they are assassinated by him or they may just surrender their authority to the little horn. After that, the little horn gains dominance over the whole empire. Daniel 7:20 says he "looked more imposing than the others" (NIV). This man outshines all the rest. He has an irresistible charisma. The other kings hand over their power to him. The little horn is the Antichrist. His initial influence is relatively small. That's why he is seen as a *little* horn. A horn represent power. But this man has made a deal with the devil. Remember when Satan took Jesus on a high mountain and showed him all the kingdoms of the world. There he offered to give all that to Jesus, if he would only bow down and worship him. The offer that Jesus refused in Matthew 4, this man accepted. In the same way Satan entered into Judas,[4] Satan enters into the Antichrist and gives him supernatural power.[5] Daniel 8:24–25 says, "His power will be mighty, but not by his *own* power, And he will destroy to an extraordinary degree And prosper and perform *his will*; He will destroy mighty men and the holy people. And through his shrewdness He will cause deceit to succeed by his influence; And he will magnify *himself* in his heart" (NASB).

This man will enter the scene as a profound peacemaker. He initially comes riding on a white horse,[6] symbolic of victory. In the middle of the tribulation period that brief time of peace will be followed by bloodshed, famine, and death. But initially he will speak peace; and the world will celebrate his ability to solve insurmountable problems. He will probably have a solution to the Palestinian/Israeli conflict that nobody else can solve. He will likely bring peace to the Middle-East and to the world for that matter. He will make a covenant with Israel which he will break after three and a half years.[7] The Antichrist will go into the inner sanctuary of the Temple and present himself as God and demand that the whole world worship him as God.[8] Daniel calls this act of desecration, the abomination of desolation in Daniel 12:11.[9] Jesus prophesied it in Matthew 24.[10] This little horn, John calls Antichrist. Paul calls him "that man of sin . . . the son of perdition."[11]

John's readers had been taught from Daniel's prophecies and Jesus's teachings. So, when John opens our text with the words, "Dear children, this is the last hour; and as you have heard that the antichrist is coming," much of what I have just shared with you would have come to mind. Remember, John is also the one who wrote the book of Revelation. Paul had also been teaching on this subject.[12] In 2 Thessalonians 2 he goes into detail about the coming of Antichrist. But John does not just talk about the Antichrist.

## IMMEDIATE CONCERN REGARDING THE MANY ANTICHRISTS

John's more pressing concern is the many antichrists that had already come and were seducing the people of God. "Dear children, this is the last hour; and as you have heard that the antichrist is coming, *even now many antichrists have come*. This is how we know it is the last hour" (emphasis mine). John is not saying the Antichrist has come; he is saying the spirit of antichrist is at work even in his day. This is the focus of John's warning in our text. The prefix, anti, can mean "instead of, in place of," or it can mean "against, in opposition to."[13] In the case of the Antichrist, he presents himself in place of the true Christ. He is a counterfeit of Christ. So, in that sense he is Antichrist. And the many antichrists present their false gospel instead of the real thing. However, the primary thought behind the term is the opposition to Christ and His followers. The Antichrist and the many antichrists operate deceitfully; but it is all done *against* the Lord.

John says, "Even now many antichrists have come. *This is how we know it is the last hour*" (emphasis mine). What does John mean in this verse by the phrase, *the last hour*? That sounds like it would refer more to our day than to his. However, New Testament writers called the period between the first coming of Christ and the second coming of Christ, the last hour, the last days, and the last times.[14] Notice how the author of Hebrews uses the term. Hebrews 1:1–2 says, "In the past God spoke to our ancestors through the prophets at many times and in various ways, but *in these last days* he has spoken to us by his Son, whom he appointed heir of all things, and through whom also he made the universe" (emphasis mine, NIV). In reference to the 120, on the Day of Pentecost, Peter said, "No, this is what was spoken by the prophet Joel: '*In the last days*, God says, I will pour out my Spirit on all people" (emphasis mine, Acts 2:16–17, NIV). Why did they speak in those terms? They did not know chronologically when the Lord would return. They knew the signs that Jesus had told them in Matthew 24. But Jesus Himself said, "But about that day or hour no one knows, not even the angels in heaven, nor the Son, but only the Father. Be on guard! Be alert! You do not know when that time will come" (NIV).[15]

One of the signs of the last days is *many antichrists*. In Matthew 24:3 the disciples came to Jesus privately and asked Him, "Tell us, when will these things be? And what will be the sign of Your coming, and of the end of the age?" (NKJV). In answer to their question, the first thing Jesus said was, "Take heed that no one deceives you. For many will come in My name, saying, 'I am the Christ,' and will deceive many" (NKJV). Later in that discourse He warned them saying, "For false christs and false prophets will rise and show great signs and wonders to deceive, if possible, even the elect."[16] The spirit of antichrist is a spirit of deception. John is warning his readers of the deception.

In 2 Timothy 3:13 Paul said, "Evildoers and impostors will go from bad to worse, deceiving and being deceived" (NIV). There is a progression of evil in the world. We see it going on in our lifetime. At the same time there is a progression of light. The kingdom of God is advancing toward the purposes of God. But evil men "will go from bad to worse, deceiving and being deceived." The increase in world-wide communication certainly facilitates that. Through the internet, deception is now available to most teenagers in America. There is the possibility for the spread of the gospel to every nation: something that will happen in the end times.[17] But there is also the possibility for the spread of deception: something that is currently happening.

## ADDITIONAL INFORMATION ABOUT THESE ANTICHRISTS

John gives us additional information about who these antichrists are. In verse 19 of our text, he says, "They went out from us, but they did not really belong to us. For if they had belonged to us, they would have remained with us; but their going showed that none of them belonged to us." So, these are people who once professed Christianity. They were in the church. However, it seems they were never really born again.[18] The fact that they did not stay and continue in the faith, was for John, evidence that "none of them belonged to us." They did not share in the koinōnia life of God and of the community of believers.[19] They were related to us the same way Judas was related to the twelve. Judas participated in the external activates of preaching the gospel along with the others.[20] No one but Jesus knew his true condition. On the surface, he looked like the other eleven apostles. But in the end, he proved to be a devil.[21] Implied in John's statement is another test of genuine Christians: they *continue* in the faith.[22]

The language here clearly indicates these antichrists left of their own accord. They were not thrown out of the church. But in time they showed their true colors and left. Remember the Parable of the Wheat and Tares that Jesus gave in Matthew 13? A farmer sowed good seed, wheat, in his field. But during the night, an enemy sowed tares in the field. His workers later saw the tares growing with the wheat. They asked the farmer if he wanted them to pull out the tares. But he said that in doing that, they would also pull up the wheat. Therefore, he told them to just let the tares and wheat grow up together until the harvest. So, what we have in the church is a combination of wheat and tares: some genuine believers and some superficial professors. This is why the tests that John gives us in this epistle are so important. People need a way to make sure their salvation is real and that they are indeed a child of God. So, the first thing that John tells us about these antichrists is that they separated themselves from the community of true believers. And by doing that they demonstrated that they were not genuine members of the Body of Christ.

These antichrists are also denying the most fundamental doctrines of the faith. Consider 1 John 2:22–23: "Who is the liar? It is whoever denies that Jesus is the Christ. Such a person is the antichrist—denying the Father and the Son. No one who denies the Son has the Father; whoever acknowledges the Son has the Father also" (NIV). The critical issue here is who is Jesus? Is He the divine Son of God or not? Notice how John puts the Son on equal basis with the Father in this text. The Gnostics were denying the true nature of Jesus as fully man and fully God. Various sects would deny that reality in one way or another. We talked about some of those Gnostic errors in chapter five. But these errors continue today in cults like Jehovah's Witness, Unity, and Church of Latter-Day Saints. All of these groups fit into what John describes as antichrists. I know some very nice people in the Mormon religion. But this doctrinal issue is a deal breaker when it comes to salvation. It's not enough to give some limited recognition to Jesus. It's not enough to accept Him as a prophet or an angel or religious leader. He is God manifested in the flesh. There is salvation in no other name.[23] Jesus stated the case plainly in John 14:6, "I am the way and the truth and the life. No one comes to the Father except through me"

(NIV). He is the only way to the Father. To reject the divinity of Jesus is to not have the Son. And to not have the Son is to not have the Father. First John 2:23 states it very simply. "No one who denies the Son has the Father; whoever acknowledges the Son has the Father also." Every liberal preacher who denies the full divinity of Jesus is an antichrist. The seminaries are full of them. Some mainline denominations are full of them. There are many antichrists all around us today. They have departed from the faith just like these people in the first century whom John calls antichrists.

Recognizing the humanity of Christ is also essential. John begins this epistle talking about the incarnation. And he addresses this issue again in the fourth chapter, verses two and three. "This is how you can recognize the Spirit of God: Every spirit that acknowledges that Jesus Christ has come in the flesh is from God, but every spirit that does not acknowledge Jesus is not from God. This is the spirit of the antichrist, which you have heard is coming and even now is already in the world." (NIV). He issues the same warning in his second epistle (1:7). Everything depends on our doctrine of Christ.

Isn't it interesting that this is the one thing the world asks us to compromise? They talk about all the things we have in common: "We all want to alleviate human suffering. We all want to live in peace. We all worship God in one way or another. Some of us call Him Allah; some call Him Zeus, some use the name Jehovah. But it really doesn't matter. In reality, we're all serving the same God. Living in peace with one another is more important than these little differences. You can pray to God. Just don't use the name Jesus. When you insist that Jesus is the only way of salvation, you're just being bigoted and unreasonable. There are many ways to heaven. And God has many names. So, let's find our common ground and not bicker over the differences." That is the reasoning of our pluralistic society. It is in direct opposition to what John is saying in our text. If you deny the Son for who He is, you do not have the Father. It is only through the Son that you can be in relationship with the Father. First John 5:12 makes this very straightforward statement: "Whoever has the Son has life; whoever does not have the Son of God does not have life" (NIV).

It has even become popular in some Christian circles to say something like this. "It really doesn't matter what you believe, as long as you're sincere," or "God doesn't want us to get hung up on doctrine; the important thing is that you love people." Well, loving people is important. John has already told us that in this chapter. But so are our beliefs. What you believe drives your thinking, and what you think drives your behavior. That's why John and Paul and the other apostles wrote all these letters. These letters are full of doctrine. Being sincerely wrong can lead to hell and destruction. John is telling these Christians to hold tenaciously to the truth. Don't be seduced or deceived by the antichrist spirit that is in the world. Try the spirits to make sure what you're hearing is truth.

Earlier in this epistle, John has given the test of righteousness and the test of love. Now he is giving the test of truth.[24] These antichrists departed from the truth and thereby proved to not be genuine Christians. There is pressure in our society to compromise truth. We cannot do that, and we will not do it. It matters what you believe!

The significance of that is evident in a story that occurred in 2010. A nurse gave dialysis patient, Richard Smith "a drug that induces paralysis, instead of a [prescribed] antacid" he was supposed to receive. "The packaging looked the same and he grabbed the wrong package." The nurse believed he was administering the right medication. But his belief was wrong. Richard Smith died of respiratory arrest.[25] It mattered what that nurse believed. It mattered a lot. In fact, it was a matter of life and death. Make sure you know what you believe. Stay rooted and grounded in the truth found in the Bible. Never depart from it.

# Endnotes: Chapter 9

1   1 John 2:15, NIV.

2   Smalley, 91: "The absence of the article indicates not only that the concept symbolized by *antichristos* had by now become personalized (cf. 2 Thess. 2:1–12; also *antichristoi*, "antichrists" in this v), but also that the term itself had passed into current (technical) use as a proper name (so Westcott, 70)."

3   Cf. Dan. 5.

4   Cf. John 13:27.

5   Cf. Rev. 13:4; 2Thess. 2:9; Dan. 8:24.

6   Rev. 6:2. As a counterfeit of the true Prince of Peace, the Antichrist will present himself as a peacemaker. The real Prince of Peace is riding a white horse in Rev. 19:11. Cf. W. A. Criswell, *Expository Sermons on Revelation: Five Volume Complete and Unabridged in One*, Vol. 3, 1962 (Grand Rapids: Zondervan, 1978) 91.

7   Cf. Dan. 9:27.

8   2 Thess. 2:4; Rev. 13:14–15.

9   Dan. 9:27; 11:31. This desecration of the sanctuary was foreshadowed by the actions of Antiochus IV Epiphanes in about 167 B.C. W. A. Criswell, *Expository Sermons on the Book of Daniel*, Vol. 4 (Grand Rapids: Zondervan, 1972) 78.

10  Matt. 24:15; Mark 13:14. Notice that Jesus is predicting this as a future event. Paul prophesied it in 2 Thessalonians 2:4 and John prophesied it in Revelation 13:14–15.

11  2 Thess. 2:3, KJV.

12  2 Thessalonians was written about A.D. 51. First John was written sometime between A.D. 85 and 95. So teaching on the subject by the apostles had been going on for many years. For details of the dating see introductory notes for each of these epistles in the *NIV Study Bible*.

13  Colin Brown, ed., Vol. 1, s. v. "Antichrist" by E. Kauder, 124.

14  Cf. Heb. 1:2; 2 Tim. 3:1; 1 Pet. 1:20; 4:7; 1 Cor. 10:11; Barker, ed. *The NIV Study Bible*, s. v. "1 John 2:18" by Donald Burdick, p. 1908. Zodhiates, *The Epistles of John* (p. 106) writes, "*Eschate* is the feminine of *eschatos* (2078), last. It does not necessarily mean *husteros* (5306), concluding, terminal, final."

15  Cf. Matt. 24:36; 25:13; Luke 12:40; Acts 1:6–7.

16  Matt. 24:24, NKJV.

17  Cf. Matt. 24:14; Mark 13:10.

18  In contrast, those referred to in Heb. 6:4–5, 2 Pet. 2:20–22, and Jude 12 seemed to have apostatized from the real experience.

19  Burdick (pp. 194–195) sees a play on the words "*ex hemon*" in this verse. He sees the first occurrence as locational, indicating they were once present in the congregation physically, but then went out. In contrast, he sees the second

occurrence as descriptive of character, meaning they did not share the same spiritual life.

20  Cf. Matt. 10:1–8.

21  John 6:70–71.

22  Cf. 2 Cor. 13:5.

23  Cf. John 1:1–4, 14; Heb. 1:1–3; Acts 4:12.

24  James M. Boice, *The Epistles of John: An Expositional Commentary* (Grand Rapids; Baker Books, 2004) 67.

25  Christina Carson, "Nurse Gives Patient Paralytic Instead of Antacid," *ABC News*, Nov. 21, 2011. Retrieved Oct. 5, 2017 at http://abcnews.go.com/Health/nurse-patient-paralytic-antacid/story?id=14997244.

# CHAPTER 10

# Protection from Deception: The Anointing
## 2:18–27

Little children, it is the last hour; and as you have heard
that the Antichrist is coming, even now many antichrists
have come, by which we know that it is the last hour. They
went out from us, but they were not of us; for if they had
been of us, they would have continued with us; but they
went out that they might be made manifest, that none of
them were of us. But you have an anointing from the Holy
One, and you know all things. I have not written to you
because you do not know the truth, but because you know
it, and that no lie is of the truth. Who is a liar but he who
denies that Jesus is the Christ? He is antichrist who denies
the Father and the Son. Whoever denies the Son does not
have the Father either; he who acknowledges the Son has
the Father also. Therefore let that abide in you which you
heard from the beginning. If what you heard from the
beginning abides in you, you also will abide in the Son
and in the Father. And this is the promise that He has
promised us — eternal life. These things I have written
to you concerning those who try to deceive you. But the
anointing which you have received from Him abides in
you, and you do not need that anyone teach you; but as
the same anointing teaches you concerning all things, and

is true, and is not a lie, and just as it has taught you, you
will abide in Him.

1 John 2:18–27, NKJV

---

Expository Message

In our last chapter, we focused on the warning John gives in verses 18–19
concerning the antichrist spirit. He reminds his readers of previous teaching
concerning the Antichrist who would come with such cunning deception
that the vast majority of world will follow him. But more specifically, John
is concerned with the "many antichrists" who were already seducing people
away from the truth. In verse 26 John says, "These things I have written
to you concerning those who try to deceive you." It was a very real threat;
and John wants them alerted to the dangers.

The danger is no less today. In fact, the deception intensifies as history
marches toward the end.[1] John's warning is for us! It is a mistake for anyone
to pridefully assume he is above the possibility of being deceived. Smarter
men than you and I have been deceived. I found it heartbreaking to read
Clark Pinnock's beautiful, brilliant insights on the Trinity; then find him
moving dangerously toward universalism in his book, *Flame of Love*.[2] How
are the mighty fallen! It doesn't just happen to intellectuals either. Spiritual
people fall as well. William Branham was a man mightily used in healings
and the word of knowledge. God even used him to raise the dead. Yet in
the latter years of his ministry he fell into terrible error, even thinking he
was the end time Elijah and forerunner to Christ's return.[3] Many followed
him in the deception. The person who thinks he doesn't need to pay
attention to John's warnings is the person in the greatest danger. "Pride
goes before destruction, a haughty spirit before a fall" (Prov. 16:18, NIV).
The warning John is giving in our text is for everyone. We dealt with his
warnings about antichrists extensively in chapter nine.

But John does something else in our text even more helpful. He teaches
us how to avoid being deceived. God has made two key provisions for us
that will protect us from deception, if we will avail ourselves of them.[4] One
is the anointing explained in verses 20 and 27. The other is the apostles'
teaching referenced in verse 24. In this chapter we will deal with the first

of these provisions: the anointing. We will deal with the apostles' teaching in chapter eleven.

## THE ANOINTING IN BELIEVERS

In verse 20 John calls their attention to the anointing: "But you have an anointing from the Holy One." The English word "anoint" means "to smear or rub with oil . . . [or] to apply oil to as a sacred rite. . . ."[5] The term John uses here has its roots in the Old Testament practice of anointing kings, priests, and prophets. First Samuel 10:1 narrates the anointing of Saul as king. "Then Samuel took a flask of olive oil and poured it on Saul's head and kissed him, saying, 'Has not the Lord anointed you ruler over his inheritance?'" (NIV). Notice, even in the Old Testament, the ritual is in response to what God has initiated. It doesn't make God do something. It recognizes and symbolizes what He has done.[6] From that day forward, Saul is often referred to as the anointed of the Lord. Later Samuel anoints David king of Israel. First Samuel 16:13 says, "So Samuel took the horn of oil and anointed him in the presence of his brothers, and from that day on the Spirit of the Lord came powerfully upon David. Samuel then went to Ramah" (NIV). Notice here the Scripture makes a clear link between the anointing and the coming of the Spirit of God on David. That association is very important. That's a couple of examples of kings being anointed. In Exodus 30:30 we have one of several passages that talk about priests being anointed for service unto God. "Anoint Aaron and his sons and consecrate them so they may serve me as priests" (NIV). Here the anointing is linked with consecration unto God. In 1 Kings 19:16 God tells Elijah to anoint Elisha as a prophet to take his place. What we need to see is that the Old Testament tradition included a kingly anointing, a priestly anointing, and a prophetic anointing.

All three of these offices culminate in the ultimate prophet, priest, and king: The Messiah. Christ is another word for Messiah. The Greek word translated Christ in the New Testament is *Christos*. What does that word mean? It means the Anointed One.[7] Jesus is the Christ, the Anointed One. He carries the kingly, priestly, and prophetic anointing. Hebrews 1:9 quotes Psalm 45:7 in reference to Jesus. "You have loved righteousness and hated wickedness; therefore God, your God, has set you above your companions by anointing you with the oil of joy" (NIV). The anointing on Jesus exceeds all those Old Testament anointings. His anointing is the ultimate anointing. He is the Christ, the Anointed One.[8] Remember at His baptism the Spirit descended upon Him in the form of a dove. John the Baptist testified, "I saw the Spirit come down from heaven as a dove and remain on him. And I myself did not know him, but the one who sent me to baptize with water told me, 'The man on whom you see the Spirit come down *and remain* is the one who will baptize with the Holy Spirit.' I have seen and I testify that this is God's Chosen One" (emphasis mine, John 1:32–34, NIV). The Spirit would come on Samson at times and give him supernatural strength.[9] The Spirit came upon Jahaziel in 2 Chronicles 20:14 and he prophesied. The anointing came on various people at times in the Old Testament. But the Holy Spirit took His permanent dwelling in Jesus.[10] John 3:34 tells us Jesus was given the Spirit without limit. So, we have seen Old Testament examples of the anointing. All of those were simply foreshadowing the Anointed One, Christ our Lord.

Now let me bring this anointing down to you and me. Acts 11:26 says, "The disciples were called Christians first at Antioch" (NIV). The Greek word translated Christian is *Christianos*. It is obviously from the Greek word for Christ which is from the Greek word *chriō* which means to rub with oil.[11]

In 1 John 2:20 John writes, "But you have an anointing from the Holy One." The Holy One is Christ.[12] His anointing flows down on us. He is the head and we are the body.[13] We do not have an anointing separate from His. We are partakers of His anointing. Psalm 133:1–2 says, "Behold, how good and how pleasant it is for brethren to dwell together in unity! It is like the precious ointment upon the head, that ran down upon the beard, even Aaron's beard: that went down to the skirts of his garments" (KJV). His anointing runs down on us. We are Christians. We share in His anointing.[14]

John uses a play on words in our text that is obscured in the English translations. In verses 18–19 he warns of the Antichrist and many *antichristoi*; the word comes from the combination of *anti* and *Christos*.[15] Then he contrasts that in verse 20 by saying, "But you have an anointing from the Holy One" (*chrisma*). They are anti *christos*. You have *chrisma*. Verse 22 adds, "Who is a liar but he who denies that Jesus is the Christ?"

*Christos!* Then in verse 27 he comes back to the word translated anointing, *chrisma*. So, this anointing is a key distinctive of true believers versus the antichrists.

What is this anointing in 1 John 2:20? It is the Holy Spirit who comes into a person's life when that person becomes a Christian.[16] Keep in mind John is speaking to Spirit-filled believers. The baptism in the Holy Spirit was the norm for the early church. In Samaria, when people were converted under Philip's preaching, they didn't stop there. Peter and John came to lead them into the fullness of the Spirit.[17] When Paul encountered elders in Acts 19 who had not experienced the fullness of the Spirit, he led them into that experience. Some teachers interpret John in the context of today's lukewarm church. The believers in John's day were not half in. They were believers filled with the Spirit of God.[18]

John says to them, "But you have an anointing from the Holy One, and *you know all things*" (emphasis mine). That is not the best translation of the phrase at the end of that sentence. The New International Version is much better. "But you have an anointing from the Holy One and *all of you know the truth*" (emphasis mine).[19] All believers have received the anointing and can therefore know the truth because of the anointing.

Notice the flow of verses 20–21 in the New International Version. "But you have an anointing from the Holy One and all of you know the truth." The all-important truth that they know is that Jesus is the Christ. This is what the antichrists were denying according to verse 22. All of you know the truth. In verse 21 John says, "I do not write to you because you do not know the truth, but because you know it and because no lie comes from the truth." Then, in verse 22, He exposes the lie that he's dealing with. "Who is the liar? It is whoever denies that Jesus is the Christ." See how beautifully that flows?

John is teaching the "priesthood of all believers," a significant concept brought back by Martin Luther in the Reformation.[20] John puts it this way in Revelation 1:5–6, "Unto him that loved us, and washed us from our sins in his own blood, And hath *made us kings and priests* unto God and his Father; to him be glory and dominion for ever and ever. Amen" (emphasis mine, KJV). We are all kings and priests unto God. Not just a select few, but all who are in the family of God.[21] Peter says we are a royal priesthood, a holy priesthood.[22] John is recognizing the priesthood of all believers when he writes, "All of you know the truth." You don't need a pope to dictate interpretation of Scripture to you. You have an anointing that illuminates the word to your heart. You don't need a Jim Jones to tell you to drink the Kool-Aid. And you don't need to let the antichrists step into the position that belongs solely to the Holy Spirit (the Spirit of Truth).

## CHARACTERISTICS OF THE ANOINTING

In verse 27 John gives additional insight on the anointing. "But the anointing which you have received from Him abides in you, and you do not need that anyone teach you; but as the same anointing teaches you concerning all things, and is true, and is not a lie, and just as it has taught you, you will abide in Him." Consider with me the anointing of the Holy Spirit in the believer.

He abides in you. The Greek word translated abides is *menō*. It is sometimes translated continue, remain, tarry, dwell. It is a major theme in our text and in this epistle. John is assuring believers the Holy Spirit does not come and go. He remains. God's Spirit is joined to the believer's spirit according to 1 Corinthians 6:17.

In our circles it is common for someone to pray that the anointing would rest upon the service. Technically that is not correct. The anointing is in you. The anointing abides in you. You are anointed by the Holy Spirit whether it feels like it or not. The anointing is in each individual Christian; and when we come together, the anointing is in us collectively. The real issue is how yielded we are to the anointing. Manifestations are more pronounced where people are operating in faith and obedience to the Holy Spirit. But God understands what we are saying when we ask Him to anoint the service. We're simply asking God to direct the service and help us yield ourselves to His leading. So, it's not a significant problem if we don't say it all just right. The Holy Spirit abides in us, and that brings stability to our lives. He is there sustaining us and strengthening us so that we're able to persevere. In John 14:16 Jesus promised that He would abide with us forever.

The anointing teaches *concerning all things* according to verse 27. Since He is God and knows all things, there is nothing beyond His ability to address in our lives. He doesn't teach all things. There are a lot of things we don't know. But He teaches *concerning* [Greek: *peri*] all things. He will tell us what we need to know when we need to know it.

His guidance is never wrong. "But as the same anointing teaches you concerning all things, *and is true*, and is not a lie" (emphasis mine). In other words, you can rely on what He tells you. In fact, John wants these believers to rely on the anointing. That is something we should take away from our study today. Rely on the anointing! The Holy Spirit will never mislead you. Yes, that is somewhat subjective. But we will see in the next chapter that the other provision, the apostles' teaching, is an objective safety net to make sure we're hearing correctly. You can trust the anointing to lead you into truth.

What does John mean by the phrase, "And you do not need that anyone teach you"? That's exactly what John is doing in this epistle; he is teaching them. But we have to understand this phrase in context. The Gnostics were leading people astray by telling them they needed their "advanced" teaching.[23] They were presenting themselves as people who had special insight that others don't have. And by the way, that is how cults operate today as well. John is saying in verse 21, "I have not written to you because you do not know the truth, but because you know it, and that no lie is of the truth." You already have the message that leads to salvation. The Gnostic teachings cannot take you any higher than that. In verse 24 he tells them to let the original teaching they have already received remain in them.

How does the Holy Spirit teach the believer? He gives intuitive insight on truth. He is the Spirit of truth. Jesus said in John 16:13–14, "But when he, the Spirit of truth, comes, he will guide you into all the truth. He will not speak on his own; he will speak only what he hears, and he will tell you what is yet to come. He will glorify me because it is from me that he will receive what he will make known to you" (NIV). The Holy Spirit always glorifies Jesus. He will take the truth that Jesus has given and declare it to us. He will impart understanding.

Have you ever been reading a scripture that you have read a hundred times when, suddenly, revelation of what that verse is saying flashed into your heart. You didn't reason it out with your mind. The Holy Spirit simply showed it to you in your spirit. The knowledge He gives is an intuitive knowledge. In Matthew 16:13 Jesus asked His disciples this question, "Who do people say the Son of Man is?" (NIV). The disciples began to throw out answers. Some say John the Baptist, some Elijah, some say Jeremiah. Then Jesus changed the question. "Who do you say I am?" (NIV). Immediately it came to Peter. "You are the Messiah, [Christ] the Son of the living God" (NIV). That was teaching by the Holy Spirit! Jesus said to Peter, "Blessed are you, Simon son of Jonah, for this was not revealed to you by flesh and blood, but by my Father in heaven" (NIV).

The teaching of the Holy Spirit is not book knowledge. It is not reasoning power. It is spiritual perception of truth: understanding that only He can give. It happens at a deeper level than teaching from man. I can communicate words in this book, but only the Holy Spirit can take those words and bring spiritual insight. Paul dealt with this distinction in 1 Corinthians 2. In verse 9 he quotes, "Eye hath not seen, nor ear heard, neither have entered into the heart of man, the things which God hath prepared for them that love him" (KJV). In other words, the natural senses cannot discern these things. But Paul then adds in verse 10, "But God hath revealed them unto us by his Spirit" (KJV). The anointing teaches us. He teaches us Spirit to spirit. Since He is the Spirit of Truth, He enables us to distinguish between truth and error, right and wrong, what we should do and what we should not do.[24] Have you ever heard someone preaching on the radio or on television, and just knew in your heart something was wrong with that message? You might not be able to put your finger on what it is, but you knew it wasn't something you could follow. That was the anointing guiding you. When someone gives a prophecy, there is often a witness in one's spirit that it was from God. Or the Holy Spirit may tell you it was from the flesh, and not from God. We are to prove all things.[25] We prove prophecy by the written word of God and by the internal witness of the Spirit. We can all operate in that because we all have the Holy Spirit in us. And He will guide us into all truth.

In 1976 Jeanie and I had been married about a year and lived in Texas. We were young Christians, very zealous for the Lord. I was doing some Bible teaching at that time. We were approached by the associate pastor in our church. He was an intelligent, charismatic man about forty years old. We attended some of the meetings he and his wife led. One day they sat us down and talked with us about joining a special group of young couples that they would be mentoring. They talked about how exclusive the group would be and how much potential they saw in us. Everything they said was very flattering, and the opportunity to connect with them really sounded exciting. We told them we would pray about it. When we prayed, Jeanie and I both felt a strong caution from the Holy Spirit. The anointing was teaching us what to do in that situation. We didn't need any human to tell us what to do. The Holy Spirit was telling us. We declined their offer, and they were very disappointed. But they did get some other young couples to join them. Shortly after that, to our surprise, they broke away from the church. They took the group to California, and from what I can understand those young couples ran into serious financial and marital problems. The wonderful utopia they promised did not happen. That is an example of the anointing teaching us and leading us.

I have had the same kind of experience with people teaching doctrines that on the surface sounded biblical, yet the Spirit would caution me. Before Jeanie and I got married, I visited a large Christian commune in Dallas. The people there were very friendly. I had no experience with that sort of thing. They showed me Bible verses about the early church having all things in common.[26] Intellectually it sounded right. But I felt a heaviness in the whole experience. I couldn't identify what it was, but in my spirit, I knew something was wrong with the whole thing. I did not join the commune. Later it totally fell apart. John wants his Christian readers to know they can depend on the anointing to teach them what is right and what is wrong. And if they will follow the leading of the Spirit, they will not follow the Gnostics who are trying to lead them out of orthodox Christianity.

Unbelievers don't have this anointing.[27] They cannot receive the Holy Spirit.[28] Therefore, they don't have the same capacity to discern truth from error.[29] Paul explains this in 1 Corinthians 2:14. "But the natural man does not receive the things of the Spirit of God, for they are foolishness to him; nor can he know them, because they are spiritually discerned" (NKJV). In Matthew 13 the disciples asked Jesus about the difference in the way He spoke to the multitudes versus the way He taught them. Jesus answered in verse 13, "Because they seeing see not; and hearing they hear not, neither do they understand" (KJV). The multitude could hear what He was saying with the natural ear, but the Holy Spirit was not making the meaning known to them.

Do you have any idea how privileged we are to have the anointing? The insight you have concerning the kingdom of God is not there because of your intellect. There are people much smarter than us that simply don't get it. But the anointing shows us the truth. Jesus said to the disciples in Matthew 13:16–17, "But blessed are your eyes, for they see: and your ears, for they hear. For verily I say unto you, That many prophets and righteous men have desired to see those things which ye see, and have not seen them; and to hear those things which ye hear, and have not heard them" (KJV). My heart is filled with gratitude for the anointing that abides in us. There are many times I would have been shipwrecked along the way, were it not for His guidance. Many prophets and righteous men in ages past would have loved to enjoy the privilege we experience as children of the Most High God. May we never take that for granted!

# Endnotes: Chapter 10

1 Cf. 2 Tim. 3:1–13.

2 Clark H. Pinnock, *Flame of Love: A Theology of the Holy Spirit* (Downers Grove, IL: InterVarsity Press, 1996) 21–48, 185–246. Cf. John MacArthur, *The MacArthur New Testament Commentary: 1–3 John* (Chicago, IL: Moody Press, 2007) 225.

3 Roberts Liardon, *God's Generals: Why They Succeeded and Why Some Failed* (Tulsa, OK: Albury Publishing, 1966) 320–344.

4 Cf. 2 Pet. 1:3; 1 Cor. 10:13.

5 *Merriam Webster's Collegiate Dictionary*, 10th ed., s. v. "Anoint," 47.

6 The ordinance of water baptism is an external rite that recognizes the spiritual transformation that has occurred in the person's heart. It was when they believed, that Philip baptized people in Samaria (Acts 8:12). The spiritual experience preceded water baptism in Acts 10:45–48. The rite alone is ineffectual unless the person has believed in the heart (Rom. 10:9–10).

7 Robert W. Yarbrough, *1–3 John: Baker Exegetical Commentary on the New Testament* (Grand Rapids: Baker Academic, 2008) 150, 166. The root of *Christos* is *chrio* which means "to rub with oil", hence anoint.

8 Cf. Acts 10:38; Luke 4:18.

9 Judges 13:25; 14:5–6, 19. Other examples of the Spirit coming on people in the Old Testament, but not remaining on them, can be found in Judges 3:10; 6:34; 11:29; 1 Sam. 10:10; 2 Chron. 15:1; 24:20.

10 Of course, this refutes the Gnostic heresy of Cerinthus that the anointing left Jesus at the cross. Cf. Marvin R. Vincent, *Vincent's New Testament Word Studies*, 1903, s. v. 1 John 2:22. Accessed in electronic data base: Biblesoft 2000.

11 James Strong, *New Exhaustive Strong's Numbers and Concordance with Expanded Greek-Hebrew Dictionary* (Originally published: The Exhaustive Concordance of the Bible, Cincinnati: Jennings & Graham, 1890. Accessed in electronic data base: Biblesoft 2000) s. v. "NT:5548."

12 Cf. John 6:69 (NIV); Mark 1:24; Luke 4:34; Acts 3:14; 4:27. The Holy One in the Old Testament is God, the Father (Ps. 71:22). Of course, all that the believer has from God comes only through Christ. Following the pronouns in this text from verse 20 through to verse 28 ("when he shall appear") tends to confirm Christ as *the holy one* in this context. See Robert Yarbrough, p. 150 for further discussion.

13 Cf. Eph. 1:22; 4:15; 5:23; Col. 1:18; 2:19.

14 The anointing is a unifier of the true Body of Christ. There is one Spirit in my Baptist brother, my Methodist sister, my black brother, my white brother, etc. Ephesians 4:4 reminds us there is *one body, one Spirit*. And yet the anointing distinguishes us from those who are not genuine believers.

15  Strong, s. v. "NT:500."

16  Some try to equate the anointing with the word of God. But Donald Burdick (p. 197) points out "there is no Scripture that refers to the Word of God as an anointing." However, in verse 24 John anchors his readers in the apostles' teaching. Therefore, he balances the subjective leading of the Spirit with the objective adherence to Scripture.

17  Cf. Acts 8:14–16.

18  While initiation into the faith is absolutely essential, Peter tells believers to grow (2 Pet. 3:18). The use of the Greek present tense in Eph. 5:18 indicates we are to be continually filled with the Spirit. The fact that the Spirit abides in every believer does not mean that we are not to continue pursuing growth in God, as long as what we are pursuing is biblical.

19  Cf. Burdick, 198; A. T. Robertson, *Robertson's New Testament Word Pictures*, 1930, s. v. "1 John 2:20." Accessed in electronic data base: Biblesoft 2000.

20  Martin Luther, *Commentary on the Epistles of Peter and Jude*, (Originally published: *The Epistles of St. Peter and St. Jude*, Minneapolis, MN: Lutherans in All Lands Co., 1904. Reprint, Grand Rapids: Kregel Publications, 1982) 88–89.

21  Cf. Jer. 31:33–34; Heb. 8:10–11.

22  1 Pet. 2:5, 9.

23  Burdick, 206. Jude refers to these Gnostics as sensual, having not the spirit. They do not have the anointing, but you (as a Christian) have it.

24  Just as the Urim and Thummin showed Israel the right path versus the wrong path in the Old Testament, the anointing provides counsel to the believer in the New Testament. Ex. 28:30; Num. 27:21; John 14:26; 16:13.

25  1 Thess. 5:21. Cf. 1 Cor. 14:29.

26  Cf. Acts 2:44.

27  Cf. John 3:3, "Except a man be born again, he cannot see the kingdom of God" (KJV).

28  John 14:17.

29  Cf. 1 John 5:20.

# CHAPTER 11

# Protection from Deception: Apostolic Teaching 2:18–29

Children, time is just about up. You heard that Antichrist is coming. Well, they're all over the place, antichrists everywhere you look. That's how we know that we're close to the end. They left us, but they were never really with us. If they had been, they would have stuck it out with us, loyal to the end. In leaving, they showed their true colors, showed they never did belong. But you belong. The Holy One anointed you, and you all know it. I haven't been writing this to tell you something you don't know, but to confirm the truth you do know, and to remind you that the truth doesn't breed lies. So who is lying here? It's the person who denies that Jesus is the Divine Christ, that's who. This is what makes an antichrist: denying the Father, denying the Son. No one who denies the Son has any part with the Father, but affirming the Son is an embrace of the Father as well. Stay with what you heard from the beginning, the original message. Let it sink into your life. If what you heard from the beginning lives deeply in you, you will live deeply in both Son and Father. This is exactly what Christ promised: eternal life, real life! I've written to warn you about those who are trying to deceive you. But they're no match for what is embedded deeply within you—Christ's anointing, no less! You don't need any of their so-called teaching. Christ's anointing teaches you the truth on everything you need to know about yourself and him, uncontaminated by a single lie. Live deeply in what you were taught. And now, children, stay with Christ. Live deeply in Christ. Then we'll be ready for him when he appears, ready to receive him with open arms, with no cause for red-faced guilt or lame excuses when he arrives. Once you're convinced that he is right and righteous, you'll recognize that all who practice righteousness are God's true children."[1]

1 John 2:18–29, *The Message*

## Expository Message

John is dealing with the danger of deception. Many antichrists were active in John's day and many antichrists are active today. This epistle is particularly applicable to us today because there is so much deception going on all around us. It is in the world, but, more alarming, the spirit of antichrist is operating in the church, seeking to lead people astray.

In this passage, John identifies two provisions of the faith that will protect believers from deception. We talked about the first one in chapter ten: the anointing which is the Holy Spirit in the believer. Verse 27 says, "But the anointing which you have received from Him abides in you, and you do not need that anyone teach you; but as the same anointing teaches you concerning all things, and is true, and is not a lie, and *just as it has taught you*, you will[2] abide in Him" (emphasis mine, NKJV). They have already been experiencing the benefits of the Holy Spirit leading them into truth. John is telling them to continue in that. It was the Holy Spirit who brought conviction of sin into their hearts and led them into believing on the Lord Jesus Christ. So, they know, by experience, what John is talking about. Verse 28 begins with this imperative, "And now little children, abide in Him" (NKJV). John's instruction is that they would continue to dwell in Christ and rely on the Holy Spirit.[3]

We, as believers, have the assurance that the Holy Spirit will always be there for us and do His part. We will enjoy protection from deception as we listen to His promptings and follow His leading. He will show us the difference between truth and error; He will give us all the revelation we will ever need. We don't have to look to Gnostics or spiritual gurus for that. That was the subject of chapter ten. The anointing is one protection from deception.

Now we examine the second protection available to the believer, the apostles' teaching. Again, the key concept is to continue in what God has already given. The Greek word translated *abide* is *menō*. It occurs six times in the verses we are examining and twenty-six times in John's epistles.[4] This is an ongoing theme in John's message to believers. Continue in the Holy Spirit and in the teaching you have already received. Our focus today is on verse 24. "Therefore let that abide in you which you heard from the beginning. If what you heard from the beginning abides in you, you also will abide in the Son and in the Father" (NKJV).

## COMMAND FOR CONTINUANCE

Consider the command stated in that first sentence. "Therefore let that abide in you which you heard from the beginning" (NKJV). That translation is a bit awkward. The New International Version is a little easier to follow, "See that what you have heard from the beginning remains in you." The Living Bible says, "So keep on believing what you have been taught from the beginning." And the Message paraphrases it this way. "Stay with what you heard from the beginning, the original message."[5]

What was the original message? It was "Jesus Christ and Him crucified."[6] It was the message of Jesus's death, burial, and resurrection brought to them by the apostles.[7] In a broader sense, it was the apostles' testimony and teaching that they had received in their initial experience. It was said of the early church in Acts 2:42, "And they continued stedfastly in the apostles' doctrine and fellowship, and in breaking of bread, and in prayers" (KJV). Continuing in "the apostles' doctrine" is what John is talking about in our text.

The apostles' teaching was built upon two things: (1) the Old Testament (the Greek version of the Old Testament, called the Septuagint, being the Bible they commonly used) and (2) the teaching that Jesus had given them before His crucifixion and ascension.[8] Based on the truths they learned from Jesus, including His interpretation of the Old Testament, the apostles brought the gospel to the Jews and the gentile world. So, what is John referring to in verse 24 of our text when he writes, "Which you heard from the beginning"? He is referring to the message they received in the beginning of their Christian experience. He is referring to the gospel message they got from the apostles' preaching. The apostles' message was first given orally. But it was eventually written and distributed to the early church as the gospels, the book of Acts, the epistles, and the book of Revelation. From our perspective today, the protection that John is pointing to is the Bible, the Old and New Testament. The first protection that we dealt with last week is the anointing, the Holy Spirit in the believer. The second protection is the word of God. We are to rely heavily on these two provisions.

John is particularly concerned about the apostles' teaching about Christ and the essential gospel message of salvation. Notice the two verses just before this one. First John 2:22–23 says, "Who is a liar but he who denies that Jesus is the Christ? He is antichrist who denies the Father and the Son. Whoever denies the Son does not have the Father either; he who acknowledges the Son has the Father also" (NKJV). The gospel message of salvation focuses on Jesus and His work of redemption.[9] There is salvation in no other name, and He must be accepted for who He is.[10]

We live in an increasingly pluralistic society. The environment in America is not the same as it was in 20th century. In the past, most people professed the fundamental tenets of biblical morality and reverence for God. Even though they were not all Christians, most acknowledged at least an intellectual assent to basic Christianity. That is not so much the case today. Secular law is less in line with biblical mandates. With the influence of internet teachings, false doctrine and belief in foreign gods are more and more common. Many young adults have abandoned their Christian roots for atheistic and agnostic positions. Since 1994 there has been a steep decline in the belief of fundamental Christian doctrines. Recent studies have shown that in America, belief in Jesus's resurrection and in the deity of Christ, that Jesus is the Son of God, has declined from 87% in 1994 to 65% in 2014.[11] That's more than a 20% drop in 20 years. If we project that trend into the future, we have an alarming situation. Even now many antichrists have come! The number of adult Americans who believe in the Virgin Birth is already down to 57%.[12] So, we're not talking about a problem that just happened in the first century. We're talking about major deception that is going on all around us today. It is a very real issue. If it is not an issue for you, it is likely an issue for your children and grandchildren. If we don't teach the emerging generation the truth, they are vulnerable to the lies of the many antichrists.

In many cases, we are getting people to come to church; but we are not establishing them in the truths of the gospel.[13] The goal has been numbers into a building instead of committed disciples of the Lord. In days gone by, sermons were generally longer than they are today. Most churches had Sunday School teaching every week, not to mention Sunday night services. And some churches had catechism, designed to insure understanding of the basic tenets of the faith. Today entertaining programs often replace those teaching events. Bible reading outside of the church has also declined from 43% in 2004 to 33% in 2014.[14] None of these trends are headed in the right direction.

Awhile back I was approached by a pastor who was recruiting me to come on staff as a teacher. He said his gift was evangelism, and he needed a teacher in the church. This was a minister in his forties who had pastored for several years. He had talked with the Assemblies of God about bringing his church into their denomination. So, I was pretty sure I knew his position on the baptism in the Holy Spirit and the gifts of the Spirit. However, in the conversation, I suggested we talk about doctrine, just to make sure we were on the same page on key issues. He looked at me and said, "Oh no, I don't want you to teach doctrine. Just teach the Bible and how to live a Christian life." I'm thinking, how do you separate the two? The Bible is full of doctrine, and the Christian life is based on sound doctrine. At this point, I had decided that teaching under this man's leadership would not work. So, I didn't argue the point.

He is a good man. I don't know how effective his evangelism is, whether he is really bringing people to repentance and biblical faith in Christ or whether he is just leading them in the sinner's prayer and inviting them to join the group. I can't make that judgment. I am convinced that this pastor is a sincere follower of Christ. He is simply operating out of what he knows. His church seemed to be focused on social interaction and the satisfaction people were getting from that. I think he realized there needed to be more depth. This was a gifted leader seeking to reach people for Jesus. He was not a liberal pastor who denied the key points of the gospel. Yet he didn't want any doctrine taught. I interpreted that to mean, keep it all palatable to those who come. Don't teach things that might upset someone. People want to know how to have a good marriage, how to manage their finances, how to raise their kids. The congregation was mostly composed of young families. But don't teach doctrine! That position explains some of the statistics I just read to you. It portrays a failure to understand the necessity of sound doctrine, not just on a doctrinal statement somewhere but in the hearts of the believers. You can't preach the word without preaching doctrine. The epistle we are currently studying is a doctrinal message.

The point of this story is that the church today is vulnerable to antichrist deception. This was a good pastor with good intentions. He was focused on growing his church. But he did not have an adequate appreciation for the importance of believers being grounded in the essential truths of the faith.[15] We are pursuing the wrong goals. The goal Jesus gave us in Matthew 28:19 is "Therefore go and make disciples of all nations" (NIV). In the next verse He says, "Teaching them to obey everything I have commanded you" (NIV). The goal is not to get a bunch of people in a building on Sunday morning. That's the way the church measures success today.[16] But we are to teach them to in accordance with all the things Jesus commanded. Teaching is an essential part of the goal.

Paul wrote in 1 Timothy 4:13, "Until I come, devote yourself to the public reading of Scripture, to preaching and to teaching" (NIV). He continued in verses 15–16, "Be diligent in these matters; give yourself wholly to them, so that everyone may see your progress. Watch your life and doctrine closely. Persevere in them, because if you do, you will save both yourself and your hearers" (NIV). The idea that it doesn't matter what you believe is totally foreign to John and Paul. Listen to what Paul tells the church in Colossians 2:6–7. "Therefore as you have received Christ Jesus the Lord, *so* walk in Him, having been firmly rooted *and now* being built up in Him and established in your faith, just as you were instructed, *and* overflowing with gratitude" (NASB). He is saying essentially what John is telling believers in our text. Stick with what you heard from the beginning of your experience in Christ. Stay rooted and grounded in the apostles' teaching. Let the word of Christ dwell in you richly.[17] He continues in Colossians 2:8–10. "See to it that no one takes you captive through philosophy and empty deception, according to the tradition of men, according to the elementary principles of the world, rather than according to Christ. For in Him all the fullness of Deity dwells in bodily form, and in Him you have been made complete" (NASB).[18] Paul's way of avoiding deception is very much in line with what John is telling his readers. Second Timothy 3:13–14: "But evil men and impostors will proceed *from bad* to worse, deceiving and being deceived. You, however, continue in the things you have learned and become convinced of, knowing from whom you have learned *them*" (NASB). So, the warnings and counsel of Paul affirm what John is giving here. This call to be steadfast in the word is prominent in the New Testament.[19]

We have seen that "which you heard from the beginning" is the gospel that led them to Christ at the beginning of their Christian experience. That gospel which was based on Christ's teachings and what He accomplished at the cross was brought to them by the apostles. So, John is telling these believers to abide in the apostles' teaching. It is authoritative. It comes from people who personally learned at the feet of Jesus. Their message is tried and proven. Stick with the teaching you already have. Don't abandon it for some mystical knowledge that a Gnostic says you need to have. Verse 21 says, "I have not written to you because you do not know the truth, but because you know it, and that no lie is of the truth." The gospel you have received is true. There is no lie in it. There is nothing in it that needs to be corrected. First John 2:24: "Therefore let that abide in you which you heard from the beginning."

I talked with a young woman awhile back who was excited about her church. Her comment to me was, "We have a very progressive church!" That took me back a bit, because I knew that could mean one of two things. It could just mean that they had adapted their methods to the current culture, that they had a coffee shop, that they were up to date on their technology, and their worship songs are relatively current. If that is what she meant, there is nothing wrong with it. We want to reduce communication barriers that might hinder us expressing the gospel to the people we're trying to reach. However, it is easy to inadvertently change the *message* while changing the *methods*. If we mean, by progressive, we are following the moral trends of "political correctness" in secular society, that is a concern. If progressive means we now accept gays into the ministry, abortion, and co-habitation of unmarried couples, then that is a problem. If progressive means abandoning the commandments of God, the things Jesus told us to observe, then it will not produce good results. The Bible does not tell us to be progressive. It tells us to be faithful, to abide in the doctrines of Scripture, to not forget the covenant, to live according to the word of God.[20]

When Israel got progressive in the wrong way, God confronted them in Jeremiah 6:16. "This is what the Lord says: 'Stand at the crossroads and look; ask for the ancient paths, ask where the good way is, and walk in it, and you will find rest for your souls.'" (NIV). God was saying to those people, "You need to come back to the paths that I have given you to walk in, *the ancient paths*. Their response is immediately recorded. "But you said, 'We will not walk in it'" (NIV). In verses 17–19 God says to them, "I appointed watchmen over you and said, 'Listen to the sound of the trumpet!' But you said, 'We will not listen.' Therefore hear, O nations; observe, O witnesses, what will happen to them. Hear, O earth: I am bringing disaster on this people." (NIV). God has shown us the way in His word. If we will abide in His word, and let His word abide in us, we will not be deceived, and we will be okay.

Years ago, I was in a church that dealt with an antichrist spirit. I was not the pastor, but I knew some of the people involved quite well. A man came into the church, introduced as Brother Woods. He was about fifty years old and not particularly handsome. But he claimed to have insights into the Bible that few people had. I don't remember exactly the teachings he had, but it related to the seed of the serpent and unusual teachings about the fall of Adam and Eve and the verse where Adam said of woman, "This is now bone of my bones, and flesh of my flesh."[21] I think he got these ideas from Gnostic writings. Be careful when you leave the Scripture and find truths that nobody knows but a few of the informed. There are all kinds of Gnostic teaching floating around on the internet, portrayed as "deeper" insights than the church is teaching. Let's stick with the word of God. There is plenty in the Bible to learn. There is a lot about Ezekiel's visions that I still don't know. Gnostic writings and cultic literature are dangerous because there is an antichrist spirit, a deceiving spirit, behind it. Brother Woods became a recognized teacher in the church. In time he seduced two of the most beautiful women in the church through his teaching. They were about thirty years old. A good twenty years younger than him. Both women were pretty, but one was movie-star pretty. Both were married to good Christian men. One couple was very involved in the church. The other couple was more on the fringes. Both women had grown up as Pentecostals. But Brother Woods' teaching was new and exciting. He had insights the pastor did not have. The novelty of his teaching was intriguing, and the way he communicated it was flattering. He convinced these two women that if they got pregnant by him they would give birth to a special seed. The children born of their union would have a very important role in God's program for end times. He was driven by the lust of the flesh and controlled by a seducing spirit. The women were seduced by the pride of life and the promise of greatness. Both women got pregnant by Brother Woods. Their marriages were destroyed. They left the church. Destruction followed that antichrist spirit. Before this man came, you would have never guessed these women would have fallen into such error. It was a sad story for some people I love and care for very much.

John is telling his readers to *abide*, stay with, the truth in Scripture. Don't follow some extra-biblical teaching that will lead you astray. Yes, we grow in the grace and knowledge of the Lord Jesus Christ.[22] But we do that on the inspired teaching in the word of God. We build on the firm foundation of Christ and we never, never depart from it.

Paul wrote in 1 Corinthians 3:11, "For other foundation can no man lay than that is laid, which is Jesus Christ" (KJV). The message of Jesus as the Christ is foundational to all other understanding. Without that foundation, there is no salvation.[23] "Whoever denies the Son does not have the Father either" according to verse 23 of our text. "He who acknowledges the Son has the Father also." This is nonnegotiable truth that we must never compromise. Salvation is through Jesus alone. Anyone who says they know God, but denies the deity of Christ, is antichrist and does not know the Father or the Son.

## REWARD OF CONTINUANCE

Now consider with me the reward of obeying the command to abide in the apostles' teaching. Verse 24 of the text says, "If what you heard from the beginning abides in you, you also will abide in the Son and in the Father." The result will be continued fellowship with the Son and with the Father. This is John's goal for these believers. Remember his purpose for writing this letter is set forth in chapter 1 verse 3. "We proclaim to you what we have seen and heard, so that you also may have fellowship with us. And our fellowship is with the Father and with his Son, Jesus Christ" (NIV). That purpose runs all through this epistle. And John is saying in our text, one key for that to happen in your life is that you hold to the word of God. You abide in the word and let the word abide in you.

"Then Jesus said to those Jews who believed Him, 'If you abide in My word, you are My disciples indeed. And you shall know the truth, and the truth shall make you free'" (John 8:31–32, NKJV). So here is additional blessing: spiritual freedom. If you abide or continue in My word: That means you read it, meditate on it, and let it be the rule of your life. "If you abide in My word" two things are assured. You really are one of His disciples. You're not just a superficial professor of faith, but you prove yourself to be the real deal. Secondly you will know the truth as revealed in the word; and that truth will set you free. You will live in freedom from the tyranny of sin.

Remember what John told the young men in 1 John 2:14. "I have written to you, young men, because you are strong, and the word of God abides in you, and you have overcome the evil one" (NASB). They overcame the wicked one because *the word of God abides* in them. They were strong in the Lord and the power of His might because the word of God abides in them. Our victory is found in letting the word, that which we heard from the beginning, abide in us.

The promise in 1 John 2:25 is another reward of doing this. "And this is the promise that He has promised us — eternal life" (NKJV). When people hear the words *eternal life* they usually just think everlasting life, unending life. But the eternal life God gives has a certain quality to it. It is God's life. It is life full of love, joy, peace, righteousness, and hope.[24] If you are born again, you are already living in eternal life. The life of God is in you, in the person of the Holy Spirit. We are now limited in our capacity to experience the completeness of this life while in these mortal bodies. One day the full manifestation of the sons of God will be revealed. Then this eternal life will shine forth in us with the full glory God has called us to. But even now we enjoy a quality of life that is rich and full because of our fellowship with the Son and with the Father. Abiding in the word assures an on-going fellowship with the Father and the Son. It assures us of eternal life. In fact, fellowship (*koinōnia*) with the Son and the Father is equivalent to eternal life.[25]

Additionally, abiding in Him now prepares us for His coming. The result is confidence at Christ's return. Verse 28 says, "And now, little children, abide in Him, that when He appears, we may have confidence and not be ashamed before Him at His coming" (NKJV). When all is right in our relationship with Him, we love His appearing. We look forward to His return. It is a blessed hope that sustains us through the trials and persecutions of this life. Verses 28 and 29 are transitional statements. Verse 28 introduces the theme of Christ's coming, which will be expounded further in chapter 3. Verse 29 summarizes the theme of righteous behavior which John has taught in chapters 1 and 2 and will continue to deal with throughout the epistle.

Let me summarize the two major provisions against deception that John discusses in the text. The first is the anointing (the Holy Spirit) who leads us into truth. We are to rely upon His guidance and obey His promptings. The second provision is the apostles' teaching which we have in the word of God. We are to embrace this word, cherish it, and live by it. We are not to abandon the foundations of our faith. We are, according to Jude 3, to "contend for the faith that was once for all entrusted to the saints" (NIV). If we will do that, we will stand and not fall. Jude 24–25 seems to be a fitting way to conclude this chapter. "Now unto him that is able to keep you from falling, and to present you faultless before the presence of his glory with exceeding joy, To the only wise God our Saviour, be glory and majesty, dominion and power, both now and ever. Amen" (KJV).

# Endnotes: Chapter 11

1   Peterson, The Message: *The New Testament in Contemporary Language*, 591–592.

2   Some manuscripts have *"meneite"* which could be translated as future tense (NKJV) or as imperative (NIV). Other manuscripts have *"menete"* which is present tense, translated as continuing action, *"you are abiding."* There are good arguments for each position. Cf. Burdick, 207; Zodhiates, *The Epistles of John*, 153.

3   On this command to "abide," Burdick writes, "Both the present tense and the inherent meaning of the verb call for continuing action" (p. 208).

4   Zodhiates, *The Epistles of John*, 136.

5   Peterson, *The Message: The New Testament in Contemporary Language*, 591.

6   1 Cor. 2:2, KJV.

7   Cf. 1 Cor. 15:1–5.

8   Cf. Matt. 28:19–20. In addition to all He taught the disciples before His death, Jesus taught them during the 40 days between His resurrection and ascension (Luke 24:27; Acts 1:3).

9   Paul's stated concern in 2 Cor. 11:3–4 is that believers' minds would be "corrupted from the simplicity that is in Christ" (KJV).

10  Acts 4:12. A major debate in our society is whether a person can worship God, the Father, without recognizing Jesus as God, the Son. John categorically denies that possibility. Christians must never compromise the honor God has bestowed on the Son just to get along with infidels.

11  George Barna and David Barton, *U Turn*, 30 (using data from their research and from Harris Interactive, "America's Belief in God, Miracles, and Heaven Declines" reported at http://www.newsweek.com/rethinking-resurrection-176618).

12  Ibid. The 57% is as of 2014.

13  However, church attendance in America has also declined. Cf. Barna and Barton,138.

14  Ibid., 138. This is based on national surveys conducted by the Barna Group in 2004 and 2014.

15  Benjamin Franklin once said, "An ounce of prevention is worth a pound of cure." If you have ever tried to reason with someone who has fallen under the spell and deception of false doctrine, you know it is easier to teach them the truth as a preventive measure than to rescue them once they've fallen. It's like having good anti-virus software in contrast to cleaning up a computer virus.

16  A pragmatism that puts greater emphasis on external signs of success than fidelity to God's word must be avoided. The high ideals of Scripture should be our beginning point.

17  Col. 3:16.

18    Peter also warns, "Therefore, dear friends, since you have been forewarned, be on your guard so that you may not be carried away by the error of the lawless and fall from your secure position" (2 Pet. 3:17, NIV).

19    Paul insists elders be "Holding fast the faithful word as he hath been taught, that he may be able by sound doctrine both to exhort and to convince the gainsayers" (Titus 1:9, KJV).

20    1 Cor. 9:19–23 seems to imply that we should adapt our methods/approach in order to reach the lost. However, the overwhelming weight of Scripture is that we would be steadfast and faithful to God's word.

21    Gen. 2:23, KJV.

22    Cf. 2 Pet. 3:18; 1 Pet. 2:2.

23    Paul tells the Ephesians that the household of God is "built upon the foundation of the apostles and prophets, Jesus Christ himself being the chief corner stone" (Eph. 2:20, KJV).

24    In John 15 Jesus teaches the necessity of abiding in Him and the fruitfulness that accompanies that.

25    Burdick, 192.

# CHAPTER 12

# Royal Privilege
# 3:1-3

Behold what manner of love the Father has bestowed on us, that we should be called children of God! Therefore the world does not know us, because it did not know Him. Beloved, now we are children of God; and it has not yet been revealed what we shall be, but we know that when He is revealed, we shall be like Him, for we shall see Him as He is. And everyone who has this hope in Him purifies himself, just as He is pure.

John 3:1-3, NKJV

## Expository Message

This passage begins with a call to attention: *Behold*. There is a tone of wonder and astonishment in what is about to be addressed. The Greek word is *idete*. It is more than a call for attention. It is an imperative to consider and perceive the truths that are about to be explored.[1] Spurgeon said, "It is as if the man of God said, 'Stand still, and consider the extraordinary love of God.' . . . Look at it microscopically. Study it. . . . and pry into this secret . . . inwardly digest, and still behold again."[2] A quick glance is insufficient for what John is about to present. Ponder, perceive, and understand its depths. As we receive the revelation in verses 1–2, the practical results described in verse 3 are manifested in our lives.

There is an interesting focus on seeing, perceiving, and knowing in this text. Verse 1 opens with this command to see and perceive the manner of love God has bestowed upon us. In that same verse John tells us the world can't see, perceive, know or recognize what we are in Christ. Then in verse 2 he says it has not yet been revealed, made manifest (or seen) what we shall be. But we know; we see or understand that when Christ shall be made manifest (or seen), we shall see Him as He is. The concept of seeing and perceiving is pervasive in these first two verses.

"Behold, what manner of love the Father has bestowed on us." Take time to consider thoroughly the glorious love God has given you, that you could be called a child of God! Compare His love to all other expressions of love. Ponder the extent and quality of His love toward you. It is absolutely unselfish and generous. The Phillips translation says, "Consider the incredible love the Father has shown us." Stephen Smalley translates it, "Consider how lavish is the love that the Father has showered upon us."[3] The New International Version begins with, "How great is the love the Father has lavished upon us." The vastness, quality, and degree of this love is an enriching contemplation.

## OUR FATHER'S LOVE

First, consider the kind of love the Father bestowed on us. It is a love that originates with God. It flows out of who He is. Therefore, it is eternal. Kent Henry wrote a song taken from Jeremiah 31:3 in which God says to His people, "I have loved you with an everlasting love."[4] The only reason we have any standing before God is that He loved us out of His own choice from the foundation of the world. "God is love" (1 John 4:8, KJV). It is His nature to love, but more specifically it is His choice to love you. Ephesians 1:3 says, "Blessed be the God and Father of our Lord Jesus Christ" (KJV). Isn't there something in you that cries out, "Blessed be my heavenly Father for His great love toward me," even as we read these words? Ephesians 1:3–4 continues, "Who hath blessed us with all spiritual blessings in heavenly places in Christ: According as he hath chosen us in him before the foundation of the world, that we should be holy and without blame before him in love" (KJV). It was His idea to redeem you. He set all this in motion. The old song expresses it well.

The love of God is greater far than tongue or pen could
ever tell.
It goes beyond the highest star, And reaches to the lowest
hell . . .
O love of God, how rich and pure! How measureless and
strong!
It shall forevermore endure, The saints and angel's song."[5]

The angels may sing along with us. But as redeemed sinners, we know a
depth of that love they can only desire to look into.[6] We are privileged to be
His very own children. Ephesians 1:5 goes on to say, "Having predestinated
us unto the adoption of children by Jesus Christ to himself, according to
the good pleasure of his will" (KJV).

It is an undeserved love. It is not based on any qualities in us. For we
were dead in trespasses and sin, without hope. It never was dependent on
our performance. God didn't start loving us because Christ died on the
cross. Christ died on the cross because the Father loved us. His love is the
first cause of it all.[7] In Romans 5 Paul talks about God loving us even when
we were in all-out opposition to Him. We were His enemies, throwing off
the rightful authority of the Creator. As Isaiah 53:6 puts it, "All we like
sheep have gone astray; we have turned every one to his own way" (KJV).
That states our problem quite well. "We have turned every one to his own
way." The crime is rebellion. The crime is independence from the Creator.
Your actions may or may not have been inappropriate as far as society is
concerned. The world may consider you a very good person. But if you are
going your own way, instead of submitting yourself to God's way, you're
guilty. Yet the Father so loved us that He sent His only begotten Son to
rescue us.[8] "But God demonstrates his own love for us in this: While we
were still sinners, Christ died for us" (Romans 5:8, NIV).

It is only when we appreciate our own sinfulness and helplessness, that
we can appreciate the wonder of His love toward us. People who think
God was lucky to get them will never grasp the extent of God's love. The
bad news of our sinful state precedes the good news of God's redemption.
Some people only want to hear the positive. "Talk about my good qualities.
Encourage me with talk about my value. Build my self-esteem." No, that

is not the pathway to real joy. Joy comes when we see God's love toward us, and we see it against the backdrop of our own corruption and lostness.

God told Ezekiel to cause Jerusalem to know her abomination.[9] God always deals with the truth, the whole truth, and nothing but the truth. When God found Israel, she was like a newborn, lying in her own blood. Her navel cord was not cut. She was thrown out in an open field and left to die. That is a picture of the state you and I were in without Christ. But God says in Ezekiel 16:6, "And when I passed by you and saw you struggling in your own blood, I said to you in your blood, 'Live!' Yes, I said to you in your blood, 'Live!'" (NKJV). Do you remember the day He said to you, "Live"? Oh, what compassion and love!

Consider the pure, redemptive love the Father has bestowed upon you. One reason Christians are weak in their walk with God is that they don't obey this command. Their time is consumed with considering other things. They consider the latest news. They know the NFL scores. They know the latest fashions and fads. But they don't dig into the depths of what God has done for them. They don't ponder these things. They don't meditate on the goodness and mercy of God. We will see in verse 3 that there are practical benefits to be enjoyed by those who will do what John is telling us to do. Don't pass over what he is about to say too quickly. "Behold what manner of love the Father has bestowed upon us."

Understand this love is transforming! "We love him, because He first loved us" (1 John 4:19, KJV). Grasping the depth of His love toward us ignites a love in our hearts toward Him. We don't love God because someone told us to. You can't do it on that basis. It begins with seeing; it begins with seeing His love toward us. That is first. Our love is a response to His love. Romans 5:5 says, "God's love has been poured out into our hearts through the Holy Spirit, who has been given to us" (NIV). How has God bestowed His love on us? He has poured that love out in our hearts by the Holy Spirit. He doesn't just love us by some external decree. But He makes it personal and effectual. He puts His love in our hearts. That makes it transformational. It's not a distant love. It's intimate and changes us from the inside out.

## OUR ROYAL PRIVILEGE

Consider the royal privilege we enjoy because of the Father's love toward us. "Behold what manner of love the Father has bestowed on us, *that we should be called children of God!*" (emphasis mine, 1 John 3:1). God publicly owns us as His own. He gives us the family name. We are adopted with all the legal rights of inheritance.

Paul writes to Christians in Romans 8:15–16, "For you did not receive the spirit of bondage again to fear, but you received the Spirit of adoption by whom we cry out, 'Abba, Father.' The Spirit Himself bears witness with our spirit that we are children of God" (NKJV). We have the witness of the Spirit inside confirming our relationship with the Father. Christians are to live in that assurance. We do not live with a "hope so" mentality. We are not just hoping we will go to heaven when we die. We are not waiting until we die to know. It's too late to do anything about it at that point. Do you know that you're a child of God? If not, God wants to make that matter clear to you. John gives tests in this epistle that we can use to affirm that reality. Listen to the assurance Paul had as he faced death. In 2 Timothy 4:6–8 he wrote:

> The time of my departure is at hand. I have fought a good fight, I have finished my course, I have kept the faith: Henceforth there is laid up for me a crown of righteousness, which the Lord, the righteous judge, shall give me at that day: and not to me only, but unto all them also that love his appearing (KJV).

That's the way a Christian is to die, in full assurance of God's favor. That's the way we are to live. First John 4:13: "This is how we know that we live in him and he in us: He has given us of his Spirit" (NIV). Do you have that inner witness of the Spirit that you belong to the Lord? If not, ask God to give you that assurance. It is a privilege available to every child of God.

Back in Romans 8 Paul elaborates on the wonderful privilege of sonship. In verse 17 he writes, "And if children, then heirs; heirs of God, and joint-heirs with Christ" (KJV). Paul is dealing with the legal aspect of our sonship. God's choice is to share all that He has with us, just as He shares it all with Christ. Can you wrap your mind around that? It would be gracious of God to just let us into heaven as lowly servants. I'm amazed He would even let me into heaven. That is amazing love. But His love takes us higher than that. His love bestows all His goods on us. His love gives us a place at the family table. His love makes us joint-heirs with Christ. Are you basking in the incredible love God has lavished upon you? Are you realizing something of the kind of love the Father has toward you?

Have you embraced your new identity in Christ? This is a fundamental key to victory. *In Christ* we are fully accepted by the Father.[10] His grace has made us something we could never climb up to ourselves. His hand has reached way, way down and pulled us up from our debauchery and crowned us with His righteousness.

The King James Version of 1 John 3:1 stops short of the full impact intended: "Behold what manner of love the Father has bestowed on us, that we should be called children of God!" The best manuscripts add these two Greek words, *kai esmen*, which simply mean, *"and we are!"*[11] It's not just that we are *called* children of God; we really *are* His children. Paul uses the metaphor of adoption to explain our legal standing before God as His children. But John's focus is regeneration. We are called children, and we are His children. The Greek word translated children is *tekna*, a term of affection.

John's statement in 1 John 3:1 flows out of something introduced in the previous verse. 1 John 2:29 says, "If you know that He is righteous, you know that everyone also who practices righteousness is born of Him" (NASB). This is the first time John has referred to the new birth in this letter. It introduces a new section in the epistle. The theme of practicing righteousness runs throughout this epistle. In the first two chapters Paul calls people to godly behavior based on their fellowship with the Father and the Son. "If we say that we have fellowship with Him and *yet* walk in the darkness, we lie and do not practice the truth" (1:6, NASB). "By this we know that we have come to know Him, if we keep His commandments. The one who says, 'I have come to know Him,' and does not keep His commandments, is a liar, and the truth is not in him" (2:3–4, NASB). "The one who says he is in the Light and *yet* hates his brother is in the darkness until now" (2:9, NASB). "Do not love the world nor the things in the world. If anyone loves the world, the love of the Father is not in him"

(2:15, NASB). John is countering Gnostic error, error that says my daily obedience to God is not that important[1]. It's a popular error today. That's why this epistle is so vital to the church today. We must understand that genuine Christianity is demonstrated by godly living.

John will continue this theme of right living in chapter 3. But he will base it on something introduced in chapter 2, verse 29: the new birth. We are not only children by adoption, we are not just legally called children of God, but that's what we really are. Any person who has been born again, born of the Spirit, has received the very nature of God Himself. And that nature is characterized by righteousness. Peter exhorts believers to behave, "As obedient children, do not be conformed to the former lusts *which were yours* in your ignorance, but like the Holy One who called you, be holy yourselves also in all *your* behavior; because it is written, 'YOU SHALL BE HOLY, FOR I AM HOLY'" (1 Pet. 1:14–16, NASB). The wholesale rejection of holiness in our churches is absolutely contrary to everything the apostles taught. John now points to this new nature as the source of our godly behavior, and our godly behavior as evidence that we have truly been born again and have the Father's nature. "If you know that He is righteous, you know that everyone also who practices righteousness is born of Him." We have the Father's DNA, and that DNA produces the fruit of righteous behavior. If righteous behavior is not being produced, then the assumption is that the new nature is not present. We will deal with this more extensively later in chapter 14.

John introduces another subject in verse one that will be expanded on later: the world's attitude toward believers. Even though we are children of God destined for greatness, the world does not see that in us. As far as they are concerned, we're just ordinary people with the same destiny they have. If they could see the reality, they would open up to the gospel and receive it. If they could suddenly see our destiny compared to their destiny, they would run to the cross for salvation. And we try to communicate that when we preach the Gospel. God is "not willing that any should perish, but that all should come to repentance."[12] This great salvation is available to "whosoever will." John 1:12 says, "But as many as received him, to them gave he power to become the sons of God, even to them that believe on his name" (KJV). Any sinner who will bow the knee to Christ as Lord

---
[1]

and receive His forgiveness can become a child of God. God will not push him or her away. He will grant to the repentant person the right to become a child of God. It is the most amazing offer that's ever been made: an invitation to be "born, not of blood, nor of the will of the flesh, nor of the will of man, but of God."[13]

"Therefore the world does not know us, because it did not know Him." They couldn't recognize God in Christ, and they won't recognize God in you. These things are spiritually discerned, and the natural man does not discern them.[14] Therefore, don't be surprised if the world doesn't recognize you as God's child, destined for greatness. John 1:10–11 makes this statement about Jesus. "He was in the world, and the world was made by him, and the world knew him not. He came unto his own, and his own received him not" (KJV). That was Jesus's experience. Then He says to His followers in John 15:18–20,

> If the world hates you, you know that it has hated Me
> before *it hated* you. If you were of the world, the world
> would love its own; but because you are not of the world,
> but I chose you out of the world, because of this the world
> hates you. Remember the word that I said to you, "A slave
> is not greater than his master." If they persecuted Me, they
> will also persecute you; if they kept My word, they will
> keep yours also (NASB).

So, we do not look to the world for affirmation of who we are. The Spirit bears witness with our spirit that we are the children of God.

Verse 2 in our text begins with this affirmation, "Beloved, now we are children of God." This is in perfect accord with what the best manuscripts say in verses one: *and we are.* Where there are minor differences in the manuscripts used for translating the Bible, there is so often little consequence of the difference. This is a perfect example. To translate verse one with this addition phrase, "and we are," adds some punch to John's statement. But it doesn't change what John is saying. Verse 2 says the same thing loud and clear, "Beloved, now we are children of God." Therefore, such differences are little cause for concern.

In verse 2 the Greek word, *nun*, translated "now," is placed at the beginning of the sentence for emphasis.[15] We are *now* children of God. If you have been born again, you will never be more of a child of God than you are right now. We're not waiting to become children of God. We are already His dear children. We still come short of His glory. We have a lot to learn and a lot of rough edges to be knocked off. But our Father takes us into His arms as His dear children even *now*. And we are to rest in that fact.[16] Understand God's attitude toward you as His child. Do not let the devil tell you that God doesn't like you. Don't let him tell you that you're second class in God's eyes. "Now we are the children of God." That is your current identity.

We have pondered the kind of love the Father has bestowed upon us. We have considered the royal privilege of being called children of God, and actually being made His dear adopted children and His children by the new birth as well. Those are two ways of looking at this filial relationship we have with the Father: adoption and regeneration. Regeneration means we have been recreated at a higher state; we have been born again; we are now a part of a new creation, a new humanity redeemed by the sacrifice of Calvary.

Get an understanding of your *identity* in Christ. It will ground you in your walk with God. In chapter thirteen, we will begin in the middle of verse two and talk about our *destiny* in Christ. The revelation of identity and destiny, as addressed by John in verses one and two, can have a powerful impact on our daily lives. We will see that when we study the connection between what John says in verses one and two with the practical results he declares in verse three. "And everyone who has this hope in Him purifies himself, just as He is pure" (NKJV). Notice, John does not say he *should* purify himself. That is implied and clearly stated in other New Testament passages. But the effect of having this hope in Christ *is* purifying. It motivates us to greater heights and goals. We are no longer so enticed by what the world has to offer. Houses, cars, bank accounts are as nothing compared to the glory that awaits us. All that the flesh and the world can offer is trivial compared to the love God has lavished upon us, that we should be called the children of God, and we are! May the Lord fill your heart with gratitude toward the Father for His unfailing, abundant love for you.

# Endnotes: Chapter 12

1 Zodhiates, *The Epistles of John,* 159. Thayer's definition (NT:1492) includes this idea of getting knowledge and understanding of any fact.

2 Charles H. Surgeon, "'And We Are': A Jewel from the Revised Version," sermon preached Dec. 19. 1886. Accessed at The C. H. Spurgeon Collection on CD-ROM (AGES Software, Inc., 1998).

3 Smalley, 138.

4 Kent Henry, "I Have Loved You," Integrity's Hosanna! Music. Retrieved Nov. 15, 2017 at www.ccli.com.

5 Fettke, ed., s. v. "The Love of God," by Fredrick M. Lehman, 220. The following stanza is said to have been penciled on the wall of a narrow room of an asylum by a man said to have been demented. The lines were discovered after his death. "Could we with ink the ocean fill, and were the skies of parchment made; Were every stalk on earth a quill, And every man a scribe by trade: To write the love of God above Would drain the ocean dry, Nor could the scroll contain the whole Though stretched from sky to sky." Ben Glanzer, "Music of the Message: The Story of 'The Love of God,'" retrieved Nov. 15, 2017 at https://www.ministrymagazine.org/archive/1950/09/the-story-of-the-love-of-god.

6 Cf. 1 Pet. 1:12.

7 Spurgeon, "'And We Are': A Jewel from the Revised Version." Accessed at The C. H. Spurgeon Collection on CD-ROM.

8 John 3:16.

9 Ezek. 16:2.

10 Eph. 1:6.

11 Burdick, 230–231.

12 2 Pet. 3:9, KJV.

13 John 1:13, KJV.

14 1 Cor. 2:14.

15 This comes, of course, after the word translated beloved in which John addresses his readers.

16 Some commentaries emphasize the contrast between what we are now and what we shall be and put a negative light on what we are now. This is not John's intent. As he did in 2:12–14, John is affirming these believers. He is speaking in a positive tone about what we are now and about what we shall be.

# CHAPTER 13

# Glorious Destiny
## 3:1–3

> Behold what manner of love the Father has bestowed on
> us, that we should be called children of God! Therefore
> the world does not know us, because it did not know Him.
> Beloved, now we are children of God; and it has not yet
> been revealed what we shall be, but we know that when
> He is revealed, we shall be like Him, for we shall see Him
> as He is. And everyone who has this hope in Him purifies
> himself, just as He is pure.
>
> 1 John 3:1–3, NKJV

### Expository Message

In chapter twelve we examined the first half of that text. We talked about
the love God has bestowed upon us. We talked about the high privilege
of being adopted into the family of God and the new nature we have
receive by being born of the Spirit. All of that is already ours. Verse 2
says, "Beloved, *now* we are children of God" (emphasis mine). We are not
waiting for that to happen. It is already our reality! However, the glory
of all that is shrouded in a mortal body. The reality is not evident for all
to see. By all outward appearances we look no different than the world.[1]
"Therefore the world does not know us, because it did not know Him."
Just as the world did not recognize Jesus for who He is, the world does not

recognize the Holy Spirit in us and our relationship with the Father. But that does not change who we really are. Verse 2 begins with this sentence: "Beloved, now we are children of God." That is our *identity* in Christ. That is who we really are. And it is imperative that we know who we are in Christ. Knowing our identity in Christ and meditating on these truths has a powerful sanctifying influence on our lives.

In the middle of verse 2 John moves his attention from our identity to our *destiny* in Christ. If you have been born from above, you're a new creation in Christ; your destiny is altogether different from that of an unbeliever. The world is moving on a path toward destruction, shame, and everlasting separation from God. The Christian is moving toward everlasting joy and glory. Look again at John's words in verse 2. "And it has not yet been revealed what we shall be, but we know that when He is revealed, we shall be like Him, for we shall see Him as He is."

## OUR DESTINY

Think about your destiny in Christ. This is the great hope of our salvation. John says, "We shall be like Him." I cannot imagine anything better than that! John is talking about the resurrection of our bodies into a glorified state.

We are currently in mortal bodies, bodies with frustrating weaknesses and limitations, bodies that get tired, bodies that get sick, bodies that age and decay. The Holy Spirt does quicken these mortal bodies.[2] We can testify of times when God has supernaturally healed our bodies. Physical healing is a part of the earnest of our inheritance.[3] It is available to us right now. But a healing does not change the basic makeup of these corruptible bodies. Even though Jesus raised Lazarus from the dead, Lazarus eventually died. No matter how diligent you are to care for your body, it will still decay with age and eventually die. Hebrews 9:27 says, "It is appointed unto men once to die, but after this the judgment" (KJV). These mortal bodies have an expiration date on them. What we need is a body that will last for an eternity. We need glorified bodies like the one Jesus has.

The world looks at these outside containers and says, "What's the big deal; you look the way I look; you're no different than I am." "It has not yet been revealed what we shall be," John says. The new creation within us has not yet been make manifest. That happens at the resurrection of the just.[4]

In Romans 8:18 Paul wrote, "For I consider that the sufferings of this present time are not worthy to be compared with the glory that is to be revealed to us" (NASB). That's a perspective that we will talk more about. You deal with the current sufferings and difficulties in the context of God's long-term plan for your destiny. God never meant for this life to be heaven on earth. "The just shall live by faith."[5] The fullness of our inheritance is yet to come.

"For the earnest expectation of the creation eagerly waits for the revealing of the sons of God" (Rom. 8:19, NKJV). The revealing of the sons of God! That's what John is talking about in our text. First John 3:2 says, "It has not yet been revealed what we shall be." Paul says, "The creation eagerly waits for the revealing of the sons of God." They're talking about the same thing.

> For the creation was subjected to futility, not willingly, but because of Him who subjected it, in hope that the creation itself also will be set free from its slavery to corruption into the freedom of the glory of the children of God. For we know that the whole creation groans and suffers the pains of childbirth together until now. And not only this, but also we ourselves, having the first fruits of the Spirit, even we ourselves groan within ourselves, waiting eagerly for *our* adoption as sons, the redemption of our body" (Rom. 8:20–23, NASB).

That is a vivid description of our current state. "Even we ourselves groan within ourselves." No matter how much faith you have, you're not going to change God's overall plan. We await the redemption of our bodies. And we do that with eager expectation of glory.

The Greek word translated hope has a different meaning than the way we use the English word hope. When we say hope it is usually said like a wish. "I hope it doesn't rain tomorrow." But when you read the word *hope* in the Bible it means confident expectation.[6] We have absolute confidence that God will raise our bodies from the dead.[7] "Being confident of this very thing, that he which hath begun a good work in you will perform it until the day of Jesus Christ" (Phil. 1:6, KJV).

"The day of Jesus Christ!" Paul is talking about the return of Christ. That is supposed to be our focus. That is the finish line we are running to. "Looking for that blessed hope, and the glorious appearing of the great God and our Saviour Jesus Christ" (Titus 2:13, KJV). Are you living for that day? There's nothing wrong with setting goals in this life. In fact, it can help us be disciplined and accomplish more of what we need to do. But the one goal we must always keep in view is that day when we will meet the Lord in the air—that day when we will be resurrected from the dead—that day when "in a moment, in the twinkling of an eye" we will be changed.[8] This mortality will put on immortality. We will be given a glorified body like the one Jesus has. In 1 Corinthians 15 Paul declares that we will be raised incorruptible.

> For this corruptible must put on incorruption, and this mortal must put on immortality. So when this corruptible shall have put on incorruption, and this mortal shall have put on immortality, then shall be brought to pass the saying that is written, Death is swallowed up in victory (1 Cor. 15:53–54, KJV).

No more death; no more sickness; no more pain; no more temptation; no more disappointments. Our salvation will then be complete!

In 1 Thessalonians 5:23 Paul addressed three aspects of our salvation. As he closed his letter he wrote, "Now may the God of peace Himself sanctify you entirely; and may your spirit and soul and body be preserved complete, without blame at the coming of our Lord Jesus Christ" (NASB). Paul identified three parts of our being that need sanctification: spirit and soul and body. When you were born again, your spirit was made perfect. Your spirit was joined with the Holy Spirit according to 1 Corinthians 6:17. When Christ returns for His church, we will receive glorified bodies. Philippians 3:20–21 affirms this: "But our citizenship is in heaven. And we eagerly await a Savior from there, the Lord Jesus Christ, who, by the power that enables him to bring everything under his control, will transform our lowly bodies so that they will be like his glorious body" (NIV). This is the stage of salvation John is talking about when he writes, "We shall be like Him." We look forward to that as our ultimate destiny. We eagerly wait for the full salvation of these bodies.

The salvation of the soul is what God is working on in the here and now. Paul described the process in 2 Corinthians 3:18. "But we all, with unveiled face, beholding as in a mirror the glory of the Lord, are being transformed into the same image from glory to glory, just as from the Lord, the Spirit" (NASB). There is a maturing process going on in your soul as you walk with the Lord daily. There is a sanctification process. There is a development of the character of Christ as our minds are being renewed and we embrace His ways of doing things. We are growing in the grace and knowledge of our Lord.[9] The hammer and anvil of trials and hardships are often involved. Paul described some of the hardships and persecutions he was enduring. Then he wrote, "For our light affliction, which is but for a moment, is working for us a far more exceeding and eternal weight of glory" (2 Cor. 4:17, NKJV). That part of salvation does not happen at the resurrection. It is happening in the here and now. The extent to which you cooperate with the work of the Holy Spirit in this life determines a level of development that affects your eternal future. When you receive a glorified body, you will still be you! The very presence of evil will be gone. No more flesh to contend with. Praise God! But the resurrection does not develop the soul. The resurrection transforms the body. What's my point? Your cooperation with God's program for your life in the here and now is extremely important. It is working for you a far more exceeding and eternal weight of glory. Don't neglect the things of God. Your place in the kingdom of God is being chiseled out in the context of your obedience to God's plan now.[10]

"And it has not yet been revealed what we shall be, but we know that when He is revealed, we shall be like Him, for we shall see Him as He is." How will we see Him as He is? We will see Him as He is because we will be like Him.[11] We will be elevated into a capacity to see better than we can now see. "For now we see through a glass, darkly; but then face to face: now I know in part; but then shall I know even as also I am known" (1 Cor. 13:12, KJV). The Greek word, *opsometha,* carries the idea of seeing with understanding or perception.[12] The reason we will see Him as He is and the reason we will know even as we're known is the transformation that takes place when we receive a glorified body and are freed from the limitations of our mortality. Ray Stedman illustrates this by his relationship with his dog. Your dog does not know you as he is known.[13] He can't enter into a complete understanding of a human being. He can jump up and down and wag his tail when you get home. He can relate to you at a level. But the limitations of his capacity are there. He would need a major transformation in order to know you as he is known. "For now we see through a glass, darkly; but then face to face: now I know in part; but then shall I know even as also I am known." At Christ's coming we will get the transformation we need in order to see Him as He is.

The Greek particle, *hoti*, in 1 John 3:2 can be translated "for" or "because of." That's the way the New King James Version translates it. "But we know that when He is revealed, we shall be like Him, for we shall see Him as He is." Translating it that way, it means our transformation to be like Him is caused by seeing Him as He is. That is a possible translation. However, other scholars recognize an equally acceptable translation in which *hoti* is translated "that;" and this is the more common way the word *hoti* is translated in the New Testament.[14] Then it means "we shall be like Him, [that or so that] we shall see Him as He is." Either way, the end result is twofold: (1) we will be resurrected in His likeness, and (2) we will see Him with a much fuller understanding and depth. "For now we see through a glass, darkly; but then face to face: now I know in part; but then shall I know even as also I am known."

We will experience a glorious transformation when resurrected. However, that does not mean we become gods or become divine. That is forever reserved for God alone. Mormons and other cults teach their followers will become gods. That is heresy. Infinite omniscience and omnipotence belong to God alone. In an open vision, God gave me some insight into this subject. I saw the difference between what I will be versus what Christ is forever. I saw the light, love, and glory flowing out of His being. I knew He was the source of all that. We are honored to reflect that Light. He is the Light.[15] As the moon and stars reflect the glory of sun, but the sun is the source of that light, we will forever show forth His light, glory, and love. His love has been poured out in our hearts and His glory will be manifested in our resurrected bodies. We are destined for greatness. If you and I were to see a glorified saint today, we would be tempted to worship that saint, but we would not be authorized to do so.[16] Worship is for God alone. In Revelation 19:10 John received a message from a heavenly being. John said, "And I fell at his feet to worship him. But he said to me, 'See that you do not do that! I am your fellow servant, and of your brethren who have the testimony of Jesus. Worship God!'" We will be changed at the resurrection of the just. We will receive a glorified body like Jesus has. But we will never be God. We will never receive worship. It will be our glory to give worship to our Creator and Redeemer. God alone is God!

So, we have considered the manner of love the Father has bestowed on us. He has made us His children. We are that already. And we shall be glorified with Christ at His coming. It is our destiny and the hope of that is ever before us. Verses 1–2 assures us of that.

## OUR RESPONSE TO REVEALED DESTINY

Now John states in verse 3, *our response* to these revelations. The practical result is godly conduct. First John 3:3 says, "And everyone who has this hope in Him purifies himself, just as He is pure." As pointed out in the previous chapter, that verse does not say he *should* purify himself. That is implied here and is clearly stated in other New Testament passages. But the effect of having this hope *is* purifying. It motivates us to put away ungodliness and prepare for His coming. It lifts our goals to a higher plane. The more we see our current identity and future destiny in Christ, the more we live for spiritual things, rather than the beggarly elements of this world. Like the old song says:

> Turn your eyes upon Jesus,
> Look full in His wonderful face.
> And the things of earth will grow strangely dim,
> In the light of His glory and grace."[17]

What has your attention? Whatever it is, it will profoundly affect the path you take. That's why John begins our text with the word *Behold*. It calls for our attention. But more than that, it calls upon us to ponder, consider, meditate on the things he writes in the first two verses. "Behold, what manner of love the Father has bestowed upon us that we should be called the children of God." If we think about His love toward us, if we consider what He has done for us, if we focus on His plans for us and the glory He has prepared for us, it will automatically affect us in positive ways.[18]

It will motivate us to behave in accordance with who we are and where we're going. This is why these truths are so important. They have practical implications. The more we study them and mediate on them, the more this hope captures our hearts and the more we live for eternity. Obeying John's command to *behold* the truths recorded in verses 1–2 produces the results recorded in verse 3. "And everyone who has this hope in Him purifies himself, just as He is pure."[19]

Verse 3 does imply that we should purify ourselves, "just as He is pure." This theme of practical righteousness is prevalent throughout this epistle. In the verses following our text, John will expound upon that concept. It is an important theme in Paul's letters as well. For example, Paul concludes 2 Corinthians 6 in verses 18, "I will be a Father to you, And you shall be My sons and daughters, Says the LORD Almighty" (NKJV). Notice how closely this matches John's statement in verse one of our text. Then in the next verse, 2 Corinthians 7:1, Paul gives the logical response to these promises. "Therefore, having these promises, beloved, let us cleanse ourselves from all filthiness of the flesh and spirit, perfecting holiness in the fear of God" (NKJV). Whose responsibility is it for the cleansing in this verse? Let us cleanse *ourselves*. "But," someone might say, "I thought only God could cleanse sin?" Only God can remove the guilt and shame of our disobedience. Only the blood of Jesus can remove the stain of sin. But God requires us to act in faith. God requires us to cooperate with what He desires to do for us. That's why there are so many imperatives in the New Testament. Remember how Paul taught in the first half of Ephesians all the wonderful privileges and provisions that are ours in Christ by grace? Then in the second half of the book he tells us how we are to respond to those provisions. He begins the transition in Ephesians 4:1–2: "As a prisoner for the Lord, then, I urge you to live a life worthy of the calling you have received. Be completely humble and gentle; be patient, bearing with one another in love" (NIV). That's a pattern we see often: a revelation of what

God has already done for us as His dear children, followed by exhortations of how we are to respond to His grace. Ephesians 4:25–29 says,

> Therefore each of you must put off falsehood and speak truthfully to your neighbor, for we are all members of one body. "In your anger do not sin": Do not let the sun go down while you are still angry, and do not give the devil a foothold. Anyone who has been stealing must steal no longer, but must work, doing something useful with their own hands, that they may have something to share with those in need. Do not let any unwholesome talk come out of your mouths, but only what is helpful for building others up according to their needs, that it may benefit those who listen (NIV).

Paul goes on and on telling Christians to respond to God's love and grace by putting away behavior that offends or grieves Him.[20] The revelation of God's grace teaches us "to say 'No' to ungodliness and worldly passions, and to live self-controlled, upright and godly lives in this present age, while we wait for the blessed hope—the appearing of the glory of our great God and Savior, Jesus Christ" (Titus 2:12–13, NIV). It's so consistent with John's message.

Look at John's instruction at the end of chapter two in this epistle. First John 2:29: "If you know that He is righteous, you know that everyone who practices righteousness is born of Him" (NKJV). The new nature is evidenced by a life that *practices righteousness.* I am alarmed at the "Christians" who deny this fact. How many people today claim to be born again, yet their lives are characterized by lying, cheating, fornicating, and maligning others. According to John, their claim is unfounded. This error of claiming relationship with God while living an unrighteous life is not new. When Israel went into sin and idolatry, they kept their form of godliness. They kept their religious rites and rituals. They claimed righteousness because they had done the external rituals. They even drew near to God with their lips; but God said their hearts were far from Him.[21] God confronted them in Isaiah one, declaring His displeasure with their superficial religion and calling them to true holiness. Ritual can never replace relationship. Form can never replace substance. Pretense can never replace a sincere consecration to God.

In 1 John 2:28 the apostle gives a powerful motive for living in fellowship to the Lord, obeying His commandments, abiding in Christ: "And now, little children, abide in Him, that when He appears, we may have confidence and not be ashamed before Him at His coming" (NKJV). John sets forth two possibilities for the Christian at Christ's coming. One is that we would be ashamed at His appearing, caught off guard, and unprepared. We see the shame on Adam and Eve after they had disobeyed the Lord's command to not partake of the tree of knowledge of good and evil. When we have sinned, our tendency is to draw back from the Lord in shame. We experience that even now in our walk with God. At His appearing everything hidden will be brought to light. Even a cup of water given in His name will be rewarded. But we will also give account for every idle word.[22]

I have heard some teachers recently say that only good things will be brought up at the Judgment Seat of Christ. It will only be a time of rewards and rejoicing. But this is not what Paul says in 2 Corinthians 5:10. "For we must all appear before the judgment seat of Christ, so that each of us may receive what is due us for the things done while in the body, whether good or bad" (NIV). Notice the words *good or bad*. "That each of us may receive what is due us for the things done while in the body, whether good or bad." Paul punctuates that in verse 11 with these words, "Knowing therefore the terror of the Lord, we persuade men" (KJV). I do not believe that any Christian will be punished for his sins at the Judgment Seat of Christ. Jesus bore our punishment on the cross. But even in this life, we bear the consequences of our choices and actions.[23] And those choices will have eternal consequences when we stand before the Judgment Seat of Christ. I suspect a common and sad phrase will be: "what might have been." What would your life and my life be, had we fully served the Lord. Revelation 21:4 says that God will wipe away every tear from our eyes in heaven. I suspect some of those tears will be shed at the Judgment Seat of Christ. The possibility that John wants us to avoid is that we would be "ashamed before Him at His coming." We avoid that by abiding in Him now. We avoid that by purifying ourselves now. We avoid that by living with our eyes fixed on His coming and making preparation for that day.

The other possibility is that we would have confidence, joy, and commendation at His coming. The word translated *confidence* commonly refers to openness, boldness, or freedom to speak.[24] Rather than being overwhelmed by our accountability, we would meet the Lord with confidence and assurance because we've done what He's told us to do and lived pleasing to Him. A worker does not dread the review of his work when he knows in his heart he has done what his boss wanted him to do. He actually looks forward to his boss' approval the way Paul did in 2 Timothy 4:6–8 where he said:

> The time of my departure is at hand. I have fought a good fight, I have finished my course, I have kept the faith: Henceforth there is laid up for me a crown of righteousness, which the Lord, the righteous judge, shall give me at that day: and not to me only, but unto all them also that love his appearing (KJV).

> William Borden was born November 1, 1887 into privilege and wealth. By high school graduation he was already committing himself to God's call to the mission field. Reportedly he wrote in his Bible, "No reserves." During his first semester at Yale University, he started an early morning prayer group. By the time he was a senior, 1000 of Yale's 1300 students were meeting in such groups. Upon graduation Bill Bordon turned down high-paying job offers and reportedly added two more words in his Bible, "No retreats." Completing studies at Princeton University, he sailed for China to minister to Muslims. On his way he stopped in Egypt to study Arabic. But in Egypt he was stricken with spinal meningitis and died at age 25. It is said that in his Bible, underneath the words "no reserves" and "no retreats," Bordon had written the words, "No regrets."[25]

When we live for God with "no reserves" and "no retreats" we can come before Him at the Judgment Seat of Christ with "no regrets." That's the way to live. Paul said, "We make it our aim . . . to be well pleasing to Him."[26] Every decision is based on what would please the Father. When you live with that mindset, you love His appearing! You look forward to His coming with confidence and hopeful expectation. Is that your relationship with the Lord today? It is available to all who will embrace it.

# Endnotes: Chapter 13

1   Of course, the light that is in us should shine forth in the form of good works. But, as a whole, the world does not discern that being from the Father any more than it discerned Jesus's good works as being from the Father. Otherwise, they would not have crucified Him.

2   Rom. 8:11.

3   An earnest is a small portion that is given to insure the full inheritance at a later time. Most of us understand earnest because we put down earnest money during the process of buying a house. It assures the seller of the validity of our full intentions while we prepare for close. Ephesians 1:13 says you "were sealed with that holy Spirit of promise, Which is the earnest of our inheritance until the redemption of the purchased possession" (KJV). The earnest of our inheritance is available to us now by faith, but we must wait until the resurrection to receive the full inheritance.

4   We are eagerly waiting for the manifestation of the sons of God. Christians should think often about the promise of His coming as a source of comfort (1 Thess. 4:13–18) and hope. It puts the trials of life in proper perspective.

5   Heb. 10:35–38, KJV.

6   Burdick, 235.

7   Cf. Rom. 8:29.

8   1 Cor. 15:52, KJV.

9   Cf. 2 Pet. 3:18; Rom. 12:2; 2 Pet. 1:5–8.

10   Cf. Rev. 22:12; Matt. 25:14–30; 1 Cor. 3:12–15; 2 Cor. 5:10.

11   The *hoti* clause may indicate the condition for seeing Him as He is, or the cause of being like him. I personally believe that in this passage, likeness to Jesus is the condition, not the result, of seeing Him face-to-face. Burdick, 234: "Only those who are like Christ will see Him just as He really is." However, Westcott is correct in his assessment that either interpretation is grammatically possible, and either interpretation is scriptural. Westcott, 99. Smalley (pp. 146–147) believes the preferable interpretation is to see the transformation as a result of the vision.

12   Spiros Zodhiates, *The Complete Word Study Dictionary: New Testament*, 1052. *Opsometha* is the future tense of *optanomai* (NT: 3700).

13   Ray Stedman, *Expository Studies in 1 John: Life by the Son* (Waco, TX: Word Books, 1980) 201–202.

14   Stedman, 200–202. See Westcott, 99–100. According to James Strong's Concordance, the KJV translates "*hoti*" with the English word "that" 606 times and with the English word "for" 255 times and with "because" 176 times.

15   Cf. John 1:4–9.

16   In his book, *The Weight of Glory*, C.S. Lewis wrote, ". . . the dullest most uninteresting person you can talk to may one day be a creature which, if you saw

it now, you would be strongly tempted to worship. . . ." "The Weight of Glory Quotes," *Goodreads*. Retrieved Nov. 22, 2017 at https://www.goodreads.com/work/quotes/1629232-the-weight-of-glory.

17  Ric Simeson, ed., *The Best of Lift Him Up* Helen (Nashville, TN: Benson Music, 1994), s. v. "Turn Your Eyes Upon Jesus," by Helen H. Lemmel, 53.

18  1 Thess. 4:18 also recommends these truths as a source of comfort for believers.

19  The phrase "in Him" in verse 3 means our hope in Christ, although the hope in Christ does reside in the believer's heart and is nurtured by meditating on the promises stated in verses 1–2.

20  I learned early in ministry that people may respond well to the news of what God has done for us and less enthusiastically to the responsibility to respond to God's grace in obedience. Years ago, I was teaching a group of people through the book of Ephesians. As I taught the first three chapters, the hearers celebrated the teaching and expressed how much they were enjoying my ministry. As I taught through chapters four and five, the mood changed. Some got so upset they went to the senior pastor and complained that I was embarrassing them by exposing some of their activities that were supposed to be kept secret. They demanded that I apologize. Since I did not know their secret sins, I told the senior pastor that I was simply expounding the passage and would only apologize unless someone could show me where I had departed from Scripture. No one could do that, so I stood my ground. It was an uncomfortable experience, but a lesson well learned.

21  Isa. 29:13 Cf. Isa. 1:10–20; 2 Tim. 3:5.

22  Cf. Matt. 10:42; 12:36.

23  Cf. Heb. 12:5–13; Rev. 2–3. We can get some insight on what the Judgment Seat of Christ might be like by examining Jesus's words to His people in Revelation 2–3. There He dealt with both the positive and the negative.

24  Smalley, 130.

25  While it is commonly reported that Borden had written the inspirational words, "no reserve, no retreat, no regret," in his Bible, that Bible has not been recovered, and that part of the story cannot be historically corroborated. Jason Casper summed up this issue well when he wrote, "Ultimately, it is not Borden's words but rather his life that have had the greatest impact." Jason Casper, "The Forgotten Final Resting Place of William Borden, "*Christianity Today*, February 2017. Retrieved Nov. 22, 2017 at https://www.christianitytoday.com/history/2017/february/forgotten-final-resting-place-of-william-borden.html. Cf. Hubert Culbertson, "No Reserves. No Retreats. No Regrets," Southern Nazarene University missions course material. Retrieved Nov. 22, 2017 at https://home.snu.edu/-hculbert/regret.htm; "William Whiting Borden." *Wikipedia*. Retrieved Nov. 22, 2017 at https://en.wikipedia.org/wiki/William_Whiting_Borden.

26  2 Cor. 5:9, NKJV.

# CHAPTER 14

***

# Power of a New Nature
# 3:4–10

Whoever commits sin also commits lawlessness, and sin is lawlessness. And you know that He was manifested to take away our sins, and in Him there is no sin. Whoever abides in Him does not sin. Whoever sins has neither seen Him nor known Him. Little children, let no one deceive you. He who practices righteousness is righteous, just as He is righteous. He who sins is of the devil, for the devil has sinned from the beginning. For this purpose the Son of God was manifested, that He might destroy the works of the devil. Whoever has been born of God does not sin, for His seed remains in him; and he cannot sin, because he has been born of God. In this the children of God and the children of the devil are manifest: Whoever does not practice righteousness is not of God, nor is he who does not love his brother.

1 John 3:4–10, NKJV

---

## Expository Message

The term "born-again" has become so common in our culture that it is specifically defined in Webster's Dictionary.[1] Vast numbers of Americans, about 130 million, claim to be born again.[2] But the question must be asked. Are all these people really born again? Would they pass the test that John gives in this text? Of course, a more personal question is would I pass the test. In this chapter, we will examine John's test of righteousness.

The heart of John's message here is found in verse 7. "Little children, let no one deceive you. He who practices righteousness is righteous, just as He is righteous." The danger of deception is still on John's mind. He has talked about it earlier in this letter. He is addressing an error preached by Gnostics that tells Christians that the way they live their daily lives has little bearing on their eternal destiny.[3] The important thing is having mystical knowledge of God. Obeying the commandments of God is not all that important, as long as you have had the experience and gotten the revelation. The error is called antinomianism.[4] It minimizes the significance of sin in a person's life. It declares people righteous even when their behavior is unrighteous. Deception is subtle; it appeals to what people want to hear, and it contains enough truth to sound right. John writes as a concerned pastor and spiritual father. Hear the tenderness in his voice, "*Little children*, let no one deceive you" (emphasis mine).

In the preceding verses John talked about the wonderful privilege that is ours in being made the children of God. What an awesome expression of love that God would call us His children and make us His children through the new birth. John says in verse 3 of this chapter, "And everyone who has this hope in Him purifies himself, just as He is pure" (NKJV). It would be absolutely illogical to embrace this relationship with God, and not conform to His values. It would be illogical to know the holiness of God and His love toward us, and not purify ourselves, just as He is pure. Peter says it this way, "But like the Holy One who called you, be holy yourselves also in all *your* behavior because it is written, 'YOU SHALL BE HOLY, FOR I AM HOLY'" (1 Pet. 1:15–16, NASB). "Little children, let no one deceive you."

Are there people today being deceived by the same error that John is contending with in these antinomian Gnostics? I would suggest to you, this is perhaps the most prevalent error you will find in the church today. People love to hear they can have their cake and eat it too. They love a message that tells them all they have to do is say a little prayer, perform a little ritual, and heaven is their home, regardless of how they live. So, they say the prayer; they jump through a few religious hoops; then they go on about their lives the same way they always did. But John says, "That is not the way it works, don't be deceived; don't be lead astray by enticing promises that are not consistent with the truth." Real righteousness is reflected in real behavior. "He who practices righteousness is righteous." Claiming righteousness is not enough. Joining the church club is not enough. Saying prayers and performing rituals is not enough. "You must be born again."[5]

The new birth is absolutely essential. It is something that only God can do for a person. The church can't do it for you. The individual can't do it for himself. Only God can grant the miracle of new birth. When it happens, the fundamental nature of the individual is transformed. The person becomes a new creation in Christ, "old things are passed away; behold, all things are become new" (2 Cor. 5:17, KJV). John says, when that has really happened, there comes a profound change in the way the person lives. If there is no significant change, then the transformation of new birth has simply not happened. The person may have had an emotional experience. The person may have "turned over a new leaf." The person may have even become religious. But the new birth sets the person on a new direction in life. That's how you know it has really happened.

Each year 200,000 abortions are acquired in America by people who claim to be born-again. In 2008 the Guttmacher Institute found that 65% of abortions in America were performed on people who claimed to be Christians.[6] I find in those statistics a disconnect between claiming to be righteous and really being righteous. "Little children, let no one deceive you. He who practices righteousness is righteous." Studies by the Barna Institute have found no substantial differences between the moral behavior of Christians and non-Christians in America.[7] Beloved, these things ought not to be! "For instance," Barna writes, "we know that in most instances, the attitudes, values, and behavior of born-again Christians are very similar to those of the non-born-again public."[8] I am simply showing you how relevant John's message, specifically our text, is for us today.

In addressing this danger of deception, John presents three crucial concepts about the matter. He actually states these concepts twice using three parallel statements.[9] First, sin is rebellion against God. John deals with that in verse 4 and again in verse 8a. Secondly, sin is treason against Christ and His purposes. He deals with that in verse 5 and in verse 8b.

Finally. sin is contrary to the new nature (verses 6 and 9).[10] Verse 10 is a summary statement which also introduces the next section.

## SIN: REBELLION AGAINST GOD

Sin is rebellion against God. A cavalier attitude toward sin is foundational to the error John is addressing. Unbelievers are not alarmed about their sin. They see is as the common weakness of humanity. They excuse it in a variety of ways. "Perhaps it is just a psychological problem provoked by a troubled childhood. Maybe it's just the way I cope with stress. Or maybe there is nothing wrong with it at all. If society says homosexuality is okay, then it must be okay. Every other unmarried couple cohabitates, why shouldn't we. Besides there is more government aid if you don't actually marry. Everybody cheats on their income tax." On and on, people discount the problem of sin. For those people to be genuinely born again, their conscience must be awakened to the true nature of their condition and behavior. There must come a personal awakening to the seriousness of the matter. So, John tells his readers how serious it is.

First John 3:4 says, "Whoever commits sin also commits lawlessness, and sin is lawlessness." The Greek word translated sin is *hamartia*. It literally means, "missing the mark,"[11] as if you would shoot an arrow and it falls short of the target. It is coming short of the standard that God has set, whether it be sins of commission or sins of omission. "Whoever commits sin also commits lawlessness." The word translated lawlessness is *anomia*. *Nomos* is the Greek word for law. The prefix "a" is a negation, just as it is in English. So, to be lawless, as John uses the word here, is to be without law, in contempt of the law, or in violation of the law.[12] It carries the idea of revolt and rebellion.[13] So sin is more than a mistake. It is more than a failure. It is more than simply falling short of the mark. It is rebellion against the authority of God. It's akin to the revolt of Lucifer and his demonic followers. It is willfully going against the commandments and law of God.

When we talk about lawlessness, don't confine your thinking to the Law of Moses. That covenant with Israel was an expression of God's law. But we must go further back than that. Adam and Eve were lawless when they partook of the forbidden fruit. They violated the expressed will of the

Creator. Lucifer was lawless when he rebelled against God. The boundaries of righteousness proceeds from the very nature of God. For that reason, His law is absolute and eternal. It sets limits on mankind based on the principle of love. It sets limits based on the way man is designed to function and the way the creature is to relate to the Creator.[14] Many dismiss the commandments of God because we are not under the Law of Moses. Truly, we are not under the Law of Moses. As gentiles, we were never under the Law of Moses. But we are accountable to the law of love that proceeds from God's very nature. The two great commandments are that we love God with all our heart, soul, and mind; and that we love our neighbor as we love ourselves.[15] That is the way man is created to function. That is consistent with who God is and who we are designed to be. The idea that we are free to be lawless because we are not under the Law of Moses fails to recognize all that.

We are responsible to submit to God's authority and His commandments. That's why John wrote earlier in this epistle, "He who says, 'I know Him,' and does not keep His commandments, is a liar, and the truth is not in him" (2:4, NKJV). Sin is not just a little mistake that God ought to forgive. Sin is defiance against the authority of God Himself. Sin includes more than the atrocities and debauchery that refined society would reject. Sin is going my own way, insisting on my independence from God, in whatever way we do that. When some people go their own way, they sin in gross, despicable ways. Society, as a whole, recognizes their behavior as sin. Others go their own way in more refined, socially acceptable ways. Their sin of greed might be interpreted as diligence and success by social standards. Their prideful pursuit of respectability might be misconstrued as integrity and righteousness. Jesus dealt with respectable sinners when He dealt with the priests and Pharisees. They were the most difficult to reach. Sin is not defined by social standards. Sin is defined by who God is and who we are designed to be. Sin is selfishly going our own way. That is the heart of the matter. We are either surrendered to God and subject to His will, or we're going our own way—and the latter is rebellion. Isaiah 53:6 states it in these terms: "All we like sheep have gone astray; we have turned every one *to his own way*" (emphasis mine, KJV). John wants his readers to see the sinfulness of sin. He wants them to recognize it as a revolt against God. It must not be minimized or excused. It is worse than you think. It is rebellion or lawlessness.

In verse 8 of our text, John further exposes the seriousness of sin. "He who sins is of the devil, for the devil has sinned from the beginning." The archenemy of God is the devil. In the face of God's goodness toward him, Lucifer rose up in rebellion against God and persuaded others to join him against God. "When you sin," says John, "you are siding with God's enemy. You are not residing on neutral ground. You are not living in a demilitarized zone. You have chosen your side with the devil himself." And it is an extremely dangerous thing to make yourself God's enemy. It is an extremely disloyal thing to side with God's adversary.

One way people justify their sin is to say it is not hurting anybody else. But that is never true. Every action is like throwing a pebble into a pond. It always has a ripple effect. Adam and Eve's sin affected others. David's sins affected his family and the nation of Israel. No man is an island.[16] Sin is never neutral. It affects your destiny. It affects other people. When you sin, you are siding with God's archenemy. In the strongest possible terms, John is telling his reader to recognize the seriousness of your sins. Never, never discount it as insignificant.

## SIN: TREASON AGAINST CHRIST

John also teaches that sin is treason against Christ. The reason Christ came at the incarnation was to take away our sins, not to overlook them. Verse 5 says, "And you know that He was manifested to take away our sins, and in Him there is no sin."

Sin is inconsistent with who Christ is. Our text says, "In Him there is no sin." He has never sinned, though tempted in every way possible (Heb. 4:15, NIV). He is the pure Lamb of God who takes away the sin of the world (John 1:29–34). Think about what it cost Him to take away your sin and my sin. He left the glories of heaven. He set aside His divine prerogatives. He trod the dusty roads of Jerusalem. He bore the reproach of the scribes and Pharisees. He was wounded for our transgressions. He was bruised for our iniquities. Because of my sin, He was crucified in humiliation and shame. He endured unimaginable pain and suffering on the cross to take away my sin. How can I love sin that cost Him so much?

175

How can I embrace and justify that which cost Him His life? Jesus did not come to "lovingly" tolerate your sin. He came to rid you of it! "You shall call His name Jesus," the angel said to Joseph, "for He will save His people from their sins" (Matt. 1:21, NASB). Did He come to save you from hell? Yes, but only by first saving you from your sins. Some preaching today proposes a Jesus who saves from hell but does not save from sin. It is tragically misleading. It produces people in church whose moral behavior is the same as the non-born-again public. It misleads unbelievers because they see professors of Christianity doing the same things they do. They can discern no real value in Christianity. This half-gospel produces tragic results at every turn. First and foremost, "He was manifested to take away our sins." Otherwise, we could never be fit for heaven, and we can't function as salt and light while here on earth.[17]

Do you want rid of your sin? If so, you are in agreement with the Savior. Do you want a so-called salvation that overlooks your sin and leaves you in your sin? If so, you have missed the point of His coming. He came to take away your sin, not to excuse or tolerate it, but to obliviate it. It's not just a salvation from the penalty of sin. It is a full salvation that breaks the power of sin off your life. Romans 6:14 says, "For sin shall no longer be your master, because you are not under the law, but under grace" (NIV). Grace is operating to free you from sin's dominion. Grace does not excuse sin. Grace empowers us to overcome it in Christ's name. John says to his readers, "You already know what I am saying; apply it to your lives." "And you know that He was manifested to take away our sins."

Verse 8 puts it in even stronger terms. "For this purpose the Son of God was manifested, that He might destroy the works of the devil." The works of the devil are sin and rebellion against God. When we sin, we are cooperating with the works of the devil. We are helping his cause. There is no such thing as neutral ground. You're either subject to God and working for God, or you're following the lusts of the flesh and working for the devil. Jesus told the Pharisees, "You belong to your father, the devil, and you want to carry out your father's desires. He was a murderer from the beginning, not holding to the truth, for there is no truth in him. When he lies, he speaks his native language, for he is a liar and the father of lies" (John 8:44, NIV). There Jesus exposed two works of the devil: murder and lying. Murder sets man against man, brother against brother, sister against sister. The desire of evil toward another always originates from one source, the devil. Those ensnared in anger, hatred, and unforgiveness always have a reason they feel that way. Yes, the devil probably did give you a reason. But that never justifies living in that attitude of heart. We will see in the latter part of 1 John 3 a great emphasis on loving one another. It is an important test of our real relationship with God. Seeking good for others is in line with the heart of God. Seeking bad for someone else is in line with the heart of Satan. Love works no ill toward his neighbor.[18] Murder in all its forms is from the devil.

Jesus also exposed the devil as the source of all lies. Oh, what sorrow and pain the devil has brought in people's lives through his lies. Lying is his major weapon. He used two fundamental lies on Eve: (1) God does not have your best interest in mind, and (2) the consequences of disobeying God won't be so bad; you will actually be better off ignoring His command. Those are lies he continues to use over and over. He maligns God. He convinces people God is an old fuddy-duddy who doesn't want them to have fun. He convinces them that God is mean and really doesn't like people. Ironically, that is the devil's attitude toward people. The devil only comes to kill, steal, and destroy.[19] Just look at all the twisted, distorted views of God out there, and you will see how much Satan lies about God. God loves all the people He created. He is not willing that any would perish, but that all would come to repentance.[20] He has demonstrated His love in sending His own Son to die for our redemption. God is love. If people could only see God for who He is and know His heart for what it is, many would run to Him for help. But the devil lies, and lies, and lies. He has blinded them to the truth.[21] The second lie is to minimize the significance of sin. That is what John is countering in our text. The serpent told Eve, "You shall not surely die."[22] "I know God said you would die if you disobeyed, but that's not going to happen.[23] In fact, you will get what you want, and there will be no negative consequences." Isn't that the way Satan talks to you when he is trying to lead you into temptation. He always minimizes the significance of the disobedience. He convinces you nobody will know; it's no big deal. The deception that John is countering in our text begins with a minimization of sin. From that foundation is built the false idea that a person can live in sin and still fellowship God and one day go to heaven.

From the day Lucifer became the devil, he works in opposition to God. God seeks to bring people into a place of freedom and fellowship with Him. Satan seeks to entangle them in bondage and rebellion against the God who loves them. From the beginning he has established a kingdom to thwart the purposes of God. He has built up strongholds and lies that oppose the purposes of God. Jesus came to destroy all that. He broke its power by His death and resurrection. He continues to destroy the works of the devil in our lives, if we walk in the Spirit. He heals, and delivers, and changes the hearts of mankind. He exposes the lies of Satan and establishes people in the truth. It is our privilege to be co-laborers with Him in all this.[24] We are soldiers of the cross. We contend with the evil one for the souls of men.[25] It makes no sense that we would participate in the works of the devil. It makes no sense that we would live like the devil when we are children of God. We will not work for the devil and claim allegiance with God at the same time. We recognize sin as a betrayal of the purposes of Christ. We recognize it as rebellion against the Father. And we can have nothing to do with it.

So, John has shown us the seriousness of sin. He has described it as rebellion against the Father. He has also shown how it is antagonistic to the person of Christ and the purposes of Christ. Finally, in this text he shows us that sin is contrary to the new nature.

## SIN: CONTRARY TO THE NEW NATURE

In verse 6 John writes, "Whoever abides in Him does not sin. Whoever sins has neither seen Him nor known Him."[26] That is a shocking statement. But what John says in verse 9 is even more shocking. "Whoever has been born of God does not sin, for His seed remains in him; and he cannot sin, because he has been born of God" (1 John 3:9). If you can read those words without some sense of alarm, you've either attained to a level of sainthood most of us only dream of, or you have lost touch with the convicting power of the Holy Spirit, or you simply don't comprehend what is being said. Let's focus on verse 9 since it makes the stronger declaration. "Whoever has been born of God does not sin." How does that statement line up with your personal experience? "And he cannot sin, because he has been born of God." If we take those statements at face value, we have to wonder if anybody is truly born again. It certainly cannot be said of Richard Tow that he *does not sin*. And I know by personal experience that I certainly can sin quite easily. What is John telling us? There have been six or seven basic interpretations proposed.

Some have thought these verses teach sinless perfectionism: that a Christian can get so sanctified that he lives above the possibility of committing an act of sin. I have only known a few people who held this opinion.[27] They usually make distinctions between willful sins and unintentional sins in order to justify the position. But there are insurmountable problems with that interpretation. First, John is talking about all born-again Christians, not just super saints who have attained to sinlessness. It says, "Whoever has been *born of God* does not sin" (emphasis mine). It does not say, "Whoever attains to super sanctification does not sin." There is a problem with that interpretation right there in the verse. But the big problem is this. It violates other passages that plainly say that Christians, born of God, do sin. In fact, John says in 1:8 of this epistle, "If we say that we have no sin, we deceive ourselves, and the truth is not in us" (KJV). How plain is that?[28] The verse prior to that says, "If we walk in the Light as He Himself is in the Light, we have fellowship with one another, and the blood of Jesus His Son cleanses us from all sin" (NASB). That's a promise to Christians. If we never commit a sin, then we don't need the blood of Jesus to cleanse us of sin. But we are taught to pray daily, "Forgive us our sins, for we also forgive everyone who sins against us" (Luke 11:4, NIV). One thing is abundantly clear. John cannot be talking about individual acts of sin in our text. It would contradict what he has already taught in this epistle: "If we confess our sins, He is faithful and righteous to forgive us our sins and to cleanse us from all unrighteousness. If we say that we have not sinned, we make Him a liar and His word is not in us" (1 John 1:9–10, NASB). Then in 2:1 John writes, "My little children, I am writing these things to you so that you may not sin. And if anyone sins, we have an Advocate with the Father, Jesus Christ the righteous" (NASB). That is the message. Don't sin. Don't take sin lightly. Resist temptation. But if you do fail, God has made a way for you to clear that up. Jesus is our High Priest. Jesus is our Advocate. His blood cleanses sin. "If we confess our sins, He is faithful and righteous to forgive us our sins and to cleanse us from all unrighteousness." Aren't you glad for that?

We have seen in this letter both words of warning and words of comfort.[29] That is not only true of this epistle, but it's true of the whole Bible. The warnings protect us from presumption and abuse of the grace of God.[30] The words of comfort protect us from discouragement and despair.[31] Both are needed because we often find ourselves in a struggle against sin. Paul described the experience in Romans 7 and 8. We love God; we love His law. However, there is a propensity toward sin in our flesh that we have to reckon dead; we have to deny the flesh its expression and walk in the Spirit. There are besetting sins that we have to lay aside and run our race with perseverance.[32] So when we deal with the subject of sin we must embrace the whole counsel of God.[33] We must balance the warnings with the comfort and assurance in Scripture. We must balance the assurances with the warnings. Spiritual health is found in that balance. I say that because our text today should awaken the presumptuous person to the danger of living in willful sin. It should not bring despair to the sincere follower of Christ who is given assurances in other passages. If you are sincerely seeking to live pleasing to the Lord, then John's message to you is this. Don't sin. But if you have a failure, you have an Advocate. You have a provision for cleansing. First John 1:9 assures us, "If we confess our sins, He is faithful and righteous to forgive us our sins and to cleanse us from all unrighteousness." It is clear to me that John could not possibly be talking about individual acts of sin in our text. It would contradict what he has already said. So, we set aside the sinless perfection interpretation.

Some people reconcile 1 John 3:9 with other verses by saying John is just talking about the ideal that Christians ought to shoot for. But the language of the text does not allow that at all. John is not using the subjunctive mood in the Greek text, but the indicative. He does not say the born-again Christian *should* not sin, although that is true. He is dealing with reality. He says he does not and even cannot sin. John is not presenting an ideal. He is stating a fact.

Some explain this passage as saying the new nature does not sin and cannot sin. In fact, I was taught that years ago. It is true that the new nature does not and cannot sin. But that is not what John is saying in this passage. He is addressing the behavior of the believer as a whole person. He says, "*Whoever* [not whatever] has been born of God does not sin" (emphasis mine). The subject is the person, not the nature. The whole context of the chapter argues for that understanding. Romans 8 teaches that we as believers must choose to walk in the Spirit, rather than walk in the flesh. If we choose to sin, we cannot deny responsibility by saying the devil made me do it or the flesh made me do it. God holds us, as a person, responsible for our behavior. The desires of the new nature are always righteous. But John is addressing the person's behavior.

This interpretation is actually a common error today. Ironically it portrays the very thinking of the Gnostics that John is correcting. The idea that I have a revelation or a standing or imputed righteousness that makes my behavior irrelevant is exactly what John is contending with. Let me show you the subtlety of this. It begins with a biblical truth. In Romans 4 Paul teaches that when we put our faith in Christ we receive, as a gift, the righteousness of Christ. It is imputed to us. At the moment we receive Christ, we are declared righteous. I will never be more righteous than the day I received Christ.[34] I will never be more justified than the day I received Christ. We do not go about trying to establish our own righteousness by our performance; we rely on the righteousness of Christ imputed to us by faith.[35] The righteousness of Christ in us produces good works, but our confidence is always in the righteousness of Christ. So far, so good. But all this breaks down when people begin to minimize the importance of that imputed righteousness bearing the fruit of righteous behavior. If the life of God is in a person, it will be expressed in that person's behavior. That is John's point in our text. To live a life contrary to the holy nature of God and then claim to be born of God is a lie according to John.

A popular teaching today is that when you got saved your sins past, present, and future were all forgiven. So, don't get all concerned about the sins in your life, God has already taken care of all that. Again, there is some truth here, but enough error to make it dangerous. The cross provided atonement for the sins of the whole world. First John 2:2 tells us that. And that includes all your sins: past, present, and future. However, that provision must be appropriated by faith. Just because the blood of the cross atoned for the sins of the whole world does not mean the whole world will be saved. There are plenty of scriptures that tells us people must receive that by faith in order to enjoy its benefits. An unwillingness to recognize the need to appropriate God's provision, has led many into the error of universalism. Just because Christ's atonement on the cross was sufficient for the whole world does not mean the whole world will receive that by faith. In fact, multitudes continue in unbelief.

When you came to Christ and were born again, you received forgiveness for past sins. In the present, when you exercise the faith to confess your sins; God is faithful and just to forgive you (according to 1 John 1:9) and cleanse you of all unrighteousness. That does not automatically happen to me because I got saved fifty years ago. I have to appropriate that in the now. And it is inconceivable that I could now receive forgiveness for sins I plan to commit in the future. Where's the repentance in that? The provision for your past, present, and future sins is there in the cross. But we must appropriate that by faith in the way Scripture tells us to appropriate it. So, watch out for doctrines that sound ever so sweet, but don't actually line up with what the Bible tells us to do. First John 1 clearly tells us we have to deal with our sins, not ignore them. And we have to deal with them in the context of time. Part of the argument for this error is the fact that God is above time. That is true.[36] But we are not God, and we are not able to live above the parameters of time. We have to deal with sins in the context of time. I can and must ask for forgiveness for my past sins. As I proceed in life and when I fail, I must deal with those sins as they occur. I can't ignore them or discount them as insignificant or already processed when I got born again. If I commit a sin tomorrow, I will need to go to the Lord tomorrow and process that with Him. The processing is not just acknowledging that I did it, but also turning from it in repentance. You may say, why do we need to be so precise. It is the subtly of these errors that makes them so dangerous. They sound good on the surface, but they lead people down a path that takes them further and further from the truth. If something doesn't agree with the Bible, we need to identify where it has strayed from the truth and correct it.

The Gnostics made an arbitrary distinction between the spiritual and material. They did that in their Christology which we talked about in earlier chapters. They also did that in their concept of sin, separating the spiritual standing from the physical behavior. They claimed to be righteous because of a spiritual, esoteric knowledge and experience. Yet their daily lives did not manifest that righteousness. They lived contrary to what they claimed to be. However, they said it doesn't matter because what we do in terms of physical behavior does not and cannot affect our spiritual standing. John says, "hogwash." "He who practices righteousness is righteous."

The modern Gnostic language goes something like this. I had a spiritual experience. I said the sinner's prayer. They told me I was born again. I now have the imputed righteousness of God. Nothing can change that. My ungodly behavior past, present, and future is already forgiven through the cross. Regardless of how I live, I am on my way to heaven. The flaw in the logic is this: If you really were born again, you will live according to that new nature, not according to the old nature that you were following in the past. Jesus said you know a tree by the fruit it bears. Listen to His words in Luke 6:43–46:

> For there is no good tree which produces bad fruit, nor, on the other hand, a bad tree which produces good fruit. For each tree is known by its own fruit. For men do not gather figs from thorns, nor do they pick grapes from a briar bush. The good man out of the good treasure of his heart brings forth what is good; and the evil *man* out of the evil *treasure* brings forth what is evil; for his mouth speaks from that which fills his heart. Why do you call Me, "Lord, Lord," and do not do what I say? (NASB).

Then He talks about the importance of doing what He tells us to do. John's teaching in our text follows the same line of reasoning. So, this idea that John is just talking about how the new nature is righteous, and not referring to the whole person's behavior is simply not true to the text.

Other erroneous attempts to explain verses 6 and 9 include making an arbitrary distinction between willful sins and less serious sins. The Catholic Church draws a distinction between mortal sins and venial sins. Nothing in the text supports that.

Another approach complicates the matter by saying John is dealing with different Gnostic errors in chapter one than here and needs to say different things to address them. But the fact is he says what he says in verse 9, and that approach does not explain it. Some approach it by adding conditions. If the person abides in Christ, he will not sin.[37] But adding to a passage to make it say something different than what it clearly says is not an acceptable solution. There are some prominent scholars that project John's statements in verse 9 into the eschatological future when Christ returns. But that "fails to preserve the integrity of John's indicative declarations" in the text.[38] None of these interpretations adequately explains John's statements in our passage.

So, what does John mean in verses 6 and 9? The answer lies in the Greek grammar he employs. All the verbs for committing sin are in the present tense in these verses. The present tense in Greek usually depicts continuous action or habitual behavior. There are contexts where the present tense is not used that way.[39] But John is obviously using the present tense as continuous action. Otherwise he would be contradicting his own statements in chapter one.[40] And we know he would not do that under the inspiration of the Holy Spirit. So, in verse 6 and 9 John is talking about lifestyle. The New International Version and others reflect that in the translation. Listen to those verses from the New International Version. "No one who lives in him *keeps on sinning*. No one who *continues to sin* has either seen him or known him" (emphasis mine). Verse 9 says, "No one who is born of God will *continue in sin*, because God's seed remains in them; they cannot *go on sinning*, because they have been born of God" (emphasis mine). That captures John's thinking.

The person who is genuinely born again will not and cannot live a sinful life over the long run. Why, because the new nature influences him toward righteousness. The Holy Spirit convicts him of sin, and he is internally disturbed to the point that he turns from the sin back to God. It is simply not his nature to continue in sin. Will he fail from time to time? Absolutely. That is why we need to confess our sins daily. That's why we need an Advocate with the Father. Even when walking in the light, we will need the blood to cleanse us from specific sins. But the overall tenor of a person genuinely born again is one of righteousness, rather than sinfulness. He is walking in the light, not walking in darkness. The illustration has been around as long as I can remember, but it makes the point so well, I will use it. A pig may fall into the mud, and a sheep may fall into the mud. The difference is the pig will lay down in the stinky mud, wallow in it, and enjoy it. In contrast, the sheep may fall into the mud. But it will be uncomfortable for him because that environment is contrary to his nature. He will struggle in that context and climb out of the mud. The pig is perfectly happy to stay there.[41] John's point is that the divine nature in the true believers compels him toward righteousness.

Another reason this text is true is found in the chastening or correction of the Lord. It is not John's focus here, but it is an important factor. God will not allow a true child of God to continue in sin without correction. Hebrews 12 tells us to receive God's correction in our lives because God does that so we can be partakers of His holiness. Hebrews 12:8 makes this distinction between those who have been born again versus those who have not been born of the Spirit. "But if you are without discipline, of which all have become partakers, then you are illegitimate children and not sons" (NASB). Hebrews 12:6 says, "For those whom the Lord loves He disciplines, And He scourges every son whom He receives" (NASB). People who have not been born again can continue in sin because God does not intervene with correction the way He does with those who are truly His. Do you remember how miserable David was when he sinned? In Psalm 32:5 he tells of his repentance. But the verses before that describe the misery he experienced that brought him to repentance. "When I kept silent *about my sin*, my body wasted away Through my groaning all day long. For day and night Your hand was heavy upon me; My vitality was drained away *as* with the fever heat of summer" (NASB). By the time Nathan got to David, he was ready to repent. David could not be content living in unconfessed sin. God also sent a prophet to confront his sin. God did not leave David in his sin. He chastened him and brought him around. What happened to Jonah when he ran from God? He could not continue in that direction, because God made it too miserable to do so. Think about the way Peter felt when he denied the Lord. He experienced godly sorrow that led to repentance. The thought of his own disloyalty to Jesus broke him down. Matthew 26:75 says, "He went out and wept bitterly" (KJV). Do you know how Peter felt? Have you ever failed the Lord in ways that broke your heart? Not because you got caught, but because you never wanted to fail Him that way! You never wanted to betray His love in the way you betrayed it. The repentance is not just a sorrow over the consequence of sin. That may be a part of the lesson. But deeper than that, your new nature is absolutely opposed to such disloyalty. The honest desires of the new nature, the conviction of the Holy Spirit, divine correction from the Father all work against the continuance in sin for the true child of God. "No one who is born of God will continue in sin, because God's seed [*sperma*] remains in them; they cannot go on sinning, because they have been born of God."[42]

John says in verse 10 of our text, "In this the children of God and the children of the devil are manifest: Whoever does not practice righteousness is not of God, nor is he who does not love his brother." The last statement points to the study we will have in our next chapter. Regardless of what people claim, if they continue in sin, undisturbed and unchanged, they have not been born again. The external behavior is clear evidence that the internal nature is not right.

My heart goes out to those who have been misled to believe they are safe when they are not. Can you imagine the horror for a person like that on judgment day? To discover it was all a lie. To realize there is no going back and redoing the past. Now is the day of salvation. Now is the acceptable time.[43] Now is the time to change course. It will be too late on that day. John gives this test, so that no one will be deceived. "Little children, let no one deceive you. He who practices righteousness is righteous, just as He is righteous." If you are not practicing righteousness, if the Holy Spirit is putting His finger on sins that need to be addressed, this is a good time to get that all cleared up before God. Just bow your head, allow the Holy Spirit to show you the sin, ask God's forgiveness and enablement for the changes needed. He is eager to help you in that process.

# Endnotes: Chapter 14

1   *Merriam Webster's Collegiate Dictionary*, 10th ed., s. v. "Born-again," 133.

2   Albert L. Winseman, "Who Has Been Born Again," *Gallup News*, Jan. 18, 2005. Retrieved Dec. 1, 2017 at http://news.gallup.com/poll/14632/who-has-been-born-again.aspx. Gallup polls in 2004 indicate 41% of Americans consider themselves "born-again" Christians. Current population is about 325 million (http://www.worldometers.info/world-population/us-population/). Although these statistics are somewhat dated, the calculated total of 133,250,000 is indicative of the vast numbers who claim to be born again.

3   Cf. 1 John 1:6–8; 2:3, 26, 29.

4   Cf. Chapter 5 in this book, entitled "Combating Gnostic Error."

5   In John 3:7 (KJV) Jesus made this statement to a religious, moral man. Righteous behavior does not produce a righteous heart; but a righteous heart produces righteous behavior. And a righteous heart is only in those who have been born again.

6   Barna and Barton, 109.

7   Ibid., 101.

8   Ibid., 144.

9   One reason for the threefold presentation is to emphasize the importance of what he is saying.

10  Each category bears a direct relationship to the Trinity. The first deals with rebellion against the Father. The second deals with disloyalty to the Son; and the third addresses the inconsistency of sin in regard to the Holy Spirit.

11  J. R. W. Stott, *The Epistles of John: An Introduction and Commentary*, 4th printing (Grand Rapids: Eerdmans, 1971) 122.

12  *Thayer's Greek Lexicon* (NT:458) provides the following definition for "*anomia*." "1. properly, *the condition of one without law— either because ignorant of it, or because violating it. 2. contempt and violation of law, iniquity, wickedness. . . .*"

13  Burdick, 237.

14  For example, man is not designed to receive worship. He is designed to find fulfillment in worshipping the Creator. That is not so because of the Law of Moses, it is inherent in who God is and who people are. The order of reality requires it to be so.

15  Matt. 22:35–40. Cf. Rom. 13:10.

16  Cf. Rom. 14:7.

17  Cf. Matt. 5:13–17.

18  Cf. Rom. 13:10.

19  John 10:10.

20  Cf. John 3:16; 2 Pet. 3:9.

21  2 Cor. 4:3–4.

22 Gen. 3:4, KJV.

23 Satan even questioned whether God had said it. He also brings confusion and causes people to doubt what God has said.

24 Cf. 1 Cor. 3:9.

25 Cf. Eph. 6:10–12.

26 The Greek words, *horaō* (translated seen) and *ginōskō* (translated known) are in the perfect tense which indicates action completed in the past with ongoing results. With the negative *ou* and *oude* associated with these words, John seems to have in view a person who has never known the Lord, never been born again.

27 There was a group in one church I attended that got deceived into thinking they had attained to sinless perfection. I don't know how anyone could come to such a conclusion, but these people insisted they no longer sinned at all. They split off from the church because of that doctrine.

28 Cf. Raymond E. Brown, 83.

29 In this epistle, John provides a balance of comfort and warning. The person living in presumptuous sin should be alarmed by our text. However, the person who is sincerely seeking to live pleasing to the Lord and failing some along the way should take comfort in what John tells us in 1 John 1:7–2:2.

30 Cf. Rom. 6:1–2; Jude 4.

31 Cf. Ps. 103:13; Rom. 8:28–29; Jude 24–25; Phil. 1:6.

32 Cf. Heb. 12:1.

33 Cf. Acts 20:27; Rom. 11:22.

34 A newborn baby is as right with his father as a fully mature son. The mature son can handle more responsibility, but he is no more accepted in the family as the infant. We are to grow and mature, but that does not change our right standing with the Father. Cf. 1 Pet. 2:2; 2 Pet. 3:18.

35 Cf. Phil. 3:9.

36 Cf. Chafer, Vol. 1, 216–217; Lewis, *Mere Christianity*, 166–171.

37 Living in sin is inconsistent with abiding in Christ. In verse 6 John does not seem to be setting up two categories of Christians, those who abide (fellowship) in Christ and those who do not. From John's perspective every Christian abides in Christ. Claiming to be a Christian and not abiding in Christ is not an acceptable position to take.

38 Burdick, 245.

39 Daniel Wallace interprets these verbs as gnomic present, rather than customary present, stating 1 John 5:16 as an example of the gnomic. However, his explanation of the passage as a projected eschatological reality is simply not true to the language of the text. Wallace, 524–525. In defense of the continuous action interpretation, George Ladd, *A Theology of the New Testament*, (Grand Rapids: Eerdmans, 1974) rev. ed., 1993, writes (p. 663), "This is a very plausible

and consistent interpretation and cannot be rejected because it is based on grammatical subtleties. Tenses in Greek did mean something."

40  This conclusion comes after careful consideration of the other proposed interpretations. None of those provide a viable explanation of the text. Therefore, one comes back to the obvious, but with additional assurance that it is the right interpretation. John is using the present tense here as it is usually used. He is talking about continuous action rather than individual acts of sin.

41  I heard this illustration in a sermon over 50 years ago. The earliest source I could find was a sermon preached by Charles Spurgeon in 1863 entitled "The Sinner's Advocate." Accessed at The C. H. Spurgeon Collection on CD-ROM (AGES Software, Inc., 1998).

42  1 John 3:9, NIV. There is a growing process in relationship to a seed, beginning at the time of conception. Children of God *cannot go on sinning* because they have been born of God. However, there is a growth process in which the child develops and looks and behaves more and more like the father. In time, he puts away childish things and operates at a higher level of maturity.

43  2 Cor. 6:2.

# CHAPTER 15

# Loving One Another
## 3:11–15

For this is the message which you have heard from the beginning, that we should love one another; not as Cain, who was of the evil one and slew his brother. And for what reason did he slay him? Because his deeds were evil, and his brother's were righteous. Do not be surprised, brethren, if the world hates you. We know that we have passed out of death into life, because we love the brethren. He who does not love abides in death. Everyone who hates his brother is a murderer; and you know that no murderer has eternal life abiding in him.

1 John 3:11-15, NASB

## Expository Message

Now John zeros in on relationships. Christianity is about relationships. The two great commandments are about relationship with God and relationships with others. And Jesus said the whole Law stems from these two great commandments.[1] We take up a subject today that is of supreme importance to our spiritual wellbeing.

John has been emphasizing the necessity of righteous living. He has presented that as evidence of real Christianity. Last week the text ended in verse 10 of 1 John 3. "In this the children of God and the children of the devil are manifest: Whoever does not practice righteousness is not of God, nor is he who does not love his brother" (NKJV). There are two tests here which are really just one, looked at from two different perspectives. The way we can know who is really a Christian and who is not is by applying these two tests. First is the test of practicing righteousness, keeping God's commandments, living a godly lifestyle. "Whoever does not practice righteousness is not of God." That is a good summary of what John has been saying in the preceding verses. The second test is the test of love: "Nor is he who does not love his brother." That looks forward to what John is about to say. The tests are really two sides of the same coin.[2] For me to practice righteousness, I must love my brother and treat him accordingly. For me to love my brother, I must do him right; I must practice righteousness. To fulfill the two great commandments is a description of practicing righteousness. It is, however, helpful to look at each side of the coin. We will now examine this test of love in 1 John 3:11-15.

## THE MESSAGE

John introduces this discussion by reminding his congregation of *the message*. This message they had "heard from the beginning" of their Christian experience.[3] John wants them to connect what he is about to say with what they already know. In 2:7 he did the same thing, pointing them back to what they had already been taught. He is not teaching them a new doctrine; he is calling on them to continue in what they already know. Throughout this epistle he uses phrases like "which you heard from the beginning" (2:24); "you know" (3:5, 15); and "we know" (3:2; 5:18, 19, 20).[4] Continue in that! Don't let the Gnostics lead you away from it. So, he begins in verse 11, "For this is the message which you heard from the beginning"

And what is the message he is reminding them of? It is "that we should love one another." John has mentioned this subject a couple of times, earlier in this letter.[5] But now he focuses on it as an exhortation and as a test of real faith in Christ. His subject is not love in general, but our love for *one another*, our love for fellow Christians. The word brother or brethren appears seven times in verses 10 through 15.[6] In other places, we are commanded to love unbelievers, just as God loves them (John 3:16). Jesus said, we are to love our enemies.[7] But that is simply not John's subject here.

How are your relationships with fellow believers? Are you loving them? Are you avoiding them? Are you angry at them? Have you said things about them that you shouldn't have said? Is there resentment in your heart against any brother or sister in Christ? John's message in our text raises all those questions. It's as if he is shining a spotlight in our hearts and exposing any secret animosity that might be hiding there. "For this is the message which you heard from the beginning, that we should love one another."

There are many verses in the New Testament that tell us how to treat "one another." Let me just mention a few. Perhaps the most foundational and important are the words of Jesus in John 13:34: "A new commandment I give to you, that you love one another, even as I have loved you, that you also love one another" (NASB). Surely these words were in John's mind when he wrote our text. When Jesus tells us to keep His commandments, this commandment is on the list. We are to love one another. Anytime we are not doing that, we are grieving the Holy Spirit and disobeying a commandment from the Lord. We are to love one another, in the same way Jesus loved us—not as that other Christian is loving us, but as Jesus has loved us! Why is that important? If I use the other Christian's behavior as my standard, and that person is living below the standard, I am sure to come short of the true standard. But if I will hold to the standard Jesus has exemplified, then I am pursuing the right goal, and I may inspire my brother or sister to come up to that standard as well. "Love one another, even as I have loved you [in the same way I loved you as I unselfishly laid down My life for you]." Do not let other people set your standard of integrity and obedience. If you respond to them the way they are acting toward you, that's exactly what you're doing: you're letting them set the standard for your life. Is that the power you want to give that person? No, do not let other people determine who you are. Let the word of God be your guide. Follow that, regardless of what anybody else does. Don't be reactive; be proactive in your approach.

Several places in the epistles we told to "love one another."[8] I will not quote those. But I want you to see from Scripture what loving one another looks like.

> Romans 12:9–10 says, "Let love be without hypocrisy [Let it be sincere and genuine, without pretense]. Abhor what is evil; cling to what is good. Be devoted to one another in brotherly love; give preference to one another in honor" (NASB). The way we treat *one another* matters so much.
> Romans 15:7: "Accept one another" (NASB).
> Romans 16:16 tells us to "greet one another" (NASB). When you won't speak to another believer, you're violating that commandment.
> Ephesians 4:2 talks about us "bearing with one another in love" (NKJV). There are some people, even believers, that you just have to bear with.
> Ephesians 4:3: "Endeavoring to keep the unity of the Spirit in the bond of peace" (NKJV).
> Colossians 3:12–13 tells us to "put on tender mercies, kindness, humility, meekness, longsuffering; bearing with one another, and forgiving one another, if anyone has a complaint against another; even as Christ forgave you, so you also must do" (NKJV).
> First Thessalonians 4:18: "Comfort one another" (KJV).
> First Thessalonians 5:11: "Edify one another" (KJV).
> Hebrews 10:24: "Consider one another" (KJV).
> James 5:16 says, "Confess your faults to one another and pray for one another" (KJV).
> First Peter 3:8–9: "Having compassion for one another; love as brothers, be tenderhearted, be courteous; not returning evil for evil or reviling for reviling, but on the contrary blessing" (NKJV).
> First Peter 4:9 says, "Be hospitable to one another" (NASB).

And there are others. But all those "one another" passages can be summed up in the message John gives in our text: "We should love one another."

It is a very big deal with God, if that is not happening in your life. Don't think your prayers can be effective, if you are not loving one another.[9] Don't expect God's blessing on your life, if you're not loving one another. You can read your Bible every day, pray three times a day, and tithe 20%, but none of that is a substitute for loving one another. Jesus said in John 13:35, "By this all men will know that you are My disciples, if you have love for one another" (NASB). We know we're the real deal by the love we have for one another. John makes that very clear in verse 14 of our text. But notice, even unbelievers will use this as an indication of our authenticity. That's why it is so damaging to the cause of Christ when Christians get into conflicts and do not resolve them in love. Of course, everybody thinks it's the other person's fault. "If that person would just come around and do right, everything would be fine." But God is looking at you and at me and saying, "You're my child. You do right regardless of what they do." Romans 12:18 says, "If it is possible, as much as depends on you, live peaceably with all men" (NKJV).

To reinforce the message, John gives an example of the opposite. He often uses contrasts to make his point clear. "Not as Cain, who was of the evil one and slew his brother" (1 John 3:12). Instead of loving Abel, his brother, Cain became jealous and envious of him. They were the first two children of Adam and Eve. Cain became a farmer and Abel became a shepherd. They both were religious. In today's terms, they both went to church. They both brought an offering to God. Cain brought a grain offering from his fields. Abel sacrificed a lamb from his flock. The problem came to a head when God accepted Abel's offering, but rejected Cain's. Genesis 4:4–5 says, "And the Lord had regard for Abel and for his offering; but for Cain and for his offering He had no regard. So, Cain became very angry and his countenance fell" (NASB).

We do not know for sure why God accepted Abel's offering and rejected Cain's offering. It could have been that God required a blood sacrifice that foreshadowed Christ and the cross. If that were the case, all Cain needed to do was to trade some of his grain to Abel for a lamb and make that sacrifice. It is possible that was a factor. However, the exact wording of the text is informative. It doesn't just say that God rejected the offering. It says, "The Lord had regard for *Abel* and for his offering; but for *Cain* and for his offering He had no regard" (emphasis mine). There was something about *the man*, something about the heart condition of the man that was either accepted or rejected.

I think it's logical to infer from the story and from John's commentary in our text, that Cain's heart was not right when he brought his offering in the first place. God's rejection of the offering was a merciful call to repentance. To receive the offering from someone who brings it in the wrong spirit, would be misleading. Cain's heart was not right, and this incident brought all that to light. When God is not honoring our offerings and sacrifices, the best thing we can do is humble ourselves, and ask Him what we need to do to get it right. That was not Cain's response. Cain's response was to sulk. He got mad at God, rather than humbling himself and opening his heart for correction from God. His countenance fell. The passage then focuses on Cain's anger.

"Then the Lord said to Cain, 'Why are you angry? And why has your countenance fallen?'" (Gen. 4:6, NASB). That is an amazing demonstration of God's love and mercy. Here is a man whose heart is full of hate and anger. He is jealous of Abel. He is mad at God.[10] Yet no judgment falls. Instead, God condescends to reason with him. "Why are you angry? Let's talk about this, Cain. Are you really being reasonable?" It was an opportunity for Cain to take a second look at his response. Often, our first response to a situation is too impulsive and self-centered. The failure and rejection were understandably painful for Cain. Our first inclination may be to find someone else to blame. But what Cain needed to do was take responsibility for his own failure and simply correct it. That is the opportunity God is giving him.

In Genesis 4:7 God says to him, "If you do well, will not your countenance be lifted up? And if you do not do well, sin is crouching at the door; and its desire is for you, but you must master it" (NASB). "The decision lies with you, Cain. You can 'do well' (do the right thing) or you can choose to not do well (take the wrong course of action). If you do the right thing, if you get your heart right before Me and bring the offering I require, you will be accepted just like Abel was." God was offering Cain that opportunity. God is no respecter of persons.[11] On the other hand, God speaks this warning to Cain. "And if you do not do well, sin is crouching at the door; and its desire is for you, but you must master it." There are two or three possible interpretations of that statement. To address those would take too much time.[12] But a probable meaning is this. "Like a wild lion, sin is right there at your door, waiting to pounce on you. You should conquer it. You can rule over it, by My grace. But if you don't make the right choice here, you're going to be overcome by the anger and hate in your heart. A worse thing will come upon you. You are angry at Me because I'm not doing what you think I ought to do. You have resented your brother and are angry with him. This is not going to turn out good for you, if you don't make the right decision now while you have the opportunity to do so."

The next verse tells us the decision Cain made. "Cain told Abel his brother [some versions say talked with Abel]. And it came about when they were in the field, that Cain rose up against Abel his brother and killed him" (Gen. 4:8, NASB). The envy and hate in Cain's heart produced an act of murder.[13] "Sin will take you further than you wanted to go, keep you longer than you wanted to stay, and cost you more than you wanted to pay."[14] Never forget that. When Cain was talking with God about his offering, I doubt Cain could foresee the end result of the anger that was in his heart. The more he nurtured the offense, the more it consumed his heart and soul.

Remember the offense Esau had against Jacob. You could hardly blame him for being upset over Jacob's manipulation and deceit. I can easily see how Esau justified that resentment toward his brother. But what happened to Esau? The resentment turned to bitterness. It ruined his spiritual relationship with God. His heart became so hardened that he eventually couldn't find place for repentance.[15] Listen to what Hebrews 12:14–17 says about that.

> Pursue peace with all men, and the sanctification without which no one will see the Lord. See to it that no one comes short of the grace of God; that no root of bitterness springing up causes trouble, and by it many be defiled; that *there be* no immoral or godless person like Esau, who sold his own birthright for a *single* meal. For you know that even afterwards, when he desired to inherit the blessing, he was rejected, for he found no place for repentance, though he sought for it with tears (NASB).

Esau had problems in his own heart. But, instead of resolving those problems, he focused on the wrong Jacob had done to him.[16] The anger he harbored in his heart turned him into a bitter, hardened, unrepentant person. Cain and Esau are two serious warnings against nurturing offense in the heart.

A choice, a decision, is a powerful thing. It points you in a direction, and the tendency is to continue in that direction. Have you ever gone snow skiing? You are standing on the hill about to make a decision. You set yourself off in a direction. Once you push off, the momentum of that push and the gravity on that slope propels you forward in the direction you chose. It's difficult to stop once you launch in a direction. Cain's decision moved him in a direction. He had opportunities to repent. But his choices accelerated his descent.

In Genesis 4:9 we see the mercy of God at work, even after Cain murdered his brother. God took the initiative and approached Cain with another question, "Then the Lord said to Cain, 'Where is Abel your brother?'" (NASB). Why did God ask that question? God knew where Abel was. But He asked the question to stir Cain's conscience toward repentance. As bad as it was, Cain could have still humbled himself, confessed his sin, and cried out to God for mercy. But he had hardened his heart before, and now he continues to harden his heart. His response to God is curt and disrespectful. "I do not know. Am I my brother's keeper?" (NASB). There is no fear of the Lord in his words. It's as if he is even questioning God's right to ask the question. With that refusal to repent, God pronounces the judgment associated with Cain's choices.

John contrasts Cain's attitude toward his brother with the command to love. Cain is an example of what not to do. He is an example of someone who fails the test of genuine Christianity. From the beginning, he is "of the evil one." Instead of yielding himself to God, Cain followed the same path Lucifer took. The prideful insistence on his own way, the harboring of resentment and hate toward God and toward his brother, all of which culminated in the act of murder. It manifested his true nature. The choices he made proved that he was of the evil one and not of God. Jesus saw the same thing in the Pharisees who opposed him and used similar terminology with them. In John 8:44 He said to them, "You are of your father the devil, and you want to do the desires of your father. He was a murderer from the beginning" (NASB). In verse 15 of our text John says, "And you know that no murderer has eternal life abiding in him." A hateful stance against anyone, but especially a fellow believer, is, in its essential nature, murder. When a person hates another and keeps on hating that other person, it is evidence that person does not have eternal life abiding in him. It is proof that he or she is not a Christian. First John 3:15 makes that clear: "Everyone who hates his brother is a murderer; and you know that no murderer has eternal life abiding in him."

## THE TEST

John gives the test of love in 1 John 3:14. "We know that we have passed out of death into life, because we love the brethren. He who does not love abides in death" (NASB). It's easy to claim to be a Christian. But it is not always easy to live that out in practice. It's not always easy to love *all* my brothers and sisters in Christ. Sometimes they do things that I don't agree with. Sometimes they do things to me that are hurtful and harmful. If I am walking in the flesh, I will respond to them just like the world responds. If I will walk in the Spirit, I will overcome the temptation to respond in like kind; instead, I will love them for His name sake.[17]

The new nature we have received in Christ is a loving Spirit. That influence continually prompts us to love others. The Holy Spirit convicts us of unforgiveness, hate, and resentment. As we discussed in the previous chapter, that influence in the core of our being produces righteous behavior and love for fellow believers.[18] It is a natural expression of who the true believer really is. "But the fruit of the Spirit is love, joy, peace, longsuffering, gentleness, goodness, faith, Meekness, temperance" (Gal. 5:22-23, KJV). All of those terms are manifestations of love. All of those characterize what John says is evidence of the life of God in a believer.

Our love for fellow believers is evidence "we have passed out of death into life." That is an interesting phrase. In this context, what does it mean to abide in death? It is described in Ephesians 2 as (1) existing in "trespasses and sins" (2) walking "according to the course of this world" (3) operating "according to the prince of the power of the air, of the spirit that is now working in the sons of disobedience" (4) living "in the lusts of our flesh, indulging the desires of the flesh and of the mind," and (5) being "by nature children of wrath" (NASB). That was our state of existence before we were born again. We walked in darkness. We lived to fulfill the lusts of our heart and mind. We were separated from God. Our existence was outside the realm of God's fellowship. We were of the devil, under his control, connected to him as part of the world. Our spirit was not alive unto God. Our spirit was not in touch with God. Our spirit was not drawing upon the life of God.

The new birth moved us from that realm of existence into the kingdom of God's light and love.[19] We are now part of God's family, under His blessing and protection. We are now connected with God in a vibrant way. Ephesians 2:6 says He has "raised us up with Him, and seated us with Him in the heavenly places in Christ" (NASB). A dramatic transformation has taken place. We no longer abide in a place of hate, resentment, and unforgiveness. That is altogether contrary to who we are in Christ. The real Christian may have moments of anger that he needs to confess and be forgiven of, but he does not continue in attitudes of unforgiveness, anger, and bitterness toward other people, especially Christians. That's the test. "We know that we have passed out of death into life, because we love the brethren. He who does not love abides in death."

How do we live according the message or command that John gives us in this text? It all sounds good, but most of you have lived long enough to know it can be challenging at times. If that were not the case, all the exhortations that we read earlier (to bear with, and forgive, and endeavor to keep the unity) would not be necessary. We have to make the decision to pursue love.

How do we cooperate with God in all this? We rely on the anointing to lead us. Remember how John counseled us to do this in 2:27? "As for you, the anointing which you received from Him abides in you, and you have no need for anyone to teach you; but as His anointing teaches you about all things, and is true and is not a lie, and just as it has taught you, you abide in Him" (NASB). The Holy Spirit will tell you how to behave, what to do in specific situations. He will prompt you in the right direction. You have to obey those promptings. But it is a wonderful gift from God; right there in your innermost being is the One who teaches you to love. He sheds His love abroad in your heart, and He inspires you to behave in loving ways.[20]

We keep ourselves in the love of God, praying in the Holy Spirit. Jude 20–21 tells us to do that. You can't neglect this great salvation and expect to live victoriously at the same time.[21] It was never designed to work that way. So, we stay in the word of God. We stay in prayer. We build ourselves up in faith, so that we are prepared and equipped for those people who rub us the wrong way. First Thessalonians 4:9–10 says, "Now as to the love of the brethren, you have no need for anyone to write to you, for you yourselves are taught by God to love one another; for indeed you do practice it toward all the brethren who are in all Macedonia. But we urge you, brethren, to excel still more" (NASB).

Does it seem strange to you that on the one hand John says if you "have passed out of death into life," if you're really a Christian, you *will* love the brethren. That is stated as a fact, as something inevitable. On the other hand, he tells us in verse 11 "that we *should* love one another" (emphasis mine). Why is it not one or the other? How can it be a factual test and an exhortation at the same time? We get some light on this from Paul's statements in 1 Thessalonians 4. Paul commends them for loving one another, even "all the brethren who are in Macedonia" Then he adds, "But we urge you, brethren, to excel still more." It is impossible for us to love the way God loves without the new nature.[22] It is the new nature that enables us to love. Yet our will is not taken out of the picture. We are to cooperate with the promptings and desires of the new nature, by choice. We are not to grieve the Holy Spirit; we are to cooperate and obey Him. That produces loving behavior in our lives. And we are to grow and mature in our capacity to do that. It happens as we yield to the Holy Spirit; but, the fact that it happens is evidence that we are authentic Christians.

We obey the word of God in these matters. We do what He tells us to do, regardless of how we feel about it. In America, we tend to understand love as an emotion. We think that way not only in terms of romantic love, but also brotherly love. So, when we hear the exhortation to love one another, we think it means we ought to feel a certain way toward them. But feelings are always secondary. They come as the result of other things.[23] Love is, in its essence, a matter of the will and the action that is taken by choice. In 1 Corinthians 13 love is described with fifteen action verbs. Paul does not talk to us about how we should feel. He talks to us about how we should *act*, how we should treat other people. When someone slaps you on the cheek, you don't have to feel a certain way to turn the other cheek. You just have to make a choice and do it.

I have found in my own experience: my feelings will tend to follow my choices and actions. When someone does me wrong, if I take offense, and respond in the flesh, if I strike back or if I pull back and sulk, my feelings will tend to follow and reinforce those choices. I will find myself nurturing the offense and becoming more resentful toward the person. The choice I make, sets the course, just as it did with Cain and Esau. On the other hand, if I will obey the commandments that I find in the Sermon on the Mount, my feelings will go in a different direction. Jesus said, "Whoever slaps you on your right cheek, turn the other to him also. If anyone wants to sue you and take your shirt, let him have your coat also. Whoever forces you to go one mile, go with him two" (Matt. 5:39–41, NASB). From that, I understand that mere passivity is not enough. I have to take action to bless the other person.[24] I have to go that extra mile. When I do that, as unto the Lord, something wonderful happens in my heart. I actually want to see that person helped. I actually want my actions to bear good fruit. Our minds tend to rationalize and justify the actions we have taken. When a person slaps me on the cheek, if I slap him back, I will tend to justify that action. "That guy deserved that; he would have kept hitting me if I hadn't done it; besides, he would hurt other people if somebody didn't teach him a lesson." That postures me to continue on that course. On the other hand, when he slaps me, if I turn the other cheek, I will tend to reinforce and affirm that behavior in my mind. "Thank God, I did what Jesus told me to do; I hope it softens that guy's heart; I pray God would grant him mercy and repentance. Maybe he will come to the Lord." A right choice will set you on a course that tends to gain its own momentum. Additionally, obedience to the word of God is an act of faith. You don't have to feel anything to simply do what God has told you to do in His word. And when you do that, God honors the act of faith with His grace. That's what happened when you got saved. You heard the word of God. You acted in obedience to that word. And when you did, God gave you eternal life. When you simply obey God's word, grace comes in.

Let me share a resent experience that illustrates this. When I moved into my house and met my next-door neighbor, I tried to talk to him about the Lord. His response let me know he did not want to pursue the conversation, so I respected that. About a year ago I saw him blowing his leaves into my yard. My initial response was, "How would you like it, if I blow my leaves into your yard." But I knew that wasn't right, so I just forgave and overlooked the offense. During the year, we strongly suspect he is letting his dog into our backyard to relieve himself, so it doesn't mess up his yard. That is something we contend with when we mow. When the leaves fell this year, it came at a time when we were very busy. We went to Texas to check on my parents, and several other things came up. As a result, we were very late in picking our leaves. He got his leaves up, but the wind kept blowing our leaves into his yard. Now it was tempting to just let Mother Nature vindicate me. But I knew that was not right. So, I made a priority of getting my leaves picked up as soon as possible. But I did not stop there. I went to his yard and meticulously got all the leaves off his lawn. What did that do for me? It actually made me feel love toward the man. God honored the act of faith and obedience with His grace. I found it easy to pray for his salvation. I don't know how he will respond to that. The principle I'm teaching is what happens *in me* when I choose that course of action. You do what's right, and let the feelings follow. Cain chose to do what was wrong, and the wrong feeling intensified. But it also works that way on the positive side, especially because God honors the act of faith. Love is a choice. It is choosing to seek the highest good for the other person. It is acting in accordance with that goal.

You might find some comfort in what I am about to share with you. God is not saying you have to *like* everybody. There are some people you will naturally like. There are some people you won't like. The commandment is to *love* them whether you *like* them or not. We think of love as being on a continuum that goes from neutral, to like, to love. We think we have to like someone before we can love them. But liking and loving are simply two different things. Love is a choice to seek their wellbeing. Love has to do with the actions I take toward that person. Often God will reinforce those actions with feelings of care and compassion toward them. Then it really gets easy. But if the feelings don't come, just keep treating them right anyway. You can love people that you don't like, if you will choose to do so. Liking is a product of personal preferences and interests. I enjoy the company of people with interests similar to mine. I like people whose opinions fit well with my ideas. I am attracted to people who give me something I want, in terms of respect, support, and affirmation. That's just the way we are wired. It's okay to like some people more than others. It's not okay to behave unloving toward the ones you don't like.

I have learned all that through personal experience. But I was encouraged to find C. S. Lewis saying some of the same things in his book, *Mere Christianity*.[25] It has worked for him. It has worked for me. I am growing in my ability to do that, and I want to grow more in my love toward the family of God. We will be spending a lot of time together in eternity with all our brothers and sisters in Christ.

The message John brings in our text is "that we should love one another." Are you doing that, no exceptions? If so, it is evidence you are a child of God. Is there someone that you're having a hard time loving? Don't wait for the right feeling; take the action Jesus tells you to take. Let your choices and actions toward that person be characterized by love.

# Endnotes: Chapter 15

1   Cf. Matt. 22:37–40.

2   Burdick, 260: "The two phrases together set forth the two sides of the ethical test of sonship. . . ."

3   Cf. Burdick, 260: ". . . 'from the beginning' has several possible interpretations, depending on the context in which it appears."

4   As translated in the NASV.

5   1 John 2:10–11; 3:10.

6   John is speaking from a familial perspective. The family relationship is expressed in verse 1 of this chapter and continues into our text. Donald Burdick (p. 260) writes, "Bultmann holds that the term 'brother,' here and in 2:10; 3:15; and 4:20, is not to be limited to fellow Christians, but means 'neighbor.' John, however, explicitly limits the term to the person who has been born of God (5:1)."

7   Matt. 5:44. Cf. 2 Cor. 5:14–15, 20; 1 Thess. 3:12, "And the Lord make you to increase and abound in love one toward another, *and toward all* men" (emphasis mine, KJV).

8   Cf. Rom. 12:10; 13:10; 1 Pet. 1:22; 1 John 3:23; 4:7; 2 John 1:5.

9   Cf. 1 John 3:22–23; 1 Pet. 3:7–9.

10   God asked Jonah a similar question for similar reasons (Jonah 4:4). Amazing grace, how sweet the sound!

11   Cf. Acts 10:34.

12   Charles Spurgeon's sermon entitled "To Those Who Are Angry with Their Godly Friends" does a masterful job of dealing with this subject. I am indebted to him for the imagery of the crouching lion. Accessed at The C. H. Spurgeon Collection on CD-ROM (AGES Software, Inc., 1998).

13   The Greek word, *sphazō*, translated "murdered" in 1 John 3:12 originally meant "to slay by cutting the throat" as a butcher would do. Abel's was a violent death, further illustrating the evil in Cain's heart. Vincent, s. v. "1 John 3:12."

14   Ravi Zacharias is credited with this saying at Goodreads. com. Retrieved Dec. 7, 2017 at https://www.goodreads.com/quotes/746709-sin-will-take-you-farther-than-you-want-to-go.

15   Cf. Heb. 3:13. Persisting in sin has a hardening effect on the soul.

16   Cf. Matt. 7:3–5.

17   John is simply giving the test in our text. But in Galatians 5:16–25, Paul discusses the decisions we have to make on a daily basis in regard to the conflicting desires we experience. John will expound on the exhortation and the test as he continues in the letter.

18   Cf. Chapter 14 in this book entitled, "The Power of a New Nature."

19   Col. 1:13.

20   Rom. 5:5.

21  Cf. Heb. 2:3; Eph. 5:18.
22  It is beyond the scope of this study to explain actions by unbelievers that seem very loving. Many such actions are, in reality, motivated by well-masked selfishness; and, therefore, do not qualify as *agapē* (God's kind of love). However, there is a common grace (not saving grace) from a loving, merciful Creator that is enjoyed by all humanity.
23  Cf. Archibald D. Hart, *Unlocking the Mystery of Your Emotions* (Dallas, TX: Word Publishing, 1989).
24  Cf. Matt. 5:44; 1 Pet. 3:9.
25  Lewis, *Mere Christianity,* 129–133.

# Chapter 16

&#x269C;&#x2022;&#x25C9;&#x2022;&#x269C;

# This Is Love
# 3:16–18

> We know love by this, that He laid down His life for us;
> and we ought to lay down our lives for the brethren. But
> whoever has the world's goods, and sees his brother in
> need and closes his heart against him, how does the love
> of God abide in him? Little children, let us not love with
> word or with tongue, but in deed and truth.
>
> 1 John 3:16–18, NASB

## Expository Message

Our text in chapter fifteen began in 3:11: "For this is the message which you have heard from the beginning, that we should love one another" (NASB). John is obviously continuing with that theme. In verse 14 he gave this test of love. "We know that we have passed out of death into life, because we love the brethren. He who does not love abides in death" (NASB). The person who is really saved (the person who is truly born again) loves fellow Christians. The new nature within him is expressed in love toward others, especially toward believers. The Pharisees that Jesus dealt with claimed to love God and to love their neighbors. But, in reality, they despised the common people,[1] and they ultimately so hated Jesus that they orchestrated his crucifixion. They were religious. They talked a good talk. But when it came down to how they treated people, it was obvious that the love of God was not in their hearts.

In contrast to that, the early church was so full of God's love that they were sacrificially giving to one another. In addition to the 120 disciples, 3,000 more were saved on the Day of Pentecost. Acts 2 says their lifestyle was consistently characterized by prayer, Bible study, the Lord's Table, and fellowship with one another. The word translated "fellowship" in Acts 2:42 is koinōnia. It means to share, participate, partner with, or to have in common.[2] In 2 Corinthians 9:13 Paul used the word in reference to providing material goods to those in need. In his introduction to his first epistle, John invites people into this koinōnia enjoyed by the early church. First John 1:3 says, "What we have seen and heard we proclaim to you also, so that you too may have fellowship [koinōnia] with us; and indeed our fellowship [koinōnia] is with the Father, and with His Son Jesus Christ" (NASB). This theme of koinōnia continues to be on John's mind as he writes this text.

How is this level of koinōnia possible? It is only possible as people operate in the love of God. It is something that issues from the new nature and is expressed by believers toward one another. Acts 2:43–47 says,

> Everyone kept feeling a sense of awe; and many wonders and signs were taking place through the apostles. And all those who had believed were together and had all things in common; and they *began* selling their property and possessions and were sharing them with all, as anyone might have need. Day by day continuing with one mind in the temple, and breaking bread from house to house, they were taking their meals together with gladness and sincerity of heart, praising God and having favor with all the people. And the Lord was adding to their number day by day those who were being saved (NASB).

That is a beautiful picture of the church alive and well. Miracles are happening. People are getting saved. Christians are in unity with one another, enjoying the fellowship they have together while serving the Lord. What is the key to all that happening? The love of God is overflowing in believers' hearts.[3] It is shortly after the Day of Pentecost. These believers have been filled with the Spirit. They are walking in the Spirit. And they are treating one another right. That is a picture of what John is shooting for in our text. He was there in Acts 2, experiencing it. He knows it is possible. And he knows how good it is when it's happening. So, in 1 John 3:11 he reminds them of the message preached from the beginning: "That we should love one another" (NASB).

The Greeks had four words for love. Broadly speaking, *philia* is a friendship kind of affection, *storgē* is similar to *philia*. It is the kind of affection family members have for one another. *Erōs* is sexual love. The word John is using here is *agapē*. It is God's kind of love. It is an unconditional, unselfish love.[4] To some degree, John's readers understood his meaning, by the Greek word that he used. But John has given this agapē love as a test of real salvation.[5] It is extremely important that Christians know what he is talking about. So in our text today, he gives further clarification of what he means by the word "love."

## LOVE EXEMPLIFIED

Love is exemplified in Christ. John begins verse 16, "We know love by this." The best definition I can give you of this love is to show it to you in concrete terms. Turn your attention to the cross, and you will see love in action. John does not get bogged down in abstract concepts. "We know love by this, that He laid down His life for us." Look at what Jesus did for you at the cross; experience the reality of that. That's how you know what love is. Jesus is the personification of love.

Everything Christ did for us is an expression of unselfish love. Read Philippians 2 and ponder His willingness to step down out of heaven into our fallen world. The incarnation was an expression of agapē. He saw our need, and He stepped into the mess to deliver us. Real love is not something you can do at a distance. It compels you to get involved with the problem. He laid aside His rights of deity. He became a man. He served others, rather than looking out for his own interests. He healed the sick, delivered the oppressed, and fed the multitudes. All that was motivated by love. The gospels often tell us how he was moved with compassion and took steps to relieve suffering and pain as a result.[6] He healed the two blind men in Matthew 20 because He "had compassion on them."[7] In Mark 8 he fed the multitude for the same reason. Compassion for hurting people brought Him to earth, and compassion compelled Him to serve others. Although He is Lord of all, He washed the disciples' feet; then told them to serve each other in the same way.[8] John 3:16 tells us this love compelled the Father to send the Son, and that same love caused the Son to come to our rescue. We learn about this love by everything Jesus did.

But the greatest demonstration of love was when He laid down His life for us on the cross. He had given His time and energy in service. He did not cling to the glories that were His in heaven. He laid it all aside for us. He gave His back to the whip for us. There He stands at the cross with only a seamless robe to cover His nakedness. That too is given up, so that He is there with nothing left to give but His life.[9] Does He stop there? Does He call 10,000 angels to end the sacrifice?[10] No, He willingly offered up Himself for our salvation. No man took His life; He willingly gave His life for our salvation.[11] This agapē love voluntarily gives to others. The main characteristic of this love that John wants us to understand is its sacrificial nature. It is selfless. It is focused on the needs of others. It is willing to suffer loss in order to rescue the one in need.

Do you remember the time John's mother came to Jesus and asked that John and James might sit at Jesus's right hand and left hand in the kingdom? That really upset the other disciples. They were not operating in love. They were each pursuing their own self-interest.[12] John's mother was being selfish in her request, wanting her boys to get the best spots. The disciples were responding in a competitive, selfish spirit. All of that was the very opposite of what John is calling for in our text. He had learned it from Jesus. Now He is passing on what he learned. Jesus contrasted the way His kingdom operates with that of the world. The world pushes and shoves to get on top. Once there, they make everybody serve them. But Jesus's kingdom operates in reverse of that. In His kingdom, you humble yourself and serve others. And that's what demonstrates your greatness. He uses His own example to drive home the point. In Matthew 20:28 He says, "Just as the Son of Man did not come to be served, but to serve, and to give His life a ransom for many" (NASB). That's the example John points to in our text as the ultimate demonstration of what love is.

## LOVE EMULATED

Love is to be emulated by us. In the last half of verse 16, John applies this principle of sacrificial love to us. "And we ought to lay down our lives for the brethren." We should meditate much on the sacrifice Jesus made for us. But we must not camp there forever. At some point, we must get up and do likewise. In all this teaching, John is talking about our lifestyle. He is not talking about occasional acts of benevolence. The Message translates it this way: "This is why we ought to live sacrificially for our fellow believers, and not just be out for ourselves."[13]

Our lives should be characterized by self-sacrifice. It's so contrary to the way the world lives. They are looking out for number one. They may camouflage it with sweet talk and an occasional act of benevolence. But, on the whole, they are about taking care of themselves. That may spill over to family, because family is an extension of self. But the love John is talking about is not natural to the human race. Some of the other loves expressed through other Greek words are. But agapē is a love that comes by way of the new nature. That is why it is such a good test as to whether a person is truly born again.

The natural man is selfish. Divine love is unselfish. That is the primary difference. "And we also ought to lay down our lives for the brethren." The Greek word translated *ought to* is not a suggestion. It is a moral obligation, a debt that is owed.[14] Remember how David treated Mephibosheth kindly for Jonathan's sake. He brought Mephibosheth to his table and treated him like his own son.[15] You may see a brother in need and say, "That person has never done anything for me." And that may be true. In fact, he may never do anything for you. But Jesus said, "To the extent that you did it to one of these brothers of Mine, *even* the least *of them*, you did it to Me" (Matt. 25:40, NASB).[16] The debt we owe is to Jesus. It is a debt beyond anything we could fully repay. But that debt compels us to treat His brethren with kindness, even more, to lay down our lives for them.

> George Atley . . . was engaged in the Central African Mission. [In 1989] he was attacked by a party of natives. He had with him a Winchester repeating rifle with ten loaded chambers. The party was completely at his

mercy. . . . [But the evidence indicates he made a choice to not use his rifle against them.] He [apparently] concluded that if he killed them it would do the mission more harm than if he allowed them to take his life. . . . When his body was found in the stream, his rifle was also found with its ten chambers still loaded.[17]

George Atley considered the eternal wellbeing of those natives more important than his own life. That is the kind of unselfish love God puts in the believer's heart.

## LOVE EXAMINED

Love is examined more fully in verse 17. There John gives a practical, everyday example of what he is talking about. "But whoever has the world's goods, and sees his brother in need and closes his heart against him, how does the love of God abide in him?"[18] There are three dynamics in this scenario. (1) The person has the resources to help the one in need. It doesn't mean he is rich. But he could help the person. (2) He knows about the brother's need. The Greek word, *theōreō*, translated "sees," implies a long look, long enough to understand the circumstances of the case.[19] There is wisdom in knowing where you are investing the resources. I see panhandlers standing at street intersections in Springfield. People drive by and put money into their hands. It is not a wise way to give. I suspect much of the funds go to support the addiction that has the man in a needy state to begin with. Are you ultimately helping him? Would you buy him more heron with the funds? Would you bring him a bottle of whiskey? But in many cases, that is where it winds up. I have been involved in benevolence ministries for many years. Understanding the circumstances of the case enough to really help the person is important. Love is seeking the individual's highest good. It is not just doing what he wants you to do. John does not pause to address matters like this. But the Bible teaches us to be good stewards of our resources.[20] John is focused on the importance of acting in compassion toward the one in need.[21] (3) "And closes his heart against him" He may have felt an initial compassion for the person, but out of his own greed, he shuts that down, and does not help him. Then John asks the rhetorical question, "How does the love of God abide in him?" Of course, the obvious answer is that it doesn't.

James provides a rich commentary on our text.

> What use is it, my brethren, if someone says he has faith but he has no works? Can that faith save him? If a brother or sister is without clothing and in need of daily food, and one of you says to them, 'Go in peace, be warmed and be filled,' and yet you do not give them what is necessary for *their* body, what use is that? Even so faith, if it has no works, is dead, *being* by itself. But someone may *well* say, "You have faith and I have works; show me your faith without the works, and I will show you my faith by my works" (Jas. 2:14–18, NASB).

In other words, what's inside is demonstrated by what action we physically take. Talk is cheap. John makes that point in verse 18 of our text. "Little children, let us not love with word or with tongue, but in deed and truth."[22]

There is always the danger that we would deceive ourselves into thinking we're loving people, simply because we embrace the concept. We hear sermons like this, and we say, "Amen. Love the brethren. That is so important." But then we encounter a need, and we pass right by it without rendering any true help.[23] I've known people who could talk about love with such a sentimental, soft voice it would almost bring you to tears. Yet their lives were characterized by utter selfishness.

Several years ago, Jeanie and I were at a pastors' convention in Palm Springs, California. From our motel you could see the mountains in the distance. There on the horizon was the Big Bear resort area. At an open-air restaurant we could hear people discussing their experiences there. God used that setting to speak a word to Jeanie. He showed her how easy it is to look at those mountains, think about those mountains, talk about them, and hear others talk about them until you subtly convince yourself that that you've actually been there. In truth, you have never set a foot on that ground. You may know something about the area and the activities that go on there. But you have never experienced it for yourself. For you, it is only an imaginary experience. Intending to do something, is not the same as actually doing it. Fanaticizing about personal sacrifice, is not the same as actually making the sacrifice. Knowing someone who does it, is not the same as doing it yourself. Being a part of an organization where others are sacrificing, does not necessarily mean that you're sacrificing.

So, the question that must be asked is this. Are you personally helping other people? Is it just something that you claim vicariously from being a member of an organization? Is it just something that you think about doing? Sometimes the people who are insisting that institutions meet needs, are the least willing to make any personal sacrifices for it to happen. How many politicians want a generous welfare system with *your* tax money? What they really want is the votes. They're not making a personal sacrifice. They are looking to gain from it all. It doesn't count for righteousness. It is entirely selfish in nature.

The key issue John is dealing with is the difference between a selfish life and an unselfish life.[24] Sometimes people join an organization because they see it as a way to tap into resources. They are selfish people who do not want to work. Paul dealt with people like that in Thessalonica. They wanted to lay around and take it easy while the others provided for them. Paul admonished them in his first letter, but it didn't do any good.[25] So in his second letter he lays down the law that if they would not work, neither should they eat. This is what he writes in 2 Thessalonians 3:10–12.

> For even when we were with you, we used to give you this order: if anyone is not willing to work, then he is not to eat, either. For we hear that some among you are leading an undisciplined life, doing no work at all, but acting like busybodies. Now such persons we command and exhort in the Lord Jesus Christ to work in quiet fashion and eat their own bread (NASB).

To meet the needs of a lazy person, may do him more harm than good. He needs some motivation to work and live an honorable life. Proverbs 16:26 says, "The person who labors, labors for himself, For his hungry mouth drives him on" (NKJV). If that's the motivation he needs to work, we should not take it away from him. It is just as selfish to be lazy and live off the hard work of others as it is to be stingy and not share resources with those who need help. Paul deals with these matters in his epistles.[26] Paul confronts the heart condition of the one needing help.

But John is not addressing those issues. He focuses on the other side of the situation, the heart condition of the one with resources to give. He is only dealing with stinginess in the potential giver, just as Jesus did in in Matthew 5:42. "Give to him who asks of you," Jesus said, "and do not turn away from him who wants to borrow from you" (NASB). He is making a general statement about the way we should respond to those in need. It corresponds to John's words in our text. Do these statements by Jesus and John contradict what Paul says in 2 Thessalonians? No, Jesus and John are only addressing one side of the equation. They are not going into the details that Paul speaks to. That's why we must always take the whole counsel of God in Scripture, and not let one proof text define our whole understanding of a subject. What does the Bible, as a whole, say about the matter?

We must also consider the context in which a message is given in Scripture. In our text, John is talking about how we respond to other believers.[27] He uses the words "brother" and "brethren" over and over. He is not talking about the way we should respond to the world and unbelievers. We should be loving toward them. There are other passages that inform us about that.[28] But, in our text, John is talking about seeing a fellow believer in need. Keep in mind, John has also given us some meaningful tests that let us know whether a person who claims to be a Christian, really is a Christian. For example, in 1 John 2:29 he writes, "If you know that He is righteous, you know that everyone also who practices righteousness is born of Him" (NASB). How many times have you seen people who live in open sin, demanding the church to obey our text? But do they really qualify as the *brother* John is talking about here? John is talking about people who demonstrate Christian lifestyle and have a valid need. In those situations, he is saying to the Christian with resources, "You have an obligation to help that brother or sister. You should understand the matter well enough to actually be helping him. But if he needs your help, and you can help, then do it. Don't just talk about it. Don't try to get others to make the sacrifice. You help that brother or sister in Christ."

By its nature, mercy gives to people who don't necessarily deserve it.[29] We must not excuse our own obligation to give by finding faults in the recipients of our help. Our text today does not address the heart condition of person receiving help. John's concern is about the potential giver shutting off compassion toward the one in need. Love gives. Love sacrifices for the sake of another. Jesus's sacrifice on cross is the highest demonstration of that. We must guard our hearts and keep them soft and tender and willing to share anything the Lord would prompt us to give.[30] It is better to be too generous, too merciful, than to pull back in selfishness and refuse to help others.

In Matthew 7:21 Jesus said, "Not everyone who says to Me, 'Lord, Lord,' will enter the kingdom of heaven, but he who does the will of My Father who is in heaven *will enter*" (NASB). The commandment we have from Christ is that we would love one another, just as He has loved us.[31] That's John's message in our text. The love is expressed in practical works of kindness. May God give us a heart to actually do that and not just talk about it.

# Endnotes: Chapter 16

1   Cf. John 7:49.

2   Thayer, s. v. "NT:2842."

3   Years ago, people sang, "Give me that old time religion." The second verse says, "Makes me love everybody, makes me love everybody, makes love everybody, and it's good enough for me." The song itself may be passé, but the truth declared in that verse is eternal. Genuine relationship with God will cause a person to love others. "Old Time Religion," by David Houston, *Metro Lyrics*. Retrieved Dec. 15, 2017 at http://www.metrolyrics.com/old-time-religion-lyrics-david-houston.html.

4   C.S. Lewis, *The Four Loves*. Retrieved Dec. 15, 2017 at https://www.youtube.com/watch?v=-GMYXRE1A1I and https://archive.org/details/TheFourLovesCSLewisPart3ErosSexualLove. I am only giving imprecise, general definitions in passing. Cf. Law, 70–72.

5   To emphasize the distinction between agapē and the other expressions of love, I sometimes use agapē as an adjective modifying the English word love.

6   Cf. Matt. 15:32; 20;34; Mark 1:41; 5:19; 6:34; 8:2; Luke 7:13.

7   Matt. 20:34, KJV.

8   Cf. John 13:14.

9   Spurgeon, "The Death of Christ for His People." Accessed at The C. H. Spurgeon Collection on CD-ROM (AGES Software, Inc., 1998).

10  Cf. Matt. 26:53.

11  Cf. John 10:18.

12  Cf. Phil. 2:4–5; Jas. 3:14–15.

13  Peterson, *The Message: The New Testament in Contemporary Language*, 593.

14  Friberg, s. v. "*opheilō*." Also see Thayer. s. v. "NT:3784."

15  2 Sam. 9:6–7, 9.

16  Matt. 25:34–36, "Then the King will say to those on His right, 'Come, you who are blessed of My Father, inherit the kingdom prepared for you from the foundation of the world. For I was hungry, and you gave Me *something* to eat; I was thirsty, and you gave Me *something* to drink; I was a stranger, and you invited Me in; naked, and you clothed Me; I was sick, and you visited Me; I was in prison, and you came to Me." (NASB). Time and money are two important ways to give.

17  Paul Lee Tan, ed., *Encyclopedia of 7700 Illustrations: Signs of the Times*, 1979 (Rockville, MD: Assurance Publishers, 1985) s. v. "His Unused Rifle Was Loaded" by *Heart and Life*, p.1176-1177. Cf. Victor Zalakos, "George Atley." Retrieved Dec. 15, 2017 at https://www.mail-archive.com/rangernet@ebible.org/msg05693.html.

18  By changing from the plural, brethren, to the singular, brother, John brings the exhortation to a personal, practical level. Stephen Smalley (p. 197) astutely points out, "It is easier to love 'mankind' as a whole and in theory than (say) to help a particular brother who needs, and deserves, our cash.".

19  Zodhiates, *The Complete Word Study Dictionary: New Testament,* p. 733: "To look closely at. To gaze, to look with interest and for a purpose, usually indicating the careful observation of details." Cf. Stott, p. 144.

20  Cf. Prov. 18:9; 21:20; Matt. 25:14–30; Luke 16:11.

21  Cf. Deut. 15:7–11.

22  Phillips translation says, "My children, let us love not merely in theory or in words—let us love in sincerity and in practice." J. B. Phillips, *The New Testament in Modern English*, rev. ver. (New York: The Macmillian Co., 1972) 504.

23  Cf. Jas. 1:22–25.

24  The kingdom of Satan is a kingdom of selfishness. The kingdom of God is a kingdom of love. John has compared the hate in Cain to the love in Christ. But what drives hate in a person's heart? Is it not selfishness, love of self and disregard for the needs of others? Animosity toward anyone or anything that gets in the way of number one, springs from a self-centered orientation. Hate strikes out against anyone that appears to obstruct the wishes of self. Why did Cain hate Abel? Abel's righteousness exposed Cain's wickedness; Abel got what Cain wanted, the favor of God. Of course, Cain refused to enter into that favor through submission to God in the way Abel did. Selfishness is the root of hate.

25  Cf. 1 Thess. 4:11–12.

26  In 1 Tim. 5:3–8 Paul deals with other issues related to this subject. He does not indiscriminately throw money at needs. We are to be wise stewards of the resources God entrusts into our care, but we are to do so with a generous heart of love.

27  Cf. Burdick, 269; Robert Yarbrough, *1–3 John: Baker Exegetical Commentary of the New Testament,* 205.

28  The story of the Good Samaritan (Luke 10:25–37) deals with the issue of compassion and benevolence in broader terms than John does in our text. The Christians actions toward *all* people should be characterized by love. Galatians 6:10 provides a healthy perspective on the matter. "So then, while we have opportunity, let us do good to all *people*, and especially to those who are of the household of the faith" (NASB).

29  Cf. Titus 3:5, "Not by works of righteousness which we have done, but according to his mercy he saved us" (KJV).

30  Cf. Prov. 4:23.

31  John 15:12, NASB. Express the same unselfish attitude that He expressed toward us.

# CHAPTER 17

# Good Conscience
## 3:18–24

My little children, let us not love in word or in tongue, but in deed and in truth. And by this we know that we are of the truth, and shall assure our hearts before Him. For if our heart condemns us, God is greater than our heart, and knows all things. Beloved, if our heart does not condemn us, we have confidence toward God. And whatever we ask we receive from Him, because we keep His commandments and do those things that are pleasing in His sight. And this is His commandment: that we should believe on the name of His Son Jesus Christ and love one another, as He gave us commandment. Now he who keeps His commandments abides in Him, and He in him. And by this we know that He abides in us, by the Spirit whom He has given us.

1 John 3:18–24, NKJV

### Expository Message

The Apostle Paul said to the Sanhedrin in Acts 23:1, "I have lived in all good conscience before God" (NKJV). That statement summaries the theme of this chapter. Do you live in all good conscience before God? He later said to Governor Felix, "I myself always strive to have a conscience without offense toward God and men."[1] What does Paul mean by those statements? How do we live in all good conscience? What are the benefits of doing that? John is answering some of those questions in our text. He has laid the foundation by teaching the importance of embracing truth, practicing righteousness, and loving one another. Now he points us to a condition in which we enjoy peace of mind, confidence before God, and answered prayer.

Many Americans enjoy watching the 1947 movie, "It's a Wonderful Life," during the Christmas holidays.[2] The film excels in celebrating biblical values, values that support a meaningful, fulfilling life. God wants all His children to live a wonderful life. Such a life is experienced when we live in all good conscience toward God and men. There may be external trials and difficulties. Those trials may be very challenging. We're not necessarily talking about an easy life. Paul's life was anything but easy. But when we live in all good conscience, the soul is at rest and all is well inside the heart.

In the text, John addresses two conditions of the heart. In verse 20 the conscience is troubled and condemning.[3] In verse 21 the conscience is affirming and free of condemnation. We will examine those two conditions in reverse order because I want us to first see the way things ought to be and, then, talk about how we deal with the accusations of conscience.

## AFFIRMING CONSCIENCE

Verse 21 begins, "Beloved, if our heart does not condemn us." What does that look like? What are the benefits of a clear and affirming conscience? Peace of mind is first. Look at verse 19. "And by this we know that we are of the truth, and shall assure our hearts before Him" (NKJV). I think the New International Version makes the last part of that verse easier to understand. "This then is how we know that we belong to the truth, and *how we set our hearts at rest in his presence*" (emphasis mine). Is your heart at rest? "There remains, therefore, a rest to the people of God," (Heb. 4:9, NKJV). It is a state of mind where we are at peace with God; we are at peace with other people; and we are at peace with ourselves.

You have a relationship with yourself that is intricately connected to your relationship with God and with others. It includes self-talk; it includes the meditations of your heart; it includes the voice of your conscience.

When the conscience is not condemning us, we have, not only peace *with* God, but also the peace *of* God ruling our hearts.[4] Everything is perfectly lined up with God and with His will. Have you experienced that? Totally *at rest* in His presence! We used to sing about it.

> Peace, peace, wonderful peace coming down from the Father above.
>
> Sweep over my spirit forever I pray, with fathomless billows of love.[5]

That is a taste of heaven on earth: the full assurance that we are exactly where God wants us to be, doing exactly what He wants us to do. This place of rest is not dependent upon external circumstances. It is simply knowing that God is pleased, and there is nothing limiting our assurance and intimacy with Him.

Verse 19 points back to verse 18 as instruction on how we enjoy this.[6] "And by this we know that we are of the truth" (NKJV). He has just spoken about loving in deed and truth. Now he talks about knowing "that we are of the truth." You have to know that before you can set your heart "at rest in his presence." To be "of the truth" simply means you are indeed a child of God, walking in truth. How do we know we are really a child of God? Everything John has said in this epistle helps us answer that question. But John is specifically referring to verse 18. "My little children, let us not love in word or in tongue, but in deed and in truth" (NKJV). The assurance proceeds from the objective evidence of how we are conducting our lives, especially in our relationships with one another.[7] Do your actions toward other believers demonstrate love? Are there specific things you do that indicate genuine concern for their wellbeing? If so, the knowledge of those facts will produce a sense of wellbeing and peace in your own conscience. "By this," by the way we treat other believers, we enjoy assurance of our salvation and we enjoy peace of mind.

John identifies another benefit of a good conscience in verse 21. "Beloved, if our heart does not condemn us, we have confidence toward God" (NKJV). Boldness or confidence before God is the second benefit I want to talk about.

Back in 1 John 2:28, John addressed the issue of confidence before God. "Now, little children, abide in Him, so that when He appears, we may have confidence and not shrink away from Him in shame at His coming" (NASB). That verse focused on having confidence at the Judgment Seat of Christ: not being ashamed at His coming. Our current text focuses on the present: our confidence as we stand before God *now*, especially when we come before Him in prayer. Did you notice those last two words in verse 19, "Before Him"? On the one hand, we are always "before Him." We live our lives *before Him*. We maintain an awareness of His presence at all times. It is a source of comfort, and it is a source of accountability. But when we come to Him in prayer, without any other distractions, we are especially aware of the fact that we are standing or bowing *before Him*. That is when it is extremely important to enjoy a sense of assurance and confidence before God. Hebrews 4:16: "Therefore let us draw near with confidence to the throne of grace, so that we may receive mercy and find grace to help in time of need" (NASB). The Greek word translated confidence in that verse is the same word translated confidence in our test: *parrēsia*. It implies the freedom to speak openly and frankly, like you can with a close friend.[8] "Beloved, if our heart does not condemn us, we have confidence toward God."

In Genesis 18 God is about to send judgment on Sodom and Gomorrah; He lets Abraham in on the secret. Abraham is the only person God tells. Lot lives in Sodom, but God doesn't tell him. He tells the man who lives in all good conscience. Abraham begins to pray with amazing boldness. Genesis 18:23 says that Abraham came near to the Lord and said, "Will You indeed sweep away the righteous with the wicked?" (NASB). Listen to his appeal in verses 24–25.

> Suppose there are fifty righteous within the city; will You indeed sweep it away and not spare the place for the sake of the fifty righteous who are in it? Far be it from You to do such a thing, to slay the righteous with the wicked, so that the righteous and the wicked are treated alike. Far be it from You! Shall not the Judge of all the earth deal justly? (NASB).

Those words may sound presumptuous to our ears. But God was pleased with Abraham's prayer. Abraham had that kind of boldness in prayer because his heart was surrendered to the Lord. He was sold out to the will of God. He was actually praying according to the will of God. The intercession needed to happen. Abraham was perfectly in line with God's desire that none would perish, but that all would come to repentance.[9] Although there were not even ten righteous in that city, God spared Lot and his family in answer to Abraham's prayer. It was bold intercession. Abraham could do that because of his intimacy with God. His conscience was completely clear. The prayer got an answer.

This boldness before God spills over into boldness before man. When the conscience is free and clear of all offense, then the person knows God is with him. And if God be for us, who can be against us.[10] "The righteous are bold as a lion." In fact, Proverbs 28:1 draws this contrast. "The wicked flee when no one is pursuing, But the righteous are bold as a lion" (NASB). An accusing conscience will make a coward out of a person. If the devil can't get you to rebel against God and sin willfully, his next best move is to bring you under a condemning conscience. It will keep you quiet when you need to speak up. Just as you need to make a stand, it will say something like this: "Who are you to stand up for righteousness. You remember that little fit you threw the other day. What if these people knew about that? You had better just walk away and let somebody talk to them, somebody who is qualified to do it." And so, you are neutralized by your own conscience. An accusing conscience cows the person down. Remember when the scribes and Pharisees brought to Jesus a woman taken in adultery. They were laying a trap for Jesus. But Jesus just stooped down and wrote on the ground. Then He said to them, "He that is without sin among you, let him first cast a stone at her" (KJV). Their response is recorded in John 8:9, "And they which heard it, being convicted by their own conscience, went out one by one, beginning at the eldest, even unto the last" (KJV). They walked away with their tails tucked between their legs because they were convicted by their own conscience.

An uncondemning conscience means boldness before God and boldness before men. Look at Elijah as he confronts King Ahab and tells him there will be no rain until he (Elijah) commands it. Watch him on Mt. Carmel confront the prophets of Baal.[11] Look at Daniel when he reads the decree to make no petitions, except to the King of the Medes and Persians. He boldly opens His window and defies the decrees of men.[12] Look at Peter and John as they stand before the Sanhedrin and defy their command forbidding them to preach Jesus.[13] "The wicked flee when no one is pursuing, But the righteous are bold as a lion."

Our tendency is to rush into prayer without giving due attention to the voice of conscience. For prayer to be effective, we must be able to speak with a confident expectation that God hears us and will answer the prayer.[14] We cannot pray in full faith when our conscience is condemning and accusing us. We must first resolve those issues. Then we can pray effectively. There have been times when I would get down to pray, and just have this nagging sense that something is not right. I am not sensing in my heart the liberty and freedom that ought to be there. If I don't stop and deal with that, I will not be able to pray effectively. I should not proceed just tolerating a condemning conscience. I should resolve the issues, then make my requests unto God. We'll talk about how to do later in this chapter.

But first look at the other benefit of a good conscience in 1 John 3:22a: "And whatever we ask we receive from Him" (NKJV). Answered prayer is promised to the person who lives in all good conscience. How can God promise such a thing? The person who lives in all good conscience is submitted to Him and makes requests He can safely answer. When we respond to the conviction of the Holy Spirt in our conscience, we are resolving issues that take us out of the will of God. We are aligning ourselves with God.[15] Therefore, we do not pray amiss that we would consume it on our own flesh.[16] We pray according to the will of God. First John 5:14 specifically addresses that. "This is the confidence which we have before Him, that, if we ask anything according to His will, He hears us" (NASB). Our conscience will alert us, before we take an action. So, if I start to pray amiss and my conscience is sensitive to the Holy Spirit, I will experience a caution through my conscience. Right there, right then my conscience will alert me to the error, before I even make the mistake. That's when I adjust the prayer under the direction of the Holy Spirit. The Holy Spirit will enable me to pray according to the will of the Father.[17]

Jesus never prayed amiss. He did always those things that please the Father, including the way He prayed.[18] And He prayed with bold assurance that the prayers would be answered. And they were answered! He is the model that we are to follow. Look at His boldness in prayer at Lazarus's tomb. Standing there before the dead body, He prays, "Father, I thank You that You have heard Me. I knew that You always hear Me" (John 11:41, NASB). That is spoken out of a clear conscience. That is the confidence John is talking about in our text. Now hear the authority of Jesus's prayer: "Lazarus, come forth!" And what happened? The prayer got answered. Lazarus did come forth.

That kind of boldness is possible for us, "in Christ." Jesus said, "Most assuredly, I say to you, he who believes in Me, the works that I do he will do also; and greater works than these he will do, because I go to My Father" (John 14:12, NKJV). I have a lot to learn; but I am pursuing that place in God where my prayers get answered the way Jesus's prayers got answered. My standard is not the status quo of a lukewarm church. My standard is Jesus. I want more boldness in prayer. I want more answers to prayer. And one thing that must be in place for that to happen is a heart that does not condemn. The foundation for authoritative prayer is a clear conscience.[19]

Isaiah 58 provides an Old Testament counterpart to what John is teaching here. There God confronted Israel for thinking they could live contrary to the commandments of God, just do some religious stuff, and enjoy the blessings. In Isaiah 58:6 God says, "Is this not the fast which I choose, To loosen the bonds of wickedness, To undo the bands of the yoke, And to let the oppressed go free And break every yoke?" (NASB). He goes on to talk about feeding the hungry, housing the homeless, and clothing the naked. He is talking about an unselfish life spent in the interests of others.[20] Verses 8 and 9 describe the blessings that would follow.

> Then your light will break out like the dawn, And your recovery will speedily spring forth; And your righteousness will go before you; The glory of the Lord will be your rear guard. Then you will call, and the Lord will answer; You will cry, and He will say, "Here I am" (NASB).

That's what a life of obedience looks like. "Then you will call, and the Lord will answer." First John 1:21–22 says, "Beloved, if our heart does not condemn us, we have confidence before God; and whatever we ask we receive from Him, because we keep His commandments and do the things that are pleasing in His sight" (NASB).

Now we have seen the benefits and beauty of living in all good conscience. But we also need to know how to do that. How do we keep our conscience free and clear of condemnation? Let's go back to verse 20 and address the problem of an accusing conscience.

## ACCUSING CONSCIENCE

Verse 20 says, "For if our heart condemns us" (NKJV). How do we deal with that? How do we maintain a good conscience? First, by living in obedience to God! We already talked about the way verse 19 refers back to verse 18, concerning our attitudes and actions toward fellow believers. Treating others right is a big part of this. Then, verse 22 tells us that a clear conscience and authority in prayer are ours "because we keep His commandments and do those things that are pleasing in His sight" (NKJV). That does not mean we earn answers to prayer. The moment we think like that, we shut ourselves off from the flow of grace and don't get answers to prayer.[21] God is never our debtor. He gives to us generously out of His grace. All that we receive is by the grace of God, not by our own works of righteousness.[22] However, living in obedience to Him positions us to pray right and receive out of His goodness. When we "keep His commandments and do those things that are pleasing in His sight" (NKJV), we are submitted to Him and can be trusted with spiritual authority.

The conscience is a moral compass that God has built into man's design. It is part of the image of God that we enjoy.[23] God is a moral being; and so are we. The animal kingdom does not have this sense of moral accountability. Your pet dog may lick your hand and snuggle up to you; but it's because you feed him well, and he likes what he gets from you. He does not feel any moral responsibility. Instincts may motivate him to defend his provider. But that's it. I watched a National Geographic documentary about lions. When a male lion defeats the dominate male and takes over the pride, he ruthlessly kills all the cubs sired by the previous male. He does not brood over that terrible act of violence. He feels no remorse whatsoever. He has simply done what his instincts tell him to do; and that's that.

But humans have a sense of conscience. The conscience may be ill-informed. If it is violated it may be defiled or even become seared and virtually inoperative.[24] But all people are equipped by God with a conscience and are accountable to God for responding to that moral sense of right and wrong. It is an important factor in evangelism. It is even more important for the believer. We are responsible to maintain a clear conscience before God.[25] Even if our conscience is incorrect or inadequate in its knowledge, we are not to violate it.[26] We may need to inform it from the word of God. But the conscience is to be maintained free of accusation and offense. Paul taught these things in Romans 14 and 1 Corinthians 8. We don't have time to go into the specifics.[27] But the dictates of conscience depend upon the knowledge that the person has. It is not infallible. Its dictates can be too strict or too lax.[28] But it is an immediate gage that should never be ignored.

The first and most important thing we do to maintain a good conscience is to keep God's commandments and do those things that are pleasing in His sight. The word of God teaches us those commandments. John talks about living in obedience to God's commandments throughout this epistle. He is confronting the false teachings of the Gnostics who would minimize the importance of doing that. We have the sure word of God to show us what to do in keeping God's commandments. We also have the Holy Spirit to convict us and instruct us in righteousness. If we will listen to His guidance, we will do those things that are pleasing to the Father. These behaviors can be objectively seen by others, but they are also known by the person doing them. I know whether I was kind to the clerk at the store or unkind. I know it; and it registers on my conscience. When my conscience is reporting back to me that I am keeping God's commandments and living pleasing to Him, then my heart does not condemn me. I have a clear conscience. That is John's main message in the text.

On the dashboard of my car are gages that warn me if the oil pressure is too low or if the cooling system is too hot. If I forget to fasten my seatbelt, I am alerted to that fact. If a door is ajar, the system will tell me there is a problem.[29] Those gages could be wrong, but they're usually telling me something I need to know and pay attention to. Our conscience serves us in the same way. It tells us something is wrong: something needs to be attended to. It's not enough to acknowledge the warning. That's a first step. But if the temperature warning light is on, I must search that out and correct the cause of the problem.

What am I to do about an accusing conscience? How am I to clear up the accusations? I do that by subjecting myself to the scrutiny of the Holy Spirit. When I sense that all is not well in the conscience, I may not know at first why that is so. It may first come as a rather vague, general discomfort of spirit: a kind of dull, deadened feeling inside. That's when you have to take time before God and ask Him to show you what's wrong. In Psalm 139:23–24 David prayed, "Search me, O God, and know my heart: try me, and know my thoughts: And see if there be any wicked way in me, and lead me in the way everlasting" (KJV). It takes courage to pray that prayer. We're asking God to turn His search light on our soul and search out any violations of right and wrong.

Look at 1 John 3:20. "For if our heart condemns us, God is greater than our heart, and knows all things" (NKJV). The verdict of conscience is not the final word. God knows more than our conscience knows. Now that statement can be a word of warning or a word of comfort depending on the situation.[30]

If my conscience is accusing me, and I submit that to God, I may find that God knows more about the depth of my sin than my conscience was even telling me. My conscience may be telling me I should not have made that unkind remark to my sister in the Lord. But as I deal with that before God, He may show me more. He may show me the pride that was behind it all. It wasn't just that one act; the whole unloving attitude was wrong. I may begin to see other occasions when I have acted that way toward other people and just dismissed them as insignificant. The Holy Spirit may show me the case is worse than I thought. Will I allow Him to probe and get at the root of the matter? As He does, I must confess the sin and turn from it. I may have to go ask people to forgive me. Clearing the conscience can be hard work.

When we help people deal with addictions, this is step 4—11 of the twelve-step program. That's eight of the twelve.[31] Too many people try to get free from habits and additions without addressing issues of conscience. Guilt is a heavy weight to bear. It's hard to get answers to prayer, if we won't clear the conscience. It's not likely that the person will get free and stay free from addiction. When we can't get answers to prayer, it may be time to respond to conscience and deal with the violations.

Clearing the conscience is not something you can do with a general confession that just says, "God forgive me for all the bad things I've done." You cannot repent of those things as a bundled package. You have to turn from each wrong behavior. And before you can turn from it, you have to acknowledge the specific problem. We like the old song that says, "Count your blessings, name them one by one." That is a good thing to do. But sins have to be named one by one as well. It's not that we have sinned in general. There are specific commandments that we have violated. There are specific people that we have wronged. We have to deal with the specifics of sin.

"For if our heart condemns us, God is greater than our heart, and knows all things." I find much comfort in that verse. God has not left us to deal with our sins alone. He has provided all things that pertain to life and godliness.[32] He has made provision for our sin. To maintain a pure conscience, we must avail ourselves of the provisions of the new covenant.

The verdict of our conscience is not the final word. There is a higher court. We can appeal to God and even ask for His help.[33] "My little children," John wrote in chapter 2:1, "I am writing these things to you so that you may not sin" (NASB). If we don't sin, our conscience is free of condemnation. This is ideal. But it's what John says next, that is so comforting. "And if anyone sins, we have an Advocate with the Father, Jesus Christ the righteous; and He Himself is the propitiation for our sins" (NASB). God has made a way for us to clear the conscience. Hebrews 9:14 says, "How much more will the blood of Christ, who through the eternal Spirit offered Himself without blemish to God, cleanse your conscience from dead works to serve the living God?" (NASB). The blood of Christ is there for the unbeliever if he will turn from his sin and put his faith in Christ. But that same blood is also there for the believer who sins. First John 1:7: "But if we walk in the Light as He Himself is in the Light, we have fellowship with one another, and the blood of Jesus His Son cleanses us from all sin." (NASB). Walking in the light includes our willingness to submit to the scrutiny of the Holy Spirit; allow Him to shine the light upon our sin, so that we can repent of it. Then the promise is that "the blood of Jesus His Son cleanses us from all sin." You are not stuck with an accusing conscience. God has made a way for us to clear these things up.

We have to be willing to open our hearts to Him and walk through the process. But it is certainly worth it. First John 1:9 continues, "If we confess our sins, He is faithful and righteous to forgive us our sins and to cleanse us from all unrighteousness" (NASB).

Let me just mention three ways that people commonly deal with an accusing conscience that do not work. One is to offer God dead works, in place of repentance. Instead of clearing up the violation that the conscience is testifying against, they get more religious: they do more good works. Dead works can be actions we would consider bad, or they can be actions we would consider good. They are works done outside the life of God, works not initiated by the Holy Spirit. The conscience will continue to condemn, if we try to substitute good works in place of confessing and repenting of the sin conscience is alerting us to. Another mistake is to justify the violation in our minds. Conscience is condemning us of something we are doing wrong, and we begin to rationalize and excuse ourselves, instead of receiving the correction. The third error is the most common: ignoring the matter as insignificant. Conscience is registering a condemnation, but we just live with the discomfort as a normal part of life. Biblically, it is not normal and should not be considered normal, to live with an accusing conscience. We should be living in all good conscience and enjoying unobstructed intimacy with God.[34]

Sadly, most Christians live under a cloud of guilt, an accumulation of little unattended matters.[35] In that state, the devil robs us of our confidence before God. He steals our peace; he steals our joy; he obstructs answers to prayer that might have been. He is the accuser of the brethren, and he is busy doing his work.[36] But we can cut him off at the knees, if we will pause long enough in our busy lives to do it. It takes some time with God to do this. But it is the best time you will ever spend. Instead of walking around under a cloud of self-condemnation, you can be walking on air. You can be praying with confidence. You can have boldness before God and before man. The conscience has to be cleared of its accusations, and we have to live in obedience to His commandment.

Verse 23 says, "And this is His commandment: that we should believe on the name of His Son Jesus Christ and love one another, as He gave us commandment" (NKJV). John brings all this down to one commandment with two components: believe and love. Our faith must be in Christ and not ourselves. We must know that walking in God's commandments is only possible by the grace of God. We live by the faith of the Son of God. We live in dependence upon Him and His work in our behalf. We manifest that faith by loving one another.

It's a wonderful life when the conscience is cleansed of all accusation. And God has made that available to you and me. He is no respecter of persons.[37] If you want it, and are willing to walk in it, it can be yours. Do you want it?

# Endnotes: Chapter 17

1   Acts 24:16, NKJV.

2   "It's a Wonderful Life" was a movie produced and directed by Frank Capra, based on a story written by Phillip Van Doren Stem. The movie is widely viewed as a Christmas tradition.

3   Warren W. Wiersbe, *Be Real* (Wheaton, IL: Victor Books, 1984), 130: "A 'condemning heart' is one that robs a believer of peace. An 'accusing conscience' is another way to describe it." Concerning *kardia* (translated heart), Donald Burdick writes (p. 272), "John uses the term to refer to the inner man with special emphasis here on the conscience and the feelings."

4   Compare Phil. 4:7 with Rom. 5:1.

5   Fettke. Tom, ed., s. v. "Wonderful Peace," by Warren D. Cornell, p. 500.

6   Burdick, p. 271.

7   Smalley, 201: "John is saying that loving behavior is a means of being reassured in the searching presence of God."

8   Thayer, s. v. "NT:3954."

9   Cf. 2 Pet. 3:9.

10  Cf. Rom. 8:31.

11  Cf. 1 Kings 17:1; 18:17–40.

12  Cf. Dan. 6:1–28.

13  Cf. Acts 4:19–20.

14  Cf. Mark 11:24.

15  Cf. Ps. 66:18; Mark 11:25.

16  Cf. Jas. 4:3.

17  Cf. Rom. 8:26–27.

18  Cf. John 8:29.

19  There is much teaching available about knowing your authority in Christ. That is something we need to know. But we must be willing to keep our conscience free of condemnation in order to operate in that authority effectively.

20  Cf. Acts 10:38.

21  Cf. Phil. 3:3.

22  Cf. Rom. 4:4; 11:6; Gal. 2:21–3:3: Eph. 2:8–9; Phil. 3:9.

23  Cf. Gen. 1:26–27.

24  Cf. Rom. 2:15; 1 Tim. 4:2; Titus 1:15.

25  Cf. 1 Tim. 1:19; 3:9; 2 Tim. 1:3; 1 Pet. 2:19; 3:16.

26  Cf. Rom. 14:14, 20, 23; 1 Cor. 8:7–11.

27  Watchman Nee, *The Spiritual Man: In Three Volumes*, Vol. II (New York: Christian Fellowship Publishers, 1968) pp. 106–127 provides an insightful discussion of conscience.

28  The person with a dull, insensitive conscience needs to be exposed to truth. Hopefully it will awaken his conscience. That way conscience can serve him as its designed to do, and God can lead him to repentance.

29  David L. Allen, *1–3 John: Fellowship in God's Family*, Preaching the Word Series, R. K. Hughes, gen. ed. (Wheaton, IL: Crossway, 2013) p. 163.

30  Smalley, 203. Scholars are divided as to whether John intends to warn or comfort with this statement. The immediate context persuades me that his intention is to comfort. However, God's knowledge of our sins transcends the conscience and is, therefore, more through than the human conscience. On the other hand, He is good and His mercy endures forever (Ps. 136:1; Eph. 2:4; 1 Pet. 2:10). When we appeal our case to God, we are coming to our Father, as well as our Judge.

31  *Twelve Steps and Twelve Traditions*, 40th printing (New York: Alcoholics Anonymous World Services, 1988) 5–9.

32  2 Pet. 1:3.

33  Cf. Rom. 8:32–34.

34  Cf. Heb. 10:22.

35  Cf. Song of Solomon 2:15.

36  Rev. 12:10.

37  Cf. Acts 10:34; John 3:16, "Whoever believes."

# Chapter 18

# Testing the Spirits
## 3:23–4:6

This is His commandment, that we believe in the name of His Son Jesus Christ, and love one another, just as He commanded us. The one who keeps His commandments abides in Him, and He in him. We know by this that He abides in us, by the Spirit whom He has given us. Beloved, do not believe every spirit, but test the spirits to see whether they are from God, because many false prophets have gone out into the world. By this you know the Spirit of God: every spirit that confesses that Jesus Christ has come in the flesh is from God; and every spirit that does not confess Jesus is not from God; this is the *spirit* of the antichrist, of which you have heard that it is coming, and now it is already in the world. You are from God, little children, and have overcome them; because greater is He who is in you than he who is in the world. They are from the world; therefore they speak *as* from the world, and the world listens to them. We are from God; he who knows God listens to us; he who is not from God does not listen to us. By this we know the spirit of truth and the spirit of error.

1 John 3:23–4:6, NASB

Expository Message

John has been giving objective tests of true salvation. First John 3:23 is a good summary of what he has been saying. "This is His commandment, that we believe in the name of His Son Jesus Christ, and love one another, just as He commanded us."[1] The belief or faith that John is talking about always expresses itself in the person's behavior.[2] It's not just a philosophical assent to truth. It is a commitment to walk in the truth. We act on what we really believe.[3] To believe in "the name of His Son Jesus Christ" is to put your trust in Him and commit yourself to Him. That kind of belief is demonstrated by the way we love one another. The actions of anyone who professes Christianity can be objectively observed and evaluated.

John follows up in verse 24. "The one who keeps His commandments abides in Him." That's an observable, object test. You can look at a person's life and make some determination as to whether that person is a real Christian or not. Only God can make the final determination. But we are given objective criteria that should first be applied to ourselves, then applied to those who say they are Christians.[4] This is particularly important when it comes to leaders and teachers. We are supposed to examine their lives for evidence that their walk is consistent with their talk. Paul wrote in 2 Timothy 3:10, "You, however, know all about my teaching, my way of life, my purpose, faith, patience, love, endurance" (NIV). We don't just have the right to examine these things; we have a responsibility to do so. We don't do it with a critical spirit. We don't do it with a harsh desire to find something wrong. We do it with a meek, humble spirit; but we do it. John will address that responsibility more fully in chapter 4 of this epistle.

In 3:24 the apostle gives a subjective test. "We know by this that He abides in us, by the Spirit whom He has given us." "The Spirit Himself bears witness with our spirit," as Paul put it in Rom. 8:16 (NKJV). There is a very real interaction that we have with the Holy Spirit. We are aware of His presence operating in our lives. We cannot see Him with the natural eye, but we know when we have grieved Him. We know when He is speaking to us and guiding us. We know when He is empowering us to pray according to the will of God.[5] We have a very real relationship with the Holy Spirit that the world does not know or understand. John makes

234

the point again in verse 13 of the next chapter. "By this we know that we abide in Him and He in us, because He has given us of His Spirit" (NASB).

That test is very subjective, and John understands that. It's something that goes on internally and is very hard to identify objectively. So immediately after his statement in 3:24, John gives a word of caution and provides an objective way to make sure it is the Holy Spirit and not some other spirit.[6]

## A WORD OF CAUTION

John begins chapter 4 with this word of caution in verse 1. "Beloved, do not believe every spirit." We have an adversary who counterfeits the things of God. There is a cosmic conflict going on the spiritual realm, and, whether we like it or not, we are in the middle of it. Paul gives a similar warning in Ephesians 6:11–12.

> Put on the full armor of God, so that you will be able to stand firm against the schemes of the devil. For our struggle is not against flesh and blood, but against the rulers, against the powers, against the world forces of this darkness, against the spiritual *forces* of wickedness in the heavenly *places* (NASB).

God is working in our behalf to bring us into the full manifestation of His purposes and good plans for our future. Satan, the adversary, is working in opposition to that. His main strategy is deception. He often transforms himself into an angel of light and his ministers present themselves as ministers of righteousness.[7] He is a liar from the beginning and the father of lies.[8] The more effective you are for God, the more he wants to trip you up and neutralize your testimony.

John says, "Do not believe every spirit." Why? "Because many false prophets have gone out into the world." Prophets are people who speak under the inspiration of God. Spiritual leaders in the church are supposed to be speaking under the inspiration of the Holy Spirit. First Peter 4:11 says, "If anyone speaks, let him speak as the oracles of God. If anyone ministers, let him do it as with the ability which God supplies" (NKJV).

The New Testament church is to be a prophetic people.[9] John is not warning against everything supernatural. That would be counter to the purposes of God. Jesus sent the Holy Spirit on the Day of Pentecost, so we could be supernaturally empowered to fulfill the Great Commission.[10] I'm amazed at the teachers who use this verse as a springboard to oppose everything that is supernatural. John is not contending for a dead orthodoxy, emptied of the life-giving anointing of the Holy Spirit. But, because we operate in the Spirit; because we operate in the supernatural; because we operate in the prophetic, we must know the difference between the genuine and the counterfeit. We must not gullibly believe every spirit. We must be "wise as serpents and harmless as doves" (Matt. 10:16, KJV). So, John tells us to "test the spirits whether they are from God."

On January 24, 1848, James Marshall discovered gold in California.[11] The "forty-niners" soon followed, and the gold rush was on.

> But would-be prospectors quickly learned that not everything that appeared to be gold actually was. Riverbeds and rock quarries could be full of golden specks that were nevertheless entirely worthless. The "fool's gold" was iron pyrite, and miners had to be careful to distinguish it from the real thing. . . . So, they developed tests to discern what was genuine from what was not. One test involved biting the rock in question. Real gold is softer than a human tooth, whereas fool's is harder.[12]

So, if the bite pressed into the metal, it was likely gold. That test was a valuable thing to know. In fact, their future depended on it.

John is telling his readers to beware. Not everyone who says, "Lord, Lord," is really following Christ. "Many false prophets have gone out into the world." Jesus said, "Beware of false prophets, who come to you in sheep's clothing, but inwardly they are ravening wolves" (Matt. 7:15, NASB).

I read an article yesterday about "a 25-year-old California man" who was playing the online game "Call of Duty." He got upset over a small bet on a game. In retaliation he did what is called "swatting." He called in "a false 911 report to get a SWAT team to descend" on the address.

The details of his false report indicated that the man at the address had already killed, was holding hostages, and was extremely dangerous. The caller mistakenly gave the wrong address; it was the residence of a person who didn't even play "Call of Duty." When the SWAT team arrived, the resident came to the door to see what was going on. "As police told him to put his hands up, [Andrew] Finch moved a hand toward the area of his waistband - a common place where guns are concealed. An officer, fearing the man was reaching for a gun, fired a single shot. Finch died a few minutes later at a hospital and was found to be unarmed." Andrew Finch is dead because someone told a lie.[13]

The old saying, "Sticks and stones may break my bones, but words will never hurt me" is far from true. Many a soul has been destroyed by the lies of the devil. Many gullible people have been robbed of their savings. Worse, many have lost their souls, by believing a lie. Truth versus error is a matter of life and death. In Andrew Finch's case it was physical death. In many cases, it involves spiritual death.

## AN OBJECTIVE TEST

So, John gives an objective test to determine whether a prophet, and the spirit behind that prophet, is speaking from God or from the devil. First John 4.2 begins, "By this you know." I'm going to tell you the test. I'm going to tell you how to tell a true prophet or teacher from a false one. "By this you know the Spirit of God: every spirit that confesses that Jesus Christ has come in the flesh is from God." That is a test that any of us can use. We simply watch and listen to the person's message and attitude toward Jesus Christ. The supernatural gift of discerning of spirits may operate, but if not, we still have this test.[14]

John is intentional about the expression "Jesus Christ." He is combating error that would separate the two. Gnostics were teaching a separation between Jesus of Nazareth (the man) and Christ (the divine). There were a variety of errors. Some said that Jesus was only a man, but the eternal Christ came upon him at his baptism. Then Christ left him before the cross, so that Jesus died as a mere man.[15] It is a twisted, inadequate view of who Jesus is. John is emphasizing the unity of the person Jesus Christ. The Son of God, the Messiah, the Christ came as the babe born in a manger whose name is Jesus. He is fully God and fully man; one person with two natures.[16]

The Mormons teach that, rather than being God, before his incarnation, Jesus was a created being, the brother of Lucifer. Jehovah's Witness teach that Jesus was Michael the Archangel before his incarnation.[17] Notice how these cults will give some honor to Jesus, but they will not honor Him as God, the Son. They deny his deity. The liberal modernist preachers do the same thing in a different way. They say Jesus was a good man, a prophet, a teacher of truth. But they deny His deity as well. These modern naturalists begin with their presupposition that the supernatural can't happen. Then they judge the Bible against their presupposition. They say it couldn't be true because it violates natural laws. But the "whole design of the Bible is to challenge presuppositions, not to be controlled by them."[18] These false teachers do not receive the revelation of Scripture. As a result, they preach a Jesus who is not divine. In 2 Corinthians 11:4 Paul warns us of those who would come preaching "another Jesus." He told the Galatians, "But though we, or an angel from heaven, preach any other gospel unto you than that which we have preached unto you, let him be accursed" (Gal. 1:8, KJV). When it comes to who Jesus is, both Paul and John are unbendable and non-negotiable in their doctrine.

Sometimes people don't know where to draw the line in their fellowship with others who claim the name of Jesus. John helps us with that. He defines the line clearly. Listen to what John says in his second epistle, verse 7–11.

> For many deceivers have gone out into the world, those who do not acknowledge Jesus Christ *as* coming in the flesh.[19] This is the deceiver and the antichrist. Watch yourselves, that you do not lose what we have accomplished, but that you may receive a full reward. Anyone who goes too far and does not abide in the teaching of Christ, does not have God; the one who abides in the teaching, he has both the Father and the Son. If anyone comes to you and does not bring this teaching, do not receive him into *your* house, and do not give him a greeting; for the one who gives him a greeting participates in his evil deeds (NASB).

It's an alarming thought that we might be sharing in another's evil deeds by condoning or supporting him. It might seem loving to do so. But John is warning us not to do it.

There is a powerful ecumenical movement in the world today. Politicians and religious leaders work with the United Nations to create world peace and form one religious system. They do not understand why people like you and me will not go along. It is because we believe the Bible. We see, in Revelation 13 and 2 Thessalonians 2, where it is all headed. Their promise of love and brotherhood will culminate in evil, oppressive control, and persecution of true believers. Its roots are in Babel, and it is an anti-God movement. We will not go along with the compromises. Instead, we will obey scriptural mandates like the one I just read. We will be called bigots, obstructionists, and be persecuted for the stand. But I would rather obey God than man.

There are many differences in interpretation of the Bible that are not grounds for breaking fellowship with other believers. For instance, some Christians believe in a pre-tribulation rapture; others think it is mid-tribulation; and some interpret it as post-tribulation. As strong as your convictions may be on those issues, it is not a valid reason for discontinuing fellowship with another Christian. We believe the gifts of the Spirit are for today. But I don't disfellowship other believers because they disagree with me on those subjects. Ephesians 4 tells us to work at keeping the unity of the Spirit in the bond of peace. Ephesians 4 is talking about unity between true believers. It is not talking about unity with those who deny Christ for who He is. The motto adopted as early as 1627 is a good rule of thumb. "In essentials unity, in non-essentials liberty, in all things charity [or love]."[20]

Why does John place so much emphasis on the incarnation? He opened this epistle talking about it. He began his gospel, "In the beginning was the Word, and the Word was with God, and the Word was God" (KJV). John 1:14 says, "And the Word was made flesh, and dwelt among us, (and we beheld his glory, the glory as of the only begotten of the Father,) full of grace and truth" (KJV). Without the incarnation, God's way of salvation falls apart.[21] For the cross to be effective for our atonement, Jesus had to be fully man. Jesus's success is our rescue from Adam's failure. In Romans 5:19 we read, "For as through the one man's disobedience the many were made sinners, even so through the obedience of the One the

239

many will be made righteous" (NASB). Adam committed one unrighteous act that plunged humanity into judgment and separation from God. Jesus committed one righteous act that provides redemption for all of Adam's race who will receive it. To redeem humanity, Jesus had to be human. He had to be the last Adam.

Remember how God gave dominion of the earth to Adam. In Genesis 1:28 God said to Adam and Eve, "Be fruitful and multiply; fill the earth and subdue it; have dominion over the fish of the sea, over the birds of the air, and over every living thing that moves on the earth" (NKJV). God delegated dominion of the earth to Adam. Adam lost that to the Serpent. Jesus took it back. He crushed the head of the Serpent on the cross and reclaimed dominion.[22] We see the celebration of that in Revelation 5 when Jesus is found worthy to open the scroll. That scroll is the title deed to creation, encumbered by Adam, redeemed by Christ.[23] "And they sang a new song, saying: 'You are worthy to take the scroll, And to open its seals; For You were slain, And have redeemed us to God by Your blood Out of every tribe and tongue and people and nation'" (NKJV). Jesus became one of us, so that He could be our kinsman-redeemer. "Therefore, since the children share in flesh and blood, He Himself likewise also partook of the same, that through death He might render powerless him who had the power of death, that is, the devil" (Heb. 2:14, NASB). He became partaker of flesh and blood so that He could die on the cross as our representative. He had to identify with us in that way to affect our salvation. He had to become fully man and suffer as a man to pay the price of redemption.

But he also had to be fully God. For a mere man could never pay the full price of our redemption. A mere man might pay the price for one man if he were sinless and qualified before God to do it. But a man or an angel could never qualify to redeem *all* of mankind. Only God could do that! Only the God-man Jesus was able to do it. His life was of endless worth.[24] His blood is of endless worth. Therefore, the full price was paid. "By this you know the Spirit of God: Every spirit that confesses that Jesus Christ has come in the flesh is from God."

In verse 3 we have the test reinforced, as John states it in negative terms as well. "And every spirit that does not confess that Jesus Christ has come in the flesh is not of God. And this is the spirit of the Antichrist, which you have heard was coming, and is now already in the world" (NKJV).

You remember our teaching in chapter two concerning the antichrist spirit. By calling it antichrist and by contrasting the error with the truth, John is leaving no room for middle ground.[25] You either confess Christ "for who He is" or you deny Him "for who He is." You are either "of God" or "not of God." For or against, which is it? What will you do with Christ? Will you receive Him for who He is and follow Him as a disciple? Or will you reject Him as Lord and Savior? People like to think they stand somewhere in the vague middle. "I don't serve Christ, but I'm not against Him either." But Jesus said in Matthew 12:30, "He who is not with Me is against Me." (NASB). Then John puts it this way in our text, "And every spirit that does not confess that Jesus Christ has come in the flesh is not of God."

This week, I was reading in a blog site called *Rational Doubt*. Linda LaScola's page is entitled "How Can Seminary-Educated Pastors Preach the Bible?" Her position, as one who rejects the reliability of Scripture, is that "Seminary-Educated Pastors" don't really believe the Bible as inspired Scripture. Their seminary education has taught them that the Bible is full of contradictions and is not authoritative; they simply ignore those facts and preach from the Bible anyway.

As I read the thread, I was grieved by comments written by people in ministry positions denying the inspiration and inerrancy of Scripture. The following are some of the comments on that site. They demonstrate how the errors John addresses in this epistle are errors we must address in today's church environment. The mindset of these "ministers" is quite alarming. The first comment is from a person who refers to himself as "Pastor Disaster." Pastor Disaster writes:

> I am currently a full-time pastor. We have several pastors that share teaching duties. So, I don't have to teach/preach every week. Being a skeptic and new agnostic, I am the only pastor here who questions the bible/god etc. To maintain my position I have to be quite stealthy. I behave as missionaries do in Christian-hostile countries. When I preach I don't violate what I hold to be true. Though I do not believe the bible inerrant or any such nonsense I find enough scripture to use to teach inclusivity, anti-dogmatism and the like. I do t (*sic*) feel the need to lie.[26]

Did you know that people who think like that are actively filling pulpits? The stealth of Pastor Disaster and those like him is the reason I say, don't just listen to what a pastor says, listen to what he avoids saying. Additionally, examine his lifestyle. Someone who uses the handle "Ctcss" responds to Pastor Disaster in this way:

> . . . I don't think it much matters whether one explicitly believes in God, or has large doubts, or doesn't believe at all. Whoever is interested in ministering brings whatever tools and compassion they have to try to help others. That's why this is so neat. It moves the silliness of 'belief vs non-belief' to the sidelines (where it belongs) and tries to express loving-kindness and help towards others.[27]

So, in their minds they claim to be taking the high ground by simply doing good works. Linda LaScola (editor of the blog site) writes:

> . . . I should add that I know of other non-believing clergy—interviewed in the study, who do their part in easing fear and guilt too—making it easier to (*sic*) people to stay within a religious community by assuring them that they don't need to believe certain things to be good people and valued members of the community.[28]

Ironically, a person who assumes the name, "Without Malice," writes a comment that is full of malice.[29] I won't take time to repeat it here.

We currently have a problem in the American church; it is a very serious problem; it is similar to the problem John was dealing with in the first century.[30] We need the instruction the Apostle John gives in this letter to deal with the problem effectively. We must apply the tests of authentic Christianity that the Apostle John provides. Writers on that blog seem to think what you believe doesn't really matter. But John's position is that it is of supreme importance.

The word translated *confess* in 1 John 4:2–3 means more than just acknowledgement of the declared truth. It includes that; but it goes beyond that. It is a commitment to the truth and to the person who is The Truth.

Even the demons acknowledged the divinity of Jesus. In Mark 1:24 an unclean spirit cried out to Jesus, "I know who You are — the Holy One of God!" (NASB). But they did not confess Jesus the way John is talking about.[31] Our text uses the same word employed in Romans 10:9, "That if you confess with your mouth Jesus *as* Lord and believe in your heart that God raised Him from the dead, you will be saved" (NASB). The confession includes public acknowledgement of the proposition, but it also includes a personal commit to it and commitment to Christ Himself.[32]

## A WORD OF ENCOURAGEMENT

For those who confess Jesus Christ, John gives this word of encouragement in verse 4. "You are from God, little children, and have overcome them; because greater is He who is in you than he who is in the world." The word of caution has been given to these Christians, but a word of comfort is in order as well. They have not been deceived by the antichrist spirit. The false prophets have not been able to lead them astray. They still need to be on their guard. They still need to prove all things and test the spirits.[33] But take heart in this: "You are from God, little children, and have overcome them." The false prophets did not prevail. You're still walking in the light.

The word translated overcome is *nikaō*.[34] The Nike brand takes its name from that Greek word.[35] It is a theme John speaks of often. How were they able to overcome? Was it because they were so clever, so insightful? No, the false prophets may have been intellectually superior to them. Was it their vast knowledge or tenacious willpower? No, it's "because greater is He who is in you than he who is in the world" (NASB). The Holy Spirit, the Spirit of Truth has protected you and guided you. You have an anointing, 1 John 2:27, that teaches you what you need to know. He is the reason you have prevailed. And He is the One to rely on in the future.

In verses 5–6 we see John's test expanded. He has given us a key doctrinal test, the incarnation of Christ Jesus. It is designed to meet the needs of his readers. It addresses the situation they are facing. It confronts errors that are being pushed by false prophets at that church. It not exhaustive. There are other tests in the Bible. God had given Israel some tests. In Deuteronomy 18:22, God tells them that if someone prophecies the future and the prophecy does not come to pass, then that was not of God. In Deuteronomy 13, God says that even if prophecies come to pass, and the prophet works signs and wonders, if he is trying to lead them astray and get them to serve some other god, then it is a false prophet. Paul says that inspired speaking should be judged. In 1 Corinthians 14:3 he says prophecy should edify, exhort, or comfort. The primary test in the New Testament is the honor and glory given to Jesus. John 16:14 tells us the Holy Spirit will glory Jesus. The more a message distracts from Jesus, the more suspect it is. We don't have time to look at all the other tests. But just realize the Bible has more to say on this subject. In this study, we simply want to understand what John is telling us in the text.

## THE TEST EXPANDED

Look at verses 5–6: "They are from the world; therefore they speak *as* from the world, and the world listens to them. We are from God; he who knows God listens to us; he who is not from God does not listen to us. By this we know the spirit of truth and the spirit of error." That last sentence lets us know that John is still showing us how to test the spirits. He has given us the doctrinal test of the incarnation. But here he expands that considerably. Notice what he says in the first part of verse 6. "We are from God." Who are the *we* in that statement? Obviously, it would include the Apostle John. Broadly speaking *we* might include all those who belong to God. But John is using the word *we* in the same way he did at the beginning of this letter. "That which was from the beginning, which we have heard, which we have seen with our eyes, which we have looked upon, and our hands have handled, of the Word of life" (1 John 1:1, KJV). "We" refers to the apostles. The person "who is not from God does not listen to us." He refuses to hear the apostles and their message. Those who know God gladly hear the apostles.

How do we hear the apostles today? We do it exactly as we're doing it right now. We read and apply the message of the New Testament. Who wrote the New Testament? The apostles and those in their teams. So, John expands the test to include the whole New Testament. Those who are of God will embrace the New Testament and receive its message. Those who are not of God will not hear it.

The principle stated in these two verses can be extended a bit further. The world loves to hear those who speak their own values, goals, and opinions.[36] They do not like to hear those who speak from God. The message from God calls them to account and makes them uncomfortable. The gospel calls on us to deny self and follow Jesus. It is not a message the flesh wants to hear. Only those who have been captured by God's love want it. Proverbs 29:27 says, "An unjust man is an abomination to the just: and he that is upright in the way is abomination to the wicked" (KJV). It's not just that their message is different. They are of a different spirit. There are two kingdoms that are opposed to one another. So here is another application. You can tell a lot about the speaker by the crowd that wants to hear him speak. If the ungodly are eating it up and loving it, it's probably a message that agrees with their carnal nature. A godly person will walk away from that speaker. On the other hand, a godly crowd will gravitate to a godly speaker.

So, what does John give us in this text? He cautions us about deception and tells us to test the spirits. He gives us an essential doctrinal test: Jesus's incarnation. The confession is not only to propositional truth, but to the *person* Christ Himself. "Every spirit that confesses that Jesus Christ has come in the flesh is from God." He encourages us in our victory over error. Greater is He who is in you than he who is in the world. Finally, John expands the test to include a willingness to hear the apostles and their doctrine. We have their doctrine in the New Testament. You are reading this book because you want to hear truth from Scripture. May that love for the truth always reside in you. Keep pursuing truth; but be discerning in the process. Don't be gullible. "Beloved, do not believe every spirit, but test the spirits to see whether they are from God."

# Endnotes: Chapter 18

1 In chapter 3, John has been exhorting his readers to love on another. His mention of the Holy Spirit in 3:24 as the affirmer of our life in God, launches him into this teaching on how to objectively test the spirits. Then notice in 4:7, he resumes his exhortation that they love one another: "Beloved, let us love one another" (NASB).

2 Colin Brown, ed., vol. 1, s. v. *"pistis,"* by Otto Michel, p. 604. Commenting on James' teaching, Otto Mitchel writes, "He demands renunciation of all conduct that conflicts with living faith and confession (1:6ff.). For him, faith and obedient conduct are indissolubly linked."

3 Cf. Jas. 2:17–20.

4 Cf. Matt. 7:15–21; Luke 6:40–49.

5 Cf. Eph. 4:30; John 16:13; Rom. 8:26.

6 Dodd, 115.

7 2 Cor. 11:14–15.

8 John 8:44.

9 Roger Stronstad, *The Prophethood of All Believers: A Study in Luke's Charismatic Theology* (London: Sheffield Academic Press, 2003), 66: ". . . just as Jesus was the Spirit-anointed prophet, so the disciples, as heirs and successors to his prophetic ministry, become a community of Spirit-baptized prophets, the prophethood of all believers."

10 Cf. Acts 1:8.

11 Richard H. Peterson, "James Marshall: California's Gold Discover," *Historynet.* Retrieved Dec. 27, 2017 at http://www.historynet.com/james-marshall-californias-gold-discoverer.htm.

12 John MacArthur, *The MacArthur New Testament Commentary: 1–3 John,* 152.

13 Benjamin Brown, "Man arrested in 'Call of Duty' 'swatting' hoax that led to fatal police shooting," *Fox News.* Retrieved Dec. 28, 2017 at http://www.foxnews.com/us/2017/12/30/man-arrested-in-call-duty-swatting-hoax-that-led-to-fatal-police-shooting.print.html.

14 Cf. 1 Cor. 12:10.

15 Walter C. Kaisere, Jr., P. H. Davids, F. F. Bruce, M. T. Brauch, *Hard Sayings of the Bible* (Downers Grove: IL: InterVarsity Press, 1996) 747. This was the Cerinthian heresy. The authors also write, "The docetic heresy, on the other hand, argued that Jesus was not a real human being (not truly 'in the flesh'), but only appeared to be human."

16 Martin Lloyd-Jones, *Life in Christ: Studies in 1 John* (Wheaton, IL: Crossway, 2002) 414.

17 Allen, 179. Cults. like Christian Science, Mormonism, and others really offer nothing new, although they proport to do so. In essence, their teachings are some variation of the old Gnostic denials of the true nature of Jesus Christ.

18 McQuilkin, 32.

19 Our text in 1 John 4 refers to Christ's first coming in the flesh. This verse may refer to Christ's second coming in the flesh. However, Burdick (p. 425) follows Lenski's lead in identifying it as a timeless present.

20 Philip Schaff, *History of the Christian Church,* Vol. 7, 1910, reprint (Grand Rapids: Eerdmans, 1977) 659.

21 Raymond E. Brown, 74, 76.

22 Cf. Gen. 3:15; Col. 2:15.

23 Criswell, *Expository Sermons on Revelation*, Vol. 3, 52–64.

24 Lloyd -Jones, 417.

25 Smalley, 223.

26 Linda LaScola blog entitled "How Can Seminary-Educated Pastors Preach the Bible," *Rational Doubt*, Sept. 11, 2014. Retrieved Dec. 28, 2017 at http://www.patheos.com/blogs/rationaldoubt/2014/09/how-can-seminary-educated-pastors-preach-the-bible/.

27 Ibid.

28 Ibid.

29 Ibid.

30 Cf. 1 Thess. 2:1-12; Titus 2:1, 7-11; Jude 4, "For certain men have crept in unnoticed. . . ."

31 Stedman, 301. Cf. Smalley, 223.

32 Burdick, 295. Burdick makes an interesting case that this passage should be translated ". . . confess Jesus-Christ-come-in-flesh," and the word "that" should not be added in the translation. He agrees with A. E. Brooke and understands the confession as referring, not just to the propositional fact of the incarnation, but of the Incarnate Christ Himself. Of course, confessing the Incarnate Christ would require agreement with the incarnation doctrine.

33 Cf. 1 Thess. 5:21.

34 *Nikaō* is in the perfect tense which "suggests a victory already accomplished, but also one which has continuing effects in the present. . . ." Smalley, 226. Cf. John 16:33.

35 Allen, 181.

36 The world's message that revolves around "self" can easily be communicated with a Christian veneer, using a few Christian terms and expressions here and there. Our discernment must see beyond the surface to the essential nature of the message. Is it self-promoting or Christ-promoting?

CHAPTER 19

# Why We Love
## 4:7–12

Beloved, let us love one another, for love is from God;
and everyone who loves[1] is born of God and knows God.
The one who does not love does not know God, for God
is love. By this the love of God was manifested in us, that
God has sent His only begotten Son into the world so that
we might live through Him. In this is love, not that we
loved God, but that He loved us and sent His Son to be
the propitiation for our sins. Beloved, if God so loved us,
we also ought to love one another. No one has seen God
at any time; if we love one another, God abides in us, and
His love is perfected in us.

1 John 4:7–12, NASB

### Expository Message

John is teaching us to love one another. That is his stated objective in this
passage. His opening sentence begins, "Beloved, let us love one another."
He teaches doctrine, but the ethical application is his purpose. "Beloved,
if God so loved us, we also ought to love one another." This is God's goal
for your life and my life, that we become people who love other people.
It's quite a journey from the selfish creature we were before we were born
again. Fallen man is nothing but a bundle of selfishness. Fallen man has

248

no capacity to love the way John is talking about here. Some people are born with sweeter personalities than others. But John is not talking about human sweetness. Human sweetness is not free from the self-interest of the old nature. Some people are sweet because they feel that gets them more of what they want than not being sweet. The love John is calling us to is unselfish, unconditional, and unchanged by the response it gets from others. Today we learn about this love. Today we learn a little more about how to love one another. I want to address in these verses, four reasons for loving one another.

## LOVE'S ORIGIN

First, love is from God. God is the source of the love we're talking about here. In the previous six verses, John has been teaching us that love must be discerning. "Try the spirits," John says in verse one of this chapter.[2] He doesn't just tell us to test the spirits, but he instructs us in how to test them. That was our subject in the previous chapter. In verse 7 the focus comes back to the imperative he stated back in 3:11. "For this is the message which you have heard from the beginning, that we should love one another" (NASB). That's the goal: "That we should love one another." Are you loving your brothers and sisters in Christ? Is that demonstrated in the way you treat them? The Pharisees of Jesus day were very religious. They attended services every Saturday. They tithed down to the penny. They studied the Bible all the time. But there was no love in their hearts toward other people. Everything they did was for themselves. Even their benevolence was for self-satisfaction and self-promotion. They weren't really loving people; they were manipulating them for their own purposes. God wants you and me to have the real thing.

Let's take a closer look at verse 7. "Beloved, let us love one another, for love is from God; and everyone who loves is born of God and knows God" (NASB). There are some subtilties in the Greek that are helpful to understand in that statement. The King James Version says, "For love is *of* God" (emphasis mine). But it should be translated "For love is *from* God." That's the way most newer versions translate it. The New International Version says, "For love comes from God." God is the source of this love. You can't manufacture it yourself. You can only get it from Him. Of course, love is *of* God. But that doesn't tell us much. John is telling us that this special kind of love is from no other spirit than the Holy Spirit.

John is also very specific about the kind of love we are to practice. The Greek brings this out, first, by attaching the article to the word agapē. It is "the" love God operates in. It is "the" love, not just love in general. It is the real, true love from above.[3] John is also using a word for love, agapē, that was not commonly used in the culture.[4] To understand John's teaching, we must be clear on what kind of love John is talking about. It is self-giving, not self-serving. It is not anything the natural man can practice. Its only source is the new nature. Only those born of the Spirit are equipped to practice it. That's why John says, "And everyone who loves is born of God and knows God." Then he states the concept again in the negative. Verse 8 says, "The one who does not love does not know God." (NASB). Either the new nature is there bearing fruit in the person's life, or the new nature is not there because the person has not been born again.[5] John is not talking about *philia* love, which can be expressed by fallen man. John is not talking about *erōs*, which is erotic love. He is talking about the love that comes from God alone. Of course, we already talked about that being a test of genuine salvation when we expounded on 3:14.

John's teaching can become very distorted, if people begin with a wrong concept of the love he is teaching. Most cults speak often about love. They lure people in with their deceptive talk.[6] Cults often use Christian terminology with their own definition attached to it. On the surface, it sounds right. But it is actually a lie. Those drawn into the Jim Jones cult were attracted to a message of love. It was a message that appealed to the carnal mind. In the end, it proved to be something altogether different from agapē. In the end, it produced death.[7]

The love John is talking about produces life. It comes from God. And because it is from God, it is something we should embrace and practice. We ought to agapē one another (unselfishly care for one another), because that motivation comes from God.

## GOD'S NATURE

Secondly, we ought to love one another because *God is love*. That is His essential nature. What does that brief sentence say to us about God?

God is personal.[8] It does not say, "Love is God." The Greek does not allow for it.[9] The overall teaching of New Testament refutes it. God is not impersonal. He is not just a force. He is not "everything." Pantheism is a lie. He is not a principle you can manipulate. A common error people make is to try to relate to God as a set of principles. If I confess this and claim that in the right way, I can have it. No, you will have it because your loving Father in heaven gives it to you. Solomon didn't even ask for wealth or honor, but God gave it to him. Why? Was it because Solomon set his heart on those things and claimed them? No, it was first because of the overflowing generosity and grace of God. He received it because he aligned himself with the heart of God.[10] God is personal. You will give account to a person. To know God is more than to know about a principle of love or some set of laws. It is person-to-person, spirit-to-spirit. "When you pray, say, 'Our Father'"[11] Talk to a person; don't try to manipulate a set of laws and principles to your own advantage.[12]

God is eternal. That's a hard concept for us to grasp, because everything else had a beginning. But God is the great "I AM."[13] He always was and always will be. He exits in the eternal present. "In the beginning God."[14] He was there before anything else was.

God is Trinitarian. He exits as three persons in perfect unity. The unity is beyond our full comprehension. But there are some things we know. We know from our text that God is love. He exits in a love relationship. The Father is giving of Himself to the Son and Holy Spirit in love. The Son loves the Father and the Spirit. The Holy Spirit bonds with the Father and the Son in love. Love is the essential character of God. Agapē love is not self-centered. First Corinthians 13:4–5 says, "Love is patient, love is kind *and* is not jealous; love does not brag *and* is not arrogant, does not act unbecomingly; it does not seek its own." (NASB). It does not seek its own; it is not selfish; is not self-centered.

Before angels ever existed, before man was created, "God is love." God was acting in love in the Trinitarian Godhead. The Father was loving the Son and the Spirit. Each person of the Godhead was *other orientated* in active love. For John's statement to be eternally true, God must be more than one person. Love only exists as it is expressed toward another. If God were a solitary individual in eternity past, He could not be love. The Muslim's God, Allah, is not love. Love must be expressed toward another.

Scripture reveals God as Trinitarian.[15] The word Trinity is not in the Bible. It is, however, a useful theological term expressing what is revealed all through the New Testament. We see all three persons active at Jesus's baptism. The Son is submitting himself to baptism "to fulfill all righteousness." The Spirit descends upon Him like a dove. The Father speaks from heaven, "This is my beloved Son, in whom I am well pleased."[16] The whole plan of redemption involves all three persons of the Trinity. Every time Jesus refers to the Father, you have a declaration of Trinitarian truth. Every time He refers to the Holy Spirit, you have a similar declaration. Listen to His words in John 14:16–17. "I will ask the Father, [1st person of the Trinity] and He will give you another Helper, that He may be with you forever; that is the Spirit of truth, [3rd person of the Trinity] whom the world cannot receive." (NASB). All that is spoken by the 2nd person of the Trinity. You cannot make any sense of the New Testament without the revelation of the Trinity. To recognize Jesus Christ for who He really is requires an acknowledgement of the Trinity. The foundation for understanding John's statement in our text is God in three persons. The Eternal Father forever exists loving the Son and the Spirit. If He existed without the Son and the Spirit, He did not exist in love.[17] The nature of God is love, eternally expressed in the Trinitarian Godhead community of three.

Why is this so very important? Nothing will affect the way you live as much as your concept of God. First it affects your worldview. "The fool has said in his heart there is no God."[18] He convinces himself, there is no God. He is a fool. Based on that fundamental error, he concludes that man is only a product of evolutionary chance. His low view of humanity sees nothing of the image of God there. For him, man is just an intelligent animal. Do you see how all that affects his choices? If the baby in a mother's womb is nothing but evolutionary material, snuff it out for convenience sake. There is no sanctity of human life in his thinking. There is no moral accountability to a personal God in his thinking. Anything goes, if there is no God. Every man for himself! Of course, there is some social restraint, if that serves his selfish ends. But all his actions are about self-interest. Even his daily work is sin. Proverbs 21:4: "An high look, and a proud heart, and the plowing of the wicked, is sin" (KJV). We would have expected the high look and proud heart to be sin. But even the plowing of the wicked is sin, because it is all done out of selfish motives.

That which you worship as god will ultimately determine what you become. Get your understanding of God right, for it is foundational to everything. Israel turned from Jehovah to idols. God spoke to them in Jeremiah 2:5. "This is what the LORD says: 'What fault did your fathers find in me, that they strayed so far from me? They followed worthless idols and became worthless themselves'" (NIV). Did you catch that last sentence? "They followed worthless idols and became worthless themselves." The King James Version says, "Have walked after vanity, and are become vain?"[19] Second Kings 17:15 gives a little fuller explanation. "They rejected his decrees and the covenant he had made with their fathers and the warnings he had given them. They followed worthless idols and themselves became worthless." (NIV). That which you follow, that which you direct your attention to and give your affection to, that which you worship, you become like it. That's why pornography and materialism are so damaging. That's why following the vanities of this world is so problematic. It changes who you are. It twists and distorts the personality. Romans 1 gives a vivid description of the changes that happen to people when they follow sin. You can't keep it external. It imprints the soul. But there is good news. When we worship God out of a sincere heart, change also occurs. And it is change for the better. Listen to Paul's declaration in 2 Corinthians 3:18: "But we all, with unveiled face, beholding as in a mirror the glory of the Lord, are being transformed into the same image from glory to glory, just as from the Lord, the Spirit" (NASB). When we see the Lord as He really is, we are transformed into His image, from glory to glory. It's progressive, but it's real.

John makes two key statements about the nature of God that must be understood together. In 1 John 1:5 he says God is light. "This is the message we have heard from Him and announce to you, that God is Light, and in Him there is no darkness at all" (NASB). Secondly, we have the statement in our text that God is love. That is restated in 4:16: "God is love, and the one who abides in love abides in God, and God abides in him" (NASB). The eternal life of God is characterized by light (which speaks of purity, truth, and holiness) and by love.[20] Those two words describe the essential nature of God. God's love is unconditional. What does that mean? It means it is not dependent on the qualities or actions of its object. God loves because He is love. Human love is a response to something attractive in the object loved. Agapē love is not God responding to us. It is proactive. It is based on who He is. Verse 10 of our text says, "In this is love, not that we loved God, but that He loved us." (NASB). The beginning point is "God is love." He initiated our salvation because He loves us. It wasn't us loving God and trying to find Him, as many false religions teach it. He is God operating out of His nature of love and reaching out to us in love. John 3:16 says, "For God so loved." (KJV). That is what initiated our salvation.

Many people erroneously set God's love in opposition to His righteousness. But that is the wrong way to think about God's character. Nothing that is truly agapē love can be unrighteous.[21] Divine love cannot exist without the quality of righteousness. And divine righteous cannot exist without this self-giving love that seeks the highest good of all. Moral responsibility toward others is based on love. If love were non-existent, there would be no sense of moral obligation. There would be no sense of right and wrong. There would be no interest in justice.[22] The pursuit of love demands righteousness, and the pursuit of righteousness is based on love that seeks the highest good of all.

The wonderful thing about divine love is that it is its own reward. If I will unselfishly pursue the wellbeing of others, and do that with a sincere heart, I will enter into their joys and successes. By that love toward others, I will vastly enlarge the scope of my own life. My life flows out to them in love. I invest my time, energy, and money into their wellbeing. I don't do it to get anything back from them.[23] My motive is not selfish; otherwise, it is not agapē love. But in the nature of things, I do receive a return on my investment. Instead of being restricted to my own selfish satisfactions, I enter into their joys.[24] I share in their lives. Their success becomes my success because I have become a part of it. Love carries its own reward.[25] We should love one another because love is consistent with the nature of God.

## LOVE'S MANIFESTATION

We should love one another because God showed us His love toward us by sending His Son to die in our place. Look at verses 9–10. "By this the love of God was manifested in us, that God has sent His only begotten Son into the world so that we might live through Him. In this is love, not that we loved God, but that He loved us and sent His Son *to be* the propitiation for our sins" (NASB). The NIV translates propitiation, "atoning sacrifice." That's easier to understand than propitiation.[26]

The cross is the ultimate demonstration of love. The fact that God, the Son, left heaven; came to earth; became a man; laid down His life for us on the cross; and took the full weight of our punishment as our substitute is the supreme revelation of love. We can see God's love expressed to us in many ways. But nowhere is it as clearly displayed as on Calvary. First John 3:16 approaches this event from the vantage point of the Son. "We know love by this, that He laid down His life for us." (NASB). That verse talks about the love Christ demonstrated on the cross. Our text focuses on the same event, but from the vantage point of the Father. "By this the love of God was manifested in us, that God has sent His only begotten Son into the world." That points us to the incarnation. "And sent His Son to be the propitiation for our sins." That points to the atonement. Without the incarnation and the atonement, we would have very limited revelation of the love of God. There would be glimpses of it. We see a glimpse of it in the exodus from Egypt. We see a glimpse of it in the mercy David received when he repented of his sins. We see a glimpse of God's love in the voice of the prophets calling Israel back to Him. His love does shine through in the Old Testament. But at Calvary it is in full view. "For God so loved the world, that He gave His only begotten Son, that whoever believes in Him shall not perish, but have eternal life" (John 3:16, NASB). Agapē is about selfless giving. God gave His best, His only begotten Son. The Greek word translated begotten is better translated "unique."[27] The NIV recognizes that. It translates our text in verse 9, "This is how God showed His love among us: He sent His one and only Son."

The revelation of love is unequivocally tied to the doctrine of Christ. People all over the world talk about love. But they do not really know love without Christ. They do not know it in the objective. For that is known by the historical event of Calvary. They do not know it subjectively. For that is known by the revelation of the Spirit. Love is learned from God's actions toward us. Love is learned by personal interaction and intimacy with Him. "The one who does not love does not know God." Knowing God experientially develops love in our hearts. It comes in by the new birth. It matures through knowing God better and better.[28]

Adam and Eve enjoyed an intimacy with God before their sin. They knew something of His tender, loving nature. But they did not know His love like we can know it. It was the fall that occasioned the greatest manifestation of love the universe has ever seen.[29] It is the fall of man that require the cross of Christ. In the cross we know love beyond anything Adam had experienced. Sending the Savior was a totally unselfish act on the part of the Father. It was the costliest act ever carried out. We can never comprehend the full cost. As parents, we can appreciate the pain a father or mother would go through in giving a son over to physical death. It is something none of us would ever want to endure. But Calvary was infinitely more than that. For Jesus suffered the spiritual death all of humanity deserved. The Father Himself had to administer that on His own Son.[30] The love of a human parent for a child is a powerful thing. But the love of the Father for His only eternal Son infinitely exceeds that. Imagine the depth of the Father's decision. Imagine the emotion. You, as a parent, can love as a finite human. The Father loves the Son as only God can. Oh, what love it would be to inspire such a sacrifice! "For God *so* loved." (emphasis mine). I hope we don't pass over the thought too quickly. Oh, how He loves you and me. "Beloved, if God so loved us, we also ought to love one another" (NASB).

## LOVE'S FULFILLMENT

The fourth reason we ought to love one another is found in God's purpose of redemption. The ultimate reason for redemption is that we would live eternally in an ontological state of love. Why did Christ come? Why did He die on Calvary as an atoning sacrifice? The atonement wasn't the objective. It was the means to an end.[31] The end goal was a people who would live forever in a condition of loving relationship with God and with one another. Verse 9 says, "By this the love of God was manifested in us, that God has sent His only begotten Son into the world so that we might live through Him" (NASB). That is the ultimate objective: "That we might live through Him." It's not just that God wants to take us out of the state of death. That's part of it.[32] But the objective is more positive than that. It is so that we may live forever with Him and be like Him. By that I mean: our nature would be the same as His nature. God is love. The goal is that we would be a people of love, that we would live in the quality of life that God lives in, eternal life—not just everlasting life, but life characterized by light and love.

Verse 12 emphasizes the "one another" aspect of this. "No one has seen God at any time; if we love one another, God abides in us, and His love is perfected in us" (NASB). The Greek word translated "perfected" is *teteleiōmenē*. Here it means to "carry through completely," to bring to the desired outcome, to accomplish its goal.[33] The accomplishment is not something static, but is ongoing: an ongoing state of love in action.[34] God sent His love through Jesus Christ. That love was manifested on the cross. At the cross our sins were dealt with so that we could be reconciled to God and live through Christ forever with God. But the love is not just toward God. We won't just be living with God. We will be living with one another. Without the love toward one another, the eternal society we call heaven could not happen. Love permeates the environment of heaven. God is working that love in our hearts right now. We are to cooperate with His objectives.

Verse 11 says, "Beloved, if God so loved us, we also ought to love one another" (NASB). I would have logically expected that verse to read something like this. "Beloved, if God so loved us, we ought to love Him back."[35] But it doesn't say that. Why? Because loving God back automatically happens when we get a revelation of His love toward us! First John 4:19 says, "We love Him because He first loved us" (NKJV). Any person who does not love God, simply does not know Him. To know Him is to love Him. But loving people is another matter. I think we can all appreciate this little poem.

> To dwell above with saints I love, that will be glory.
> But to dwell below with saints I know, now that's a different story.[36]

Why does John call us to love one another in response to God's love? First, because that is the practical way we can express our love for God. God doesn't need anything from us. He is entirely self-sufficient. It is right that we praise and worship Him. He is pleased when we do that. It benefits us to delight ourselves in the Lord in that way. But our expression of love for God is primarily found in loving His people. Matthew 25:40: "Inasmuch as you did it to one of the least of these My brethren, you did it to Me" (NKJV). We cannot see God. He does not need our help. But our brothers and sisters in Christ do.

Loving *them*, more closely reflects agapē love than loving God. Why? God is lovable! There is nothing in Him not to love. So, we can love God for who He is. But people are not always so loveable. Agapē is not dependent upon the worth or behavior of its object. God loved us when we were His enemies in rebellion against Him. When we love an unlovable person, we are operating in agapē love. When we love people because they're sweet and nice, that's *philia* love. That's our natural response to their lovable nature. In contrast, loving flawed and imperfect people is a clearer duplicate of God's agapē than loving God who is absolutely lovable.[37] "We know love by this, that He laid down His life for us; and we ought to lay down our lives for the brethren" (1 John 3:16, NASB).

On May 29, 1914 the British Liner, *Empress of Ireland,* set out from Quebec Harbor on its transatlantic journey to Liverpool, England. It was carrying 1,477 passengers and crew. In the heavy fog, the Norwegian freighter, *Storstad,* collided with the *Empress.* Within fourteen minutes, the *Empress* sunk, drowning 1,012 people.[38]

> When the *Empress of Ireland* went down with one hundred and thirty Salvation Army officers on board, one hundred and nine officers were drowned, and not one body that was picked up had on a life belt. The few survivors told how the Salvationists, finding there were not enough life preservers for all, took off their own belts and strapped them even upon strong men, saying, "I can die better than you can."[39]

They sacrificed their own lives for others. That is the kind of love John is teaching in this epistle.

Unbelievers cannot see God. They cannot see Christ dying on the cross. They can see us and how we behave. That is the demonstration of God's love that is available for them to see.[40] "By this," Jesus said, "all will know that you are My disciples, if you have love for one another" (John 13:35, NASB). In this day and hour God is manifesting His love through His people. I want people to see Him in me. I'm sure you do too. "Beloved, if God so loved us, we also ought to love one another."

# Endnotes: Chapter 19

1 John is speaking in absolute terms. The loving person does not just love his brother but loves everyone. While John's focus in this epistle is the agapē and koinōnia of believers, the nature of agapē extends beyond that to all humanity, so that the love that compelled the Father to send the Son (John 3:16) compels us to go into all the world and preach the gospel to every creature (Mark 16:15). Cf. Smalley, 237.

2 King James Version.

3 Zodhiates, *The Epistles of John,* 255. The presence of the article in the Greek implies that it is the real love, as it also does in verse 10. Cf. Burdick, 317.

4 Kittel, ed., vol. 1, s. v., *"agapao, agape, agapē tos,"* by Ethelbert Stauffer, 37. However, at the time this epistle was written, the Christian community probably understood agapē as God-like, unselfish love.

5 Cf. Gal. 5:22.

6 Cf. 2 Pet. 2:3.

7 Luke Holohan, "Horror in Jonestown: Cult survivor recalls brainwashing, blackmail & mass suicide (audio)," published Nov. 18, 2017, *US News.* Retrieved Jan. 4, 2018 at https://www.rt.com/usa/410257-jonestown-peoples-temple-massacre/.

8 Dodd, 109–110: ". . . we cannot be loved by an abstraction, or by anything less than a person."

9 Zodhiates, *The Epistles of John,* 258. The article, *ho,* is with *Theos,* making it the subject. The predicate, agapē, has no article.

10 Cf. 2 Chron. 1:11–12.

11 Luke 11:2, KJV.

12 There are obviously physical and spiritual principles that we should understand as well as possible. But our relationship with God is not about manipulating principles; it's about relating to our Father in heaven.

13 Cf. Ex. 3:14; John 8:58.

14 Gen. 1:1, KJV

15 KJV translates 1 John 5:7, "For there are three that bear record in heaven, the Father, the Word, and the Holy Ghost: and these three are one." This statement was probably not in John's original manuscript but was more likely a scribal addition. Cf. Yarbrough, 293. Nevertheless, the revelation of Trinity is in the New Testament.

16 Matt. 3:15–17, KJV.

17 Brian Edgar, *The Message of the Trinity: Life in God, Vol. in Bible Themes Series,* Ed. Derek Tidball (Downers Grove, IL: InterVarsity, 2004) 43. He writes, "Love requires a relationship; it does not exist just on its own. It must be expressed by someone and received by another. Love simply could not exist if God was a solitary, undifferentiated being rather than the dynamic, loving community of

Father, Son and Spirit. Love existed even before the world was created, for God is eternally a community of mutual love between Father, Son and Spirit."

18  Ps. 14:1, NASB.

19  Jamieson, Fausset, and Brown write concerning an idol, "Its worshippers acquire its character, becoming vain as it is (Deut. 7:26; Ps. 115:8)." Robert Jamieson, Robert, A. R. Fausset, and David Brown, *Jamieson, Fausset, and Brown's Commentary on the Whole Bible*, 1871, s. v. "Jer. 2:5." Accessed in electronic data base: Biblesoft 2000.

20  J. I. Packer, *Knowing God* (Downers Grove, IL: InterVarsity Press, 1973) 122: ". . . sentimental ideas of his love as an indulgent, benevolent softness, divorced from moral standards and concerns must therefore be ruled out from the start. God's love is holy love."

21  Law, 81. Law writes (pp.82–83), "In the popular understanding of the words, the Love of God is regarded as acting only in the direct communication of good; while judicial, punitive, and destructive energies of the Divine Nature, which are evoked by evil, are assigned exclusively to Righteousness. But this is a false antithesis, based upon an inadequate and one-sided conception of Love."

22  Law, 82–87. Law writes (p. 83), ". . . the Love of God must assert itself in infinitely intense antagonism to all that works for the defeat of the eternal purpose of Love—Love that seeks the highest moral excellence of His creatures—for which He created and governs the universe."

23  Cf. Luke 6:34–35.

24  Cf. Prov. 18:1, "He who separates himself seeks *his own* desire, He quarrels against all sound wisdom" (NASB).

25  Law, 86. Concerning love, Robert Law writes, ". . . it is not only the sum of all moral excellence, but the source of the highest moral satisfactions. . . . Each communicates himself to all and all to each. Each seeks the joy and well-being of all, and, in turn, enjoys the joy and is blessed by the well-being of all."

26  For a fuller discussion of this, see chapter 2, "Wrestling with Sin," in this book.

27  Burdick, 321. The Greek word, *monogenēs*, is better translated unique, rather than begotten. In a convincing explanation, Burdick references Hebrews 11:17 where the term is used of Isaac, who was not Abraham's "only begotten" son, but was his "unique" son of promise. "Etymologically the term comes from *monos*, 'only,' 'single,' and *gennō*, "kind." Furthermore, Burdick writes, "Moulton and Milligan explain that "only begotten" would be *monogennētos*. . . ." Cf. James Hope Moulton and George Milligan, *The Vocabulary of the Greek New Testament* (Grand Rapids: Eerdmans, 1930) 416–417.

28  Cf. Phil. 1:9; Eph. 3:14–19.

29  Spurgeon, "Love's Climax," preached Jan. 6, 1895. Accessed at The C. H. Spurgeon Collection on CD-ROM (AGES Software, Inc., 1998).

30  Cf. Isaiah 53:10; Matt. 27:46. God alone was qualified to administer this justice.

31  Law, 74.
32  Cf. Eph. 2:1–7; Col. 1:13.
33  Thayer, s. v. "NT:5048." cf. Zodhiates, *The Epistles of John,* 270. *Teteleiōmenē* is the perfect passive participle of *teleioō.*
34  Smalley (p. 248) says *teleioō* is ". . . here used in the emphatic form of the compound perfect *teteleiōmenē* and meaning ongoing fulfillment, rather than *static* 'completion.'"
35  Law, 249.
*36  Search Quotes.* Author unknown. Retrieved Jan. 5, 2018 at http://www.searchquotes.com/quotation/To_live_above_with_the_saints_we_love,_oh_that_will_be_glory. . ._to_live_below_with_the_saints_we_k/399908/.
37  Law, 76, 252.
38  "The sinking of the *Empress of Ireland,*" *A & E Networks.* Retrieved Jan. 5, 2018 from http://www.history.com/this-day-in-history/the-sinking-of-the-empress-of-ireland.
39  Knight, ed., s. v. "Salvation Army Sacrifices," by Walter Knight, p. 587. Secular sources that were accessed do not report the sacrifices made by these Salvation Army officers. It is, therefore, difficult to corroborate this part of the story from secular sources.
40  Stott, 164. Stott structures his analysis of this pericope with three reasons we are to love God: (1) God is love (2) God loved us (3) if we do love one another, God dwells in us and His love is perfected in us.

CHAPTER 20

# Blessed Assurance
# 4:13–16

By this we know that we abide in Him and He in us,
because He has given us of His Spirit. We have seen and
testify that the Father has sent the Son *to be* the Savior
of the world. Whoever confesses that Jesus is the Son of
God, God abides in him, and he in God. We have come
to know and have believed the love which God has for
us. God is love, and the one who abides in love abides
in God, and God abides in him.

1 John 4: 13-16, NASB

Expository Message

Before we get to the text today, I want to talk briefly about John's primary
reason for writing this letter. He plainly states it in 1 John 5:13. "These
things I have written to you who believe in the name of the Son of God,
so that you may know that you have eternal life" (NASB).[1] Do you believe
"in the name of the Son of God"? If so, this letter is for you, and it carries
this stated purpose, "That you may know that you have eternal life." Do
you know that you have eternal life? God wants you to know it in such a
way that your soul is at rest.[2] He wants you to know it when you are on
the mountain top. He wants you to know it in the valley. He wants you
to know and understand that your relationship with Him is solid. You are

in covenant with the true and faithful God.[3] He is your heavenly Father. You are His, and He is yours. "Behold, what manner of love the Father has bestowed upon us, that we should be called the sons of God!" (3:1, KJV). And that's what we are!

The emotional development of any child depends on a sense of acceptance and security in the family.[4] Children need to know that they are loved and wanted. They need the assurance that Mom and Dad are there for them, that their relationship with Mom and Dad is secure. Without that, their emotional development is thwarted. The same is true in the family of God. God's children need to know that God loves them unconditionally. He loves them when they are walking in victory, and He loves them when they are stumbling around and coming short of His glory. God is not fickle in His love for you and me.[5] He is committed to us and is steadfast in the relationship. Our text in this chapter ends with this statement: "And so we know and rely on the love God has for us" (NIV). That is the objective behind our text today: that you and I would "know" and *rely on* the love our heavenly Father has for us. Are you fully resting in that fact?

Years ago, I was in a legalistic church that did not establish people in assurance. The threat of God kicking them out of the family was ever present. The people in that church were sincere and loved the Lord. But they did not understand the doctrine of assurance. They did not know the value of Christians living in the security of knowing and relying on God's love and His commitment to them. Therefore, it was not a healthy environment, in that regard. I watched the anxiety in people. I watched them struggle to live up to the standard, trying harder, failing, then resolving to try even harder, and failing some more. The focus was on their own efforts and performance. Many grew weary and gave up. I have seen firsthand what happens when people are not established in grace, not living in the assurance of their salvation.[6] That's why our text is so important.

The New International Version provides a clear overall understanding of the passage. First John 4:13–16 says, "We know that we live in him and he in us, because he has given us of his Spirit. And we have seen and testify that the Father has sent his Son to be the Savior of the world. If anyone acknowledges that Jesus is the Son of God, God lives in him and he in

God. And so, we know and rely on the love God has for us. God is love. Whoever lives in love lives in God, and God in him."

Notice the two bookends in this paragraph. Verse 13 begins, "We know." For John, this knowing speaks of *assurance*. It's one of John's favorite terms. It occurs forty-two times in this short epistle. So, John begins with the subject of knowing. Then he provides three reasons for this assurance.[7] That is our theme in this chapter. The other bookend is found in verse 16. There he begins his conclusion with the statement, "And so we know." We know it so deeply and so well that we *rely upon it* in our daily lives. Fanny Crosby described that assurance in such beautiful terms.

> Blessed assurance, Jesus is mine!
> Oh, what a foretaste of glory divine!
> Heir of salvation, purchase of God.
> Born of His Spirit, washed in His blood.[8]

God wants to establish you in that blessed assurance. He wants you to enter into and abide in His rest. Are you resting in His love for you? Are you resting in His covenant commitment to you? Hear the words of Paul in 2 Timothy 1:12: "for I know [there's that word, know, again] whom I have believed [it's all about confidence in Jesus] and am persuaded that He is able to keep what I have committed unto him against that day" (KJV). Have you committed your soul to Him? Have you committed your eternal destiny to Him? Oh, the peace that is ours when we are fully persuaded like Paul was! The goal of this discussion is that you would know and rely on the love God has for you. There are three sources of assurance in our text, three ways that we know we have eternal life.

John uses a variety of terms in this epistle to speak of "eternal life." In chapter one he talks about living in fellowship or koinōnia with God and His people. His focus is on walking in the light. In chapter two he equates it with knowing God. Perhaps the two most common phrases for this reality are "born of God" and "lives [or abides] in God." That's the way he puts it in our text.

Notice his terminology of abiding in 1 John 4:12–16:

No one has seen God at any time; if we love one another, *God abides in us*, and His love is perfected in us. By this we know that *we abide in Him and He in us*, [another way to say that is to say we know that we have eternal life, or we know that we're really a Christian] because He has given us of His Spirit. We have seen and testify that the Father has sent the Son *to be* the Savior of the world. Whoever confesses that Jesus is the Son of God, *God abides in him, and he in God*. We have come to know and have believed the love which God has for us. God is love, and *the one who abides in love abides in God, and God abides in him* (emphasis mine).

John concludes that passage by declaring the two-way, mutual relationship. In this state of eternal life, we abide in God and God abides in us: a double bond. The Holy Spirit comes into this temple, and we are brought into communion with God: God in us, and us in God.

We have to understand that terminology in the context of John's objective for this letter. In this context, John is not using the term, *abide*, as a call to deeper intimacy with God. There are other passages in the New Testament that do that.[9] But John is combating the false doctrines of the Gnostics that relate to the issue of salvation. Some of them are denying Jesus's true humanity. Some are denying His divinity. In doing that, they are denying the true way of salvation through the work of the cross. John's subject is salvation and assurance of that salvation. That's why John speaks in such black and white terms. You're either walking in the light or walking in the darkness. You either know Him or you don't know Him. You're either of God or of the world. You're either born again or you're not born of the Spirit. You're either abiding in God or you're not abiding in God. In the passage before us, John is not focused on degrees of abiding. So, the objective in our passage is assurance that we are indeed children of God, born of the Spirit, and on our way to heaven. Now look with me at the three sources of that assurance in our text.

# THE SPIRIT OF GOD IN US

Verse 13 says, "By this we know that we abide in Him and He in us, because He has given us of His Spirit" (NASB).[10] The New English Bible translates it, "Here is the proof that we dwell in him and he dwells in us: he has imparted his Spirit to us." Here is the proof that you're a child of God. He has given you His Holy Spirit.[11]

Before His death, Jesus promised to send the Holy Spirit to His followers. He fulfilled that promise officially and historically on the Day of Pentecost. It was a major step in the eschatological program of God. The incarnation was pivotal in the plan of God. The cross was crucial in the plan of God. But so was the sending of the third person of the Trinity. What amazing grace that God Himself would inhabit these mortal bodies. Have you considered the grace of God that He would dwell among and even in His people? Your body is the temple of the Holy Spirit. The same Spirit that dwelt in Jesus dwells in you and me. The same Spirit that raised Jesus from the dead dwells in us.[12] It is amazing but true.

The fact that the Holy Spirit dwells in us is proof that we are born of God and are children of God. John mentioned this wonderful evidence back in 3:24. "We know by this that He abides in us, by the Spirit whom He has given us" (NASB). Now he links that with two other proofs, so that we can have absolute confidence in our relationship with the Father.

Someone might ask, how can I know that the Holy Spirit is in me? Let me give a few quick indicators of that reality. I'll do it with seven questions.[13]

(1) Does the Spirit bear witness with your spirit that you're a child of God? I'll admit that is rather subjective, but it is still very real. Romans 8:15–16 says, "For you did not receive a spirit of slavery to fall back into fear, but you have received a spirit of adoption. When we cry, 'Abba! Father!' it is that very Spirit bearing witness with our spirit that we are children of God" (NRSV). His Spirit bears witness with our spirit that we are children of God. That may come with much emotion or very little emotion. It happens at a deeper level than emotion. It happens in your innermost being. There comes a knowing, a revelation that God has forgiven you of your sins and received you as His child. John Wesley said that when it happened for him, his heart was strangely warmed.[14] The burden of guilt lifts off. The Holy

Spirit comes in and lets you know in your heart that you have been born again. John will later say in chapter five that the witness of God is greater than the witness of man. That witness in your heart is more assuring than any assurance man can give. "He who believes in the Son of God has the witness in himself" (1 John 5:10, NKJV).

Has God witnessed in your heart that you have been forgiven and received into the family of God? If not, ask Him to grant that affirmation. It is something He wants you to have. Your experience may not happen in the same way or with the same emotion as the person sitting beside you. God is very personal in His relationship with each of us. But the Holy Spirit will let you know that it is true.

(2) Do you have a desire in your heart to please God? Are you disappointed and grieved when you fail? If that is the case for you, then the Spirit of God dwells in you. Those desires come only from the new nature. The old nature is enmity against God.[15] Fallen man is not concerned with pleasing God. He is only concerned with pleasing himself. Fallen man is not grieved when he has violated the commandments of God. He is only grieved when he gets caught and suffers the consequences. In 2 Corinthians 5:9 Paul said, "So we make it our goal to please him." (NIV). That kind of desire comes from the Holy Spirit. It is evidence that we dwell in God and God dwells in us.

(3) Is there an inner struggle between good and evil in your life? On the one hand, a propensity toward sin is in you; at times you find yourself doing the wrong thing and then hating the fact that you did it. On the other hand, a love for the ways of God, the holiness of God, and the commandments of God is also present. Unbelievers only have one nature. It is a sinful nature that does not love the law of the Lord. It is a nature that is in rebellion against the authority of God. But the Christian struggles with an inner conflict because he has two natures to deal with. His old, carnal nature wants things contrary to what His new nature desires.[16] Paul testified of his struggle in Romans 7. In verse 22 he says, "For I delight in the law of God after the inward man" (KJV). Is there something down deep in your heart that delights in the ways of God? You want to live in obedience to your heavenly Father, but there are times you fail. There are times you struggle to live the way you want to live. You may think that's a bad sign. But it's actually an indication that God is in you.[17] It's an

indication that the Holy Spirit is working in you to will and do His good pleasure (Phil. 2:13).

(4) Do you have an interest in the Bible? Is there something inside, leading you to discover the truth revealed in the word of God? If so, it is the Spirit of Truth prompting those desires. The natural man does not think that way. The natural man does not respect the Bible as inspired and authoritative. He may study it for various reasons. He may have some intellectual curiosity toward it. But he does not study it as God's revelation for life and godliness. In 1 Corinthians 2:14 Paul wrote, "The person without the Spirit does not accept the things that come from the Spirit of God but considers them foolishness, and cannot understand them because they are discerned only through the Spirit" (NIV). Does your heart leap for joy when God speaks to you from His word? That kind of experience is a delightful sign the Holy Spirit is at work in your heart. He leads into truth. He alone gives a love for the truth. Do you have a love for the truth? If you do, you have a lot to be thankful for. The Holy Spirit has come in and given you that love for the things of God. The Holy Spirit teaches us the truths of the New Testament. Our reception of those truths is evidence of His activity. We will see that more clearly when we look at the second source of our assurance.

(5) Does God express His gifts in your life? First Corinthians 12 lists nine manifestations of the Spirit in the lives of believers. The operation of these supernatural manifestations is powerful evidence of the Holy Spirit. Sometimes these manifestations are spectacular. It was a spectacular manifestation of the Spirit when the lame man in Acts 3 was healed. More often the gifts operate to meet the immediate need in less dramatic ways. Have you ever had Him give you a word of wisdom? You didn't know what to do; so you asked God, and He gave you the answer. It was not just something you came up with. It was not a product of your natural logic. In a flash, He gave you the key. He showed you what to do. That's just one example of those manifestations of the Spirit. Those manifestations are another evidence the Spirit resides in you.

(6) Do you long to be with Jesus? Do you love His appearing?[18] Do you look forward to being with Him in heaven? The coming of the Lord strikes dread in the heart of the unbeliever. He does not want to think about it. He does not want to talk about it. His mind is on earthly things.[19] But the

269

Holy Spirit is preparing us for our Bridegroom. The Holy Spirit within causes us to love Jesus. The Holy Spirit brings a respect for the name of Jesus. No man can call Him Lord except by the Spirit of God.[20] It is the Holy Spirit who inspires our love and respect for Jesus.

(7) Is the fruit of the Spirit demonstrated in your life? Galatians 5:22–23 says the fruit of the Spirit is love, joy, peace, patience, kindness, goodness, faithfulness, gentleness, and self-control. I doubt any of us are fully mature in these things. But the Holy Spirit is working these graces into our lives. We may have a long way to go before the fruit is fully ripe, but there is a transformation of character going on. We will see in a moment how John focuses on love as another evidence of our relationship with God. But if there is more of this in your life than there used to be, it is a good indication the Holy Spirit is working. One proof of eternal life is the presence of the Holy Spirit bearing witness and working in the heart of the believer.[21]

## FAITH IN CHRIST AS OUR SAVIOR

The second proof that we have eternal life is our faith in Jesus as the way of salvation. John begins verse 14 with the Greek conjunction, *kai*, to indicate that he is continuing to give proof of God dwelling in us. "And we have seen and do testify that the Father sent the Son to be the Saviour of the world" (KJV). This is John's testimony. This is the report of the apostles who were eyewitnesses of Christ.[22] John is asserting his authority as an apostle. He is opposing Gnostics who bring a different message. John's message is that Jesus is the Son of God and was sent by the Father as the Savior of the world. That is the core message of the New Testament. That is the gospel in summary form. In the opening of this epistle John makes a similar assertion. There his emphasis was on the incarnation. He makes the same assertion in the opening of his gospel. The divine *Logos*, the eternal Word of God, was made flesh, and His name is Jesus! Here John's emphasis is on His purpose as Savior of the world. Wrapped up in John's statement is the atonement. For without the sacrifice of Calvary, there could be no salvation. Without the blood of Christ, there is no cleansing of sin; there is no appeasing of wrath. There is salvation in no other name but Jesus.[23] He alone was sent by the Father to be the Savior of the world.

The antichrist spirit hates that message. The antichrist spirit has its own message of love and salvation. It sidesteps the cross. It dishonors the work of Christ. It is man-centered, not God-centered. It seeks many ways and many doors. But Jesus said, "I am the way, and the truth, and the life; no one comes to the Father but through Me" (John 14:6 NASB).

I reviewed some "teaching" by Oprah Winfrey on her New Earth Web Class. She is very opposed to John's message. Her response to a lady who said Jesus is the only way, was to say, "There couldn't possibly be only one way." For her, Jesus is just one of many ways. She rejects doctrine, like the one John gives in our text. On her web class she says, "God is a feeling experience, not a believing experience. . . . If God for you is still about a belief, then it is not truly God."[24] But John says it is about a belief. It is about believing the truth, rather than a lie. There are multitudes of people feeling their way right into hell. There are many antichrists in the world today. And some of them are very influential.

In verse 15 John says, "Whoever confesses that Jesus is the Son of God, God abides in him, and he in God" (NASB). Here is our second source of assurance. We, unlike John, did not see Jesus in the flesh. But we receive the apostles' testimony that He is the Son of God, and He is the Savior of the world.[25] We embrace the witness of the New Testament. We receive that message and confess that Jesus is the Son of God. I like the first word in that verse, "Whoever." That includes me. "For God so loved the world, that He gave His only begotten Son, that whoever believes in Him shall not perish, but have eternal life"[26] The offer is universal, to all mankind: "That whoever believes in Him." Do you believe in Jesus? Do you confess Him as the Son of God? That confession is propositional in that it declares His deity, as a doctrine. But it is also experiential in that we are trusting Him as the Son of God, sent by the Father.[27] We are trusting Him as the Savior of the world, and, therefore, we are trusting Him as *our* Savior. That kind of trust translates into a commitment to follow Him. People always act on what they really believe.

There is substance in what we believe. We do not accept the New Age spirituality being propagated by Oprah and other antichrists. There are absolute truths that we can believe about God. There are absolute lies that we refuse to believe. Jesus said to the Pharisees, "You will die in your sins; for unless you believe that I am *He*, you will die in your sins" (John 8:24,

NASB). That should have been a sobering message for them to hear. Still they didn't repent. It matters what you believe! "For there is one God, *and* one mediator also between God and men, *the* man Christ Jesus, who gave Himself as a ransom for all" (1 Tim. 2:5–6, NASB). You are not in this by yourself. Your great High Priest, Jesus, is at the right hand of the Father interceding for you. Will His intercession prevail. Yes, it will. "Therefore He is able also to save forever those who draw near to God through Him, since He always lives to make intercession for them" (Heb. 7:25, NASB).

Our security rests in what Jesus has done for us, not what we can do, not our own performance. He is the Savior. He is able to save to the uttermost those who come unto God by Him. We have seen in this epistle that His influence in us produces fruit. It produces righteous behavior. It works transformation in our lives. And we are to cooperate with that work of sanctification.[28] But the reliance is always on the Holy Spirit. The reliance is always on the finished work of Christ in our behalf. That's where our confidence is. That produces peace in the soul. It's simple, but true, as stated in this children's song.

> Jesus loves me! This I know, for the Bible tells me so. Little
> ones to Him belong; they are weak, but He is strong.[29]

Our strength is in the Lord. Our confidence is in what He has already done for us. When I breathe my last breath, I hope I can say as Paul did, "I have finished my course."[30] I press toward that goal. But all my confidence will rest on Him who loved me and gave Himself for me (Gal. 2:20). That's where the assurance finds a firm foundation, the finished work of Christ in our behalf. "And so we know and rely on the love God has for us."

When live in that assurance: (1) We can keep coming to God, even when we fail. (2) We can keep trusting God, even when don't understand what's happening in our lives. We can endure the fiery trial knowing He is working all things together for our good. (3) We can keep praying, even when answers don't seem to be forthcoming. It is a blessed assurance God wants you to enjoy.

He has filled His word with many promises in Scripture to fortify that assurance. Let me just mention a few. If you confess Jesus as the Son of God, then He is your Shepherd and you are now in the Father's hand.

The Father is greater than all; no man can pluck you out of His hand (John 10:29, KJV). Do you remember that old commercial for Allstate Insurance? Their slogan was, "You're in good hands with Allstate." Well, I found something better than that in John 10:29. You're in good hands when Jesus is your Savior. You're in good hands when God holds you and protects you.

The promise Jesus makes in Hebrews 13:5 is "Never will I leave you; never will I forsake you" (NIV). It doesn't matter how hard it gets. It doesn't matter how people respond to you. It doesn't matter how you feel. Jesus will not abandon you. He is there for you always. His love is an everlasting love.[31] He loves you like the Father loves Him.[32] And besides that, the Father loves you in the same way. If while we were sinners and rebels God loved us, how much more now that we are His own children.[33] Set your feelings aside and rely on the promises of God in His word. Feelings are like shifting sand. They're not a reliable source of assurance. But God's word is settled in the heavens.[34] If you will rely on what He has said, you can live in much assurance.

Listen to the assurance Paul expresses in Romans 8:38–39.

> For I am convinced [I hope you are convinced of these things the way Paul was] that neither death nor life, neither angels nor demons, neither the present nor the future, nor any powers, neither height nor depth, nor anything else in all creation, will be able to separate us from the love of God that is in Christ Jesus our Lord (NASB).

We know that we are Christians (1) by the Spirit He has put in us (2) by the Savior we have confessed.

## THE LOVE HE EXPRESSES THROUGH US

Our assurance is also found in God's love working in and through us. Verse 16 says, "We have come to know and have believed the love which God has for us. God is love, and the one who abides in love abides in God, and God abides in him" (NASB). The Greek verbs translated "know" and "believed" are in the perfect tense. Understandably the NASB puts it in the perfect tense in English. That is a good translation. But the NIV translation is also acceptable because the perfect tense denotes an action in the past with continuing effects in the future.[35] We placed our faith in Christ the day we got saved, and we continue to believe in Him. The NIV focuses on our continued current experience. "And so we know and rely on the love God has for us." That's the continuing effect of our faith. That's our current state of assurance. We *know* and *rely on* the love God has for us. That's such a powerful statement.

The Gnostics were undermining Christians' assurance by telling them the simple gospel was not enough. They insisted that these believers needed some additional knowledge that only they could give them. They presented themselves as spiritual, and anyone not in their camp were labeled as carnal.[36] But John is reassuring believers that Jesus is enough; that they do have the Holy Spirit, regardless of what these Gnostics are telling them. He assures them that their love for one another is evidence of God abiding in them.

So here is the third source of assurance stated plainly. "And the one who abides in love abides in God, and God abides in him." Are you living in God's love? John has already set this principle forth in verse 12 where he wrote, "If we love one another, God abides in us, and His love is perfected in us" (NASB). We normally think of the word "perfected" as something flawless, something that cannot be improved upon. But that is not what the Greek word, *teleioō*, means. It is talking about God's love fulfilling its purpose when it is expressed through us. God didn't just send His love to be expressed through Jesus, as essential as that was. His ultimate intention is that His love be expressed by us loving one another.[37]

Do you have a love for your brothers and sisters in Christ? Are you moved with compassion when you see one of them in need? Does that compassion move you to try to help them? If that is happening, it is objective evidence that you have eternal life abiding in you. This is something we are all growing in; not that we have already attained, but we are pressing forward to be more like Jesus in our love toward each other. Sometimes it is simply a sensitive word of kindness. In her memoirs, *The Whisper Test*, Mary Ann Bird shares the following experience:

I grew up knowing I was different, and I hated it. I was born with a cleft palate, and when I started school, my classmates made it clear to me how I looked to others: a little girl with a misshapen lip, crooked nose, lopsided teeth, and garbled speech.

When schoolmates asked, "What happened to your lip?" I'd tell them I'd fallen and cut it on a piece of glass. Somehow it seemed more acceptable to have suffered an accident than to have been born different. I was convinced that no one outside my family could love me.

There was, however, a teacher in the second grade whom we all adored—Mrs. Leonard. She was short, round, happy—a sparkling lady.

Annually we had a hearing test. . . . Mrs. Leonard gave the test to everyone in the class, and finally it was my turn. I knew from past years that as we stood against the door and covered one ear, the teacher sitting at her desk would whisper something, and we would have to repeat it back—things like "The sky is blue" or "Do you have new shoes?" I waited there for those words God must have put into her mouth, those seven words that changed my life. Mrs. Leonard said, in her whisper, "I wish you were my little girl."[38]

A kind word can bring healing to a broken heart. Words can wound, but words can also heal. John says in verse 12, "If we love one another, God abides in us." (NASB).

Three proofs that we are abiding in God and He is abiding in us: (1) He has given us His Spirit. (2) We confess that Jesus is the Son of God. (3) We love one another. God wants you to live in the assurance of His love and acceptance. It is your privilege as a child of God.[39] "And so we know and rely on the love God has for us." Rest in that assurance.

# Endnotes: Chapter 20

1   The last phrase in the NKJV, "And that you may *continue to* believe in the name of the Son of God" is probably not in the original manuscript, a fact reflected in the NASB and NIV. However, other New Testament passages do emphasize the importance of continuing in faith (Acts 14:22; Rom. 11:22; Col. 1:21–23; Heb. 10:35–39).

2   Cf. Heb. 4:9–10; Matt. 11:28.

3   Cf. Heb. 10:16–23, NIV: "Therefore, brothers and sisters, since we have *confidence* to enter the Most Holy Place by the blood of Jesus . . . let us draw near to God with a sincere heart and with the *full assurance* that faith brings." (emphasis mine).

4   L. H. Turner and Richard West, *Perspectives on Family Communication,* 3rd ed. (New York: McGraw-Hill, 2006) 209–210. Cf. "Preschoolers: Building a Sense of Security," *Medicalrecords.com.* Retrieved Jan. 19, 2018 at https://www.medicalrecords.com/health-a-to-z/preschoolers-building -a-sense-of-security-definition.

5   Cf. Ps. 136; Hos. 11:8–9; Mal. 3:6; Jas. 1:17; Heb. 13:8. God's faithfulness to His children exceeds the faithfulness of any human father as far as the heavens exceed the earth.

6   Cf. Heb. 13:8–9; Gal. 2:21; 1 Pet. 5:12. Fear and uncertainty should not characterize the child of God. This is why knowing our identity in Christ is so important. This is why understanding the Covenant of Grace is important.

7   Stott, 165.

8   Fettke. Tom, ed., s. v., "Blessed Assurance" by Fanny J. Crosby, 345.

9   Cf. Eph. 4:14–15; Heb. 5:12–6:3; Jas. 4:8; 2 Pet. 1:5–7; 3:18.

10  Burdick, 327. The Father gave the Spirit to Christ without measure (John 3:34), but the Greek structure of 1 John 4:13 indicates the Spirit is given to the believer in limited measure. Therefore, the text is translated, "He has given of His Spirit."

11  At the new birth the Holy Spirit is joined to the person's spirit (1 Cor. 6:17; Rom. 8:9). However, believers should continue to be filled with the Spirit (Eph. 5:18) and desire empowerments of the Spirit for service (Acts 4:31; 19:6).

12  Cf. 1 Cor. 6:19; Acts 10:38; Rom. 8:11.

13  Lloyd-Jones, 468–472. I am indebted to Loyd-Jones for this very practical approach to the text in verse 13. These questions are not intended to be exhaustive.

14  John Wesley, *The Works of John Wesley,* Journal of John Wesley, chapter 2, 1774. Accessed in electronic data base: Biblesoft 2000.

15  Cf. Rom. 3:10–12; 8:7; Eph. 2:1–3.

16  Cf. Gal. 5:17.

17  Of course, Christians should be growing in grace and progressively overcoming the tendencies of the flesh. Ideally, as a believer matures, saying no to the flesh becomes more and more his pattern of life (Gal. 5:16).

18  Cf. 2 Tim. 4:8.

19  Cf. Phil. 3:19.

20  1 Cor. 12:3.

21  Cf. 1 John 5:9.

22  John says, "And we have seen and do testify," and verse 12 says, "No man hath seen God at any time." (KJV). No one has seen the Father in His essential nature (1 Tim. 6:16). Abraham, Moses, and other Old Testament saints saw manifestations of God. They saw theophanies. John and the other apostles saw God through Jesus (John 14:9). They knew He was the Savior of the world by the authority of His teaching, by the miracles He worked, by His glorification on the Mt. of Transfiguration, by the love He demonstrated even on the cross, and by the confirmation of His resurrection and ascension. John writes with the authority of an eyewitness.

23  Cf. Heb. 9:22; 1 John 2:2; Acts 4:12.

24  Oprah Winfrey, "A New Earth: Awakening to Your Life's Purpose," *New Earth Web Class*. Retrieved Jan. 11, 2018 at https://www.youtube.com/watch?v= r7MGw6koF8Q. Edwin Hamilton, Our Eyes Are Opened Ministries. Retrieved Jan. 11, 2018 at https://www.facebook.com/edwin.hamilton. 7/videos/10207565712633361/?hc_ref=ARSV61vU47TFZPbs 3nBUgbv38rYbWlQkB8n9okj5hDqLyk7jo2Z74WuU5Vht0 5ydYVU&pnref=story.

25  This also becomes our message to the world (Mark 16:15).

26  John 3:16, NASB.

27  Burdick, 330.

28  Cf. Phil. 2:12-13; Richard Tow, "The Sanctification Process," *Sermon Central*. Accessed at https://www.sermoncentral.com/sermons/the-sanctification -process-tow-sermon-on-richard-235169.

29  Anna B. Warner and David R. McGuire, "Jesus Loves Me." Retrieved Jan. 11, 2018 at https://www.musicnotes.com/sheetmusic/mtd.asp?ppn=MN0079820.

30  Cf. 2 Tim. 4:7, KJV.

31  Jer. 31:3.

32  Cf. John 15:9; 17:23.

33  Rom. 5:5–10.

34  Cf. Ps. 119:89; 1 Pet. 1:24–25.

35  Smalley, 255.

36  Cf. Burdick, 64–65; Law, 28–30.

37 Zodhiates, *The Epistles of John*, 270. Cf. Burdick, 326.

38 Rowell, ed., s. v. "Acceptance," by Mary Ann Bird (as told in her memoir entitled *The Whisper Test*), 8.

39 Consider the assurance Paul lived in (Gal. 2:20; 2 Tim. 1:12; 4:8).

# CHAPTER 21

# Freedom from Fear
# 4:16–18

And so we know and rely on the love God has for us. God is love. Whoever lives in love lives in God, and God in him. In this way, love is made complete among us so that we will have confidence on the day of judgment, because in this world we are like him. There is no fear in love. But perfect love drives out fear, because fear has to do with punishment. The one who fears is not made perfect in love.

1 John 4:16–18, NIV

## Expository Message

John continues with the subject of assurance in our text for this chapter. In chapter 20 we discussed three sources of our assurance, three proofs that we are born again, have eternal life, and are on our way to heaven: (1) By the Holy Spirit who has come into our lives (verse 13). His Spirit bears witness with our spirit that we are children of God.[1] The world cannot receive the Spirit of Truth.[2] The fact that He is at work in our hearts is evidence we belong to God. (2) By our confession of Jesus Christ as God's eternal Son and our Savior (verses 14–15). What you believe matters. Only those who put their faith in Christ are going to heaven. (3) By the love of God expressed through us in our behavior toward others (verses 12, 16).

Now John builds his teaching from those three truths, and particularly on the third one, our love for one another. For our text in this chapter, I am using the New International Version because it is easier to understand than most other versions. But even in this translation, these verses are not easy to understand. I skimmed over them for years, not really grasping what John is saying. Our primary goal in this chapter is that we would comprehend the meaning of the text. To do that, we will have to dig into the details. Some treasures in the Bible are laying right there on the surface. They are there even for the casual reader. But some are imbedded in the passage and must be mined out. The golden truth in this passage is valuable; the effort to get at it is worth it. You will find here revelation for living with peace of mind and confidence before God. If you will dig, you will find instruction for living above the fear that can torment our hearts and minds. Some texts beg the question, "How bad do you want it?" Do you want to know how to live in assurance and confidence before God? There are some answers here. May God help us find them. John, as he often does, first states his teaching in positive terms. Then he reinforces that teaching, by stating the same truth in negative terms.[3]

## CONFIDENCE THROUGH LIVING IN LOVE

In verse 17 John states the positive proposition. He begins with two Greek words that could be literally translated, "In this."[4] Our text says, "In this way." What is John referring to in that phrase? Is he referring to what he is about to say, or what he has already said? It is actually a bridge connecting what he has said with what he is about to say. In that respect, it relates to both. However, his primary reference is to what he has already said, especially in verse 16b.[5] "Whoever lives in love lives in God, and God in him." John is talking about living in love. As we live in love, our confidence and assurance blossom and become strong.

What does it mean to live in love? Look at the first sentence in verse 16. Living in love means we are increasingly knowing and relying on God's love for us. Confidence and assurance depend on our revelation of God's love for us, as His children.

Secondly, living in love means we live or abide in God.[6] We find our home in God.[7] In our daily lives we enjoy an intimate relationship with

Him. That intimate interaction affirms God's love toward us and teaches us to love others. During that intimacy, the Holy Spirit pours God's love into our hearts (Rom. 5:5). We are filled with the Holy Spirit, and that always means we are filled with love.[8] Jude addresses our responsibility to stay in the sphere of God's love through prayer. "But you, dear friends, by building yourselves up in your most holy faith and praying in the Holy Spirit, keep yourselves in God's love as you wait for the mercy of our Lord Jesus Christ to bring you to eternal life" (verses 20–21, NIV).

You can't produce this divine, unselfish love. It only comes from God. But you can cultivate it. The farmer cannot produce the life that is in a seed of wheat. He is absolutely dependent on God for the life and potential that is in the seed. But he has a choice as to what he will do with that seed. If he does nothing with it, if he just leaves it in the bag, he will not reap a harvest of wheat. The seed is there, but it has not reached full fruition. Its purpose is not being fulfilled. To use the Greek word John uses in our text, that seed is not *teleioō* which is translated "perfected." On the other hand, if he plants it, waters it, nurtures it, he will reap a harvest of wheat. "But you, dear friends, by building yourselves up in your most holy faith and praying in the Holy Spirit, keep yourselves in God's love." We can't do what only God can do. But God won't do what we are responsible to do. We are to cultivate and nurture that love that God has put in our hearts. The believer has the seed of love in the new nature. The potential of a harvest of love is there and available.

The potential in you is marvelous. God is love, and the Holy Spirit has taken up His abode in you. The question for each of us is this: what will you do with it? Will you exercise the faith, like the farmer does, to cultivate love in your life? If you will, you will live in a state of confidence and assurance before God. You will not fear the day of Judgment. The activity of that love will expel the fear of punishment. Instead, you will live in anticipation of reward and honor. Jesus said in John 15:9–10, "As the Father has loved me, so have I loved you. Now remain in my love. If you keep my commands, you will remain in my love, just as I have kept my Father's commands and remain in his love" (NIV).

Third, living in love means the love in our hearts finds practical expression in our behavior toward others, especially toward brothers and sisters in Christ. When we are living in love toward others, God's goal for sending His love to us is being realized, accomplished, or fulfilled.

One reason this portion of Scripture is hard to understand is the difficulty of translating the Greek word *teleioō* into English. The King James Version translates it with the word "perfect." That is misleading for most of us, because the word perfect for us means flawless. The defects have been corrected, and now it is perfect with no further need of improvement. That is not what John is saying here. The word *teleioō* means to fulfill its intended purpose, to complete its objective.[9] The closest English word the translators of the New International Version could find was "complete." That's closer to the meaning than "perfect." John is not saying you have to be perfect in your love toward others in order to enjoy this assurance. If that were the case, none of us would qualify in this life. John has clearly said in 1:8, "If we claim to be without sin, we deceive ourselves and the truth is not in us" (NIV). We strive toward perfection, but it is not something we attain in these mortal bodies. Even Paul said in Philippians 3:12 that he had not yet attained but was still pressing toward the mark. John is not talking about us having perfect, flawless love. He is talking about us having love that is expressed in our behavior toward others. James uses this same Greek word in reference to faith, just as John uses it in reference to love. He teaches that faith that never gets expressed in tangible, practical ways is incomplete and inadequate. In James 2:22 he says, "You see that his faith and his actions were working together, and his faith was made complete [*teleioō*]by what he did" (NIV). Whether we're talking about faith or about love, God insists that it be expressed in physical, practical ways.[10]

Look back at 1 John 4:12. "No one has ever seen God; but if we love one another, God lives in us and his love is made complete [*teleioō*] in us" (NIV)." The King James Versions says, "Made perfect." The Amplified helpfully adds the phrase, "Has run its course." So, how is the love of God brought to its intended purpose? The answer is in verse 12: "If we love one another." And of course, we know from our previous studies that love must be expressed in concrete, action. "Dear children, let us not love with words or speech but with actions and in truth" (1 John 3:18, NIV).

So here is God's plan (1) Out of love, He sent His Son to redeem us from destruction. (2) His love has been demonstrated to the world through Jesus, especially in His death on the cross. (3) His love has been planted in our hearts by the Holy Spirit in the new birth. (4) The Holy Spirit transforms our motives and character and expresses God's love through us to other people.[11] When # 4 is happening in tangible ways, then God's love is fulfilling its intended purpose, *teleioō*. "If we love one another . . . his love is made complete [fulfilled its intended purpose, completed its objective] in us" (4:12, NIV). In that state, we are living in love. We have become loving people. We are expressing God's love through our behavior toward others. All of that defines what John means at the beginning of verse 17 by the phrase, "In this way." Let us read verse 17 with that understanding. "In this way, love is made complete among us." It is fulfilling its intended purpose when it is being expressed through us toward others.

The result of that is assurance. Look at the next phrase in verse 17: "So that we will have confidence on the day of judgment." (NIV). When we are living in love toward others, we don't dread giving account of ourselves to God on the day of judgment.[12] Why should we? We are doing what He has told us to do. We are fulfilling the great commandments to love God and love our neighbors. We can actually love His appearing and look forward to His coming.[13]

Remember the Parable of the Talents in Matthew 25? The man who was stewarding five talents and the one stewarding two talents had boldness on the day of reckoning. They had done what the master wanted them to do. They had nothing to fear or dread from the master. In fact, they received commendation from him. He said to both of them, "Well done, good and faithful servant! You have been faithful with a few things; I will put you in charge of many things. Come and share your master's happiness!" (NIV). The day of judgment was nothing to fear for these men who had been faithful to the master. In contrast, the man who was stewarding one talent was full of fear. He was not doing what he was supposed to be doing. His life was characterized by fear and dread. Instead of actively investing, instead of actively seeking the wellbeing of others, he hid his talent. He failed to use the resources for their intended purpose. Listen to his statement to the master in Matthew 25:25, "So I was afraid and went out and hid your gold in the ground." (NIV). The man had no confidence before the judge. He lived in fear. He lived without assurance in his heart, even before the judgment day. When we are living in love, when we are living in obedience and are actively pursuing the wellbeing of others, we can enjoy assurance here and now and on the day of judgment.[14]

"This is how love is made complete among us so that we will have confidence on the day of judgment: In this world we are like Jesus" (4:17, NIV). That last phrase has always seemed out of place to me. I had to study it, meditate on it, and ask the Lord to help me to understand John's intent. "We will have confidence on the day of judgment: *In this world we are like Jesus*" (emphasis mine). How are we like Him in this world? We are representing the Father, expressing His love to people in concrete ways. We are making the Father known to the world by demonstrating His love in practical ways. He manifested the Father to the world; we too manifest who God is by the way we live and treat others. That is basically what John is saying in this context.[15]

The world is under the pending judgment of God. The world has no right of confidence. They are in rebellion against the Almighty. The world is appointed unto wrath.[16] You can see that wrath poured out in the last book of the Bible, John's revelation. But we are not of the world. We are in the world, but we are not of the world. God looks on us the same way He looks on His Son, Jesus. First Thessalonians 5:9–10 says, "For God did not appoint us to suffer wrath but to receive salvation through our Lord Jesus Christ. He died for us so that, whether we are awake or asleep, we may live together with him" (NIV). That verse ought to bring a lot of comfort to your heart. God has not appointed you to wrath. His program for you is that you obtain salvation through Christ. Jesus died for you, so that could happen. Jesus bore your punishment on the cross, so that God's wrath is fully appeased in regard to you.[17]

> What have I to dread, what have I to fear,
> Leaning on the everlasting arms?
> I have blessed peace with my Lord so near,
> Leaning on the everlasting arms[18]

If your faith is resting on what Jesus has already done for you, you have great cause for assurance. If the Holy Spirit is expressing His love toward others through you, you have a sound basis for confidence before God.

Listen to Jesus's prayer for us in John 17:14–18.

> I have given them your word and the world has hated them, for they are not of the world any more than I am of the world. My prayer is not that you take them out of the world but that you protect them from the evil one. They are not of the world, even as I am not of it. Sanctify them by the truth; your word is truth. As you sent me into the world, I have sent them into the world (NIV).

As the Father sent Jesus into the world to express His love to lost mankind, Jesus has sent us for the same purpose.[19] He is the light of the world.[20] He is now expressing His light in this dark world through us. He said in the Sermon on the Mount,

> You are the light of the world. A town built on a hill cannot be hidden. Neither do people light a lamp and put it under a bowl. Instead they put it on its stand, and it gives light to everyone in the house. In the same way, let your light shine before others, that they may see your good deeds and glorify your Father in heaven.[21]

The love that brings assurance and confidence is not an apathetic love. It is not a passive love. There are sins of commission that we are to avoid. But we must also live above sins of omission. The light that is in us is from God; we cannot produce it. But we can and must let it shine.

The good works Jesus talks about in Matthew 5:16 are expressions of God's love through us. The responsibility on our part is not just to avoid doing bad things to other people. It is not just the responsibility to forgive others and turn the other cheek. It includes that; but it goes beyond that. We are to be actively and proactively loving others. We are to be bringing the good news to the lost. We are to be caring for the poor and healing the downtrodden and sick. "In this world we are like Jesus." In fact, we through the enablement of the Holy Spirit, are carrying on His mission to the world. As we live in that way, we have assurance in our hearts before God.

"Whoever lives in love lives in God, and God in them. This is how love is made complete among us so that we will have confidence on the day of judgment: In this world we are like Jesus" (1 John 4:16–17, NIV). That is John's positive statement for us about confidence and assurance. Then he gives us the flip side of that in the next verse.

## CONSEQUENCE OF NOT LIVING IN LOVE

In verse 18, John addresses the subject on the negative side. We experience fear, rather than confidence, when we are not living in right relationship with God and other people. "There is no fear in love. But perfect love drives out fear, because fear has to do with punishment. The one who fears is not made perfect in love" (NIV). When a person is not living in love, then there is a consciousness that all is not right. It is impossible to live in disobedience to the Lord and enjoy His full peace and assurance at the same time.[22] Notice how John presents fear in opposition to love, and love in opposition to fear. The two are mutually exclusive. "Perfect love," John says, "drives out fear."[23] Once again, the Greek word translated perfect is *teleios*. It's the adjective form of the word translated "complete" in verse 17. John is talking about love that is fulfilling its objective. He's talking about love that is being expressed in our behavior toward others.[24] He is being very specific about the kind of love that accomplishes this.[25] It is not love that is just sentimental feelings or good intentions. Only this active, "perfect" agapē drives out fear. John is particularly focused on the fear of judgment in our text, although the principle has further application.[26] The fear of pending judgment cannot dwell in the heart of the believer who lives in obedience to God and operates in the love of God. Paul said in 2 Timothy 1:7, "God hath not given us the spirit of fear; but of power, and of love, and of a sound mind" (KJV). There, power and love are contrasted with a spirit of fear. A sound mind is contrasted with a fearful mind. And Paul clearly states that God's will for His children is that we would enjoy freedom from the kind of fear that torments the soul.

The implication of this is that fear cannot abide with a believer who lives in obedience and love. When a Christian is being tormented with a spirit of fear, deliverance begins with removing the ground that fear is standing on. The first thing to do is repent of selfishness and any area of disobedience. Address the sins of commission. Then address the sins of omission. Am I unselfishly operating in love toward others? If I am, I have every right to command the spirit of fear to leave. John's formula for living above fear is to live in love toward others. Love is the weapon that destroys fear, love expressed in good deeds toward others.

This emotion of fear provides for us a warning system that something is wrong. It is a good thing from the standpoint that we can respond to that and correct the problem.

> On March 18, 1937, a spark ignited a cloud of natural gas that had accumulated in the basement of the London, Texas school. The blast killed 293 people, most of them were children. "The explosion happened because the local school board wanted to cut heating costs. Natural gas, the by-product of petroleum extraction, was siphoned from a neighboring oil company's pipeline to fuel the building's furnace free of charge. . . . The one positive effect of the disastrous event was government regulation requiring companies to add an odorant to natural gas. The distinctive aroma is now familiar that we often forget natural gas is naturally odorless."[27]

That added odorant alerts us to a leak that could bring destruction. Fear is like that odor; it warns us of pending judgment. If we respond to it correctly, we can avoid disaster on Judgment Day. It should not be ignored. It should be addressed, by correcting the behavior that needs to be corrected. We know we have resolved the problem when the fear is gone.

John is talking about fear that has torment associated with it. There is another kind of fear that is healthy and beneficial. Fear or reverence toward God brings confidence and peace into a person's life. Let me give you some Scripture to support that statement. Proverbs 14:26–27 says, "In the fear of the Lord is strong confidence: and his children shall have a place of refuge. The fear of the Lord is a fountain of life, to depart from the snares of death" (KJV). The fear of the Lord drives other fears away. The fear of the Lord brings strong confidence to one living for God. Look at David as he faced Goliath. His reverence for God is expressed in His trust of the Lord and in his courage against the adversary. The armies of Israel were fearful of Goliath. David was so full of the fear of the Lord, he had such a regard for God, that there was no room in him left to fear man. "Fear of man will prove to be a snare, but whoever trusts in the Lord is kept safe (Prov. 29:25, NIV). Psalm 103:17 says, "The mercy of the Lord is from everlasting to everlasting upon them that fear him." (KJV). Psalm 115:11–13: "You who fear him, trust in the Lord— he is their help and shield. The Lord remembers us and will bless us: He will bless his people Israel, he will bless the house of Aaron, he will bless those who fear the Lord—small and great alike" (NIV). In our text, John is not talking about the fear of the Lord. He is talking about a fear that brings torment to the soul.

Verse 18 says, "There is no fear in love. But perfect love drives out fear, because fear has to do with punishment." (NIV).[28] In this context of pending judgment, fear arises in the heart when a person knows there is punishment ahead. Fear is an emotion that we have when we think the future, whether it be the day of judgment or three minutes from now, is not going to be good. If my car goes out of control on an icy road, my brain tells me I'm going to crash, and the natural emotion that comes is fear. If I have not been living for God, and the doctor tells me I have five days to live, the natural emotion would be fear. Paul was not fearful of death because he knew he was ready to step over that threshold. In Philippians 1:23 he even said that he had a "desire to depart and be with Christ, which is better by far." (NIV). It was not something he dreaded. Hebrews 9:27 teaches, "It is appointed unto men once to die, but after this the judgment" (KJV). Paul was not afraid of that judgment. He had lived his life for God. He had lived his life loving other people. He looked forward to His appointment with the Lord. But the man who lives selfishly, even if he is religious, will feel fear and dread when he faces death. He knows in his heart, all is not well. He anticipates punishment for his disobedience and is struck with fear. "Fear has to do with punishment." Fear is in the heart because punishment is anticipated.

The last sentence in verse 18 says, "The one who fears is not made perfect in love" (NIV). Do you see why I spent so much time explaining the Greek word that is translated "perfect"? It would be very easy for a person to read that sentence and say, "Wow, I have to be made *perfect* in love in order to be free from fear. I've tried and tried, and I can't get there. I guess I just have to live with this fear." But that kind of flawless perfection is not intended by John. John is just saying that the love in you needs to be expressed in practical actions toward others. If that is happening, it is fulfilling its purpose. Imperfect love is love that stays inside and never gets manifested in our lifestyle. This last statement in verse 18 is just the other side of verse 12. Let me lay them beside each other. Verse 12 says, "But if we love one another, God lives in us and his love is made complete in us" (NIV). Compare that to verse 18: "The one who fears is not made perfect in love" (NIV).

With all that said, let's read 1 John 4:16–18 again. See if you can make sense of it. "And so we know and rely on the love God has for us. God is love. Whoever lives in love lives in God, and God in him. In this way, love is made complete among us so that we will have confidence on the day of judgment, because in this world we are like him. There is no fear in love. But perfect love drives out fear, because fear has to do with punishment. The one who fears is not made perfect in love" (NIV).

John began this discussion on loving one another in 4:7. "Dear friends, let us love one another, for love comes from God. Everyone who loves has been born of God and knows God" (NIV). He has taught us the benefit of doing that: freedom from fear and confidence before God. Living in love boils down to simply living an unselfish life. There is no season of life where that is not expected of us. Society tells us we ought to work hard and save up so that in the latter years we can just do whatever we want to do. It's part of the American dream, and it's called retirement. But I don't find that concept in the Bible. I find instruction for laying up resources for future needs. For many, retirement can mean freedom to do more of what you feel God wants you to do, without the distraction of working a job to make a living. But for the Christian, it must never mean that I can now just live selfishly. If we embrace that lie, the golden years will not prove to be very golden. Whatever stage of life you're in, it must be about "others" or it is not love. Every stage of life is an opportunity to live unselfishly to the glory of God. "This is how love is made complete among us so that we will have confidence on the day of judgment."

# Endnotes: Chapter 21

1   Rom. 8:15–16; 1 John 5:10.

2   John 14:17.

3   Stott, 169. Cf. Smalley, 259.

4   The Greek words are *en toutō*, a phrase used often by John in this epistle.

5   Smalley, 256–257.

6   The Greek word, *menō*, translated "live" or "abide" in verse 16, means to remain, tarry, or continue. This verb is in the present tense, indicating continuous action. So, John is referring to a lifestyle of fellowship with God. In this verse John states this in terms of mutual abiding, ". . . lives in God, and God in him."

7   The Greek word, *menō*, can be translated "to dwell." In fact, the KJV uses that translation. To abide in God means to make our residence in Him. It is where we live, not just visit.

8   Cf. Eph. 5:18. The Greek verb, *plēroō*, translated "be filled" is in the present tense indicating an on-going activity.

9   Zodhiates, *The Epistles of John*, 289–290. Cf. Stedman, 329.

10  Of course, this directly confronts the Gnostic view of material matter.

11  Cf. Titus 2:14; Eph. 2:10; 1 Cor. 15:10; 2 Cor. 6:1, 6.

12  The Greek word translated judgment is *krisis*, from which we get our word crisis. For those unprepared, judgment day will be the ultimate crisis.

13  Cf. 2 Tim. 4:8.

14  In 2:28 John has already introduced the concept of confidence before the Lord when He returns. In our text he enhances our understanding of what it means to "abide in Him" (KJV).

15  Smalley, 259: "As he is (in the Father's love), so we are (in him, and therefore in the Father's love) in the world (obediently) making God's love known."

16  Cf. Rom. 2:7–8; Rev. 6:15–17; 2 Pet. 3:10.

17  Cf. Rom. 5:9.

18  Fettke. Tom, ed., s. v. "Leaning on the Everlasting Arms" by Elisha A. Hoffman, 298.

19  Burdick, 335. Drawing from Plumer, Lenski, and Dodd, Burdick writes, "Believers are like Christ in that they love as He loves." He says this view is preferable because it is drawn from the context. Cf. Smalley, 354.

20  John 1:9–10; 8:12.

21  Matt 5:14–16, NIV.

22  Cf. Ps. 119:165; Isa. 32:17; 48:18; 57:20–21.

23  The present tense verb *ballei* is a gnomic present indicating a fact that is always true. Cf. Burdick, 336.

24  Burdick, 333.

25 Wallace, 306. John emphasizes the kind of love that drives out fear by placing the Greek article with the adjective.

26 Cf. Ps. 23:4; 27:3; Prov. 28:1; Acts 4:18–19; 20:22–24; 1 John 3:21–22; 5:14.

27 Rowell, ed., s. v. "Guilt," by Sara Mosle, 103. The story was published in *The New Yorker* on May 15, 1995 as recounted by Sara Mosle.

28 The Greek word, *kolasis*, translated punishment, has in its basic meaning to curtail, to cut short, to limit, or to restrain. Cf. Zodhiates, *The Epistles of John*, 295; Stedman, 331. Being free of the limitations imposed by anxieties, tensions, stress, and other expressions of fear is a valuable thing for Christians to enjoy.

# CHAPTER 22

# Spiritual Siblings
# 4:19–5:1

We love Him because He first loved us. If someone says, 'I love God,' and hates his brother, he is a liar; for he who does not love his brother whom he has seen, how can he love God whom he has not seen? And this commandment we have from Him: that he who loves God must love his brother also. Whoever believes that Jesus is the Christ is born of God, and everyone who loves Him who begot also loves him who is begotten of Him.

1 John 4:19–5:1, NKJV

### Expository Message

In this text John is concluding his exhortation that we love one another. That is one of the three major themes in this letter: the themes of righteousness, truth, and love. This book has three cycles of teaching on those themes. Each cycle builds on the previous teaching, so that we receive ever-increasing understanding from the apostle. John's instruction may seem redundant on the surface. But he is going somewhere every time he comes back to these essential subjects. These three subjects are so important, they bear repeating. A person's eternal destiny depends on getting this right.

In your journey through school as a child, you were taught reading, writing, and arithmetic over and over. You had those subjects in the first grade at one level, then again in the second grade. The process continued each year even through high school. Why was the education system designed that way? First, we learn through repetition. Therefore, some of the material covered in the first grade was covered again in the second grade. That provided foundation for the additional concepts on the subject to be added. That process continued every year. Repetition is a fundamental principle for teaching. Secondly, these three subjects are so vital that everything else depends on them. If you don't get these down, you're in big trouble for everything else. Image trying to function as an adult without knowing how to read, how to write, and how to count. It's not something you can jump past or just skim over in your education.

The same is true for John's three themes in this letter. Righteousness, truth, and love are indispensable in the kingdom of God. John's concern in this epistle is that we know for sure that we have eternal life. He says that in 1 John 5:13. "These things I have written to you who believe in the name of the Son of God, that you may know that you have eternal life, and that you may continue to believe in the name of the Son of God" (NKJV). John is giving three tests that we can use to make sure we have been born again, we have eternal life, and we are continuing to live in that reality. So today we come to the last few words from John's exhortation about loving one another. I find in our text five assertions that fortify John's argument that we should love one another. Two of those are in verse 20, and one is in each of the other verses.

## LEARNING FROM GOD'S EXAMPLE

John's first assertion is that God has taught us to love one another by His own example toward us. Verse 19 says, "We love Him because He first loved us." The New King James Version has stayed with the King James Version, but the manuscript evidence is that the pronoun translated "Him" is not in the original text.[1] I was a bit disturbed to learn that because I have so much emotional attachment to the King James Version of that verse. I do love *Him* because He first loved me! And John is not denying that. In fact, it is included in his statement. But the statement is broader than that. In the context, it especially includes our love for one another.

Our capacity to operate in divine love is solely generated by Him first loving us. The way we know this love at all is by what He has done for us. "By this we know love, because He laid down His life for us" (3:16, NKJV). He has revealed His love to us through Jesus, especially at the cross. He has put that love in our hearts through the new birth. It is only *because He first loved us* that we have any understanding of divine love. It is only *because He first loved us* that we have the capacity to love. Keep in mind that we're talking about agapē love, not *philia* love—not natural, human love. That is very important for understanding verse 20. We can love "because He first loved us."

The excuse for not loving has been removed. God has poured His love out in our hearts. We have the blessed Holy Spirit abiding in us. We have been given a new nature characterized by love. Is there another Christian that you just can't love? Well, the truth is you can love that fellow believer. You may not be able to *like* him. There may be things in his behavior or personality that really rub you wrong. But you can and should *love* him. That's John's point in our text. According to John, the person who cannot love another Christian must not be saved himself.[2] That is a very sobering thought.

Ponder the first two words in verse 19: "We love."[3] Can we legitimately say that along with John, *we love*? If we put that on the front door of our church, would it be true? Would those who come into the church leave saying it is true of those people? Would those I work with on the job say it is true of me? *We love.* What about your family? Is that the way your family members would describe you and the relationships at home? The real test of love is not found in those we hardly know. It is found in those who know us well. It is found in our close, daily relationships. If it could be said truthfully, it would be a powerful mission statement for any church. Very simply: *WE LOVE!* To really live that out, a lot of other things have to be in place. Hopefully, we have learned that in our study of 1 John. But God's ultimate objective for you and me is that we could say, without contradiction, "We love." The New International version is a good translation of verse 19: "We love because He first loved us." He has not only taught us to love by His own example, but He has empowered us to love by the infilling of the Holy Spirit.

# LINK BETWEEN LOVING GOD AND LOVING PEOPLE

John's second assertion is that loving God and loving people are irrevocably linked. You can't have one without the other.[4] They are two sides of the same coin. If you're a loving person, you will love God and you will love people who are made in His image. Look at the first half of verse 20. "If someone says, 'I love God,' and hates his brother, he is a liar" (NKJV). That is strong, confrontive language. John uses that language three times in this epistle.[5] First John 2:4: "He who says, 'I know Him,' and does not keep His commandments, is a liar, and the truth is not in him" (NKJV). That was said in conjunction with the test of practical righteousness. First John 2:22: "Who is a liar but he who denies that Jesus is the Christ?" (NKJV). That was said in reference to the test of truth. Now while administering the test of love John writes, "If someone says, 'I love God,' and hates his brother, he is a liar."

John is confronting the Gnostics who were claiming to be very spiritual, claiming a close, intimate relationship with God; yet they did not demonstrate that love in their relationships with people. Later the church father, Ignatius, said of them, "They give no heed to love, caring not for the widow, the orphan, or the afflicted, neither for those who are in bonds nor those who are released from bonds, neither for the hungry nor the thirsty."[6] John is confronting a pseudo spirituality that claims godliness, but never demonstrates it in the way they treat other people. Remember John's admonition in 1 John 3:18. "My little children, let us not love in word or in tongue, but in deed and in truth" (NKJV).

It's impossible for me to observe your internal love for God.[7] The way I know that is there is by the love you demonstrate in your daily relationships with people. Anyone can say, "I love God." It's something difficult to dispute. When you're worshipping God, I don't know what's really going on in your heart. Is it all for show or is it real and sincere? God knows, but I can't say with certainty. The way I can know you love God is to observe your kindness and generosity toward other people. In the final judgment Jesus will say to you and me, "To the extent that you did it to one of these brothers of Mine, *even* the least *of them*, you did it to Me." (Matt. 25:40, NASB). To the Gnostic, and hopefully never to any of us, he will say, "I was hungry, and you gave Me *nothing* to eat; I was thirsty, and you gave

Me nothing to drink; I was a stranger, and you did not invite Me in; naked, and you did not clothe Me; sick, and in prison, and you did not visit Me" NASB). Matthew 25:44–45 continues,

> Then they themselves also will answer, 'Lord, when did we see You hungry, or thirsty, or a stranger, or naked, or sick, or in prison, and did not take care of You?' Then He will answer them, 'Truly I say to you, to the extent that you did not do it to one of the least of these, you did not do it to Me (NASB).

Some segments of today's Christian community have not enjoyed much spiritual experience. They have been born again, but they have not progressed much beyond that in personal revelations. They are not taught Paul's instruction on spiritual gifts in 1 Corinthians 12. The dreams and visions that Peter talked about on the Day of Pentecost are not a part of their understanding of Christianity for today.[8] There is not as much danger of them making the error John is confronting here as for those who enjoy a more spiritual walk with God.[9] Their tendency is to live their Christianity out at a very natural, nonspiritual level. On the other hand, people in our movement must pay attention to John's teaching here and be very careful that our spirituality is lived out in practical ways. If we're not careful, we can take on a pseudo spirituality that feels right but does not pass John's love test.

I knew one brother who would spend his whole day in a prayer closet but would not go to work and provide for his family. I'm sure he was trying to advance with God. He had seen the value of a strong prayer life. But obedience is better than sacrifice. He was not attending to his first duties.[10] He was not unselfishly caring for others in tangible ways. As a result, all that prayer did not result in power and anointing. Instead his marriage eventually fell apart.

I know an extremely gifted Bible teacher who lost all her ministry potential for a similar reason. She spent hours in Bible study. If you were to ask her to vacuum the sanctuary or help in the nursery when someone didn't show up, her response was to say that was not her ministry. It had to be super spiritual or she wouldn't do it. Her influence with people dried up over time. A problem with spiritual pride sabotaged her relationships. What might have been, never happened; her potential was never realized. We know it is not efficient to tie up a gifted teacher with tasks that other people are equipped and called to do. I have been blessed with congregations that understand that. We all need to focus on our giftings as we function in the Body of Christ. On the other hand, we are never too spiritual to clean the bathrooms. We must have a heart that is willing to do whatever needs to be done to advance the cause of Christ.

After pastoring full time for a good while, I found myself needing to supplement our income by working at an auto paint shop in Iowa. My job was mostly washing cars and doing whatever else others didn't want to do. The foreman was a prideful, ungodly man who rode me hard. One day I was complaining to the Lord about my "unfair" circumstances. God answered that complaint by telling me to thank Him for caring enough to protect me from pride. That awful job was actually a gift from God and an opportunity to humble myself. I had enjoyed a long season with a lot of support from the congregation. A lot of the daily grunt work was done by others. At that point in my journey, I needed a good reminder to keep my feet on the ground and my hands to the plow. A leader who will not get his hands dirty with simple, hard work is skating on thin ice. Menial work is a good reminder of who we really are, no matter how much God uses us in spiritual things. Manual labor may not feel very spiritual, but it can be an important part of your spiritual training and development.

You cannot separate your love for God and your love for people. If you really love God, you will demonstrate that by the way you love people. "If someone says. . . ." When John begins a sentence like that, you can know he is about to correct something. He does it three times in chapter two. "He who *says*, 'I know Him,' and does not keep His commandments, is a liar (2:4, NKJV) (emphasis mine). "He who *says* he abides in Him ought himself also to walk just as He walked" (emphasis mine, 2:6, NKJV). First John 2:9 is very similar to our text. "He who *says* he is in the light, and hates his brother, is in darkness until now" (emphasis mine, NKJV). The reality of a person's relationship with God is manifested in that person's attitude and behavior toward other people.

"If someone says, 'I love God,' and hates his brother, he is a liar." Once again, John deals with these issues in very black and white terms. You either love your brother or you hate him. Don't try to claim neutral ground; there is no neutral ground to stand on. If he is in need, you either help him or you don't help him. If he has wronged you, you either forgive him or you don't forgive him. Our response is either one of love or hate. We saw that earlier in the way Cain treated his brother, Abel. His uncaring attitude blossomed into a hateful, violent murder. The nature of his murderous attitude was there long before he committed the act of murder. It resided in his heart in the seed form of jealousy and resentment. The essence of the seed and the eventual fruit were all of the same nature. Jesus taught the same thing in the Sermon on the Mount.

> You have heard that it was said to those of old, "You shall not murder, and whoever murders will be in danger of the judgment." But I say to you that whoever is angry with his brother without a cause shall be in danger of the judgment. And whoever says to his brother, "Raca!" shall be in danger of the council. But whoever says, "You fool!" shall be in danger of hell fire (Matt. 5:21–22, NKJV).

To hate your brother, and then turn around and say, "I love God," is not credible. It's self-deception. John says it's a lie. If you really love God, you will love your brothers and sisters in Christ.

## TANGIBLE OPPORTUNITIES TO LOVE PEOPLE

Now we come to the most difficult statement in our text, the second half of verse 20. John's assertion here will need some explanation. Let me state it this way. Our opportunity to love people is more immediate than our opportunity to love God. Here is the statement: "For he who does not love his brother whom he has seen, how can he love God whom he has not seen?" That statement is not easy to understand.

First, it doesn't seem consistent with what Jesus said about the two great commandments. Jesus said the first commandment is that we love God. That's the top priority. Loving our neighbor comes second. And Jesus indicates that our love for God should permeate our whole being. When asked what the first commandment is, Jesus answered in Mark 12:29–31,

"The first of all the commandments is: 'Hear, O Israel, the Lord our God, the Lord is one. And you shall love the Lord your God with all your heart, with all your soul, with all your mind, and with all your strength.' This is the first commandment. And the second, like it, is this: 'You shall love your neighbor as yourself'" (NKJV). There is an obvious priority on the first commandment to love God. If it comes down to honoring God or honoring my neighbor, the honor of God is more important. Loving God is the first commandment. Loving my neighbor comes second. It seems to me loving my neighbor flows out of my relationship with God. God has the preeminence at every turn.

The second reason John's statement initially sounds wrong is that it doesn't seem consistent with our experience. The affection I feel for God is greater and flows easier than it does toward other Christians. Why is that? God has never done me wrong. He has really treated me good. He has loved me when I was not loving toward Him. He has been consistent in His love toward me. He gives and gives and gives to me. He forgives me seventy times seventy and then some. He is always looking out for my best interest. He is perfect and lovable in every way.

I can't say that about my brothers and sister in Christ. I do have some loving, faithful spiritual siblings. But even they fail me at times, just as I sometimes fail them. God never fails us! He is never, never selfish in His dealings with us. And then there are those Christians who actually do us wrong. I know we are to forgive them and love them regardless of what they do. But in the light of all that, I find myself questioning John's reasoning in verse 20.[11] John says, if we don't love our brother whom we've seen, how can we love God whom we have not seen? My answer is "Let me count the ways. Let's see, they stab me in the back; they say hurtful things to me; they take the big piece of pie and leave me the little one. Shall I go on?" My question for John is "How can you imply it is easier to love my imperfect brother than my perfect Savior? Do you want me to recount the unjust treatment I have received from some of them?" That's been my honest response to this verse.

There is no value in speaking religious platitudes and pretending that what I have just shared isn't so. Some commentaries just repeat what John has said and then move on. But what I need is a better understanding of what John is saying. Anytime my thoughts and feelings don't line up with the Bible, either I'm not understanding the passage, or I simply need to change my thinking to come into agreement with it. Scripture itself is never wrong. Scripture is inspired by God, without error. It is there for my correction and admonition. It sits in judgment over me; not vice versa. Anytime one passage seems to contradict another, the problem is my lack of understanding. I need more enlightenment on the matter. On the surface, verse 20 seems to contradict the words of Jesus concerning the greatest commandment. Knowing all that, I spent time asking God to give me the answer to these apparent contradictions. And I think He did that for me.

The answer lies first in putting John's statement in its context. His objective is to get us to love one another. He begins this discussion in verse 7: "Beloved, let us love one another, for love is of God" (NKJV). Now what have we learned since verse 7?[12]

The love he is talking about is agapē, the kind of love God has. He is not talking about *philia*, the natural human love that we are used to operating in. Now what are some of the characteristics of the divine, agapē, kind of love? It is unselfish. It is not looking out for what I can get from the object of my love.

It is not motivated by the quality of the object. God loved us when there was nothing at all in us worthy of love. He loved because He chose to love. This exposes a fundamental flaw in my previous reasoning. Remember my list of all the good things about God, and then my list of flaws in fellow Christians? All that thinking was inconsistent with agapē. It was valid reasoning in regard to *philia*. Human, natural love, looks for qualities it admires and likes in the person and responds to those with natural affection. But agapē does not operate out of the quality of its object. It operates independent of that. So, all my argument about how nice God is and how mean Christians can be at times has no validity in understanding John's statement. John is not talking about *philia* love. He's talking about agapē.

The love John is talking about is not a feeling; it's a choice, demonstrated by action.[13] You can choose to love even when your feelings about a person don't line up with the choice. Remember how we learned that loving and liking are two different things. There are all kinds of reasons we might not like a brother or sister in Christ. That should never stop us from loving that person. That should never stop us from acting in ways that promote that person's highest good. Agapē is found in the kind of behavior we express toward another person, not in how we feel about that person. Divine love is a choice, activated by the need the object has and expressed by actions that meet that need.[14]

So, with those reminders, how can John say, "He who does not love his brother whom he has seen, how can he love God whom he has not seen?" First, he is not talking about how we feel about the object of our love. He is not talking about the worthiness of that object. He is talking about expressing our love in tangible ways. He is recognizing the fact that we have much more opportunity to express love to our brothers and sisters in Christ than directly to God.[15] God has no need. He says in Psalm 50:12, "If I were hungry I would not tell you, For the world is Mine, and all it contains" (NASB). If we are not expressing love to fellow Christians whom we can see, we are not expressing love to God. Why? Because we express our love to God primarily by ministering to His children![16]

Before leaving this verse, let me also recognize another reason we may struggle with John's statement. Perhaps we are not looking at one another in the right way. Perhaps we are operating out of a carnal mind and failing to see each other the way we are in the Father's eyes. Paul wrote in 2 Corinthians 5:14–17,

> For the love of Christ controls us, having concluded this, that one died for all, therefore all died; and He died for all, so that they who live might no longer live for themselves, but for Him who died and rose again on their behalf. Therefore from now on we recognize no one according to the flesh; even though we have known Christ according to the flesh, yet now we know *Him in this way* no longer. Therefore if anyone is in Christ, *he is* a new creature; the old things passed away; behold, new things have come (NASB).

Too often when we look at a fellow Christian, we are focused on the old nature expressing itself through his flesh, rather than discerning who that person is in Christ. He is a new creature. He may not be yielding to his new nature like he should.[17] But what you're seeing in his fleshly behavior is not who he is at the core. He is a new creature in Christ. Paul says, "Therefore from now on we recognize no one according to the flesh." We don't discern them through our fleshly mind. We don't look on outward appearances and make our determination. We discern the spirit of the person, the renewed spirit in Christ. In one place Paul said to the Corinthians, "You are looking only on the surface of things" (2 Cor. 10:7, NIV). We don't just look on outward appearances. We see our relationship with that person through spiritual eyes. We understand people from a whole new perspective.[18] The new nature in that other Christian is a beautiful, lovable creation of God.[19] The New Revised Standard Version says, "From now on, therefore, we regard no one from a human point of view" (1 Cor. 5:16). When we see that brother or sister from God's point of view, it will be much easier to love them.

It's okay to "feel" more affection toward God than toward people. That's not John's issue in our text. There are more qualities in God to admire. He has obviously done more for us than people have. So, it is natural to feel more affection toward Him. It is reasonable that our *philia* love would be greater toward God than toward other human beings. But John is talking about a divine love that is moved to meet the need of its object. Remember when Jesus asked Peter if he loved him in John 21? Peter struggled in his response because his previous denial of Jesus had crushed his self-confidence. But here's how Jesus told Peter to express his love for the Lord. "Feed my lambs . . . feed my sheep . . . feed my sheep" (KJV). Do something for those who are Mine. Demonstrate your love for Me by taking care of them.

So, we have discussed three of John's assertions. In verse 19 we're told that God has taught us to love one another by His own example. In verse 20 John made two additional assertions: (1) Loving God and loving His people cannot be separated. You can't say you love God when you're not loving His people. (2) The opportunity to love our spiritual siblings is more readily available than loving God whom we cannot see, touch, or help.[20] "If someone says, 'I love God,' and hates his brother, he is a liar; for he who does not love his brother whom he has seen, how can he love God whom he has not seen?" Now we will deal with the last two assertions.

## COMMANDMENT TO LOVE ONE ANOTHER

John's fourth assertion is that God *commands* us to love one another. Verse 21 says, "And this commandment we have from Him: that he who loves God must love his brother also" (NKJV). Notice how John graciously reasons with us about loving one another. He really doesn't have to do that. The simple truth is God commands us to do it; that alone should be reason enough.[21]

In John 14:15 Jesus said, "If you love me, keep my commandments" (KJV). Then, in that same discussion He says, "This is My commandment, that you love one another, just as I have loved you." (John 15:12, NASB). If we really love the Lord, we will keep His commandment to love one another.

It is impossible to be right with God without being right with our brothers and sisters in Christ. That doesn't mean there won't be misunderstandings. In some cases, the other party will not be willing to resolve the conflict. But for me to stay right with God, I must always behave in love toward the other party.[22] I must stay completely willing to resolve the matter. I am responsible to take the action Scripture tells me to take. It's interesting how the New Testament commands both parties to go to the other one to resolve it. Neither party has the luxury to sit back and wait for the other one to respond. In Matthew 5:24 Jesus tells me that if I know a fellow Christian is offended at me, I am to leave my gift at the altar and go be reconciled to him. On the other side of the conflict, Matthew 18:15 tells the offended party to take the initiative. Both parties have that responsibility to actively pursue a resolution.

So, the commandment to love one another is plain and clear. Whatever we may know or not know about John's rationale, the simplicity of the command can't be missed. God wants us to love one another. He wants us to express that love in tangible, concrete ways. He wants us forgiving one another, encouraging one another, serving one another, and caring for one another. We can't plead ignorance on that. We know it and happy are we if we do it.

## LOVING GOD'S OFFSPRING

John makes one more assertion in 5:1. His assertion is that if we love God, it should naturally follow we would love His offspring who are our spiritual siblings. First John 5:1 says, "Whoever believes that Jesus is the Christ is born of God, and everyone who loves Him who begot also loves him who is begotten of Him."

The main thing that distinguishes believers from nonbelievers is the new birth. "You must be born again" (John 3:7, NASB). You can agree with me about a lot of teachings. Our views on marriage and parenting may be very similar. We may both see the world headed for Armageddon. Our political views can be virtually the same. We may have many things in common and like one another for a number of reasons. But you are only my brother in Christ, if you've been born again. Nothing substitutes for the new birth. That marks the great divide in humanity.[23] The world is alienated from God and does not know God. It is our passion that they come to know God. We actively proclaim the gospel, so they can come to know God. But anyone who has not been born again is of the old creation and are separated from God—just as we were before surrendering our lives to the Lord.

On the other hand, everyone who is born again is my brother or sister in Christ. We are spiritual siblings, born of the same seed. I don't know my spiritual siblings after the flesh; I know them in the Spirit, as God's own dear children. They may belong to a different political party than I belong to. They may hold many views that clash with my views. Their interpretation of many verses in the Bible may be different than mine. But if they have been born again, they are in the family of God, and I am to treat them with love and respect as brothers and sisters in Christ.

John says, "Whoever believes that Jesus is the Christ is born of God" (5:1). There are some fundamental truths that must be embraced in order to be saved. Most of those revolve around who Jesus is and the salvation He provides. When a person really believes in something, his behavior follows that belief. If I believe Jesus is the Christ, then I believe He is the only way of salvation. I entrust myself and my eternal destiny to Him. It naturally follows that I would do what He tells me to do. One evidence that a person has been born again is that person's faith in Jesus as the Christ.

John makes this assertion in 5:1: "Everyone who loves Him who begot also loves him who is begotten of Him." Even nature teaches this principle.[24] You know the old saying, "Blood is thicker than water." It is an affirmation of the love and commitment biological siblings have toward one another. We have an affinity toward one another because we belong to the same family; we have the same parents. John uses that natural reality to argue from. If we love our heavenly Father, it's only reasonable we would also love our spiritual siblings. And we love *all* of them: red, yellow, black, and white; Republican and Democrat; conservative and liberal; kind and cantankerous; likeable and not so likeable. The basis of our affinity is our common heritage in Christ. Ephesians 2:14 proclaims, "For he is our peace, who hath made both one, and hath broken down the middle wall of partition between us" (KJV). Paul was focused on the separation between Jew and Gentile in that verse. But the principle holds true for every human affiliation. Our strongest bond is with fellow believers. It is stronger than nationality. It is stronger than ethnicity. It is ultimately stronger than biological blood ties. We must jealously honor our relationship with the Father's children, all our spiritual siblings.

Our nation has become very divided along political and even racial lines. The rhetoric that goes on in the media exacerbates the problem. More alarming, this rivalry is affecting many believers. Anything that divides God's children grieves the heart of the Father. We are to work at maintaining the unity of the Spirit among believers.[25] It's okay for Christians to disagree on political issues. It's okay to be loyal to one's nation. We can be faithful to a denominational family without having a sectarian spirit. But none of those affiliations ever justify being unloving toward any other believer. There's something wrong with a Christian who feels a rivalry against another denomination or even the church down the street. I hope the devil is not able to get Christians so focused on racial differences that they lose track of their kinship in Christ. Scripturally, our unity in Christ must take precedence over every other association. We don't just love Christians because they belong to our church or our denomination. We love them because they belong to our family in Christ. We try to help them because they are our brothers and sisters in Christ. That's John's assertion in 5:1.

He has given us good reason to love one another. John is concluding this exhortation that we practice love toward all our brothers and sisters in Christ. It's easier said than done. But it can be done, and God expects us to do it.

# Endnotes: Chapter 22

1    Burdick, 338–339. Cf. Stott, 170; Smalley, 234; Yarbrough, 266.

2    Stedman, 333.

3    The Greek word translated "we love" is in the present tense verb indicating continuing or habitual action. Cf. Burdick, 338.

4    Referencing 1 John 3:23, Stott (p. 171) considers loving God and loving people as one command. Cf. Smalley, 264–265; Dodd, p. xiv; Barclay, 102.

5    John Stott (p, 170) refers to this as "the three black lies of the Epistle." Three Black Lies would be a good title for a message on these three passages.

6    Law, 30. Cf. Burdick, 151–152. See Paul's description of some of his contemporaries in 2 Tim. 3:2–3 and James's description of pure religion in James 1:27.

7    Smalley, 263. Cf. Burdick, 342.

8    Acts 2:16–17.

9    These Christians are resistant to mysticism in any form. Therefore, they are not very open to the pseudo spirituality found in most Gnostic teaching. However, John is not rejecting all mystical experiences. The book of Revelation is sure proof of that. He is confronting mysticism that fails his three tests of righteousness, truth, and love.

10    Cf. 1 Tim. 5:8; Eph. 4:28: 1 Thess. 4:11–12. Also consider Paul's example of practical service (1 Cor. 4:12; 1 Thess. 2:9).

11    Donald Burdick (p. 340) gives textual evidence for translating this as a statement of fact rather than a question. The New International Version translates 1 John 4:20b, "For anyone who does not love his brother, Whom he has seen, cannot love God, whom he has not seen." His heart is simply not in the condition to do so.

12    Cf. chapters 19–21 of this book.

13    Lewis, *Mere Christianity,* 129–133. Cf. Dodd, 123.

14    Law, pp. 70–73, 76. Cf. John MacArthur, *1–3 John,* 171.

15    The self-deception John confronts in people who "say" they love God, but don't serve those around them can also be made against those who claim to love people on the other side of the world but won't serve the people that live within their own house. It's easy for me to say I love the people in China, but what am I actually doing that demonstrates that love?

16    Cf. Matt 25:40: "Truly I say to you, to the extent that you did it to one of these brothers of Mine, *even* the least *of them,* you did it to Me." (NASB).

17    Cf. Gal. 5:13–16; Rom. 6:12–19; 8:1–12.

18    Ladd, 510: "To be in Christ is to be a new creation by virtue of which an entirely different interpretation is given to life and its relationships. . . ."

19    C. S. Lewis, in his book, *Weight of Glory*, wrote, "It is a serious thing to live in a society of possible gods and goddesses, to remember that the dullest and most uninteresting person you can talk to may one day be a creature which, if you saw it now, you would be strongly tempted to worship. . . ." "Be Careful," *The Official Website of C. S. Lewis*. Retrieved Jan. 25, 2018 from http://www.cslewis.com/be-careful/.

20    Law, 250–252, 294. Cf. Stott, 171; Zodhiates, *The Epistles of John*, 303; Loyd-Jones, 552–556.

21    Loyd-Jones, 556. Loyd-Jones structures his message around John's arguments for loving one another. He takes one argument from each verse.

22    Rom. 12:18; Matt. 5:38–48.

23    Cf. Spurgeon, "The Works of the Devil Destroyed," preached July 1, 1883. Accessed at The C. H. Spurgeon Collection on CD-ROM (AGES Software, Inc., 1998).

24    Dodd, 125. Cf. Law, 71–72.

25    Eph. 4:1–6.

CHAPTER 23

# Connecting the Dots
# 5:1–3

Whoever believes that Jesus is the Christ is born of God,
and everyone who loves Him who begot also loves him
who is begotten of Him. By this we know that we love
the children of God, when we love God and keep His
commandments. For this is the love of God, that we keep
His commandments. And His commandments are not
burdensome.

1 John 5:1–3, NKJV

Expository Message

This text summarizes what John has been saying in this letter and
demonstrates the link between his three tests of righteousness, truth, and
love. John now connects the dots so that a clear picture emerges for what
he wants us to see.[1]

## OVERALL STRUCTURE OF THIS EPISTLE.

Consider with me the overall structure of this book. Broadly speaking,
what has John been saying and how has he communicated it in this epistle?
As we previously said, John does not follow a straight line of reasoning
like we find in some of Paul's epistles.[2] Since he doesn't do that, some

have thought there is no clear structure.[3] But there is rhyme and reason to John's approach. It's just different than we are used to in modern literature. Some divide the epistle into two parts. The first half of the book, ending at 3:10 focuses on God as light. The second half focuses on God as love.[4] That is a useful division. However, the most helpful way to approach this letter is to recognize three cycles of teaching. Within each cycle the three recurring themes of righteousness, truth, and love are addressed. Robert Law said, "It is like a winding staircase—always revolving around the centre, always recurring to the same topics, but at a higher level."[5] He uses the term "belief," instead of truth to refer to the doctrinal test of salvation. The following outline is representative of His structure:

Prologue: 1:1–1:4
1st Cycle: 1:5–2:28 (Walking in Light tested by Righteousness, Love, and Belief)
    Righteousness: 1:8–2:6
    Love: 2:7–2:17
    Belief: 2:18–2:28
2nd Cycle: 2:29–4:6 (Divine Sonship tested by Righteousness, Love, and Belief)
    Righteousness: 2:29–3:10a
    Love: 3:10b–3:24a
    Belief: 3:24b–4:6
3rd Cycle: 4:7–5:21 (Interrelations of Love, Belief, and Righteousness)
    Righteousness takes a subordinate place and is woven in with the other two themes.
    Love: 4:7–5:3a
    Belief: 5:3b–5:21[6]

## PURPOSE OF THE EPISTLE

As we have studied this letter, John's purpose has become more and more clear. His statement of purpose in 1 John 5:13 is very enlightening. "These things I have written to you who believe in the name of the Son of God, that you may know that you have eternal life, and that you may continue to believe in the name of the Son of God" (NKJV). His subject is eternal life! That is his one focus. He comes at it again and again. Why? If that is not a reality in your life, nothing else matters! If you're moving toward eternal damnation, who cares what your eschatology is. Studying the gifts of the Spirit is a waste of time without the foundation of salvation. Everything depends on whether you're born again or not. So, John gives three tests that professors of the faith are to use to make sure they are saved.

First is the test of practical righteousness. Do you live in obedience to the commandments of God? Anyone can claim to have the imputed righteousness of Christ.[7] But if that internal righteousness is not demonstrated in your moral, ethical lifestyle, it is highly suspect. First John 2:3–4 says, "Now by this we know that we know Him, if we keep His commandments. He who says, 'I know Him,' and does not keep His commandments, is a liar, and the truth is not in him" (NKJV). First John 3:7 adds, "Little children, let no one deceive you. He who practices righteousness is righteous, just as He is righteous" (NKJV).

Secondly, John administers the test of truth or belief. There are essential truths about who Jesus is and the way of salvation that are nonnegotiable. To be saved a person must embrace the humanity and the divinity of Christ. His atoning sacrifice on the cross is the only provision for salvation acceptable to the Father. Jesus is the only way of salvation. First John 2:22–23 asserts, "Who is a liar but he who denies that Jesus is the Christ? He is antichrist who denies the Father and the Son. Whoever denies the Son does not have the Father either; he who acknowledges the Son has the Father also" (NKJV). First John 4:14–15 says, "And we have seen and testify that the Father has sent the Son as Savior of the world. Whoever confesses that Jesus is the Son of God, God abides in him, and he in God" (NKJV).

Third, the test of love is essential. Evidence of the new nature is found in our behavior toward other people, especially toward other believers. You can't know and love God without it being expressed in your love toward His people. And that must be demonstrated in concrete, tangible behavior. First John 4:7–8: "Beloved, let us love one another, for love is of God; and everyone who loves is born of God and knows God. He who does not love does not know God, for God is love" (NKJV). First John 4:20–21 adds, "If someone says, 'I love God,' and hates his brother, he is a liar. . . . And this commandment we have from Him: that he who loves God must love his brother also" (NKJV).

So, John's message is this. If you have the real thing on the inside, it will manifest on the outside in the way you live your life. Your behavior will prove or disprove the authenticity of your faith. A person who claims to be born again yet lives just like the world is self-deceived. He fails to pass the tests John has presented here. The person who manifests these characteristics of righteousness, truth, and love can live in assurance of his salvation. His behavior will by no means be flawless. But the general tenor of his life will be characterized by righteousness, truth, and love.

John's paramount concern is salvation. My wife, Jeanie, summed up 1 John with this simple phrase: "Mirror, mirror on the wall, who's the saved ones after all?" First John acts as a mirror for us to determine that.[8] The tests are about salvation. They are not focused so much on the maturity level of a believer, as they are on whether a person is truly born again. John's primary aim is to equip professors of Christianity with three practical tests that manifest whether the person is really on his way to heaven or not. Throughout church history this has been needed. The tendency for people to sidestep the demands of the gospel and seek an easy believism has always been present in the church.[9] How many people have tragically slipped into eternity relying on a religious ritual; yet they did not have eternal life? How many people go to Christian churches each Sunday morning, claiming faith in Christ who have never, in fact, been born again? The message of 1 John is sorely needed today! In evangelical circles it has become very popular to lead people in "the sinner's prayer." Then we declare them "saved" because they said the words. I have led a number of people to the Lord using the sinner's prayer. It is a valid tool. But it is only an avenue of faith, not faith itself. Just as water baptism and Lord's Table are means of expressing faith. Those external activities do not, in themselves, produce the new nature. Nothing can substitute for the radical transformation that occurs in the new birth (2 Cor. 5:17; 1 Pet. 1:23). You must be born again (John 3:7). Without that transformation the person is outside the covenant of grace and lost in sin. John's one overriding concern is whether a person is truly born again and in a saving relationship with God through Christ.[10] A spiritual experience alone does not prove that. Just claiming it does not make it so. The three tests of righteousness, truth, and love must be applied. It needs to happen in all our churches.

## THREE TESTS OF SALVATION SUMMARIZED

John brings these three tests together in our text. See if you can identify them in these three short verses. "Whoever believes[11] that Jesus is the Christ is born of God, and everyone who loves Him who begot also loves him who is begotten of Him. By this we know that we love the children of God, when we love God and keep His commandments. For this is the love of God, that we keep His commandments. And His commandments are not burdensome" (1 John 5:1–3). Do you see the three tests mentioned there?

The test of truth: "Whoever believes that Jesus is the Christ is born of God." The test of love: "and everyone who loves Him who begot also loves him who is begotten of Him. By this we know that we love the children of God, when we love God." The test of righteousness: "By this we know that we love the children of God, when we love God and keep His commandments. For this is the love of God, that we keep His commandments. And His commandments are not burdensome."

The primary significance of that passage is that here John links all three tests together.[12] He connects the dots! The right belief about Jesus is linked with being *born of God.* Loving God and His children is linked with being begotten of God. And keeping God's commandments, living in obedience to God is linked with the other two tests. These function like a three-legged stool. All three tests must be given due consideration; all three characteristics must be evidenced.[13]

A common error is found in some people who think being loving toward others is the only test one must pass. They do not understand the necessity of being obedient to the commandments of God. They may not think it matters much what you believe, as long as you're nice to people. They may not think it matters much if you live by God's rules "as long as you're not hurting other people." Of course, God's commandments are designed to keep us from violating other people. But that is not always understood.[14]

During the Hippie Movement in the 1960's, people were sleeping with multiple partners and calling it love. Of course, sexual promiscuity has been going on since the beginning of mankind: as it was in the days of Noah. But that movement glamorized it as something beneficial and loving. Their thinking was that it didn't hurt anybody what two consenting adults did. But later in life those people found out it was hurting the future spouses. It was damaging their future marriages which, in turn, hurt their children. There were lots of people hurt by what they called "love." It was in violation of the commandments of God. Had they tested their concept of love using 5:2 of our text, they would have known that. Those people were operating out of a distorted definition of love. They were passing the test of love based on their own concept of what that love is. It's happening in our society today the same way. Sick, nonbiblical concepts of love are used to justify behavior contrary to the commandments of God. For many today, tolerance toward others virtually equates to love. But John's definition of agapē is anything but tolerance. In fact, he is confronting an error of the Gnostics in that regard all through this epistle. The test of love must be based on a biblical revelation of what that love is. And the test of love must be considered in conjunction with the other two tests. "By this we know that we love the children of God, when we love God and keep His commandments (1 John 5:2)."[15]

The focus of some groups is on righteousness. They rigidly adhere to the commandments of God, as they understand them. They have little compassion toward those who violate those commandments. They come across as harsh and legalistic. Their tendency is to try very hard to do right and insist on others doing the same. Rather than loving and helping those under the bondage of sin, they condemn them and reject them. The Pharisees in Jesus's day are profound examples of this. They tithed down to the penny and were proud of their adherence to the external rules laid down. They avoided anyone who might contaminate their "holiness." They were appalled that Jesus would interact with publicans and sinners as He did at Matthew's house.[16] Their focus was the test of righteousness, as they understood it. Jesus confronted their brand of legalism by telling them they were actually living in hypocrisy, even though they considered themselves the only ones who were really serving God. In Matthew 23:23–24 Jesus said to them,

Woe to you, teachers of the law and Pharisees, you hypocrites! You give a tenth of your spices—mint, dill and cumin. But you have neglected the more important matters of the law—justice, mercy and faithfulness. You should have practiced the latter, without neglecting the former. You blind guides! You strain out a gnat but swallow a camel (NIV).

They, of course, were failing the test of truth as they rejected Jesus's message, and rejected Him who is the way, the truth, and the life.[17] They were actually violating the two great commandments and were miserably failing the test of love. Had they honestly administered the test of love, they might have realized their true condition and their own need for repentance. Each of John's three tests helps properly define the others.

Doctrine is important. What you believe matters! John confronts wrong belief throughout this epistle. In fact, he does it at the beginning of our text. "Whoever believes that Jesus is the Christ is born of God."[18] Anyone who denies Jesus as the Christ, the Savior of the world cannot be saved. That truth is essential to salvation. It is a crucial test. But when a group only focuses on doctrine, they tend to become cold and out of touch with people. When that is the only test being used, their Christianity tends toward intellectual assent, rather than vital relationships with God and others. How many denominations have dried up and gone into decline while contending for their particular theological slant, all the while failing to reach people for Christ? The test of truth or belief must be administered, but it must be considered in conjunction with the test of righteousness and of love. When a group overemphasizes the test of truth and neglects the other two tests, it's easy for them to fall into moral laxity as well. Just as the Gnostics overemphasized knowledge, they rely on a creed to carry them into heaven. But the sincerity of the belief system is proven by the person's daily behavior. The two must not be separated. If my belief system does not produce practical righteousness and tangible expressions of love toward people, something is wrong.

So, in our brief text, John links the three tests together. An expression of love that does not keep the commandments of God is not biblical love. A righteousness based on anything other than faith in Christ, is not a biblical

315

righteousness. When we consider all three tests in conjunction with each other we have a valid, objective measurement of whether the person has been truly born again and is headed toward heaven.

## MUTUAL REINFORCEMENT OF THE THREE TESTS

These tests also reinforce one another. If one test is not yielding the assurance you need, apply the other tests. How do I know I love my spiritual siblings? We have talked a lot about how we answer that question. But if we are still left unsure, examine it further by applying the other tests.[19] Notice again how John recommends that in verse 2 of our text. How do I know I really love my fellow believers? "By this[20] we know that we love the children of God, when we love God and keep His commandments."[21] There the test of love is examined under the light of the test of righteousness.[22]

On the surface, it may seem like John is using circular reasoning.[23] Back in 4:20 he teaches us the way to know if we really love God is to look at the way we treat our fellow Christians. "If someone says, 'I love God,' and hates his brother, he is a liar; for he who does not love his brother whom he has seen, how can he love God whom he has not seen? (NKJV)." We examined that closely in the last chapter. In that verse, John gives a criterion for testing our love for God. We prove our love for God by the way we act toward people. In our current text, it is the other way around. The proof that we love people is evidenced by how we act toward the commandments of God. "By this we know that we love the children of God, when we love God and keep His commandments" (1 John 5:2).

Our love for people is proved by our love for God, and our love for God is proved by our love for people. Why is that so? It's the same love in the heart. Our love for God and our love for people are just two sides of the same coin. If I look at one side of a quarter and see the authentic image, I recognize it as a quarter. If I look at the other side and see the image that's supposed to be there, I have proof it's a quarter. If I look at one side and it appears genuine, but then see something wrong on the other side, then I have cause for concern. What I'm pointing out from our text today is how interrelated and interdependent the three tests are.[24]

In the long run, your behavior will tend to define your doctrine, and your doctrine will tend to define your behavior. You do what you really believe in your heart. You don't necessarily do what you *say* you believe. You act out of what you *really* believe. That's why a person who really believes in his heart that Jesus is the Christ will obey Him. He is convinced that what Jesus tells us to do can be trusted. Therefore, he does what the Lord says to do. So, sincere belief eventually defines behavior.

A person who is living contrary to his belief system will eventually change his behavior to fit his doctrine or he will eventually change his doctrine to accommodate his behavior. The incongruity of belief and behavior inside is too uncomfortable over the long run. We can live with it in the short run; but not in the long run. That's why a person's habitual pattern of life is a valid test of authentic Christianity, but his short-term behavior may not be. The Gnostic who wants to live an immoral life will twist Scripture to justify that lifestyle, if he is unwilling to repent. I learned a long time ago, when a person is claiming to be an agnostic or atheist, don't waste your time debating intellectually whether there is a God or not. Simply ask him, "If there is a God, and there is moral accountability as taught in the Bible, what are you doing right now that you would have to stop doing?" That is likely a key motive behind his intellectual position. What you truly believe matters, and it will manifest itself in behavior. The lifestyle you insist on following will influence the way you interpret Scripture. The tendency is to rationalize and justify behavior we are unwilling to change. Applying all three tests provides a through, reliable demonstration of what is really there on the inside—whether the person has eternal life or not.

## RESULTS PRODUCED BY THESE TESTS

These tests are designed to produce one of two results. Either they indicate that you are indeed born again and have eternal life, or they indicate that you are not God's child and should deal with your situation from that standpoint.

The proof that you truly belong to the Lord should produce increased assurance in your heart. Remember John's teaching on assurance in 4:13–18? It is essential to our emotional wellbeing and spiritual development. John wrote this epistle so that you could *know* you have eternal life. No Christian should live one minute under a cloud of doubt about that.[25]

Listen to his stated purpose again in 1 John 5:13. "These things I have written to you who believe in the name of the Son of God, that you may know that you have eternal life, and that you may continue to believe in the name of the Son of God." Do you know in your heart that you have eternal life? Is it for you a settled fact? Not maybe; not I hope so; not I'll find out when I die—but now, today, I know I have been born again and am a child of God. I've got a lot to learn. I've got some overcoming to do. I've got some maturing to do. But I am God's child. If you don't have that assurance, it's important to seek the Lord until the assurance is there.

At the beginning of this letter John stated his purpose in these words: "That which we have seen and heard we declare to you, that you also may have fellowship with us; and truly our fellowship is with the Father and with His Son Jesus Christ. And these things we write to you that your joy may be full" (1 John 1:3–4, NKJV). That fellowship with God and His people is only possible through the new birth. The fellowship is, in the Greek, koinōnia: a partnership and participation in the life of God. It is equivalent to eternal life. John wants us to have that eternal life and to live in the assurance that we have it. Only then can our joy be full. The joy John is talking about is not dependent on your external circumstances. There is a certain joy in buying a new car or getting the house of your dreams. But that joy comes and goes. The joy of living in fellowship with God and His people is an ongoing experience and privilege. It is something inside that sustains us even in the most difficult trials of life.[26] Everything can be going wrong around us, and we can still sing, "It is well with my soul."[27]

The value of John's letter is found in applying the tests to our own lives. By doing that we either gain assurance or we realize our need for God to transform us by His Spirit. John's approach to verifying salvation is very different than the way we usually do it. We ask people if they've been born again. If they say they have received Christ, we take that at face value and proceed. It's a valid question. A person who can reply in the positive probably does have a personal assurance of salvation. But what if the person's doctrine does not line up with the basics John teaches in this epistle? What if the person's behavior toward people is anything but loving? What if the person's lifestyle is immoral and completely contrary to the commandments of God? Do we just ignore all that? Or do the results of those tests act as caution lights, warning of something that needs to be addressed in the person's life?

On the Day of Judgment there will be people who are shocked to discover the Lord never knew them. They thought they were living their lives acceptable before God. Yet in the final analysis, Jesus tells them to depart from Him. Listen to what Jesus says in Matthew 7:21–23.

> Not everyone who says to Me, "Lord, Lord," will enter the kingdom of heaven, but he who does the will of My Father who is in heaven *will enter*. Many will say to Me on that day, "Lord, Lord, did we not prophesy in Your name, and in Your name cast out demons, and in Your name perform many miracles?" And then I will declare to them, "I never knew you; DEPART FROM ME, YOU WHO PRACTICE LAWLESSNESS" (NASB).

Not everyone who *says*, "I've been born again," has, in reality, experienced that transformation. Not everyone who goes to church on Sunday morning is a Christian. Not everyone who claims to be a Christian, is one. That's why John gives these three tests. God is not willing that any should perish. He gives us, in this epistle, a way to know one way or another right now. That way there are no unpleasant surprises in the end. I would never want one of my parishioners to hear those fatal words from the Lord, "I never knew you; DEPART FROM ME, YOU WHO PRACTICE LAWLESSNESS."

So, I ask you to consider John's three tests in your own life. Do you believe in your heart that Jesus is the Christ, the eternal Son of God, the Savior of the world, the only way of salvation? Is His love expressed in tangible, practical ways in your behavior toward other people, especially toward those of the household of faith?[28] Do you live according to the commandments of God? Is your life characterized, not by the world's standards of conduct, but by His standards, as revealed in the Bible? If your general answer to those questions is "yes," then you have eternal life and you should live in that confidence. If your general answer to those questions is "no," then now is the time to surrender your life to Christ.[29] If you will come to Him in humble repentance, He will not push you away.

He will embrace you in His arms and give you eternal life. The invitation recorded in John 3:16–17 is extended to anyone who will sincerely receive it.[30] "For God so loved the world that He gave His only begotten Son, that whoever believes in Him should not perish but have everlasting life. For God did not send His Son into the world to condemn the world, but that the world through Him might be saved" (NIV).

# Endnotes: Chapter 23

1 When I was a child, I enjoyed connect-the-dots puzzles in which the child draws lines between the dots and a picture emerges of a butterfly, a bird, or some other object. We have progressed in our study to where it is possible to connect the dots of John's message in this epistle. In the text we see the connection between the three tests, and a picture of what John is doing in this letter can now be clearly seen.

2 The common division of doctrine in the first part and exhortation in the second, as found in Ephesians and Colossians, is not there. Cf. Raymond Brown, 119. The linear logic of Romans 1–8 does not dominate John's first epistle. Dodd (p. xxii) says, "The striking aphorisms . . . do not usually emerge as the conclusion of a line of argument. They come in flashes. . . ." Burdick (p. 85) characterizes this writing as "intuitive rather than analytic and deductive." For an extensive review of attempts to organize 1 John, see Raymond Brown, 116–129. Although an examination of a book's structure is usually addressed at the beginning of a study, I postponed that until this chapter where it naturally fits into John's narrative.

3 Raymond Brown, 116–117, 124.

4 Ibid., 124. Cf. Smalley, pp. xxxiii–xxxiv; Yarbrough, 22–25.

5 Robert Law, 5. Cf. Dodd, p. xxi. Transitions in John's epistle are not clearly marked. He often uses what Raymond Brown (p. 119) calls "hinge verses" which contain themes of both the previous section and the coming section. It is, therefore, difficult to know which section in which to place the hinge verse.

6 Law, 5–24. Independent of Robert Law, Theodor Häring developed a similar structure, which was adopted by Brook (pp. xxxiv–xxxviii. Burdick (pp. 85–92), Stott (p. 55), and MacArthur, *1–3 John* (pp. 10–11) pattern their structures after that of Robert Law. Law's structure does not perfectly fit John's writing, but it is useful for organizing the message. Cf. Brown, 121–122. It's doubtful that John was thinking in terms of these three cycles when he wrote the letter. He was more likely writing out of a spontaneous, intuitive concern for the people, rather than trying to create a well-structured document.

7 The only righteousness acceptable to God is the righteousness of Christ which is imputed to the believer when he or she is born again (Rom. 3:22; 4:5–25; 5:17–21; 1 Cor. 1:30; Eph. 4:24; Phil. 3:9). But John's concern is the evidence of whether that imputed righteousness is really in the professor's heart.

8 Cf. Jas. 1:23–24.

9 The demands of the gospel are a response to God's love and do not earn salvation. However, true believers do respond to Jesus's call to discipleship (Matt. 16:24–26; Luke 14:26–27; Titus 1:16; 2:11–15).

10  John's polemical concern with Gnostic heresy is secondary, even though it is on his mind as he writes. Cf. Brooke, xxvii–xxviii, xxx.

11  The present tense for this Greek verb suggests the need for continuous faith. Cf. Smalley, 266; Burdick, 342.

12  Law, 15; Stott, 171.

13  Stedman, 338: "These three must all be present. This is the whole argument of the Epistle of John. They must all be present and in an ever-increasing degree." Cf. Brooke, 128; Loyd-Jones, 575–584.

14  These groups tend to think God's commandments are rather arbitrary and perhaps outdated. It has become popular, even in many evangelical churches, to celebrate being free from the commandments of God. In fact, those who call for obedience to God's commandments are often characterized as old fashion, legalistic people. Of course, there are people who are legalistic, and there are people who are stuck in religious traditions of the past. But living in obedience to God's commandments is not the same thing as being legalistic. Today most churches who follow this popular trend still call for some level of obedience. However, the trend is alarming. If we take that mindset to its logical conclusion, it ends in antinomianism (something John is combating in this epistle).

15  Cf. John 14:15, 23, 31; 1 John 2:5; 2 John 6; Raymond Brown, 540.

16  Matt. 9:9–13.

17  Cf. John 14:6.

18  There is disagreement among scholars as to whether belief precedes the new birth, or the new birth precedes belief. The Greek tense in this verse might suggest new birth precedes belief (cf. Stott, p. 172; MacArthur, *1–3 John,* pp. 177–178). However, Burdick (p. 343) considers this highly unlikely and says, "The point of the passage is that belief is a sign of new birth, not that belief is a consequence of new birth." Raymond Brown (p. 535) seems to agree with Burdick and writes, "Probably the Johannine writers think of believing and begetting as belonging together and simultaneous, even though confessed belief may serve as a sign of having been begotten." Cf. Yarbrough, 269; Law, 187, 262; Brooke, 128; Acts 16:31; Rom. 10:9–10, 17; Gal. 3:26; Eph. 2:8.

19  Stedman, 340–341.

20  I understand, as suggested by Yarbrough (p. 271), the "*en toutō*" here to be cataphoric (looking forward) to what follows, although the terms functions somewhat as a transition for the previous statement as well. Cf. Raymond Brown, 536–537; Brook, 129; Smalley, 267–268; Burdick, 343–344. According to Brown this would yield the following translation: "This is how we can be sure that we do love God's children: whenever we love God and obey His commands."

21  Burdick (p. 345) and Smalley (p. 268) understand the two parts of this clause virtually form a hendiadys: to love God is to keep His commandments, and the

reverse. Although the two are highly interdependent, John 14:15 seems to make some distinction between the two.

22  Cf. Dodd, 123, 125.

23  Raymond Brown (p. 537) and Smalley (p. 268) point out the somewhat circular argument John presents. For them this apparent contradiction simply reinforces the inseparability of our love for God and our love for one another. Loyd-Jones emphasizes the importance of approaching these tests by examining the whole (pp. 578–580).

24  Loyd-Jones (pp. 578–579) uses the analogy of the human body to illustrate this point. If there is life it will manifest in all the parts.

25  Cf. Dodd, pp. xliii–xliv.

26  Cf. 2 Cor. 4:16–18; 1 Pet. 1:6–9.

27  Fettke. Tom, ed., s. v. "It Is Well with My Soul" by Haratio Spafford, 493.

28  Cf. Gal. 6:10.

29  John's primary objective in giving these tests is that Christians might live in the assurance of eternal life. In a secondary way, the application of these tests may reveal the absence of eternal life in a person's life. That too is beneficial for it alerts the person of his or her need to call upon Christ for His gift of salvation.

30  Cf. John 6:37.

# CHAPTER 24

# Overcoming the World
## 5:4–5

For whatever is born of God overcomes the world; and
this is the victory that has overcome the world—our faith.
Who is the one who overcomes the world, but he who
believes that Jesus is the Son of God?

1 John 5:4-5, NASB

---

Expository Message

In this text you will find the key to your success as a Christian, particularly,
your success in overcoming the world and its influence. In 1 John 5:
1-3, John has emphasized the importance of love and of keeping God's
commandments. "Whoever believes that Jesus is the Christ is born of
God, and whoever loves the Father loves the child born of Him. By
this we know that we love the children of God, when we love God and
observe His commandments. For this is the love of God, that we keep His
commandments; and His commandments are not burdensome" (NASB).

Then in verse 4 John brings our conflict with the world back into
view. "For whatever is born of God overcomes the world; and this is the
victory that has overcome the world—our faith" (NASB). The Greek word
translated "overcomes" is *nikaō*. The brand name, Nike, comes from that
word. It means to conquer or overpower.[1] The world is trying to overpower
us with temptations, deceptions, and persecutions. But God has equipped

us to overcome the world. John's message here is a positive one. It is a message of assurance and encouragement.

Remember John's previous discussion about the world in chapter two? There he tells us to defeat the world by directing our desires toward God and away from the world's lure. The world entices us through the lust of the flesh, the lust of the eyes, and the pride of life.[2]

> Do not love the world nor the things in the world. If anyone loves the world, the love of the Father is not in him. For all that is in the world, the lust of the flesh and the lust of the eyes and the boastful pride of life, is not from the Father, but is from the world. The world is passing away, and also its lusts; but the one who does the will of God lives forever (1 John 2:15–17, NASB).

His statement in verse 17 is in keeping with the theme of our text today. There may be struggles in this life, but ultimately, we win. All the junk and temptation of the world is passing away. It has no hope of permanence.[3] But those who do the will of God abide forever.

John's progression of thought in our text today goes something like this.

1. The person who believes in Christ is born again.
2. The person who is born again loves God and loves God's children.
3. The evidence of our love for God and for His people is that we keep His commandments.
4. His commandments are not burdensome to us because we are overcoming the world's temptations.
5. We overcome the world because we have received a new nature that is compatible with God's commandments. Our new nature desires to live according to the will of the Father.
6. Through our faith in Christ as the Son of God, we overcome the world and its influence.

Notice how that passage begins in verse 1 with faith in Jesus as the Christ and concludes with faith in Jesus as the Son of God.[4] Faith is the key to our victory. The new birth is the foundation for it. John addresses: (1) our source of victory (2) our means of victory (3) our joy in victory.

## OUR SOURCE OF VICTORY

The source of our victory over the world is the divine nature we have received from the Father. Verse 4a says, "For whatever is born of God overcomes the world." The Greek word translated "whatever" is in the neuter gender. Why does John make it impersonal? Why doesn't he say "whoever" instead of "whatever"? He is emphasizing the power of the new nature, rather than the willpower of the individual.[5] The divine life within is greater than any obstacle the world has to offer. Have you ever been in an old neighborhood where the concrete sidewalks were laid years ago? There you can observe the power of life. A tiny little plant made its way through a small crack in the concrete. The plant grew and grew and grew; now you see a giant elm tree that has conquered that concrete. The life that is in that twig busted the concrete open, pushed it aside, and took over the territory.

The influence of the world presents two formidable problems for Christians. (1) Externally it asserts pressures to conform to its values and goals. It pushes its way of thinking on the believer through social rewards and punishment. It entices with its pleasures and vain glory. Through both deception and intimidation, it seeks to shape people into its mold.[6] But that is not the worst problem. (2) Residing in the believer is the flesh with desires consistent with the world.[7] The Christians has a new nature which defines his essential being, but he is not entirely rid of the old one either. The believer's spirit has been joined to the Holy Spirit and is in perfect accord with the Father. But the body is not yet redeemed.[8] The mind still needs to be freed from old patterns of thinking (Rom. 12:2).[9] The flesh is present asserting its fallen desires. Paul discusses the struggles associated with this in Romans 7. But in Romans 8 he assures victory to those in Christ "who do not walk according to the flesh but according to the Spirit." To live in victory the Christian has to continually choose to walk in the Spirit and not allow the flesh to motivate his thoughts and actions.[10] The good news is he can do that! He can do it because the new nature he has received in Christ empowers him to do it. Without the new nature it would be impossible.

The world thinks they could do good if they wanted to. They think they are masters of their own ship. But the reality is, they are blinded by the god of this world and totally under his sway.[11] C. S. Lewis addressed this in his book, *Mere Christianity*. He writes, "No man knows how bad he is till he has tried very hard to be good. A silly idea is current that good people do not know what temptation means. This is an obvious lie. Only those who try to resist temptation know how strong it is. After all, you find out the strength of the German army by fighting against it, not by giving in."[12] The battles we fight are very real. John is not minimizing all that. In fact, it is by our failure to do good through our own willpower that we learn the real secret of living victoriously. Our natural inclination is to try to do it for God. In the process of failing to do that, we discover that He will do it in and for us.[13]

It all begins with the new birth. Without that, there is absolutely no hope of pleasing God. Without the life of God that we receive in regeneration we cannot live in the commandments of God. They are an affront to everything we are and everything we want. So, John begins in 5:1 with that. "Whoever believes that Jesus is the Christ is born of God" Do we really understand the significance of the new birth? Do we fully realize the power of this new life within to prevail over the world? Regeneration changes the game altogether. It is more than adoption. Yes, we have been adopted into the family of God. "For you have not received a spirit of slavery leading to fear again, but you have received a spirit of adoption as sons by which we cry out, 'Abba! Father!'" (Rom. 8:15, NASB). Paul uses the analogy of adoption to illustrate our relationship with God in Ephesians 1:5 as well.[14] But that does not tell the full story. He also says in 2 Corinthians 5:17 that we are a new *creation* in Christ. That too is true, but it is still not a full revelation of what God has done for us. The new birth, regeneration, is something greater than creation and greater than adoption. Through the new birth, we have become partakers of the divine nature.[15] Adoption is a significant legal action. But it does not put the parent's nature in the child. God does not impart Himself to creation either. But in regeneration we are born of the divine seed.[16] In the new birth we receive the Father's DNA. It puts something of God Himself in us.[17] We receive His propensity toward love, goodness, and righteousness. We receive His righteous nature. And His nature is higher and superior to the fallen nature of the world.[18] We cannot overcome the world through our own willpower. Romans 7 is a lesson on how far that will get you. But the nature of God in us can and does prevail. That is our secret of success. "For whatever is born of God overcomes the world."

## OUR MEANS OF VICTORY

The means of our victory over the world is *faith* in Christ. Verse 4b says, "And this is the victory that has overcome the world—our faith."[19] We have seen how our own efforts to do good are inadequate. The pull of the world within and without is simply too powerful for human willpower to withstand. But God has provided us everything we need to live a godly life.[20] He has given us a new nature with new desires and new powers. "Greater is He who is in you than he that is in the world" (1 John 4:4, NASB). The evil one is in the world. The whole world lies under his sway (5:19). But in you is God Himself. In you is the Holy Spirit, and He is greater than anything the world can throw at you. If we will live in the communion of the Holy Spirit; if we will follow His leading and obey His voice, we will outmaneuver the devil. We will experience victory over our adversary. We can't do it through self-reliance, but we can do it through God-reliance. When the Holy Spirit says, "No, don't go in there. No, don't do that. No, don't say those words," all we have to do is obey His voice. We don't have to figure it all out. We don't have to be smarter than the devil. We just have to do what God tells us to do.

There is an inseparable link between faith and obedience. If we believe Jesus is who He claims to be, then we will obey Him. The obedience is an expression of the faith in our hearts. James says we demonstrate the faith that is in our hearts by what we do. Just to believe in our hearts and not act in obedience is a sure sign something is wrong. Like love, faith is more than a feeling. If it is not acted upon it is dead and ineffectual. So, faith and obedience always go together. James illustrated this in his epistle using Abraham's obedience to God's command to offer his son, Isaac, on the altar. His faith was demonstrated by doing what God told him to do. James then added another example by pointing to Rahab's actions of hiding the Israeli spies. She believed the report about God's favor on Israel, and she acted in accordance with those beliefs.[21] Genuine faith motivates the actions that result in victory.

Hebrews 11 lists mighty deeds done by the people of God through faith. Each story begins with the words, "By faith." How did Enoch overcome the world? He walked close to God. He lived to please God. How did Daniel stop the mouths of lions? He trusted God to take care of him, even when circumstances appeared to be impossible. He continued in prayer even when threatened with death. How did Moses overcome the world? Hebrews 11:24–26 tells us.

> By faith Moses, when he had grown up, refused to be called the son of Pharaoh's daughter, choosing rather to endure ill-treatment with the people of God than to enjoy the passing pleasures of sin, considering the reproach of Christ greater riches than the treasures of Egypt; for he was looking to the reward (NASB).

He forsook the world's value system and embraced God's promises. He looked beyond the immediate, temporal advantages the world offered. Instead, He made Christ his reward. By faith, he made some good choices and follow through with those choices.

Of course, the greatest example of overcoming the world is Jesus. If you want to know what overcoming the world looks like, examine His life. Look at Him in the wilderness fasting and praying, relying on the Father's strength.[22] See how He resisted Satan's temptations with the word of God.[23] Hear His thinking in the Sermon on the Mount. Watch how He loves and cares for people. Watch how He destroys the works of the devil, going about doing good and healing all those who are oppressed by Satan. See Him tenderly heal the blind and powerfully drive out demons. Listen to Him speak the truth in love to the woman at the well. Then come to the Garden of Gethsemane and see the blood mingled with sweat as He resolves to do the will of the Father, regardless of the cost. Does He lash back at the soldiers who mock and whip Him? Does He curse the Jews and Romans who unjustly crucify Him? No, He asks the Father to forgive them.[24] There He is on the cross still loving and caring for others, making sure His mother has the support she needs, granting forgiveness to the repentant thief. We do not have to wonder what John means by overcoming the world. We can see it clearly in the way Jesus lived and died. And He says to you and me in John 16:33, "These things I have spoken to you, so that in Me you may have peace. In the world you have tribulation, but take courage; I have overcome the world" (NASB). His victory over the world is the foundation for our victory over the world.

Notice in our text, verse 5, the object of our faith matters. It's not just faith in general that brings victory. The world preaches that message often. "Be positive, trust your instincts, you can do it, etc." Unfortunately, the world's message sneaks into the church at times. "It's all going to be fine. Just keep your chin up. Don't give up. Only believe; think positive." But the question we must always ask is: believe what? Where is our faith to be invested? If we are trusting in ourselves, we are operating in the world's way of thinking. It is only when we trust in the Lord that we prevail. So, 1 John 5:5 puts it this way: "Who is the one who overcomes the world, but he who believes that Jesus is the Son of God?" (NASB). It's faith in Jesus that brings victory.[25] It's resting on His promises. It's knowing Him as the Son of God, as the Christ, as the Savior of the world. It's coming to Him for strength when you're tempted and tried. It's receiving His mercy and help when you've failed. One side of victory is relying on His strength to not fail. The other side of victory is relying on His atonement when we do fail. First John 2:1–2 says, "And if anyone sins, we have an Advocate with the Father, Jesus Christ the righteous; and He Himself is the propitiation [atoning sacrifice] for our sins" (NASB). Revelation 12:11 declares our means of overcoming. "And they overcame him [Satan, the Accuser] because of the blood of the Lamb and because of the word of their testimony, and they did not love their life even when faced with death" (NASB). The blood of Jesus is a powerful weapon against the world and the god of this world. By it we are forgiven and cleansed and empowered to continue in the battle.

John's Jesus is a saving Jesus.[26] He is able to save you to the uttermost.[27] David wrote in Psalm 20:7, "Some trust in chariots, and some in horses: but we will remember the name of the Lord our God" (KJV). Are you trusting in the name of the Lord today? If so, you have nothing to worry about. You don't have to understand it all. Just trust and obey. He will never fail you. Acts 2:21 promises, "And it shall come to pass, that whosoever shall call on the name of the Lord shall be saved" (KJV). The Greek word translated "saved" is *sōzō*. Its meaning is very broad. Depending on the context it can mean heal, deliver, protect, or save.[28] Do you need a deliverance from a habit? Call on the name of the Lord Jesus for that deliverance. Do you need a healing in your body? The authority for that healing is in Jesus's name. Make Jesus the object of your faith for whatever you need. Keep your eye always on Him, "looking unto Jesus the author and finisher" of your faith.[29] He has begun a good work in you, and He will complete that work in you. "This is the victory that has overcome the world—our faith."

Remember John's invitation at the beginning of this epistle? He invites his readers into fellowship with the Father and Son and with the Body of Christ. Then in 1:4 he writes, "And these things write we unto you, that your joy may be full" (KJV). In today's text we have a key to that joy.

## OUR JOY IN VICTORY

The joy of victory over the world is experienced as we love God and keep His commandments. "For this is the love of God, that we keep His commandments; and His commandments are not burdensome. For whatever is born of God overcomes the world" (1 John 5:3–4a, NASB). The world hates the commandments of God. They view God's commandments as obstacles to their freedom and happiness. For them the commandments of God are unbearably burdensome. Why? Because those commandments are contrary to what they want to do! They want to lie, cheat, steal, commit adultery, get revenge, and live in pride. The commandments condemn the lusts and desires of their heart. So, they would, at least internally, laugh at John's statement, "And His commandments are not burdensome."

How can John make such a statement? He explains himself in verse 4: "For[30] whatever is born of God overcomes the world." The new birth changes the desires of our heart. It gives us a new disposition. The love of God has changed our orientation toward life. We no longer despise His authority over us. We now realize how much He loves us. We now know that He is always looking out for our best interest. If He sets a boundary on our lives, it is always for our highest good. The world doesn't understand that because they don't really understand God's intentions toward them. God is not trying to condemn them.[31] He is not trying to restrict their happiness. He is trying to save them from self-destruction. We have realized that through His gracious dealings with us. So, John writes in 4:19, "We love him, because he first loved us" (KJV).

And because we love Him, we want to please Him more than anything else. His will is no longer burdensome to us, it is our delight. Yes, we have to reckon the old man dead on a daily basis. We have to deny the flesh and cultivate our love for the Father.[32] But in our new nature is a love for God and agreement with His commandments. Listen to the way David talks about the commandments of God in Psalm 119 (NASB):

➢ Verse 16: "I shall delight in Your statutes; I shall not forget Your word."

➢ Verses 34–36: "Give me understanding, that I may observe Your law And keep it with all *my* heart. Make me walk in the path of Your commandments, For I delight in it. Incline my heart to Your testimonies And not to *dishonest* gain." [Is that not the cry of your heart before God? Don't you want to live well pleasing to Him? The divine nature within cries out for the commandments of God. We no longer view them as burdensome. We see them as signposts for walking in light, walking in victory and joy.]

➢ Verse 47–48: "I shall delight in Your commandments, Which I love. And I shall lift up my hands to Your commandments, Which I love; And I will meditate on Your statutes."

Later in Romans 7:22 Paul writes, "For I delight in the law of God after the inward man" (KJV). As we find our delight in the Lord, the pleasures of this world lose their appeal.

Desire is part of the human make up. The heart of every individual desires things and puts its affections somewhere. One man may love auto racing. Another may love his job. Another may love sports. Another may love video games. The list could go on endlessly. The point is this. People find something to enjoy and pursue in life. People in the world love the things of the world. They naturally pursue the lust of the flesh, the lust of the eyes, and the pride of life. They find a measure of satisfaction in those things. If we take that away and give them nothing in its place, they are left empty and despondent. There's got to be something motivating them, some reason to get out of bed in the morning. If you take away their worldly amusements and motivations and give nothing in its place, you have not really helped them at all.[33]

That is why legalism is totally ineffective. It leaves a void inside that cannot be endured.[34] Nature abhors a vacuum. If you take away the pleasures of this world, and don't replace them with the good things of God, people will return to the little this world has to offer.

The answer is to introduce them to something better—better than life itself. That process begins when we discover and experience God's love for us. "O taste and see that the Lord is good" (Ps. 34:8, KJV). Experience the relief that comes with forgiveness of sins. Experience the goodness that God pours into the lives of those who serve Him. Proverbs 10:22 says, "It is the blessing of the Lord that makes rich, And He adds no sorrow to it" (NASB). The riches are not always material goods. God has riches that far exceed those: rich relationships, rich peace and assurance, rich treasures in heaven, and whatever material wealth is in your best interest. The wonderful thing about the blessing of the Lord, it does not come with an adder's bite of sorrow. The riches that the world gives always adds its portion of sorrow. But God's blessings are rich and pure.

> Bless the Lord, O my soul, And all that is within me, *bless* His holy name. Bless the Lord, O my soul, And forget none of His benefits; Who pardons all your iniquities, Who heals all your diseases; Who redeems your life from the pit, Who crowns you with lovingkindness and compassion; Who satisfies your years with good things, *So that* your youth is renewed like the eagle (Ps. 103:1–5, NASB).

That's the God we love and serve. The better you know Him, the more you love Him. The more you experience His love and goodness, the more you want to please Him and delight His heart. Love for God makes His commandments light work indeed.[35] The new delights and desires discovered in God push out the old pursuits.[36]

Suppose you lived in a little one-room shack, squeezed on a tiny lot in a depressed part of town. The roof leaks, but at least it's a roof. The floor is dirt and there are no windows. But still, the wood stove keeps you warm in the winter. You would cling to that place because it is all you've got. People may tell you it's a dump and you ought to leave it. But it's better than living on the street and sleeping outside in the cold. People could preach to you all day long about how terrible that place is. They're not telling you anything you don't know. But all their preaching will not move you out of that shack. But suppose you receive a letter. The letter says your wealthy aunt has died and, to everyone's amazement, she left her mansion to you. It's 10,000 square feet with all new appliances and is filled with new, expensive furniture. It is completely paid for and she has included a bank account with $ 50,000 in it for maintenance and utilities. There is a beautiful garden in the back yard. How hard would it be to get you to leave that shack and move into the new mansion?

Like that letter, the gospel is good news. It offers us something far better than anything the world can give. Yes, there are things we must give up as a Christian.[37] But the exchange is "a no-brainer." We give up the corruption and eternal destruction the world has to offer. We receive, by grace, the love of God and eternal life. How does God deliver us from the beggarly elements of this world? He shows us the glorious riches of His grace in Christ Jesus. He lavishes us with His goodness.[38] He gives and gives and gives. He captures our hearts with His love. We pursue Him and keep His commandments out of a response of love toward Him. It becomes our delight to do anything we can to please Him.

The new birth changes our orientation toward the world.[39] We lose our taste for its dainties. The new birth changes our orientation toward the commandments of God. We want to do the will of our Father, and the Holy Spirit gives us the power to live that way. That which was once considered burdensome and grievous has become our delight and joy.[40] The world wonders how we can deprive ourselves of its pomp and pleasure. We wonder how they can settle for so little.

John's message is one of assurance for the child of God. The nature we have received through the new birth loves God and loves His people. For the person walking in the Spirit, the commandments of God are not burdensome at all.[41] By delighting ourselves in the will of God, we overcome the world and enjoy God's favor. The Bible is full of promises to those who overcome the world.[42] I want to close by simply sharing some of the promises Jesus makes to overcomers in Revelation 2–3 (NASB). Open your spiritual ears and let Jesus speak these words of encouragement to you.

> ➤ 2:7: "To him who overcomes, I will grant to eat of the tree of life which is in the Paradise of God."
> ➤ 2:11: "He who overcomes will not be hurt by the second death."
> ➤ 2:17: "To him who overcomes, to him I will give some of the hidden manna, and I will give him a white stone, and a new name written on the stone which no one knows but he who receives it."
> ➤ 2:26: "He who overcomes, and he who keeps My deeds until the end, to him I will give authority over the nations."
> ➤ 3:5: "He who overcomes will thus be clothed in white garments; and I will not erase his name from the book of life, and I will confess his name before My Father and before His angels."
> ➤ 3:12: "He who overcomes, I will make him a pillar in the temple of My God, and he will not go out from it anymore; and I will write on him the name of My God, and the name of the city of My God, the new Jerusalem, which comes down out of heaven from My God, and My new name."
> ➤ 3:21: "He who overcomes, I will grant to him to sit down with Me on My throne, as I also overcame and sat down with My Father on His throne."

You will never regret putting your faith in Christ and serving Him. If you haven't done that in the past, you can make that choice right where you are, right now. Simply bow your head and talk with Him about your need and your faith in His sacrifice for you as the only Savior and giver of eternal life. Ask Christ to come into your heart as Savior and Lord of your life. That simple prayer can begin a wonderful journey of knowing Him.

# Endnotes: Chapter 24

1  H.G. Lindell, Robert Scott, H. S. Jones, and R. McKenzie, *Lindell-Scott Greek-English Lexicon* (Oxford: Oxford University Press, 1843). Accessed in Electronic Database: Bibleworks. v. 6.0. 2003, *nikaō*.

2  1 John 2:16 KJV. Cf. James 1:14–15.

3  Cf. 2 Pet. 3:10–13.

4  Cf. Smalley, 267.

5  Brooke, 130. Cf. Burdick, 346. Law (p. 275) says John's use of the Greek here, "seems to emphasise, not the persons who conquer, but the Divine energy by which they conquer."

6  Cf. Rom. 12:2; Dan. 1.

7  Martin Loyd-Jones (pp. 585–594) explores this extensively. He makes the point that physically retreating from the world, for example in a monastery, is no solution to the problem. Since the world is inside us, we still have to overcome it. Jesus told us to go into the world and be salt and light (Matt. 5:13–16; Mark 16:15).

8  Cf. 1 Cor. 6:17; Rom. 7:22-23; 8:22-23.

9  Cf. Phil. 2:5; 4:6.

10  Cf. Rom. 6:11-14; Gal. 5:16–17; Col. 3:5.

11  Cf. 2 Cor. 4:3–4; Eph. 2:1–3; 1 John 5:19.

12  Lewis, *Mere Christianity*, p 141.

13  Cf. Phil. 2:13.

14  Cf. Gal. 4:5.

15  2 Pet. 1:4. In that verse, Peter links being partakers of the divine nature with escaping the corruption that is in the world through lust. Therefore, like John, Peter sees the new birth as essential for overcoming the world and its twisted desires.

16  1 Pet. 1:23.

17  Spurgeon, "Victorious Faith," preached Aug. 24, 1879. Accessed at The C. H. Spurgeon Collection on CD-ROM (AGES Software, Inc., 1998). Cf. Brooke, 126.

18  Light is greater than darkness. Darkness does not dispel light. It is the other way around. The presence of light dispels darkness. The higher life form prevails over the lower life. Man prevails over animals. Animals prevail over vegetation. Divine life prevails over the fallen, sinful nature.

19  The Greek verb tenses in the text imply both provision for assured victory and call to ongoing engagement. The present tense translated "overcomes" in verse 4a may be gnomic present (statement of a timeless fact) or progressive present (continually overcoming). The aorist participle translated "has overcome" in verse 4b points in the immediate context to the person's new birth which is

only possible because of Christ's victory at the cross (cf. Burdick, 346–347). The progressive present for both "overcomes" and "believes" in verse 5 indicate the Christian's continued believing and continued overcoming on a daily basis. Cf. Burdick, 347; Raymond Brown, 570–572; Smalley, 270–271.

20  2 Pet. 1:3–4. Cf. Rom. 8:37.

21  James 2:25.

22  Cf. Luke 4:1–14.

23  Luke 4:4, 8, 12.

24  Cf. Luke 23:34; 1 Pet. 2:23.

25  Cf. 1 Cor 15:57, "But thanks be to God, who gives us the victory through our Lord Jesus Christ" (NASB).

26  It is crucial that the Jesus we believe in be the real Jesus, as revealed in Scripture. That's why John describes Jesus as "the Christ" in 5:1 and "the Son of God" in 5:5. That's why Christology is so prominent in this epistle.

27  Heb. 7:25.

28  Strong, s. v. "NT:4982."

29  Heb. 12:2, KJV.

30  The "*hoti*" clause being introduced here explains why the commandments of God are not burdensome for the believer. Cf. Burdick, 346; Stott, 174.

31  John 3:16–17. However, God is not reconciling Himself to the world, as the Universalists might imply. He is reconciling lost people to Himself, the only source of eternal life (2 Cor. 5:18–20).

32  Cf. Rom. 6:11–13; Eph. 4:20–24; Col. 3:5–14.

33  Warren Wiersbe, ed., *Treasury of the World's Great Sermons* (Grand Rapids: Kregel Publications, 1993) s. v. "The Expulsive Power of a New Affection," by Thomas Chalmers, 120–126. Chalmers says, "When told to shut out the world from his heart, this may be impossible with him who has nothing to replace it—but not impossible with him who has found in God a sure and satisfying portion." Cf. Titus 2:11–14.

34  The Jewish leaders in Jesus's day were doing that to people, and Jesus condemned it (Matt. 23:4). Cf. Matt. 11:30.

35  Cf. William Barclay, *The Letters of John and Jude*, The Daily Study Bible Series. 1958, rev. ed. (Philadelphia, PA: Westminster Press, 1976) 104. Barclay writes, ". . . for love no duty is too hard and no task too great." Barclay illustrates this with the story of the boy carrying his lame younger brother to school every day. When someone commented, "That's a heavy burden for you to carry," the boy replied, "He's no burden, he's my brother."

36  A popular song in the 1960's was entitled "Too Busy Thinkin' About My Baby." In that song, Marvin Gaye sang, "I ain't got time to think about money or what it can buy. . . . I'm too busy thinkin' about my baby; ain't got time for nothing

else." That secular song illustrates the concept of a higher love pushing out lesser loves.

37  We cannot live in the shack and the mansion at the same time.

38  Cf. Rom. 2:4.

39  We consciously consider the world's system of rewards and pleasures as nothing to us. The old relationship no longer exists. It is dead to us, and we are dead to it (Gal. 6:14). Cf. Rm. 6:11; Gal. 2:20.

40  Denny Stevens, *The Speaking God* (Bloomington, IN: WestBow Press, 2015) 23: "God's laws are not confining and constraining as we may have once imagined. No, they are a guiding light to all that our heart truly desires."

41  For anyone who chooses to walk in the flesh, the commandments of God are burdensome. The carnal mind is always in opposition to the will of God (Rom. 8:7). Therefore, one way we can assess our spiritual condition is to examine our attitude toward the commandments of God. Are they something we resentfully do out of duty or do they portray a way of life we choose from the heart because we love the Father? Those who consider the commandments of God to be burdensome are always looking for loopholes and live their lives as close to the boundaries as they can. Those who love God and His commandments seek to live in the center of His will.

42  Cf. Rev. 21:6–7.

# CHAPTER 25

# Evidences for Our Faith
# 5:6–8

This is He who came by water and blood — Jesus Christ; not only by water, but by water and blood. And it is the Spirit who bears witness, because the Spirit is truth. For there are three that bear witness in heaven: the Father, the Word, and the Holy Spirit; and these three are one. And there are three that bear witness on earth: the Spirit, the water, and the blood; and these three agree as one.

1 John 5:6-8, NKJV

## Message

John began chapter five with this statement: "Whoever believes that Jesus is the Christ is born of God" (NKJV). Everything depends on your faith in Jesus as the One sent by the Father to save you from your sins. Remember the instruction an angel gave Joseph in Matthew 1:21. First, the angel told Joseph that the child Mary was carrying was conceived by the Holy Spirit. Then the angel said, "And she will bring forth a Son, and you shall call His name JESUS, for He will save His people from their sins" (NKJV). That passage confirms the virgin birth of Jesus. He was sent from heaven by the Father as the Messiah, the Christ, the Anointed One who would bring salvation. One evidence of a person being truly born again is that person "believes that Jesus is the Christ."

Chapter 24 concluded with 1 John 5:5: "Who is he who overcomes the world, but he who believes" (NKJV). Again, faith is an essential part of this. As we saw in that chapter, it is not just faith in general that saves us. It's faith in the person, Christ. We must believe the truth about who Jesus is. "Who is he who overcomes the world, but he who believes that Jesus is the Son of God?" Recognizing Jesus as the Son of God is recognizing His deity. It's not enough to believe Jesus was a good man or a good example to follow. It's not enough to just accept Him as a prophet or teacher. False religions and cults do that. We must believe that He is God manifested in the flesh.[1] We must believe the second person of the Trinity came into this world through the Virgin Mary; that from conception He became a man with the purpose of saving us from our sins. To believe that Jesus is the Son of God is to believe that He is truly God and truly man, not partly God and partly man, but fully God and fully man.[2] He is the unique, eternal Son of God sent to make atonement for sin. For that to happen the incarnation was necessary, and the sacrifice on the cross was necessary. As we come to 1 John 5:6 we must realize that John is now giving proof and evidence that Jesus, the man, is God the Son.[3] If everything depends on believing that, then we should carefully weigh the evidence that proves it true. Your eternal destiny depends on it! I rest my eternal soul on the fact that Jesus is *the Son of God*. Jesus is my Savior, and I have no Plan B. If it is not true, all is lost. If it is true, all is gained.

So, how do I know that Jesus is God, the Son, the Savior of the world? John begins to answer that inquiry by focusing on the means or manner of His coming.[4] Verse 6 says, "This is He who came by water and blood — Jesus Christ; not only by water, but by water and blood."

## TWO UNKNOWNS THAT MAKE THIS TEXT DIFFICULT TO INTERPRET

Scholars have identified this passage as extremely problematic. In fact, Martin Loyd-Jones says verses 6–8 are the most difficult in the Bible.[5] What makes it so difficult to interpret? There are two facts lying behind John's statement that we do not know. First, the terms *water and blood* had a meaning to John and his readers that is not explained in the text. When both speaker and hearer already have a mutual understanding of what a phrase implies, it is not necessary to explain its meaning.[6] Most scholars guess that the term "water" is a reference to Jesus's baptism in the Jordan at the beginning of His ministry, and the term "blood" is in reference to His sacrificial death on the cross.[7] His deity, as the Son of God, was supernaturally confirmed on both those occasions. So, the water and the blood probably refer to Jesus's baptism in water and His baptism in blood at the cross.[8] Jesus spoke of this baptism in blood in Matthew 20:22 when He answered the request made by the mother of His two disciples, John and James. Remember when she asked that one could sit on His right hand and the other on His left hand in the kingdom? Part of His answer, directed at John and James, was the question in Mark 10:38, "You do not know what you ask. Are you able to drink the cup that I drink, and be baptized with the baptism that I am baptized with?" (NKJV). That baptism was a baptism of suffering. In Jesus's case it was offering Himself as a sacrifice for sin, His baptism in blood. Jesus came by way of two baptisms that characterized His mission.

In verses 6–11 the Greek noun *marturia* and the verb *martureō* together occur ten times.[9] It is the prominent theme that runs through this passage. *Marturia* means "witness." We get our English word martyr from it. When we want to prove a truth in court, we call upon witnesses to substantiate that truth. The truth John is substantiating in our text is stated at the end of verse 5: "That Jesus is the Son of God." Most translations obscure the intensity of John's focus on witnesses for his case because, for the sake of variety, they translate *marturia* and *martureō* with different English words. In the New King James Version it is sometimes witness and sometimes testimony. Fortunately, both English terms do convey the idea of proof, as in a court of law. One thing we know in this passage is that John is setting forth proof that Jesus is *the Son of God*. He is calling witnesses for the case, and the testimonial proof is overwhelming. When interpreting a passage begin with what you do know and use that to help interpret the more obscure elements. Because John is clearly presenting evidence that Jesus is the Son of God, then the terms *water and blood* must flow with that theme. Interpreting water and blood as events that confirm the His deity, best fits the context. There have been a variety of interpretations suggested for water and blood.[10] But the most likely thing John is referring to in this context is the water as representing Jesus's baptism and the blood as representing His sacrifice at Calvary. That fits best with John's objective in the narrative.[11]

Some have suggested that the sacraments of water baptism and the eucharist are what John means by water and blood. But John is giving historical evidence for the fact. The sacraments are *reminders* of the historical facts.[12] It is important that we have those reminders. But they are not evidence for the case. They are reminders of the historic realities. Only in that very secondary way do they relate to John's message in the text. John is not talking about the sacraments.[13] He is pointing to historical proof that Jesus is the Christ, the Son of God.

The second unknown that makes this passage difficult to interpret is the Gnostic heresy that John is confronting. His wording in verse 6 makes it obvious that he is opposing some error that would minimize the importance of the blood. "This is He who came by water *and* blood — Jesus Christ; not only by water, but by water *and* blood" (emphasis mine). We do know that Cerinthus was in Ephesus about the time John was there.[14] So, it's a natural conclusion they were opposing one another. Cerinthus taught that Jesus was born an ordinary person, the biological son of Joseph, and there was no virgin birth. The man Jesus was godly, and at His water baptism, the Christ came upon Him and enabled Him in His ministry. For Cerinthus, Christ was a separate entity from Jesus. Christ, who was spirit, left Jesus, who was material, before His death on the cross. Thus, Jesus died as an ordinary man. Therefore, the water baptism was very important. But Jesus's death is inconsequential because it was just a man dying on a Roman cross.[15] But John is saying Jesus is the Christ. It is not two entities. He is the God-man. He is the second person of the Trinity who became man in the womb of Mary.[16] He was conceived by the Holy Spirit, born Jesus Christ, and remains that forever. So, John may be confronting that error or one like it when he writes, "Not *only* by water, but by water *and* blood" (emphasis mine). Jesus's blood sacrifice on the cross was effectual for salvation because it was God incarnate on that cross paying the price of our salvation. We cannot know for sure that Cerinthus's error is the one on John's mind when he wrote our text. But it must have been something like that. John is providing evidence that Jesus is the Son of God.

# THREE WITNESS THAT PROVE JESUS IS THE CHRIST

John identifies three witnesses that prove Jesus is the Christ, the Son of God. He first recognizes the Holy Spirit as a witness. First John 5:6 says, "And it is the Spirit who bears witness, because the Spirit is truth." In the upper room before His crucifixion, Jesus identified the Holy Spirit as the Spirit of truth. In John 15:26–27 He said to the apostles,

> But when the Helper comes, whom I shall send to you from the Father, the Spirit of truth who proceeds from the Father, He will testify of Me. And you also will bear witness, because you have been with Me from the beginning (NKJV).

Here again is testimony language. The apostles will *bear witness* of what they saw in Jesus from the beginning of His ministry. They would be witness of the fact that Jesus is the Son of God. But the emphasis in Jesus's statement is that "the Spirit of truth who proceeds from the Father, He will testify" of Jesus as the Son of God. His testimony is particularly reliable because He is the *Spirit of truth*. He not only tells the truth, but His nature is truth, and His assignment from the Father is to bear witness of the Son.

Of course, that is happening today every time the gospel is preached. It is the Holy Spirit who convinces people of the message. That has been going on for two thousand years and will continue. Every time we open the Bible and read the word of God, the Holy Spirit is there to open our understanding and apply that truth to our lives. In the next chapter, we will talk more about the subjective witness of the Spirit in our own hearts. But John's focus in this text is on the objective, historical evidence of who Jesus is.

The Holy Spirit also testified of Jesus's office and mission during Christ's lifetime on earth. For example, the Holy Spirit bore witness to Simeon that baby Jesus was the Christ. Then Simeon bore witness to this in prophesy. Luke 2:25–32:

> Now there was a man in Jerusalem called Simeon, who was righteous and devout. He was waiting for the consolation

of Israel, [he was waiting for the coming of Messiah, the Christ] and the Holy Spirit was upon him. It had been revealed to him by the Holy Spirit that he would not die before he had seen the Lord's Christ. Moved by the Spirit, he went into the temple courts. When the parents brought in the child Jesus to do for him what the custom of the Law required, Simeon took him in his arms and praised God, saying: "Sovereign Lord, as you have promised, you may now dismiss your servant in peace. For my eyes have seen your salvation, which you have prepared in the sight of all people, a light for revelation to the Gentiles and for glory to your people Israel" (NIV).

The Holy Spirit testified of Christ's coming through the Old Testament prophets. Micah (5:2) prophesied He would be born in the small village of Bethlehem. Isaiah prophesied He would be born of a virgin (7:14). Hosea prophesied His time in Egypt (11:1). There are other prophecies like these that are very specific. My point is simply this. Before Messiah came, the Holy Spirit revealed details about Jesus, that proved Him to be the Christ. During His life the Holy Spirit was confirming Jesus's Sonship by descending on Him in the form of a dove at His baptism and by the many miracles Jesus did during His ministry. Peter pointed this out in Acts 10:38–43 when he talked about,

> how God anointed Jesus of Nazareth with the Holy Spirit and power, and how he went around doing good and healing all who were under the power of the devil, because God was with him. We are witnesses of everything he did in the country of the Jews and in Jerusalem. They killed him by hanging him on a tree, but God raised him from the dead on the third day and caused him to be seen. He was not seen by all the people, but by witnesses whom God had already chosen-by us who ate and drank with him after he rose from the dead. He commanded us to preach to the people and to testify that he is the one whom God appointed as judge of the living and the dead. All the

prophets testify about him that everyone who believes in
him receives forgiveness of sins through his name (NIV).

Notice Peter's references to all the testimony of who Jesus is. This is a
good commentary on our 1 John 5 text. There are many witnesses of what
Jesus did that proved Him to be the Son of God. There are many chosen
witnesses who could testify of His resurrection as well.

It's a bit strange that John does not use Christ's resurrection as part of
his argument in our text. He makes a broad statement that is very inclusive
when he says, "And it is the Spirit who bears witness." The Holy Spirit
gives testimony in many ways that Jesus is the Christ. Paul talks about the
Spirit's involvement in Jesus's resurrection; that is the ultimate proof that
He is the Son of God. Romans 1:1–4 says,

Paul, a servant of Christ Jesus, called to be an apostle and
set apart for the gospel of God– the gospel he promised
beforehand through his prophets in the Holy Scriptures
regarding his Son, who as to his human nature was a
descendant of David, and who through the Spirit of
holiness was declared with power to be the Son of God
by his resurrection from the dead: Jesus Christ our Lord
(NIV).

Of course, hundreds of people saw Jesus in His resurrected body, over
500 at one time.[17] Can you imagine bringing into court 500 people to
substantiate one fact? The media would be all over it. You don't need that
many witnesses to make the point. But God has provided a staggering
number of witnesses to prove Jesus is His divine Son.

The coming of the Holy Spirit on the Day of Pentecost was a lasting
testimony that Jesus had ascended to the Father, His sacrifice was acceptable
for the atonement of sin, and the Father was honoring Him by sending the
Spirit in His name.[18] Like Jesus's water baptism and crucifixion, that event
was accompanied by supernatural signs as well. Throughout Acts and even
now the Holy Spirit continues to affirm the authority of Jesus's name by
signs and wonders like the healing of the lame man in Acts 3.[19] Every time
a person is born again, the Holy Spirit is bearing witness to the Son of God.

"And it is the Spirit who bears witness, because the Spirit is truth" (1 John 5:6). Having established the Holy Spirit as one witness for his case. John now comes back to the two he has already mentioned but did not identify them as witnesses. Now he brings his focus back on "the water, and the blood." "For there are three that bear witness in heaven: the Father, the Word, and the Holy Spirit; and these three are one. And there are three that bear witness on earth: the Spirit, the water, and the blood; and these three agree as one" (1 John 5:7–8).

Before we talk further about the water and the blood, we must deal with a technical point about verse 7. The words, "in heaven: the Father, the Word, and the Holy Spirit; and these three are one; and there are three who testify on earth," were not in the original text. None of the ancient Greek manuscripts have it in them. It was not even in Jerome's original Vulgate, Latin text. At some point a scribe probably added it as a comment in the margin. Later as that text was being copied a scribe probably thought it had been accidentally left out, and then added it into the Latin text. It's known as the Johannine Comma and got into Erasmus's Greek text through an interesting chain of events that I won't take time to recount. Erasmus's text became the basis for the *Textus Receptus* which was used for the King James Version.[20] The New International Version and other modern translations correctly leave it out. Everything it says is true. But it is not needed to prove the New Testament doctrine of the Trinity, and it is, frankly, a distraction from what John is saying in the text. Verses 6–8 in the New International Version reads: "This is the one who came by water and blood—Jesus Christ. And it is the Spirit who testifies, because the Spirit is the truth. For there are three that testify: the Spirit, the water, and the blood; and the three are in agreement."

The Hebrew law required two or three witnesses to substantiate a claim in court. Deuteronomy 19:15 says, "One witness is not enough to convict a man accused of any crime or offense he may have committed. A matter must be established by the testimony of two or three witnesses" (NIV). This principle was reiterated in the New Testament as well.[21] So John points out three witnesses in our text. The first is *the Spirit*. We have talked about that.

The second witness is *the water* which we understand to be a reference to Jesus's baptism. At that event John the Baptist testified that Jesus is "the

Son of God." His testimony was based on the revelation God gave him at that time. John 1:29–34 tells the story.

> The next day John saw Jesus coming toward him and said, "Look, the Lamb of God, who takes away the sin of the world! This is the one I meant when I said, 'A man who comes after me has surpassed me because he was before me.' I myself did not know him, but the reason I came baptizing with water was that he might be revealed to Israel." Then John gave this testimony: "I saw the Spirit come down from heaven as a dove and remain on him. I would not have known him, except that the one who sent me to baptize with water told me, 'The man on whom you see the Spirit come down and remain is he who will baptize with the Holy Spirit.' I have seen and I testify that this is the Son of God" (NIV).

In the waters of baptism, Jesus was authenticated as the Son of God. Supernatural manifestations from heaven affirmed who He is. First, the Holy Spirit descended upon Him in the form of a dove and resided on Him. When John the Baptist saw this, he knew that Jesus is the Messiah, the Christ, the One who baptizes with the Holy Spirit. His testimony is recorded in verse 34, "I have seen and testify that this the Son of God" (NIV). Then, the Father also spoke from heaven validating Jesus as His Son. This is recorded is in all three synoptic gospels. Matthew 3:17: "And a voice from heaven said, 'This is my Son, whom I love; with him I am well pleased'" (NIV). Jesus's public ministry was launched shortly after that. The authority of His words and the miracles of His ministry affirmed His Sonship as well.

John's third witness in our text is *the blood*. John's contention in 1 John 5:6 is that Jesus "did not come by water only, but by water and blood." That is a point of emphasis in this text. We understand the blood to be His atoning sacrifice on the cross. Let's look at three ways His death on the cross proves He is the Son of God.

The supernatural signs that accompanied the event were evidence this was no ordinary crucifixion. Darkness came over the land from noon until

3:00 pm. The verses leading up to this sign show the emphasis on the issue of His Sonship. Is Jesus the Son of God or is He not? Watch for that issue in this passage. Matthew 27:39–45:

> Those who passed by hurled insults at him, shaking their heads and saying, "You who are going to destroy the temple and build it in three days, save yourself! Come down from the cross, if you are the Son of God!" In the same way the chief priests, the teachers of the law and the elders mocked him. "He saved others," they said, "but he can't save himself! He's the King of Israel! Let him come down now from the cross, and we will believe in him. He trusts in God. Let God rescue him now if he wants him, for he said, 'I am the Son of God.'" In the same way the robbers who were crucified with him also heaped insults on him. From the sixth hour until the ninth hour darkness came over all the land (NIV).[22]

Do you see in that narrative how Jesus's claim to be the Son of God was at issue during His trial and crucifixion?

The darkness came as a sign that the sin of the world was being judged. Darkness speaks of judgment. One of the ten judgments on Egypt during the Exodus was darkness that could be felt. The tenth plague came at a time of darkness. Only those protected by the blood of the Lamb were spared.[23] When the prophets speak of judgment they often use the metaphor of darkness.[24] The Father was turning His back on the Son because Jesus was enduring the separation and punishment that results from sin.[25] The darkness was one supernatural demonstration that Jesus is the Son of God.

The second supernatural sign was the torn veil. I will deal with that in a moment. The third supernatural sign was the earthquake. This sign also speaks of God's presence and judgment.[26] Additionally it served to accommodate the next sign.

The fourth sign was the opening of graves and the resurrection of many Old Testament saints. What a powerful demonstration that this was no ordinary crucifixion, that Jesus is the Son of God, His Christ. Matthew 27:51–53 says,

At that moment the curtain of the temple was torn in two from top to bottom. The earth shook and the rocks split. The tombs broke open and the bodies of many holy people who had died were raised to life. They came out of the tombs, and after Jesus' resurrection they went into the holy city and appeared to many people (NIV).

Here is additional witness. Many saints came out of their graves and what? "They went into the holy city and appeared to many people." That alone should have been convincing!

Now Matthew seals the significance of these signs as testimony of Jesus's divinity by quoting the response of centurion and the other soldiers who were guarding Jesus. "When the centurion and those with him who were guarding Jesus saw the earthquake and all that had happened, they were terrified, and exclaimed, 'Surely he was the Son of God!'" (Matt. 27:54). What is John proving in our text? "Surely this was the Son of God!"

The fulfillment of Old Testament prophecies concerning this event also proved Jesus to be the Messiah. David prophesied details of His crucifixion in Psalm 22. That Psalm foretells the cry, "My God, My God, why have You forsaken Me?" Psalm 22:16–18 says,

Dogs have surrounded me; a band of evil men has encircled me, they have pierced my hands and my feet. I can count all my bones; people stare and gloat over me. They divide my garments among them and cast lots for my clothing (NIV).

When these details came to pass in Jesus's life, they served to identify Him as the Christ. Isaiah prophesied Jesus's substitutionary death. Isaiah 53 talks about His rejection, His sorrows, His suffering.

But he was pierced for our transgressions, he was crushed for our iniquities; the punishment that brought us peace was upon him, and by his wounds we are healed. We all, like sheep, have gone astray, each of us has turned to his own way; and the Lord has laid on him the iniquity of us all" (Isa. 53:5–6, NIV).

We do not have time to fully explore these witnesses of Jesus as the Son of God, but I give these as examples of that testimony.[27]

The fulfillment of Old Testament typology in the sacrificial system was additional proof. Think about the thousands of blood sacrifices offered at the temple. Every time a lamb was slain it pointed to *the* Lamb of God who takes away the sin of the world.[28] Every year at Passover, Israel is to act out God's solution to the sin problem. When the High Priest went into the Holy of Holies once a year to apply the blood on the mercy seat, it was an act of faith looking forward to the blood of Jesus. Jesus was declared to be the final sacrifice when the veil of the temple was rent from top to bottom.[29] That was God's declaration that Jesus is the acceptable sacrifice for sin. That was the Father's witness that He is the Son of God, just as He claimed to be. Trace the testimony of Scripture concerning the blood, and you will see it all pointing to the Son of God laying down His life at Calvary for our redemption. No wonder John forcefully says in our text, 1 John 5:6, "This is He who came by water and blood — Jesus Christ; not only by water, but by water and blood."

The testimony that Jesus is the Christ, the Son of God is overwhelming. To reject it is to call God a liar. To accept it is to receive eternal life. I'm not just talking about accepting it at an intellectual level. That needs to happen. But the belief in the Son of God goes beyond that. It is a belief that captures the will and heart so that we throw ourselves entirely on His mercy and give ourselves entirely to His service.

Do you believe that Jesus is the Christ, the Son of God in that way? If so, your heart should be filled with much assurance. For John has given us every reason to trust Him and rely on His grace. Whoever believes in Him will not perish, but have eternal life!

# Endnotes: Chapter 25

1   Cf. 1 Tim. 3:16.

2   This terminology comes from the Niceno-Constantinopolitan Creed developed at the Council of Chalcedon in 451 A.D. using E. R. Hardy's translation in *Christology of the Later Fathers*, 1954, p. 373 as quoted in Alan Richardson, ed., s. v. "Christology" by George S. Hendry, 57–58. Cf. John 5:18; Phil. 2:6; Heb. 1:1–3: 4:14–15.

3   Brooke (p. 137) writes, "*eis to en eisin*] Are for the one thing, tend in the same direction, exist for the same object. They all work towards the same result, the establish of the truth that Jesus is the Christ, the Son of God." Addressing John's purpose in this passage, Stott (p. 176) says, ". . . the reasonableness of believing in Jesus is grounded upon the validity of the testimony which is borne to Him."

4   Brooke, 135. Brooke says the phrase *di' hudatos kai haimatos* "should express means by which the 'coming' was accomplished, or elements by which it was characterized." *Vincent's New Testament Word Studies* says, "It is not merely the sense of accompaniment, but also instrumentality, i. e., 'by, through, by means of.'" Water and blood are thus the media through which Christ the Mediator worked, which characterized the coming." Vincent, s. v. "1 John 5:6."

5   Loyd-Jones, 617.

6   Stott, 177: "There can be little doubt that John was using an expression which was already familiar to his readers, either through his own teaching or through that of the false teachers, and which is not readily understood by us."

7   Burdick, 364–371; MacArthur, *1–3 John*, 191–196; Smalley, 277–282; Stedman, 349–353; Wiersbe, *Be Real*, 174–176; Yarbrough, 282–284. Some see verse 6 as referring to the historical events and verse 8 to the sacraments. Dodd, 127–131; Law, 121–121; Stott. However, Burdick (pp. 370–371) argues convincingly against that position. Cf. Boice, *The Epistles of John*, 132–134; Raymond Brown, 584.

8   Chuck Smith, "C2000 Series in 1 John 5," Blue Letter Bible. Retrieved Feb. 20, 2018 at https://www.blueletterbible.org/Comm/smith_chuck/c2000_1Jo/1Jo_005.cfm.

9   Cf. Burdick, 368.

10  Zodhiates, *The Epistles of John* (pp. 328–331) sees the water and blood as indications of Jesus's humanity and purpose. He understands the water as representative of the natural birth (as in John 3:5). The strength of his argument is the focus on the incarnation which is an obvious interest for John from the beginning of the epistle. However, it fails to give adequate weight to the witness/testimony theme in John's narrative. It also does not explain John's

confrontive words, "not only by water, but by water and blood." Cf. Raymond Brown, 595.

11  Some identify our text with John 19:34. "But one of the soldiers pierced His side with a spear, and immediately blood and water came out" (NASB). The phrase "water and blood" are used in both passages, although in the opposite order. Both passages address issues of witness/testimony. However, there are significant differences in context and in the way the terms are used in John 19 compared to 1 John 5. John 19:34 is primarily attesting to the actual death of Jesus and the fulfillment of prophesy (John 19:35–37). The 1 John 5 text is addressing proofs that Jesus is the Son of God. Both passages likely have indirect allusion to cleansing since those two elements are prominent throughout Scripture as symbols of that. Raymond Brown (pp. 596–598) provides interesting comments concerning the salvific symbolism of the water and blood. Given the challenges in simply arriving at the basic interpretation of 1 John 5 text, I chose not to bring John 19:34 into the discussion. Cf. Smalley, 278; Stott, 177–178; Yarbrough, 282.

12  Cf. 1 Cor. 11:24–25.

13  F. F. Bruce, *The Epistles of John: Introduction, Exposition and Notes* (Grand Rapids: Eerdmans, 1979) 118–121. Concerning verse 6, Brooke (p. 135) insists, "The tense of *elthōn* excludes any primary reference to the Christian sacraments. . . ." Cf. Law, 119–123; Zodhiates, *The Epistles of John*, 328.

14  Irenaeus, *Against Heresies*, The Ante-Nicene Fathers, edited by Alexander Roberts and James Donaldson (Grand Rapids: Eerdmans, 1950) 3. 3.4.

15  Law, 92–94; Cf. Burdick, 366; Dodd, 130; Smalley, 278–280.

16  Cf. Luke 1:28–35; John 1:1–4, 14; 1 John 4:2–3.

17  1 Cor. 15:6. Cf. Acts 1:2–3.

18  Cf. John 14:26; 15:26; 16:7.

19  Cf. Acts 4:10.

20  William Barclay, *The Letters of John and Jude.*1958 (Philadelphia, PN: Westminster Press, 1976) 110–111; James M. Boice, *The Epistles of John*, Raymond E. Brown, 775–787.

21  Matt. 18:16; 2 Cor. 13:1. Cf. Deut. 17:6; Robert Yarbrough, *1–3 John*, 284.

22  Cf. Mark 15:29–33; Luke 23:39–44.

23  Exod. 10:21–23; 12:1–12, 29–30.

24  Cf. Isa. 5:30; 8:22; 13:10–11; Amos 5:18–20; Zeph. 1:14–18.

25  Cf. Matt. 27:46; Mark 15:34; 2 Cor. 5:21; Barker, ed., *The NIV Study Bible*, s. v. "Matt. 26:39, cup" by Ralph Earle and W. W. Wessel, p. 1482, and "Mark 15:34" by W. W. Wessel & W. L. Lane, p. 1526.

26  Cf. Exod. 19:18; Ps. 18:7; Isa. 13:9–13, 29:5–6; Jer. 10:10.

27 Herbert Lockyer, *All the Messianic Prophecies of the Bible* (Grand Rapids: Zondervan, 1973) provides extensive teaching on this subject including prophetic significance of Old Testament rituals and offerings.

28 Cf. John 1:29; Rom. 3:21–26; 5:9; Eph. 1:7; Col. 1:14; Heb. 12:24; 13:12, 20–21; 1 Pet. 1:18–20; 1 John 1:7; 2:2; Rev. 1:5; 5:8–10.

29 Matt. 27:51. Cf. Gen. 4:4; Exod. 12; Lev. 16; Heb. 9–10.

# CHAPTER 26

Believing God's Testimony
5:9–13

If we receive the witness of men, the witness of God is greater; for this is the witness of God which He has testified of His Son. He who believes in the Son of God has the witness in himself; he who does not believe God has made Him a liar, because he has not believed the testimony that God has given of His Son. And this is the testimony: that God has given us eternal life, and this life is in His Son. He who has the Son has life; he who does not have the Son of God does not have life. These things I have written to you who believe in the name of the Son of God, that you may know that you have eternal life, and that you may continue to believe in the name of the Son of God.

1 John 5:9-13, NKJV

## Expository Message

We will begin this study with the last verse of the text in 1 John 5:13. "These things I have written to you who believe in the name of the Son of God, that you may know that you have eternal life, and that you may continue to believe in the name of the Son of God." Notice first that John is writing this epistle primarily to Christians.[1] "These things I have written to you who believe in the name of the Son of God." There are statements in the letter that secondarily speak to nonbelievers. He indirectly confronts Gnostics who have rejected the true message of Jesus Christ. He indirectly informs the world that their anti-God kingdom is passing away. Non-Christians can benefit from reading this book. In fact, God might even use it to lead them to Christ. But it's helpful to know John's target audience: "You who believe in the name of the Son of God."

In contrast, John wrote his gospel to unbelievers. He makes that clear in John 20:30–31.

> Therefore many other signs Jesus also performed in the presence of the disciples, which are not written in this book; but these have been written so that you may believe that Jesus is the Christ, the Son of God; and that believing you may have life in His name" (NASB).

Implied in that statement is a target audience of unbelievers. Notice his purpose statement there in verse 31. "But these are written so that you may believe that Jesus is the Christ, the Son of God, and that believing you may have life in His name."

What does John want his readers to believe? "That Jesus is the Christ, the Son of God." What was the object of faith John focuses on in our text? "These things I have written to you who believe in the name of the Son of God" (1 John 5:13). The language in our text is very similar to his language in John 20:31. The critical issue is believing in Jesus as the Son of God, believing that His is who He claimed to be and that the Father has verified that as true. The purpose behind John's gospel is that people would have eternal life by believing in Jesus. "And that believing you may have life in His name" (John 20:31). His name represents who He is. He is the one and only Savior. He is God, the Son. He is the Christ, the Anointed One, Messiah. There is salvation in no other name.

The kernels of truth in these two verses, John 20:31 and 1 John 5:13. are profound. Nothing is more basic to the gospel than this. "And that believing you may have life in His name." Do not miss the connection in John 20:31 between believing in Jesus for who He is and in having eternal life. That is a vital connection in John's theology. "These are written that you may believe that Jesus is the Christ, the Son of God, and that believing you may have life in His name." Let me lay beside that 1 John 5:11–12, "And this is the testimony: that God has given us eternal life, and this life is in His Son. He who has the Son has life; he who does not have the Son of God does not have life." So, John's purpose behind his *gospel* is that people would come to faith in Christ.

John's purpose in *this epistle* is that Christians would enjoy assurance of that faith and continue in it. "These things I have written to you who believe in the name of the Son of God, that you may know that you have eternal life, and that you may continue to believe in the name of the Son of God" (1 John 5:13). The idea of continuance is found in the Greek present tense.[2] John wants to confirm these people in their faith and fortify them against the temptation to abandon it for Gnostic error.[3] The practical value of 1 John for us is that we may enjoy strong assurance that we do indeed have eternal life abiding in us. That assurance fortifies us against deception and strengthens our walk with God. It adds boldness to our testimony and to our prayer life, as we will see later in this final chapter of 1 John.

In chapter 25 we looked at three objective proofs that Jesus is the Son of God. That text, 1 John 5:6–8, in the New Living Translation says,

> And Jesus Christ was revealed as God's Son by his baptism in water and by shedding his blood on the cross—not by water only, but by water and blood. And the Spirit, who is truth, confirms it with his testimony. So, we have these three witnesses—the Spirit, the water, and the blood— and all three agree.[4]

Christianity is grounded in objective, historical reality. God intervened in human history by sending His Son into the world. Christ was in fact born of the Virgin Mary. At His baptism the Holy Spirit descended upon Him in the form of a dove in confirmation of His messiahship. The Father spoke out of heaven, "This is My beloved Son in whom I am well pleased,"[5] in confirmation of His divinity. At His crucifixion there were detailed prophesies fulfilled and miraculous signs confirming Him as the Son of God. After His resurrection hundreds of people witnessed Him in His glorified body. Witnesses saw Him ascend into heaven. The coming of the

Holy Spirit on the Day of Pentecost confirmed His authority. Millions of transformed lives over the centuries all declare Jesus to be the Son of God.

## EXTERNAL WITNESS FROM THE FATHER

Now in our text today, John reminds us that God Himself was behind all those historical events. Those objective, historical facts are external witness from God verifying Jesus as the divine, Sent One. Men were involved. They gave their testimonies. For example, John the Baptist testified that Jesus is the Christ. The apostles bore witness to what they saw. John was even one of the three apostles on the Mount of Transfiguration who saw the glory of Christ and heard the voice of the Father on that mountain. There on the Mount of Transfiguration the Father gave direct testimony of Jesus when He said, "This is My beloved Son, in whom I am well pleased. Hear Him!"[6] At that event the Father's made a direct statement out of heaven. But in verse 9 of our text, John wants us to understand that behind all those events in history is the Father Himself giving testimony in behalf of His Son.

The testimony of the water, the blood, and the Spirit are ultimately the Father's witness of who Jesus is.[7] Therefore, we are confronted with the witness of God Himself! First John 5:9 says, "If we receive the witness of men, the witness of God is greater; for this[8] is the witness of God which He has testified of His Son." Receiving the witness of men is something we do on a daily basis. We could not enter into contracts, operate the judicial system, or buy products on credit without receiving the witness of men. It is commonly understood that we do receive the witness of men. Then John argues from the lesser to the greater.[9] If we regularly receive the witness of men, we should surely receive the witness of God. The witness of God is infinitely more reliable than the witness of men. The reliability of a witness depends on that person's knowledge and integrity. Obviously, God's witness is greater than the witness of man. As to knowledge, He is omniscient. As to integrity, He is the thrice Holy One of eternity. Therefore, it is unthinkable that we would reject God's testimony. God has borne witness of His Son through the water, the blood, and the Spirit. These three witnesses are in full agreement because they all come from the same source, the Father.[10] The testimony of the Father concerning His

Son is flawless and absolutely reliable. It is God Himself who has declared Jesus to be the Son of God. In verses 6–9 we are talking about the external, concrete, objective, historical testimony of God that Jesus is the Christ, the Son of God, the Savior of the world.

Where is the witness or testimony of God recorded? Do we not find it plain and clear in the Bible? For you and me today, God's testimony comes to us in Scripture.[11] Second Timothy 3:16 says, "All scripture is given by inspiration of God" (KJV). It may include the testimony of man. The Gospel of John and John's epistles are that apostle's testimony. However, since God inspired the writing, it is more than John's testimony.[12] It is God's testimony concerning His Son. All of the Bible is ultimately given that we might believe on the Son and have eternal life. Jesus said to the Jewish leaders, "You study the Scriptures diligently because you think that in them you have eternal life. These are the very Scriptures that testify about me" (John 5:39, NIV). The Scriptures are God's testimony of Jesus. Later in that conversation Jesus said to them, "If you believed Moses, you would believe me, for he wrote about me. But since you do not believe what he wrote, how are you going to believe what I say?"[13] On the road to Emmaus, after His resurrection, Jesus used the Scriptures to show His followers that He is the Christ who would suffer for their salvation. Luke 24:27 says, "And beginning with Moses and all the Prophets, he explained to them what was said in all the Scriptures concerning himself" (NIV). The Bible is God's testimony of His Son. It is the word we proclaim. It is authoritative and powerful because it is God's word.

How are people saved? They hear the proclamation of God's testimony concerning His Son. Romans 10:14 asks a series of rhetorical questions: "How then shall they call on him in whom they have not believed? and how shall they believe in him of whom they have not heard? and how shall they hear without a preacher?" (KJV). The process begins with God's testimony of His Son recorded in the Bible. When the preacher declares God's testimony, the hearer must make the decision to either receive that testimony as true or to reject it as false. It is logical that he would receive God's testimony, because it is absolutely reliable; it is greater than the testimony of man. It is the Holy Spirit who enables the hearer to realize this is a true testimony from God. But still the choice to receive or reject that testimony rests with the hearer.

Come back to our text in 1 John 5:9: "If we receive the witness of men, the witness of God is greater; for this is the witness of God which He has testified of His Son." We are saved when we receive the testimony of God concerning His Son. What is the Father's testimony concerning His Son? "And this is the testimony: that God has given us eternal life, and this life is in His Son" (1 John 5:11). The gospel declares the coming of Christ to provide salvation for all who will receive Him.

Let me give just a few verses from John's gospel to illustrate how Scripture declares God's witness of Jesus as an offer of salvation. John 3:16 is classic. "For God so loved the world that he gave his one and only Son, that whoever believes in him shall not perish but have eternal life" (NIV). John 3:18 continues, "Whoever believes in him is not condemned, but whoever does not believe stands condemned already because they have not believed in the name of God's one and only Son" (NIV). Speaking of Jesus, John 1:12 says, "Yet to all who did receive him, to those who believed in his name, he gave the right to become children of God" (NIV).

So, God sends you and me, as His ambassadors, with His testimony concerning Jesus.[14] His testimony is called the gospel. It is God's witness that He has sent His Son to pay the penalty of our sin, to reconcile us to God, to give us eternal life. The Son laid down His life on the cross to make atonement for our sin. All who will receive the Father's testimony concerning His Son and throw themselves on His mercy, will be forgiven of sin, will be born again, and will become children of God, rather than enemies of God. Our commission in Mark 16:15–16 is to, "Go into all the world and preach the gospel to all creation. Whoever believes and is baptized will be saved, but whoever does not believe will be condemned" (NIV).

I hope you see these two truths: (1) The Bible is God's testimony concerning Jesus as the Son of God, the only Savior. (2) People receive eternal life when they receive God's testimony and place their faith in Christ. Receiving eternal life comes only to those who put faith in the testimony God has recorded in His word. God has provided external, objective, historical proof of Jesus as the provider of eternal life.

## INTERNAL WITNESS FROM THE HOLY SPIRIT

When we receive God's testimony concerning Jesus, and are, therefore, born again, we then receive an additional witness.[15] We receive an internal witness.[16] God's Spirit bears witness with our spirit that we are a child of God. Our text puts it this way in 1 John 5:10: "He who believes in the Son of God has the witness in himself" (NKJV). The order that John gives is important. It does not say, "He who has the witness in himself, believes." Believing God's word (believing God's testimony concerning His Son) comes first.[17] Faith is not based on a feeling. Faith is based on God's promises and provision. When a person takes God at His word and puts his faith in Christ based on God's testimony in the word, that person receives eternal life. That person is born again. Then comes this wonderful inner witness of the Spirit that he is a child of God.

When you are leading a person to the Lord, tell that person what God has said in His word about Jesus. Tell him what God says about sin and his need for Jesus and his inability to save himself. Tell the gospel message of Jesus's death and resurrection. Give him the promise from Scripture that whoever confesses his sins and put his faith in Christ will be saved.[18] Invite that person to believe God's testimony and receive eternal life. People are saved by taking God at His word and receiving Christ as their Savior. There is reason behind it all, but it is not reasoning power alone that brings people to Christ.[19] Without faith it is impossible to please God.[20] It is putting one's faith in the testimony God has given us in His word.

This is also essential to living in *assurance* of salvation. If your assurance is based on feelings, you are going to be up and down in your walk with God. One day you may feel saved, and the next day you're not so sure. Feelings are volatile. But the word of God abides forever.[21] If the Scripture says that God gave His Son and "whoever believes in him shall not perish but have eternal life," then it is true Sunday when I'm feeling spiritual, and it is equally true Monday when I am feeling numb and out of touch with God. The word of God abides forever! You relied on it the day you received Christ, and you can rely on it from then on.

If someone asks you how you know you're saved, the first answer is because God has *said,* "Believe in the Lord Jesus, and you will be saved."[22] I have put my faith in Christ. "I know whom I have believed, and am convinced that he is able to guard what I have entrusted to him until that day."[23] I trust the fidelity of God's word. That's the first answer. Then we can boldly add: His Spirit bears witness with my spirit that I am a child of God.[24] Our text in verse 10 parallels that Romans 8:16 statement. "He who believes in the Son of God has the witness in himself." There is a knowing in our hearts that confirms and fortifies the faith we exercised in God's word.[25] Have you received that affirmation in your spirit that you're a child of God? It's a different kind of knowing, but it too is very, very real.

I have the assurance of God's word! Additionally, I also have the assurance of the witness in my spirit that I am a child of God. John has written this epistle so that we can enjoy full assurance. He gives two foundations for that assurance in our text: the external testimony of God's word and the internal witness of the Spirit. "O taste and see that the Lord is good."[26] We have experienced His goodness and mercy. We have experienced firsthand His love poured out in our hearts. Someone has well said, "The man with an experience is never at the mercy of a man with an argument."[27] It is mighty hard to tell a man who has eaten Braum's ice cream that it's not tasty. You could give me ten reasons Braum's pecan chocolate tastes bad, and all your arguments would roll off me like water off a duck's back. I ate some and it tasted really good. Don't tell me there's no God. He walks with me and talks with me every day. Do you remember the blind man that Jesus healed in John 9? The Pharisees tried to persuade him that Jesus was a fraud. His counter to all their arguments was, "one thing I know, that, whereas I was blind, now I see" (KJV). Has Jesus brought a change in your life? Has He changed the way you think about sin? Has He put a love in your heart for the Father? That is mighty strong evidence that you're a child of God.

## BELIEVING GOD'S TESTIMONY

The testimony of God concerning His Son confronts people with a decision. Will you accept God's testimony, or will you reject it? We may quote John 3:16 to a person and his reply might be, "I don't believe in the Bible." Then what he is saying outright is that he does not receive the testimony of God. That's a fatal mistake. Hopefully he will reconsider. To reject God's testimony is to reject the only hope of salvation. We will not try to rationalize him into the kingdom, for his carnal mind is enmity with God.[28] No matter how sound the reasoning, he would not accept it. Anyone who refuses God's testimony of His Son is lost. It's the condition he's already in.[29] He simply refuses the only cure for that fallen condition.

First John 5:10b says, "He who does not believe God has made Him a liar, because he has not believed the testimony that God has given of His Son."[30] The highest appeal to reason is what God says. He is infinitely smarter than multitudes of men. The unbeliever would like us to make our appeal based on something greater than the word of God. But there is nothing greater for that appeal. It would be laughable to offer the reasonings of Einstein, rather than God's reasons. We make no appeal to anything beyond the word of God, because there is nothing greater that we can resort to. We must offer you the testimony of God and let you receive it or reject it. That's what Jesus commanded us to do. We are to go into all the world and proclaim the gospel, proclaim God's testimony of Jesus recorded in Scripture. Mark 16:16 then adds, "Whoever believes and is baptized will be saved, but whoever does not believe will be condemned" (NIV). The process is really quite simple. We declare the Father's testimony of His Son. Those hearing that declaration choose to either receive it or reject it.[31] "He who does not believe God has made Him a liar, because he has not believed the testimony that God has given of His Son."

To believe or not to believe is a moral choice, not an intellectual one. The evidence of these truths is overwhelming. There is no excuse for not receiving the testimony. In fact, rejecting the message is equivalent to calling God a liar. Can you imagine a court proceeding in which witnesses are called? In comes God Himself and gives witness to the truth. When He steps down from that witness stand, it would be preposterous to require another witness. He is the final word. How could anyone demand more proof?

"Unbelief is not a misfortune to be pitied;" John Stott wrote, "it is a sin to be deplored."[32] The carnal mind has a very different evaluation of unbelief from what God says it is. The nation of Israel wandered around in the wilderness until all but two fell over dead. What was the cause of that terrible tragedy? It was very simply because of their unbelief.[33] Why did the Pharisees reject Jesus? Was it an intellectual struggle? No, Jesus told them in John 5:40, "You are not *willing* to come to Me that you may have life" (emphasis mine). Their issue was in regard to the will, not the intellect. They were choosing other things.[34] They did not choose to receive the testimony God gave concerning His Son. John 3:19 explains it this way. "And this is the condemnation, that light is come into the world, and men loved darkness rather than light, because their deeds were evil" (KJV). As long as men justify their unbelief on the basis of inadequate intellectual proof, they will never be saved. The proof is more than adequate. It comes down to either accepting it or rejecting it. "And this is the testimony: that God has given us eternal life, and this life is in His Son" (1 John 5:11). There's only one place you can get eternal life. It is found in Jesus or it is not found at all.

John offers only two courses of action and only two destinations. He does not complicate the matter with subtleties. The truth is very simple. Either you receive the testimony of God or you reject it. Either you receive Christ as your Lord and Savior or you reject Him. Either you embrace the truth God gives in the gospel or you call God a liar. The consequences of these decisions are also very clear. If you believe God's testimony and receive Christ, you have eternal life. If you reject God's testimony, you are already under condemnation for your sin. You have called God a liar and rejected His only remedy for your condition. You will die in your sins. When a man is dying of cancer and his doctor offers him the only treatment that will cure him, if he refuses that treatment, is his death the doctor's fault? Jesus is the only cure for the terminal disease of sin. But God has provided the perfect cure. What will you do with the cure God has provided?

Look how simply John states it in 1 John 5:12. "He who has the Son has life; he who does not have the Son of God does not have life." Nothing could be more politically incorrect than that statement. John is not trying to be politically correct. He is seeking to be biblically correct. And every one of us must do the same. In this society, you can forget about being politically correct if you're going to be biblically correct. Jesus is the only way of salvation. He paid an unimaginable price for your salvation. Mohammad did not pay such a price. Buddha did not pay the price. Joseph Smith paid no such price. Jesus alone has purchased salvation. He alone has it to give! Life is in Him. Outside of Him there is no life. The life is in the Son. "He who has the Son has life; he who does not have the Son of God does not have life."

John is closing the body of his letter in verse 13. He will add some postscripts, but verse 13 summarizes his overall objective for the document.[35] Our text in verses 6–12 has naturally led us to this statement.[36] "These things I have written to you who believe in the name of the Son of God, that you may know that you have eternal life, and that you may continue to believe in the name of the Son of God." This eternal life is described in 1 John 1:3 as fellowship "with the Father, and with his Son Jesus Christ" (KJV)."[37] God does not give eternal life as something apart from Himself. The life is found in our relationship with God through Christ. We will spend eternity enjoying that loving interaction. As Christians, we now have eternal life in Christ. It is the source of our joy and peace. It is our power to live life to the fullest.

Nothing is more important than having eternal life. Nothing is more important than being in right relationship with God through Christ. The good news of the gospel is that this eternal life is available to all who will receive it. "For the wages of sin is death, but the gift of God is eternal life in Christ Jesus our Lord."[38]

# Endnotes: Chapter 26

1 Cf. Boice, *The Epistles of John,* 136; John Painter, *1, 2, and 3 John,* Sacra Pagina Series, vol. 18, D. J. Harrington, ed. (Collegeville, MN: The Liturgical Press, 2002) 314; Zodhiates, *The Epistles of John,* 369.

2 Zodiates, 368–371.

3 Smalley, 291: ". . . an undercurrent of *exhortation* is discernible in these vv. The author wishes to reassure his orthodox Christian readers of the rightness of their belief . . . In a situation of conflict, where different estimates of the person of Jesus were being debated, such readers may well have doubted the reality of their own spiritual experience. They may have even been inclined to abandon their faith in Christ altogether. John seeks to confirm these members of his church in their faith, and to persuade them to maintain it constantly" (emphasis Smalley's). Cf. Raymond Brown, 634; Stott, 184; Yarbrough, 288, 290, 297; 1 John 2:24–28; Acts 14:22; Rom. 11:20–22; Heb. 10:35.

4 *Holy Bible, New Living Translation.* 1996 (Carol Stream, IL: Tyndale House Publishers, 2004).

5 Matt. 3:16–17, KJV.

6 Matt .17:5, NKJV.

7 There are not four witnesses in this passage, but three, all of which are declarations from the Father of who Jesus is. Dodd, 132; Stott, 181. Contra: Raymond Brown, 587, 600.

8 Law, 404. Following the lead of Haupt and Weiss, Law describes the meaning in this way: "Because this (namely, the triple witness cited in the preceding verse) is the witness of God, because God *hath* borne witness concerning his Son" (emphasis Law's). Cf. Burdick, 373; Smalley, 283; Stott, 181; John 5:36–37; Heb. 2:4.

9 Burdick, 372. Cf. Num. 23:19; Titus 1:2; Heb. 6:18.

10 Stott, 181.

11 Spurgeon, "The True Position of the Witness Within." Preached Aug. 11, 1878. Accessed at The C. H. Spurgeon Collection on CD-ROM (AGES Software, Inc., 1998). Spurgeon says, "The basis of faith is the testimony of God concerning His Son—the testimony of God as we find it in holy Scripture." Cf. Boice, *The Epistles of John,* 134; Ironside, pp. 202–204.

12 Cf. 2 Pet. 1:19–21.

13 John 5:46–47, NIV.

14 Cf. 2 Cor. 5:18–20.

15 Zodhiates, *The Epistles of John,* 355: "The moment a man acknowledges God's testimony of His Son as true, then the miracle of faith is activated and he becomes a child of God."

16  The Reformers termed this *"testimonium internum Spiritus Sancti."* Boice, *The Epistles of John,* 135. Cf. Loyd-Jones, 633.

17  Stott, 182; Law, 125; Smalley, 286; C. H. Spurgeon, "The True Position of the Witness Within," preached Aug. 11, 1878. Accessed at The C. H. Spurgeon Collection on CD-ROM (AGES Software, Inc., 1998).

18  Cf. Rom. 10:13; 1 John 1:8–9; 2:2.

19  Cf. 1 Cor. 1:17–25; Col. 2:6–8.

20  Heb. 11:6.

21  1 Pet. 1:23–25 Cf. Ps. 119:89, 160; Matt. 4:4.

22  Acts 16:31, NIV.

23  2 Tim. 1:12, NIV.

24  Rom. 8:16. Cf. Rom. 9:1; Gal. 4:6.

25  Cf. 1 Cor. 2:11–12.

26  Ps. 34:8, KJV.

27  Leonard Ravenhill, "Leonard Ravenhill Quotes," *Christian Quotes for Reflection and Imagination.* Retrieved March 1, 2018 at http://quoteschristian.com/leonardravenhill.html.

28  Rom. 8:7. Cf. 1 Cor. 1:21.

29  Cf. John 3:18.

30  Raymond Brown (p. 590) writes concerning John's use of the perfect tense translated, "has made God a liar" in 1 John 5:10b, "This is the first of three consecutive perfect tenses in three lines (make, believe, testified), which give the tone of enduring stance rather than a single action."

31  Of course, the ability to believe comes through the influence of the Holy Spirit. He convinces of sin, of righteousness, and of judgment (John 16:7-11). While the freewill of man is honored, the is no room for boasting, even concerning the choice made. "By the grace of God, I am what I am" (1 Cor. 15:10).

32  Stott, 182.

33  Heb. 3:16–19; 4:2.

34  Cf. John 5:44.

35  Dodd, 133.

36  Law, 405. Cf. Burdick, 384–385. Verse 13 also provides transition to his postscript concerning confidence in prayer (verses 14–15).

37  Stott, 183; MacArthur, *1–3 John,* 197. Cf. Barclay, 113; Smalley, 288.

38  Rom. 6:23, NKJV.

CHAPTER 27

# Praying with Confidence
## 5:13–15

These things I have written to you who believe in the name of the Son of God, that you may know that you have eternal life, and that you may continue to believe in the name of the Son of God. Now this is the confidence that we have in Him, that if we ask anything according to His will, He hears us. And if we know that He hears us, whatever we ask, we know that we have the petitions that we have asked of Him.

1 John 5:13-15, NKJV

## Expository Message

The problem of unanswered prayer! It's a major source of frustration for most Christians. Why aren't my prayers being answered? Why are some prayers answered and others are not? Why do some people seem to get answers to prayer easier than others? Have you ever been puzzled with questions like that? I certainly have, and I have watched many others struggle with those issues as well. It is demotivating when we are not seeing our prays answered. Most shrug it all off as just some mystery that can't be explained. And there is an element of mystery in prayer. God does not always explain everything He does.[1]

However, most of the problem is our lack of understanding as to the purpose of prayer and how it works. I knew one Bible teacher who threw his Bible away and stopped going to church because God did not answer a specific prayer. He was convinced that God *should* have answered the prayer. He had fasted and prayed fervently for the answer. Many others were praying as well. When the answer did not come, he was devastated. He was convinced that God had failed him. In reality, he simply did not understand how prayer works. The man died a few years ago. He never fully recovered from the incident. That is an extreme case. Most people respond to unanswered prayer by simply going through the motions of prayer as a duty, with little expectation of results. On the surface they pray, but they really don't engage the process at a spiritual level. I'm talking about the demotivation of not getting answers to prayer. The best solution to that problem is to learn how to pray effectively so that answers come. Allowing for some mystery in the process, let me just say, prayer works when we are working it in the right way, according to its designed purpose. The goal for this study is that we would gain a better understanding of that purpose and become more effective in our prayers.

Our text in chapter 26 concluded with 1 John 5:13. In that verse John stated his purpose for writing this letter. "These things I have written to you who believe in the name of the Son of God, that you may know that you have eternal life, and that you may continue to believe in the name of the Son of God." John is talking to Christians, and his objective is that we would live in full assurance of our relationship with God, that we *may know* that we have *eternal life*. He used different terminology to state this purpose at the beginning in 1 John 1:3–4. "That which we have seen and heard declare we unto you, that ye also may have fellowship with us: and truly our fellowship is with the Father, and with his Son Jesus Christ. And these things write we unto you, that your joy may be full" (KJV). "Eternal life" is living in vital "fellowship" and interaction with God. It is not anything independent of God. It is God sharing His life with us. It is connection; it is relationship.

Nothing is more vital to enjoying that relationship than prayer. It is, therefore, a natural progression of thought for John to talk about confidence in prayer right after addressing assurance of eternal life.[2] And that's what he does in verses 14–15 of our text. "Now this is the confidence that we have in Him, that if we ask anything according to His will, He hears us.

And if we know that He hears us, whatever we ask, we know that we have the petitions that we have asked of Him." We have assurance of eternal life. We know that we are God's children. Based on that relationship and assurance we also have confidence in answered prayer.

In this epistle John gives us four conditions for confident prayer. I want us to look at those now. They are somewhat progressive. One condition is found in 1 John 5:13.

## ASSURANCE OF ETERNAL LIFE

Our assurance of eternal life is based on the three objective tests given in this letter (the tests of righteousness, truth, and love), and the inner, subjective, witness of the Holy Spirit mentioned in 5:10. The foundation of our confidence in prayer is our relationship with God through Christ. John began this chapter with this declaration in verse 1. "Whoever believes that Jesus is the Christ is born of God" (NASB). Through faith in Christ we can be born again, we can become children of God. That status alone gives us favor with God. We are in the family. We are God's children. And because we are His children we have access to Him.

Do you know that you have eternal life? Do you have the assurance in your heart that you are a child of God? John's primary objective in writing this epistle is that we would live in that assurance. Without that assurance we cannot have confidence in prayer. Confidence in prayer is based on knowing we are accepted in the family because of Jesus.[3] We are not praying to a distant, disinterested deity somewhere out there in outer space. We are coming to our heavenly Father. When the disciples asked Jesus to teach them to pray, His first instruction was that we begin with these two words, "Our Father."[4] That's where effective prayer always begins. It begins with the assurance that we have eternal life. It begins with the affirmation that God is our Father.

With that, we must understand that it is our Father's good pleasure to give us the kingdom.[5] Prayer is not a process by which we overcome God's reluctance to give us good things. There are obstacles to overcome. The flesh and the world are obstacles to answered prayer. But never, never is there any problem with God's willingness to do us good. We are His beloved children. He gave the most precious thing in heaven so He could do us good. In Jeremiah. 29:11 He says, "'For I know the plans I have for you,' declares the Lord, 'plans to prosper you and not to harm you, plans to give you hope and a future'" (NIV). Any doubts about God's intentions toward us must be resolved. He is always looking to bless you in the highest possible way. He is always working things together for your good. You don't have to talk God into blessing you. That is already His intention for you. Listen to Jesus's reasoning in Luke 11:11–13.

> Which of you fathers, if your son asks for a fish, will give him a snake instead? Or if he asks for an egg, will give him a scorpion? If you then, though you are evil, know how to give good gifts to your children, how much more will your Father in heaven give the Holy Spirit to those who ask him! (NIV).

The devil is the accuser.[6] He accuses you to God. He accuses you to you. And he accuses God to you. That was his approach to Eve in the garden. There he maligned God's motives toward Eve. He questioned God's benevolence toward her. When she listened to that lie, it set her up for failure. It undermined her confidence in God. In reality, God is always for you. Our first condition for confident prayer is this assurance that we are a child of God. Back in chapter 3 of this letter, John gave another condition of confidence in prayer.

## A CLEAR CONSCIENCE

First John 3:21–22 says, "Beloved, if our heart does not condemn us, we have confidence before God; and whatever we ask we receive from Him, because we keep His commandments and do the things that are pleasing in His sight" (NASB). The same Greek word translated confidence in 5:14 is also used here in 3:21. It means boldness or freedom of speech.[7] "Beloved, if our heart does not condemn us, we have confidence before God." A sense of guilt and self-condemnation is a major contributor to our lack of confidence in prayer.[8] If there are unresolved issues of guilt, it is impossible to pray in faith. That's why the Holy Spirit will make you aware of those issues when you approach the throne of grace.⁹ He does that, so we can resolve those matters and then pray with confidence.

How do we resolve the guilt issues? First, we confess the sin as sin, knowing that God has made provision for that problem. First John 1:9–10 promises, "If we confess our sins, He is faithful and righteous to forgive us our sins and to cleanse us from all unrighteousness. If we say that we have not sinned, we make Him a liar and His word is not in us" (NASB). We don't justify the wrong behavior. We don't ignore the sense of guilt. We deal with it forthrightly by acknowledging two facts. We acknowledge the transgression. We confess the sin. *And*, we acknowledge God's provision for the problem. We rely on God's faithfulness to forgive us our sins and cleanse us from all unrighteousness.¹⁰ The second part of that is as important as the first. Sometimes people confess the sin over and over doubting God's willingness to forgive. That leaves them in a state of self-condemnation. In that state, they cannot pray in faith. We must take God at His word when He says, "The blood of Jesus His Son cleanses us from all sin" (1:7, NASB). We receive the forgiveness that Jesus purchased on the cross at a very high price.

We also repent of the sin. We turn from the wrong behavior that we confessed. We commit ourselves to living in obedience to God.¹¹ We won't live that out perfectly. We may find ourselves even coming back and asking forgiveness for the same sin again. But we must be honest in our approach to God. We must be sincere in our repentance. If we are to pray with confidence, we must pursue a life of obedience to the Lord. To live in willful sin is to forfeit confidence in prayer. In fact, God says He will not hear us if we are willfully following iniquity. I'm not talking about failures. We have just talked about His provision for that. I'm talking about a determined decision to keep a sin regardless of what God thinks about it. The Psalmist said it in Psalm 66:18: "If I regard wickedness in my heart, The Lord will not hear" (NASB). It's amazing how people think they can live in open sin, and expect God to answer their prayers at the same time. He does sometimes answer their prayer in His mercy. But He is under no obligation to do so. We can't walk in darkness and pray with confidence. We must walk in the light; then the provision of forgiveness and cleansing in the blood qualifies us for audience with God. So, 1 John 3:21–22 gives us this insight on how to pray with assurance: "Beloved, if our heart does not condemn us, we have confidence before God; and whatever we ask we receive from Him, because we keep His commandments and do the things that are pleasing in His sight."

The guilt and self-condemnation are resolved by a commitment to live in obedience to God, and a confidence in the blood of Christ to cleanse us when we come short of that. In that way, we maintain a clear conscience. Now in our text we come to another condition of confidence and success in prayer.[12]

## ASKING ACCORDING TO HIS WILL

"Now this is the confidence that we have in Him, that if we ask anything according to His will, He hears us" (1 John 5:14). The focus here is on the content of our prayers. In chapter 3 John has dealt with the importance of our lives being lived in accordance with the will of God. We have confidence in prayer and get answers because we align our lives with the commandments of God and to the very best of our ability, relying on the grace of God, we do those things that are pleasing in His sight. Here in chapter 5, John says the requests themselves need to be aligned with the will of God as well.

To fully appreciate 1 John 5:14, we need to understand the *purpose* of prayer. Most Christians wrongly think prayer is about getting God to come around to our way of thinking. When we are a new babe in Christ we pray much like infants in the natural operate. When a baby wants something, he cries for it and gets it. It is all centered on what he wants. God accommodates that in new Christians. But at some point, He expects us to grow out of that into a more mature understanding of prayer. What is the purpose of prayer and how does it work? Prayer is, for the most part, aligning ourselves with the will of God and executing that will on the earth.[13]

To understand that, let us go back to the first chapter of Genesis. Genesis 1:26 records God's intent for man. "Then God said, 'Let Us make man in Our image, according to Our likeness; and let them rule over the fish of the sea and over the birds of the sky and over the cattle and over all the earth, and over every creeping thing that creeps on the earth'" (NASB). Then in the rest of that chapter we see God delegating authority over the earth to man. Genesis 1:28 says, "God blessed them; and God said to them, 'Be fruitful and multiply, and fill the earth, and subdue it; and rule over the fish of the sea and over the birds of the sky and *over every living thing that moves on the earth*'" (emphasis mine, NASB). There is a lot of language there related to the animal kingdom. But when He says, "Over every living thing that moves," He is making a very broad statement.[14] He is delegating rulership of the earth to mankind. God has sovereignly chosen to rule the earth through man.[15] That has all kinds of theological implication that we don't have time to explore. But we need to understand how that relates to prayer.

The will of God in the earth is released through the prayers and obedience of God's people.[16] The whole Bible bears record of that fact. God did not directly deliver the children of Israel from Egyptian slavery. He did it through Moses. God did not bring Nineveh to repentance until Jonah delivered His message to them. "How then will they call on Him in whom they have not believed? How will they believe in Him whom they have not heard? And how will they hear without a preacher?"[17] Lazarus was not raised from the dead until Jesus arrived and called him forth. God could do it without our involvement, but He has chosen not to![18] He has graciously brought us into the process. That's why Paul can say in 1 Corinthians 3:9, "We are labourers together with God" (KJV). Behind our understanding of the purpose of prayer is God's decision to delegate authority over the earth to mankind.[19]

In teaching the Lord's prayer, Jesus didn't just give us words to say in prayer. He gives us the stance and attitude of mind that makes prayer effective. I've already addressed the words *Our Father*, and the positive, expectant attitude that implies. But Jesus also teaches us to pray, "Your kingdom come, Your will be done on earth as it is in heaven."[20] When we are praying, "*My* kingdom come, *My* will be done," we are likely to be disappointed in the results.[21] I'm not saying we would ever actually say those words; but, if that is our mindset, we are missing the point of prayer. James confronted that error when he said, "You ask and do not receive, because you ask with wrong motives, so that you may spend *it* on your pleasures" (4:3, NASB). They were praying with a complete misunderstanding of what prayer is all about.

In prayer, we are seeking to execute the will of the Father on earth. We are submitting ourselves and our requests to His will. Jesus is the perfect example of that. Even though He is the Son of God, still He said, "I have come down from heaven, not to do My own will, but the will of Him who sent Me."[22] So what does 1 John say? "Now this is the confidence that we have in Him, that if we ask anything *according to His will*, He hears us" (emphasis mine).

Effectiveness in prayer is not found in telling God what *I* want, then adding the tag line, "Not my will but thine be done."[23] That skirts our responsibility to discover the will of God and execute it in the earth. Sometimes it indicates a kind of fatalistic attitude toward prayer that really means, "I'll throw these requests out and hope something strikes a note with You, God. But, if the answer doesn't come easily, I'll just assume it wasn't Your will." That is very common in the American church. It's not wrong to use the words, "Not my will, but Yours, be done." Those words were used by Jesus Himself.[24] But He didn't use them as a tag line. He was completely committed to the principle.

Prayer is a process of high engagement with God in the execution of His will on earth. An important aspect of that process is the discovery of His will and the implementation of that through prayer and obedience. Since that is the case, we need to answer this question. How do we discover and know the will of God? We do that primarily through the Word and the Spirit.

The Bible provides us extensive knowledge concerning the will of God. To know what that will is we must spend time in Scripture. We read it; we study it; we meditate on it day and night. We allow it to change the way we think, so that more and more we tend to pray the will of God because everything about us is already lined up with it.[25] Paul prayed for the Colossian Christians that they would know the will of God. In Colossians 1:9 he wrote, "For this reason also, since the day we heard *of it*, we have not ceased to pray for you and to ask that you may be *filled with the knowledge of His will* in all spiritual wisdom and understanding" (emphasis mine, NASB). Rather than encouraging them to add, "Not my will but thine be done," to every prayer, Paul wants these people to know the will of God so they can intelligently fulfill their responsibility in regard to it. The more we are saturated with the word of God, the more we know the will of God. Sometimes, even when the Bible doesn't specifically address a matter, we

can apply the principles that it teaches and determine God's will for that situation. God has given us His word, so we can know His will.

He has also given us the Holy Spirit to lead us into all truth. Earlier in this epistle, John wrote, "As for you, the anointing which you received from Him abides in you, and you have no need for anyone to teach you; but as His anointing teaches you about all things, and is true and is not a lie, and just as it has taught you, you abide in Him" (2:27, NASB). Isn't it wonderful to have ongoing communication with the Holy Spirit? You start to do something, and you sense this check in your spirit, letting you know not to do that or say that. At other times, there is this confirming peace that assures us we are moving in the right direction. We are not limited to our own understanding. God has sent the Spirit of Truth to help us on a daily basis.

The Holy Spirit is particularly active in helping us pray according to the will of God. In Romans 8:26–27 we are given this wonderful assurance,

> Likewise the Spirit also helps in our weaknesses. For we do not know what we should pray for as we ought, but the Spirit Himself makes intercession for us with groanings which cannot be uttered. Now He who searches the hearts knows what the mind of the Spirit *is,* because He makes intercession for the saints according to *the will of* God (NKJV).

With the help of the Holy Spirit, we can pray according to the will of God. Sometimes He quickens our minds with an understanding as to how we should pray. Sometimes it comes in the form of deep groanings that are beyond words. Sometimes it comes in the form of unknown tongues when we don't know intellectually what the Spirit is praying, yet we are participating in our spirit.[26]

A significant aspect of effective prayer is learning to conform our requests to the will of God.[27] We come to God with a settled conviction that above all else we want His will to be done. With that mindset, the process of prayer includes discovery of the Father's will by the promptings of the Holy Spirit. Once we know the will of God on a matter, we may find ourselves making bold declarations as God's representatives on earth. We may find ourselves insisting the will of the Father be done and demanding that opposing forces bow to His will.[28] Prayer can become very authoritative as we discover and execute the will of God on earth. So, we have the essential condition in verse 14 that we ask according to His will. "Now this is the confidence that we have in Him, that if we ask anything according to His will, He hears us."[29]

## ASSURANCE THAT GOD HAS GRANTED OUR REQUEST

Having prayed according to His will, there often comes an *inner* assurance that God has granted our request. Verse 15 says, "And if we know that He hears us, whatever we ask, we know that we have the petitions that we have asked of Him." Notice, it does not say, "We know that we *will* have;" it says, "We know that *we have.*" The present tense translated *we have* means "there is a sense in which, at the moment of prayer," we know the request is granted, even though we have not yet seen the physical manifestation of the answer.[30]

In the spiritual realm, we have been given possession of the answer.[31] Jesus said in Mark 11:24, "Therefore I say to you, whatever things you ask when you pray, believe that you receive them, and you will have them" (NKJV). He is not talking about mental gymnastics. He is not talking about positive thinking. He is talking about something the Holy Spirit communicates to our spirit. Having prayed in submission to God's will, there comes a confirmation inside that God has granted the request.[32] The old timers called this "praying through." It is sticking with the prayer process until you know in your heart that God has said "yes" to the prayer. Such confidence causes us to look for it to come to pass in the natural with firm expectancy.[33]

When Jesus stood at Lazarus's tomb, He prayed, "Father, I thank You that You have heard Me."[34] He is standing there in full assurance that He is praying according to the will of the Father, and that the Father has heard Him. Based on that assurance, He then speaks to the problem in prayer, "Lazarus, come forth!"[35] It is the will of God that Lazarus be raised from the dead, and Jesus is executing the will of God through prayer. When we are operating this way, we have tenacious faith that causes the elements to bow to God's plan and purposes.

Elijah was a man of like passions like you and me. He was just as human as we are. Yet, James 5 tells us he prayed earnestly that it would not rain, and it did not rain for three and a half years. He prayed again that it would rain, and the rain came. His process of praying for rain is instructive. It begins with hearing the will of God. "Then Elijah said to Ahab, 'Go up, eat and drink; for there is the sound of abundance of rain'" (1 Kings 18:41, NKJV). He is hearing in his spirit God's intentions for Israel at that time. So, what does Elijah do? He goes on the mountain and begins to pray for God's will to be done. He understood the purpose of prayer; he understood his part in the process.[36] Having an assurance in his heart that God hears his prayer, he sends his servant to go watch for the rain clouds to come in. He expects a manifestation of his answer. But answers do not always come easy, even when it is the will of God.[37] The answer that came back from his servant was not encouraging. The servant saw no sign of rain. Many of us would have concluded at that time that it must have not been the will of God. But Elijah knew two things in his heart. He knew God had heard his prayer because he was praying according to the will of God. And he knew that God had granted his request because it was affirmed in his inner man by the Holy Spirit. So, he persevered in prayer. Six time the servant went, and six times he came back with the same report: no indication of rain. Finally, on the seventh trip the servant reports a very small cloud, about the size of a man's hand. To the weak in faith, that is not much confirmation of a pending thunderstorm. But for Elijah, it was all he needed. Not a drop of water has fallen, but Elijah acts on the confidence that God has heard him, and the full manifestation is coming. That's the way effective prayer works!

What are you believing God for? Have you determined it is according to God's will? If not, address that issue first. Relying on the word of God and the Spirit of God, discover God's will in the matter. Then pray believing; pray knowing it is your Father's good pleasure to give you the kingdom. Persevere as Elijah did until the answer comes. Don't give up. You may be ten seconds from the breakthrough!

# Endnotes: Chapter 27

1   Cf. Deut. 29:29; Hab. 2:1–4; 1 Cor. 13:9.

2   Burdick, 387. The conjunction *kai* at the beginning of verse 14 clearly indicates there is a connection between verse 13 and verse 14.

3   Cf. Eph. 1:3–4; John 16:23–24, 27; 1 John 3:1.

4   Luke 11:1–2, KJV.

5   Cf. Luke 12:32.

6   Rev. 12:10. Cf. Job 1:9–11; Gen. 3:1–4.

7   Smalley, 130. The Greek word is *parrēsia*.

8   Jack W. Hayford, *Prayer is Invading the Impossible* (Chepstow, Gwent, Great Britain: Bridge Publishing, 1985) 86.

9   Sometimes Satan, the accuser, will assail us with a false sense of guilt. When we recognize that, we deal with it accordingly. When the Holy Spirit convicts, He is specific about the sin that needs to be repented of. When Satan accuses, he tends to assault with general language such as, "You're just worthless," "You never do anything right," etc.

10  Cf. Heb. 4:16; 10:19–22.

11  Cf. John 15:7.

12  The context of 1 John 5:14 assumes praying in the name of Jesus, submitted to and invoking His authority. Cf. John 14:13–14; 15:16; 16:24.

13  We get this backwards, thinking God is there to execute our will on earth. Then we wonder why our prayers are not answered.

14  U. Cassuto, *A Commentary of the Book of Genesis*, Part 1, trans. by Israel Abrahams (Jerusalem: Magnes Press, 1978) 57: "In vs 28 the words, 'And over every living thing that moves upon the earth,' clearly do not refer to . . . hayyä in the restricted sense of the term ['beast'], but to all living beings that move on the earth. . . ." Cf. James M. Boice, *Genesis: An Expositional Commentary* (Grand Rapids: Zondervan, 1982) p. 81; Henry M. Morris, *The Genesis Record: A Scientific and Devotional Commentary on the Book of Beginnings* (Grand Rapids: Backer Book House, 1976) p. 77: "This command, therefore, established man as God's steward over the created world and all things therein." The catastrophic impact of the Fall and the scope of the redemptive process (Rom. 8:19–22) affirms this interpretation of verse 28.

15  Cf. Francis A. Schaeffer, *Genesis in Space and Time: The Flow of Biblical History* (Downers Grove, IL: InterVarsity Press, 1972) 48–50: "Furthermore, being created in the image of God frees us from the burden of thinking that whatever *is* must be *right*. We have been given dominion which puts a moral responsibility on us" (emphasis Schaeffer's); Jack W. Hayford, ed., *The New Spirit Filled Life Bible*, (Nashville, TN: Thomas Nelson, 2002) s. v. "Gen. 1:26, Dominion over . . . the earth" by R. Russel Bixler, p. 5: "God created man to be His

kingdom agent, to rule and subdue the rest of creation, including the aggressive satanic forces, which would soon infringe upon it."

16 Cf. Kaiser, et al, 742; Hayford, *Prayer is Invading the Impossible*, 106: "Prayer is essentially a partnership of the redeemed child of God working hand in hand with God toward the realization of His redemptive purposes on earth." John Wesley even said, "God will do nothing but in answer to prayer." "John Wesley Quotes About Prayer," *AZ Quotes*. Retrieved Mar. 9, 2018 at http://www.azquotes.com/author/15507-John_Wesley/tag/prayer.

17 Rom. 10:14, NASB.

18 Lloyd-Jones, 661: "This is God's way of doing things. As He has decided to order and maintain the creation through various laws that He has put into nature, so He has decided to work in the spiritual realm through prayer. God could maintain the universe without the laws of nature, but He does not choose to do it that way."

19 Hayford, *Prayer is Invading the Impossible*, 74: "God hasn't given man charge of the universe, but He did give man charge of this planet."

20 Luke 11:2, NKJV.

21 Law 304: "Prayer is a mighty instrument, not for getting man's will done in Heaven, but for getting God's will done in Earth."

22 John 6:38, NASB.

23 Contra: Zodhiates, *The Epistles of John*, 391. If the Holy Spirit has made known to us the will of God (1 John 2:27), it is not presumption to proactively pray for that to happen on earth. Of course, we must always operate with a humble heart before God, recognizing we are not infallible in our ability to hear God.

24 Luke 22:42, NASB.

25 Cf. Rom. 12:1–2; Josh. 1:8; Deut. 6:6–8.

26 1 Cor. 14:2, 18. Cf. Hayford, *Prayer is Invading the Impossible*, 125–135.

27 Dodd, 134: "For prayer rightly considered is not a device for employing the resources of omnipotence to fulfil our own desires, but a means by which our desires may be redirected according to the mind of God, and made into channels for the forces of His will."

28 Cf. Eph. 6:12.

29 Ray Stedman (p. 362) illustrates the limitations of prayer using the Sears and Roebuck catalog his family received when he was a child. He points out how futile it would be to order items not in the catalog. Within the will of God is everything we need. But when we order items outside the will of God, it doesn't work.

30 Burdick, 389; Zodhaiates, 384.

31 Andrew Murray, *The Ministry of Intercession* (Springdale, PA: Whitaker House, 1982) 92: "Faith has to accept the answer, given by God in heaven, before it is found or felt on earth."

32  Cf. Matt. 21:22.
33  He is not in a state of anxiety over the matter because he knows the answer has been granted. He is looking for the manifestation with confident expectation.
34  John 11:41, NASB.
35  John 11:43, KJV.
36  Daniel demonstrated the same kind of understanding in Dan. 9:1–3.
37  Cf. Dan. 10:12–13.

# CHAPTER 28

# Sin unto Death
## 5:16–17

> If anyone sees his brother sinning a sin which *does* not *lead* to death, he will ask, and He will give him life for those who commit sin not *leading* to death. There is sin *leading* to death. I do not say that he should pray about that. All unrighteousness is sin, and there is sin not *leading* to death.
>
> 1 John 5:16–17, NKJV

### Expository Message

Now we will consider the most serious, sobering subject in all the Bible: sin unto death. It is a very controversial subject, one that I'm tempted to avoid. But if we are to preach "the whole counsel of God" we must not side-step it.[1] We love the truth enough to deal with it.

What is the difference between "sin leading to death" and "sin which does not lead to death"? At one level all sin leads to death. Paul tells us that in Romans 6:23: "The wages of sin is death" (KJV). But John is not speaking in those general terms in our text. He is making a distinction between "sin which does not lead to death" versus "sin leading to death." The KJV simply calls it "sin unto death." What kind of sin is John talking about? Is he talking about sin of Christians or non-Christians? Is he talking about physical death or spiritual death? Those are the kind of questions that have to be answered to understand the term. We will tackle those questions in this study.

As you may recall, in chapter 27 our text was in 1 John 5:14–15. There John talked about confidence in prayer and his focus was praying according to the will of God. We will read those two verses to set the stage for this chapter. "Now this is the confidence that we have in Him, that if we ask anything according to His will, He hears us. And if we know that He hears us, whatever we ask, we know that we have the petitions that we have asked of Him." John continues with the subject of prayer in verse 16. He is still talking about praying according to the will of God in our text. "If anyone sees his brother sinning a sin *which does* not *lead* to death, he will ask, and He will give him life for those who commit sin not *leading* to death. There is sin *leading* to death. I do not say that he should pray about that. All unrighteousness is sin, and there is sin not *leading* to death" (1 John 5:16–17).

Understanding those two verses depends on how we interpret "sin leading to death." Once we know what that is, we can follow John's line of thought without much difficulty. But John does not tell us what he means by this phrase. He and his readers were, no doubt, familiar with the phrase. Therefore, it needed no explanation for them.[2] But we are not familiar with the term, so we have to figure it out as best we can. For that reason, there are various interpretations among good Bible-believing scholars. It is a passage we cannot be dogmatic about. However, we can determine what John probably means from the immediate context, the context of the letter, and other scriptures. We will approach this passage methodically by considering nine questions.

## PHYSICAL DEATH OR SPIRITUAL DEATH?

In the phrase *sin leading to death*, is John talking about physical death or spiritual death? One popular interpretation is that John is talking about God's discipline of His children even to physical death. The strength of this approach is that we know from other passages in the Bible that such a thing exists. Hebrews 12 tells us that God corrects every true child of God. We are all under the discipline of the Lord. Just like any good parent, God is teaching us in very practical ways the difference between right and wrong. He is leading us in paths of righteousness, sometimes by speaking to us through His word, and when that doesn't work, He may spank us through hard circumstances. It's easy to blame the devil, but sometimes God is allowing the consequences of bad decisions to teach us not to do that again. I have learned that He is very merciful and longsuffering, but once He sets in on us with some discipline, it doesn't stop just because we say, "calf rope."[3] It stops when He has determined the discipline has adequately taught us the lesson to be learned. It won't be one second more, and it won't be one second less. So, discipline is a part of God's program for His children. God disciplined Moses for striking the rock when he was told to speak to it. Because of that, God did not allow Moses to go into the Promised Land with Joshua and Caleb. God disciplined David for his sin with Bathsheba. He disciplined him for his pride in counting the people.[4] I have certainly learned, sometimes the hard way, that when He tells you something, pay attention and do it!

There are examples of this discipline unto physical death in the New Testament. Ananias and Sapphira lied about their financial giving to the church. They were presenting themselves as more dedicated than they really were. They were immediately struck dead. The Bible doesn't say whether they went to heaven or hell. So, we can't be sure about that. But they were probably Christians in the community of believers who died a premature death because of their sin.[5] I have seen this happen in the church over the years. It's not easy to talk about when it happens, so I just watch and learn and don't identify it as such. But I'm sure I have seen it a number of times. In Corinth there was a Christian, probably a leader, living in open immorality. Paul told that congregation to deliver him to Satan "for the destruction of the flesh, that his spirit may be saved" (1 Cor. 5:5, KJV). It would be better for the man to suffer a premature physical death than to continue in his sin.[6] And in the following verses Paul talks about how it would protect the church from corruption. That premature death didn't have to happen because the man repented. But I'm sure Paul was talking about the discipline of a sinning Christian with physical death.

In 1 Corinthians 11 Paul was correcting some abuses of the communion service. In verse 29–30 he says, "For he who eats and drinks, eats and drinks judgment to himself if he does not judge the body rightly. For this reason many among you are weak and sick, and a number sleep" (NASB).

When Paul says a number sleep, he is talking about Christians dying a physical death. So, the Bible does teach the discipline of sinning Christians with premature physical death.

However, it is very doubtful that John is talking about that in our text. The context is not physical death but spiritual death. In fact, that is the only way John uses the Greek term *thanatos* (death) in this epistle.[7] Additionally, John's use of the Greek word *zōē* (life) in this epistle is always in reference to spiritual life, not physical life.[8] First John 3:16 talks about physical death when it says Jesus laid down his life for us. But there, John uses the Greek word, *psuchē*, instead of *zōē*. Look how the word *zōē* is used in chapter five. Verse 11, "And this is the testimony: that God has given us eternal life, and this life is in His Son" (NKJV). Verse 12, "He who has the Son has life; he who does not have the Son of God does not have life" (NKJV). Verse 13, "These things I have written to you who believe in the name of the Son of God, that you may know that you have eternal life, and that you may continue to believe in the name of the Son of God" (NKJV). Those are the verses leading up to our text in verse 16, "If anyone sees his brother sinning a sin which does not lead to death, he will ask, and He will give him life [*zōē*] for those who commit sin not leading to death." Then on the other side of our text we have verse 20: "And we know that the Son of God has come and has given us an understanding, that we may know Him who is true; and we are in Him who is true, in His Son Jesus Christ. This is the true God and eternal life" (NKJV).

The context of the epistle as a whole and of the verses surrounding the text convince me John is talking about spiritual life and spiritual death. Humanly speaking, I would like it to be physical death. But if I'm honest with the passage, I must conclude that *sin leading to death* is talking about eternal damnation, spiritual death.[9]

## TWO CATEGORIES OF SINS?

Is John setting up two categories of sins, something like mortal sins versus venial sins? Medieval Catholics set up those two categories. Mortal sins are the more serious violations of God's law that turn the heart from God. If they are not repented of, they result in eternal damnation. Venial sins are less serious violations that are damaging, but do not break covenant with God.[10] However, the evidence is that these categories did not exist in New Testament times. It is very unlikely that John is setting up these two categories of sins.[11] He is obviously distinguishing a specific kind of sin from the others. But he is not suggesting we place sins in the categories of mortal and venial.

## ONE-TIME EVENT OR SETTLED CONDITION OF REBELLION?

Is *sin leading to death* a one-time event or repeated rebellion against God resulting in spiritual death? In our text, John is probably talking about repeated action in both *sin which does not lead to death* and *sin leading to death.* The Greek verb controlling verse 16 does not indicate a one-time act. John uses a present participle for sinning which suggests continuing action.[12] The aorist tense would be better suited for a one-time act. Additionally, the fact that John does not use the article with the Greek word *hamartia* (sin) also makes it unlikely that he is concerned with one specific heinous sin.[13] The context of the epistle as a whole would indicate a kind of sinning that obstinately violates the tests of righteousness, love, and truth.[14] The denial of the biblical Jesus and His atoning sacrifice would certainly mean spiritual death.

I'm not sure the modern translations of "sin leading to death" is an improvement over the simple King James Version, "sin unto death." The Greek is simply *hamartia pros thanaton.* That Greek phrase does not make clear whether the idea is that of a sin that *will* (or will not) lead to death or that of a sin that *has* led to death."[15] Since John is not suggesting prayer for the person, it's probable that the person is already in a state of separation from God that is irreversible or is irrevocably moving to it.[16]

## SOMETHING THAT HAPPENS TO CHRISTIANS OR TO NON-CHRISTIANS?

Is "sin unto death" something that can happen to a Christian or non-Christian? Verse 16 says, "If anyone sees his brother sinning a sin which does not lead to death, he will ask, and He will give him life for those who commit sin not leading to death." So far, he is without question talking about a Christian, "If anyone sees *his brother*" (emphasis mine). Some try to say he just means neighbor,[17] but that argument is just not sustainable.[18] All through this epistle John is very black and white about a person either being a Christian or not being a Christian.[19] He's not going to be vague about the matter here. In this epistle, John uses the term *brother* to refer to Christians. However, some argue he is not talking about a person who has been born again in conjunction with *sin leading to death* because John does not repeat the term brother in that sentence: "There is sin leading to death. I do not say that he should pray about that." Why should he have to repeat the term? He has already said it. The most natural reading of verse 16 is that he is referring to seeing someone considered to be a brother sin, and if it is not a sin leading to death, pray for him; if it is a sin leading to death don't pray for him.[20] John says it a bit more mildly than that,[21] but it is most reasonable that John is talking about people who have been a part of the community of faith in both cases.[22] "If anyone sees his brother sinning." Of course, John would not consider a person who commits *sin unto death* a brother, because that person has renounced the faith. But he is most likely talking about people who at some time have been a part of the orthodox community of faith.[23]

From Scripture as a whole we know this condition can happen to a person who has *never been saved,* and it can happen to someone who has *been saved* but dramatically and decisively renounces the covenant of grace. Let me give you a few examples of both.

For the Scribes and Pharisees this condition culminated in blasphemy against the Holy Spirit. We see that in Matthew 12:24, 31–32 and Mark 3:23, 28–30 where the Pharisees attributed the work of the Holy Spirit to Beelzebub (Satan). For them, "The unpardonable sin was not so much an act as a state of sin, a settled attitude that regards good as evil and evil as good."[24] Jesus said on that occasion, "He who blasphemes against the Holy Spirit never has forgiveness, but is subject to eternal condemnation."[25] The words they said were significant in that they evidenced the condition of their hearts. The blasphemy itself was rooted in their heart condition, in their determined rejection of truth. These people had never been born again, yet they came into this condition by rejecting the light they had from studying Scripture, from hearing Jesus's message, and from seeing His miracles. With all that opportunity, they firmly decided against God's way.

This is an example of people who had never been born again committing "sin unto death."

Judas was privileged to be among the twelve chosen disciples. He heard Jesus's teaching. He saw the miracles Jesus did; he even operated in miracles along with the other disciples.[26] Yet he rejected all that light and remained a thief at heart.[27] No one knew his true spiritual condition but Jesus. After his betrayal of Jesus, he felt remorse even to the point of suicide. But his heart was so hardened that he did not repent.[28] Judas sinned against light.

We are given insight on this hardening process in the case of Pharaoh.[29] Early on he saw the miracles that God worked, confirming the truth Moses and Aaron spoke to him. But his response was to reject that truth and persist in going his own way. During the first five plagues, the Bible says he hardened *himself*.[30] Then there came a point where he was so settled in his decision that *God* even hardened his heart, in recognition of the choice he had made. During the last five plagues, God initiated the hardening process.[31] Once God began to harden Pharaoh's heart, I don't believe it would have done any good to pray for Pharaoh. His decision had already been made.

I have given you some examples of people who never embraced the truth. Through their resistance to the Holy Spirit, they hardened into this state of "sin unto death." But the Bible also teaches that it can happen to people who have been enlightened by the truth and then turned from it. This called apostasy.[32]

The book of Hebrews was written to Christians who were being tempted to go back on their faith. The writer of that epistle is warning them not to do that. In Hebrews 6:4–8 he writes,

> For it is impossible for those who were once enlightened, and have tasted the heavenly gift, and have become partakers of the Holy Spirit, and have tasted the good word of God and the powers of the age to come, if they fall away, to renew them again to repentance, since they crucify again for themselves the Son of God, and put Him to an open shame. For the earth which drinks in the rain that often comes upon it, and bears herbs useful for those

by whom it is cultivated, receives blessing from God; but
if it bears thorns and briers, it is rejected and near to being
cursed, whose end is to be burned (NKJV).

That may be the most sobering word in all the Bible. But it is cautioning
Christians: those who were once enlightened, tasted the heavenly gift,
become partakers of the Holy Spirit, and tasted the good word of God and
the powers of the age to come.

Some try to explain this away by saying these people only "tasted" the
good word of God.[33] But the word translated "tasted" is *geuoami*. Tasted
is an accurate translation, but the word implies eating, and figuratively
means experiencing.[34] The whole tenor of the passage lends itself to that
understanding. The writer of Hebrews is emphasizing the accountability
because their sin is with knowledge. These are people who have been
born again and have experienced the power of God.[35] Peter writes in his
second epistle, "For if, after they have escaped the pollutions of the world
through the knowledge of the Lord and Savior Jesus Christ, they are again
entangled in them and overcome, the latter end is worse for them than
the beginning. For it would have been better for them not to have known
the way of righteousness, than having known it, to turn from the holy
commandment delivered to them" (2 Pet. 2:20–21, NKJV). And Jude 12
talks about people who are *twice dead*. This possibility of apostasy is well
documented in the New Testament.

There is no use praying for an apostate because the person has already
become set in his rejection of God. Like Esau, in Hebrews 12:14–17,
he may regret bad choices, but his heart is too hardened to find sincere
repentance.[36] "There is sin leading to death. I do not say that he should
pray about that" (1 John 5:16). Why does John say that? Because it is
useless to do so. We cannot have assurance of an answer because we are
not praying according to God's will. It is always right for us to intercede
for the salvation of others, except in the unusual case of *sin leading to death*.
In that situation the dye is already cast.

# SIN LEADING TO DEATH?

What is *sin leading to death*? It is a deliberate, persistent turning away from the truth.[37] The person committing "sin unto death" is affirming his decision against God over and over. His heart is so hardened that it will not respond to God's mercy.[38] I am reminded of C. S. Lewis's comment in his book, *The Great Divorce.* "There are only two kinds of people in the end: those who say to God, 'Thy will be done,' and those to whom God says, in the end, '*Thy* will be done.'"[39] The person who commits *sin leading to death* has trampled over God's offer of grace enough to be absolutely certain that is the course he wants to take.

"Sin unto death" is a state of sinning against light past the point of no return.[40] It is not a one-time act, like murder or suicide. It is not the result of an emotional burst of anger against God. Sometimes Christians say terribly stupid things when they're upset. God looks deeper than that; God looks into the heart. "Sin unto death" is a deep decision of the will. It is a hardening of the soul against truth into a confirmed, irreversible rejection of God. Satan is in that condition and so are the fallen angels who follow him. There is absolutely no possibility of repentance because the person no longer has any receptivity to the Holy Spirit. A person can only come to this condition after repeated rejection of truth and hardening the heart against God.

# CONTEXT OF JOHN'S STATEMENTS?

Who does John have in mind when he mentions *sin leading to death*? Most likely, he has the secessionists in mind when he talks about *sin leading to death.*[41] In the overall context of the letter, John is combating Gnostic error. Heretics have left the orthodox community, renouncing the incarnation and deity of Jesus Christ (2:19).[42] John is warning the Christian community against following their error.[43] He is also discouraging the misplaced affection of praying for them as former brothers.[44] These people are antichrists referred to in chapter two. They could have been mere professors in the Christian community or genuine believers who apostatized or a mixture of these. In any case they have made a determined, irreversible decision to reject the Christ of the Bible. They are not humbly asking for forgiveness; they are pridefully insisting that others follow them. John's instruction in verse 16 applies whether they were previously born again or not.

## PROCESS OF FALLING INTO SIN LEADING TO DEATH?

How does someone get in this state of *sin leading to death*? It only comes to those who have made a willful, determined decision against Christ after abundant light and opportunity. Hebrews 10 expresses three actions that must take place for a person to apostatize. Look for them as we read Hebrews 10:26–29.

> For if we sin willfully after we have received the knowledge of the truth, there no longer remains a sacrifice for sins, but a certain fearful expectation of judgment, and fiery indignation which will devour the adversaries. Anyone who has rejected Moses' law dies without mercy on the testimony of two or three witnesses. Of how much worse punishment, do you suppose, will he be thought worthy who has trampled the Son of God underfoot, counted the blood of the covenant by which he was sanctified a common thing, and insulted the Spirit of grace? (NKJV).

Apostasy is much more determined and resolved in its renunciation of Christ than just a person falling into sin, even gross sin. The Christian's struggles with sin are not even close to it. A persistent, evil habit does not constitute apostasy. One must purposefully, arrogantly, resolutely renounce the faith. Here are the three things that must happen: (1) "trampled the Son of God underfoot" (2) "counted the blood of the covenant by which he was sanctified a common thing" (3) "insulted the Spirit of grace" We're not talking about failure. We're not talking about being ensnared in a sinful habit. We're talking about trampling the Son of God underfoot.

When Christians read these passages, they sometimes come under the fear that they or a loved one may have done this. First of all, anyone who has any concern about it, has not done it! The person who commits *sin leading to death* has no fear of God. The person feels no conviction of sin, not because God wouldn't convict, but because he has hardened his heart to the point that all sensitivity to God's conviction is utterly lost. So, get this clear in your mind. If you have any concern whatsoever that you have blasphemed the Holy Spirit, committed the unpardonable sin, apostatized, committed *sin leading to death,* whatever term you want to use, I can tell you without reservation that you have not done it.[45] You would not care at all, if you had actually done that. Secondly, this is only possible for those who have been given truth over and over. There has to be a lot of light rejected for the soul to become this calloused.[46]

## DISCERNING SIN LEADING TO DEATH VERSUS SIN NOT LEADING TO DEATH?

How can we identify *sin leading to death,* as opposed to *sin not leading to death*? I have already given a lot of information in that regard. However, there is usually an overt, public action that evidences the reality of *sin leading to death.* For the Scribes and Pharisees, it was when they publicly called the works of the Holy Spirit the work of Beelzebub. Their determined, set rejection of Christ came to a head that day.

In John's context, it was probably when the secessionists departed from the orthodox community and publicly renounced Christ.[47] They are trampling underfoot the Son of God when they deny the incarnation and deny the deity of Jesus. They are renouncing the faith and rejecting the covenant of grace. They are publicly counting the blood of Christ as a common thing, not effectual for salvation.[48] This public renouncing of the covenant is probably how John's readers could make the determination.[49] We come to that conclusion by examining our text in the context of this whole epistle, in the context of all John's warnings against antichrist and against denying Jesus as the Son of God.[50] John has just said in this chapter, verse 12, "He who has the Son has life; he who does not have the Son of God does not have life." You can't reject the Son and still have life!

A word of wisdom is probably in order here. We should assume we are seeing in others *sin which does not lead to death* until we know, with a high degree of certainty, that it is *sin leading to death.* Mercy and humility should rule the day. In most cases, even when we discern *sin leading to death*, we should keep it to ourselves, and let it inform our own prayer life. To falsely accuse someone of *sin leading to death* could do a lot of damage. At times, a leader may have to warn the flock, just as John is doing in this epistle. There was probably some danger that natural affection toward individuals who had left the orthodox community might make Christians susceptible to their deception. I suspect that is partially why John is confronting Gnostic heresy throughout this epistle. We are to be "wise as serpents and harmless as doves."[51] It is better to err on the side of mercy than to erroneously write someone off as past redemption. With all that analysis, we now address one final question.

## JOHN'S MESSAGE IN THE TEXT?

What is John saying in our text? He makes three clear statements. And he does so with the overriding objective of promoting prayer according to the will of God, specifically prayer for one another. First, John says, "If anyone sees his brother sinning a sin which does not lead to death, he will ask, and He will give him life for those who commit sin not leading to death." John is encouraging these believers to pray for each other. When you see a Christian fall into sin, don't gossip about him, don't criticize and judge him. Pray for him that he might turn from the error of his ways and overcome the sin. Our stance toward other people should always be redemptive. James wrote, "Brethren, if anyone among you wanders from the truth, and someone turns him back, let him know that he who turns a sinner from the error of his way will save a soul from death and cover a multitude of sins" (James 5:19–20, NKJV).

Remember how Jesus treated Peter. By revelation, Jesus knew Peter would deny Him in His darkest hour. But Peter's faith did not utterly fail because Jesus prayed for him. After His resurrection Jesus restored him to fellowship and ministry as well.[52] That is the way we approach a faltering brother or sister in Christ who is *sinning a sin which does not lead to death.*[53]

Secondly, John writes, "There is sin leading to death. I do not say that he should pray about that."[54] John is not forbidding prayer for the person who commits sin leading to death. However, he is not recommending it because it will not do any good. In the context of verse 14–15, it is not according to the will of God, and the prayer will not be answered.

Finally, John tells us, "All unrighteousness is sin, and there is sin not leading to death." In comparison to sin leading to death, sin which does *not lead to death* might seem rather harmless. It is not! Persistence in sin usually leads to greater sin if not repented of. John does not want his readers to think he is minimizing *sin which does not lead to death*. He has repeatedly taught the importance of practical righteousness in our lives. No one should think that he is saying some sins don't really matter. "All unrighteousness is sin."

We have spent a great deal of this chapter analyzing the phrase *sin leading to death*. We had to do that so we could understand what John meant by the phrase. However, that is incidental to the exhortation John is giving. His main point is that we should pray for fellow Christians who are struggling with sin. With the exception of *sin leading to death*, we will always be praying in the will of God when we pray for faltering brothers and sisters in Christ. And because we are praying in the will of God, we have the promise in verse 16 that God will hear us and give life to that person. God will turn that person's heart toward Him and deliver him or her in answer to our prayer. Read the following verses with that in mind.

> This is the confidence which we have before Him, that, if we ask anything according to His will, He hears us. And if we know that He hears us in whatever we ask, we know that we have the requests which we have asked from Him. If anyone sees his brother committing a sin not leading to death, he shall ask and God will for him give life to those who commit sin not leading to death (1 John 5:14-16a, NASV).

Do you have a loved one or friend that is ensnared in sin? Take a moment and pray for that person right now. You can do that with John's assurance that you are praying in the will of God and that God will answer your prayer!

# Endnotes: Chapter 28

1 Cf. Acts 20:27. One value of expository preaching is it tends to require teaching subjects we might not choose.

2 Dodd, 136; Burdick, 391; MacArthur, *1–3 John,* 205; Smalley, 297.

3 "Calf rope" is a cry of surrender. "Definition of calf rope," *Merriam-Webster.* Retrieved Mar. 15, 2018 at https://www.merriam-webster.com/dictionary/calf%20rope.

4 Cf. Num. 20:8–12; 2 Sam. 11–18, 24.

5 Cf. Acts 5:1–11; John MacArthur, *The MacArthur New Testament Commentary: Acts 1–12* (Chicago: Moody Press, 1994) 153; Ironside, 217.

6 A course of sin is a slippery slope. We cannot be sure how far it will take us. God's discipline of premature physical death can be a merciful act on His part.

7 In 1 John 3:14 John clearly uses *thanatos* (death) in reference to spiritual death. Smalley, 188.

8 Kaiser, et al., 742–743.

9 Painter, 319; Law, 138–139. Contra: Boice, *The Epistles of John,* 142; Stott, 187; Stedman, 366–367.

10 Richardson, ed., s. v. "Mortal Sin" by William Hordern, 224; Tim Staples, "Mortal and Venial Sin?" April 14. 2014, *Catholic Answers.* Retrieved Mar. 16, 2018 at https://www.catholic.com/magazine/online-edition/mortal-and-venial-sin.

11 Raymond Brown, 615; Stott, 187–188; Boice, *The Epistles of John,* 141: "Moreover, it may also be said that such a distinction is simply not supportable from the pages of the New Testament and that John, even in this very letter, seems to contradict it (see the discussion on 3:6, 9). Old Testament law did distinguish between unconscious, unwitting sins and deliberate, willful sins (Lev. 4:2, 13, 22, 27, 5:15,17; Num. 15:27–31; Deut. 17:12). The penalty for the willful sins was physical death while the others could be forgiven." Cf. Marshall, 247; Painter, 318; Raymond Brown, 617; Smalley, 297: "But the reference is to *physical* death as the consequence of wrongdoing; whereas the present context speaks of *spiritual* life and death (note the use of zōē. 'life,' in v 16a)" (emphasis Smalley's). While this Old Testament background may have influenced John's thinking, there is not a direct correspondence between these Old Testament passages and John's text. Cf. Yarbrough, 308; Kaiser, et al., 743.

12 Brooke, 146–147; Smalley, 300. Wallace (pp. 524–525) argues against assuming the customary present in 1 John 3:6,9, pointing out the apparent contradiction with 1 John 5:16. Since one cannot be certain how John is intending the present tense in these texts, context becomes very important in the interpretation.

13 Smalley, 298; Yarbrough, 307–308: "That John does not use the definite article and seems to stress the act of sinning rather than precisely to delineate some

particular misdeed weakens the case for seeing here on specific heinous sin (cf. Westcott 1883: 192; Witherington 2006: 553)."

14  Cf. I. Howard Marshall, *The Epistles of John*, New International Commentary (Grand Rapids: Eerdmans, 1978, 247.

15  Raymond Brown, 611. Contra Burdick, 390.

16  Law, 139: "And, if it is evident that *thanatos* means spiritual death,—separation from fellowship with God,—it is also evident that sin *pros thanaton* means, not sin 'tending towards death,' but by which this fatal goal is reached." Kittel and Friedrich, ed., Vol. VI, s. v. "pros with the Accusative," by Bo Reicke, p. 725: "*hamartia pros thanaton*, 'so serious that it leads to death.'" In this text *pros* may mean "issuing in" or result. Cf. Colin Brown, ed., Vol. 3, s. v. "Appendix: Prepositions and Theology in the Greek New Testament: II, N.3 (*1 Jn. 5:16f*)" by M. J. Harris, 1205–1206.

17  Stott, 190. No matter how sincere we are, there is always the danger that we would become so preoccupied with defending a particular theological system that we fail to allow a passage to simply say what it is saying.

18  I. Howard Marshall, 246.

19  1 John 1:6, 7; 2:4, 9–11, 19, 22–23, 29; 3:1, 6–10, 14–15; 4:1–8, 13–16, 20; 5:1–5, 10–12, 16, 18–20.

20  Painter, 317.

21  John does not forbid prayer for the one committing sin unto death. He simply does not suggest it since it will not be effectual.

22  Marshall, 249–250: "The fact that John needed to warn his readers against the possibility of sinning and failing to continue in the truth and the doctrine of Christ (2:24; 2 Jn. 7–11) suggests that he did not altogether exclude the possibility that a person might fall away from the faith into apostasy."

23  Law, 137: "It is a sin which may be committed by Christians, and it is only as committed by Christians that it is here contemplated."

24  Hayford, ed., *New Spirit Filled Life Bible*, s. v. "Matthew 12:31, 32" by J. Lyle Story, p. 1312 and "Mark 3:28–30" by J. Lyle Story, p. 1355.

25  Mark 3:29, NKJV. The King James Version says, "eternal damnation."

26  Cf. Luke 9:1–6.

27  John 12:4–6.

28  Cf. Matt. 27:3–5; John 17:12; Acts 1:25.

29  Kaiser, et al., 142–143.

30  Exod. 7:13–14, 22; 8: 15, 19, 32; 9:7, 34–35; 13:15.

31  Exod. 9:12. 10:1, 20, 27; 11:10; 14:4, 8, 17. God who knows the end from the beginning prophesied this in Ex. 4:21 and 7:3.

32  Cf. Colin Brown, ed., Vol. 2., s. v. "Law" by H. H. Esser, 449: "1 Jn. distinguishes between 'sin unto death' (5:16) which is apostasy from true faith in Jesus, the

Son of God (5:1–12), and 'sin not unto death' (5:16a and 17), which can be confessed and forgiven (1:9).

33 For example: Arthur W. Pink, *An Exposition of Hebrews* (Grand Rapids: Baker Book House, 1954) 291.

34 Strong, "NT: 1089;" Bauer, Walter, *A Greek-English Lexicon of the New Testament and Other Christian Literature*, translated and edited by W. F. Arndt, F. W. Gingrich, and F. W. Danker, 3rd ed. (Chicago: University Press of Chicago, 1979) "*geuoami*, 2" 195: "to experience something, cognitively or emotionally, come to know someth (sic)."

35 Everitt M. Fjordbak, *Hebrews* (Dallas, TX: Wisdom House Publishers, 1983) 218–240; Kaiser, et al., 681–683.

36 Raymond Brown, 616: "Plummer, *Epistles* 122, explains 'the sin unto death' in terms of closing 'the heart against the influence of God's Spirit so obstinately and persistently that repentance becomes a moral impossibility.'"

37 Kaiser, et al., 743; Smalley, 300; Brooke, 146–147: "The form of expression would seem to indicate that the author is not thinking of one particular sin, definite though unnamed. 'There is such a thing as sin which leads to death.' Such a state of sin may find expression in different acts. In the author's view any sin which involves a deliberate rejection of the claims of the Christ may be described as 'unto death.' If *persisted* in it must lead to final separation from the Divine life" (emphasis Brooke's).

38 Cf. Heb. 3:13; 1 Tim. 4:1–2.

39 C. S. Lewis, *The Great Divorce* (New York: HarperCollins Publishers, 1946) 75.

40 Dodd, 136; Brooke, 145–147

41 Painter, 317–318; Law, 141; Raymond Brown, 636: "The best solution by far is that it is the sin of the secessionists. . . . When his readers came to faith and joined the Johannine Community of 'brothers,' they passed from death to life (I John 3:14). By leaving the Community the secessionists have shown that they hate the 'brothers' and have reversed the process by passing from life to death. In that sense theirs is a sin that is unto death." 1 John 2:19 may indicate that those leaving the orthodox community never had life. Brown acknowledges that possibility as well. However, as Painter points out (p. 319), the passage does not exactly say that, and we must be careful not to read more into it than what John intended. The condition of "sin leading to death" can happen in a person who never believed (but had profound opportunity to do so) or it can happen in a person who has received Christ, then later renounced faith in Him (Heb. 6:4–8).

42 Ladd, 663: "We can do no more than interpret 'sin which leads to death' in the context of the whole epistle, and understand it to be the sin of apostasy in deliberate and defiant repudiation of one's Christian faith."

43 Raymond Brown, 632: "Throughout the work his attacks on the secessionists have been provoked by the danger they presented by proselytizing his adherents." Cf. I. Howard Marshall, 245.

44 Raymond Brown, 618.

45 Lloyd-Jones, 678–679

46 Loyd-Jones, 677: "Clearly this is something that cannot exist in unbelievers generally. Unbelievers are not willful, they are not deliberate—they are just blind and ignorant. There are many in the world who say, 'I do not believe this gospel about Jesus being the Son of God; they are incapable of sin against the Holy Ghost. The people who sin against the Holy Ghost are people like the Pharisees—people who claim a knowledge and an interest and an understanding; people like those described in Hebrews 6 . . .'"

47 Law, 141: "Within the Church such sin can be manifested only in one certainly recognizable form—deliberate, open-eyed apostasy from Christ (Heb. 6:4–6)."

48 Cf. 1 John 5:6.

49 There is amazing security for those who embrace the covenant of grace. Unfortunately, we don't have time to teach that in this message, although it is an important balance to this teaching. This security, however, is found only in the covenant of Christ. When a person rejects that covenant (Heb. 10:29), he or she rejects the security that comes with it.

50 Cf. 1 John 2:18–19, 22–26; 3:7–12, 4:1–4, 15; 5:1, 5, 10–11, 20.

51 Matt. 10:16, KJV.

52 Cf. Luke 22:31–34; John 21:1–25. It is noteworthy that there is no record of Jesus praying for Judas when Jesus knew he would betray Him (Matt. 26:21–25; John 13:21–30). Judas had already hardened himself beyond repentance.

53 Cf. Gal. 6:1.

54 Most scholars see John's use of *erōtaō* regarding prayer for *sin leading to death* verses *aiteō* in reference to prayer for is sin not leading to death as simply stylistic for the sake of variety, with no discernable difference in meaning intended for the two verbs. Painter, 316; Smalley, 301. Contra Zodhiates, *The Epistles of John*, 389–392.

# Chapter 29

# Final Assurances
## 5:18–20

We know that whoever is born of God does not sin; but he who has been born of God keeps himself, and the wicked one does not touch him. We know that we are of God, and the whole world lies under the sway of the wicked one. And we know that the Son of God has come and has given us an understanding, that we may know Him who is true; and we are in Him who is true, in His Son Jesus Christ. This is the true God and eternal life.

1 John 5:18–20, NKJV

## Expository Message

John is drawing his letter to a close. He is elderly and knows this could be his last chance to equip his spiritual children for the challenges they will face.[1] The Gnostics are still calling them to a false gospel. The world is still wooing them through the lust of the flesh, the lust of the eyes, and the pride of life. On the one hand, John feels concern for their future. On the other hand, he has taught them well, and God is with them. He just wants to make sure they remember a few key points. He gives these final words of encouragement before concluding the letter.

We see in our text the heart of a pastor. He is like a mother sending her child off to school for the first time. "Now, Johnny, don't worry, Mommy will be back to get you this afternoon. Play good with the other kids and mind your teacher. I love you. Give me a hug." It's akin to Jesus's farewell address to His disciples in the upper room. It reminds me of my feelings when Jeanie and I took our oldest daughter to California for her first day of college. Our last words went something like this. "Karol, you are going to do great. Here is a little extra spending money. Your car is full of gas but watch the gage. Call us if you need anything. We'll call you tomorrow just to make sure you got settled in okay."² I had similar feeling during my last service at Grace Church. After pastoring the congregation for fourteen years, we were very close to the people. We knew God was reassigning us to a new work. But it was not easy to leave. I know exactly what I preached on that day because I wanted to really make it count. What should I tell them in that last message that would help them most? It was something I took very seriously because I wanted them to do well in my absence.

It is not hard to find an outline from our text. Each verse begins with the words *we know*. These are reminders. John has already taught these truths, but they are so important he must at least mention them again before closing the letter. In three cycles, John has administered three objective tests of salvation. We have a subjective assurance of our salvation through the inner witness of the Spirit. In verse 10 of this chapter he writes, "He who believes in the Son of God has the witness in himself." Paul says the same thing in Rom 8:16. "The Spirit Himself bears witness with our spirit that we are children of God" This apprehension of truth is very real, but it is subjective. Our eternal salvation is too important to rest on this one subjective test. So, John has added to that three objective, observable tests that can affirm our salvation. These are the tests of practical righteousness, truth (especially concerning Christ), and love expressed in observable behavior (especially toward our fellow believers). These tests can expose the absence of genuine salvation. However, John's primary purpose is that they would affirm true believers in the faith. He wants these Christians to be grounded in their assurance and, thereby, fortified against the suggestions of the Gnostics that would undermine their faith. So, in 5:13 John states his purpose for writing this letter. "These things I have written to you who believe in the name of the Son of God, that you may know that you have eternal life, and that you may continue to believe in the name of the Son of God" (NKJV). That verse was followed by a word of assurance concerning prayer in verses 14–17. Now he follows that with three final words of assurance.

## ASSURANCE OVER THE POWER OF SIN

In verse 18, John gives assurance of victory over the power of sin. "We know that whoever is born of God does not sin; but he who has been born of God keeps himself, and the wicked one does not touch him." The power of sin is something we all contend with daily. Any sincere Christian is concerned with how he can overcome it. We want to live upright, and honorably before the Lord and before people. We want to represent Him well. But in our experience, we have spent some time in Romans 7. We are well aware of our own frailty and vulnerability to temptation. We remember times when we thought we were strong, yet we failed. The battle with the world and with our own flesh is very challenging. C. S. Lewis made a statement that many of us could attest to in our own experience. "No man," Lewis writes, "knows how bad he is till he has tried very hard to be good."[3] The world thinks highly of themselves because they have set their own moral standards and done pretty well against those standards. The pole jumper who only seeks to jump four feet will probably consider himself a success. But if he will set the goal at fourteen feet he might come to a different conclusion.[4]

John has stated the seriousness of sin in 5:17 when he says, "All unrighteousness is sin" (KJV). Don't take any of it lightly. Now he turns around and balances that with this assurance in verse 18: "We know that whoever is born of God does not sin." God has given you the power to overcome it. You are no longer under its dominion. Paul stated it this way in Romans 6:14: "For sin shall not have dominion over you, for you are not under law but under grace" (NKJV). The divine influence of the Holy Spirit within you will empower you to win the battle with sin. We all have to face the battle. The battle is very real. But God has given you what you need to live above its power.

John has already said something like this back in 1 John 3:9. "Whoever has been born of God does not sin, for His seed remains in him; and he cannot sin, because he has been born of God" (NKJV). The New International Version has made this easier to understand by emphasizing the continued activity often associated with the present Greek tense. So that translation says, "No one who is born of God will continue to sin." John is not saying a Christian will never commit an act of sin. That would contradict statements he made at the end of chapter one and the beginning of chapter two.[5] In verse 16 of this chapter, he has just encouraged Christians to pray for other Christians who are sinning.[6] Like Paul, John recognizes the Christian struggle with sin. But he also assures these Christians that they can live above its power. They may not live a perfect life, but they can live a life characterized by righteousness. In 3:9 he says this is because of the new nature we have received from the Father. The new birth has given us a completely different orientation toward sin and has empowered us by the indwelling Holy Spirit to overcome.

In our text John gives the reason for our victory. First John 5:18 says, "We know that whoever is born of God does not sin; but he who has been born of God keeps himself, and the wicked one does not touch him." Theologians are divided into two camps as to whom the second part of that verse is referring: "But he who has been born of God keeps himself." This translation sees that as a reference to the Christian. It is saying the Christian does not live a lifestyle of sin. Through the power of the new nature, he guards himself against sin, Therefore Satan cannot lay hold on him. There is strong support for that translation. The Revised Standard Version embraces the other camp that takes "he who has been born of God" to mean Jesus. The Revised Standard Version capitalizes the *"He"* to indicate it is referring to Jesus and the New International Version capitalizes "One" for the same reason.

So, we have two different interpretations of the phrase. Both are plausible because the Bible as a whole teaches both truths. On the one hand, we know that the Lord is our shepherd. Ultimately, He watches over us and protects us. In John 17 Jesus talked about how He had kept the disciples while He was on the earth. Then He prayed to the Father in verse 15 saying, "I do not pray that You should take them out of the world, but that You should keep them from the evil one" (NKJV). There is no doubt the Bible teaches God's side of keeping us from the evil one. Psalm 121:4 says, "Behold, He who keeps Israel Will neither slumber nor sleep" (NASB). We draw much comfort in that fact.[7] We also know that if He withdrew His protection, we would be no match for the devil on our own.

401

So, regardless of which camp you're on concerning our text, Scripture tells us that God is protecting us from the evil one.

Equally true, the Bible teaches us to guard ourselves from the evil one. You can do this because "greater is He who is in you than he who is in the world" (1 John 4:4, NASB). You can do this only because of the indwelling of the Holy Spirit. As 1 John 3:9 teaches, it is the new nature within that empowers us to overcome. Let me give a few examples from Scripture where God puts this responsibility on us. Romans 6:11–12: "Even so consider yourselves to be dead to sin, but alive to God in Christ Jesus. Therefore do not let sin reign in your mortal body so that you obey its lusts" (NASB). That's the way we keep ourselves from the evil one. Second Timothy 2:21 says, "Therefore, if anyone cleanses himself from these *things*, he will be a vessel for honor, sanctified, useful to the Master, prepared for every good work" (NASB). James 1:27 also addresses this side of the matter. "Pure and undefiled religion in the sight of *our* God and Father is this: to visit orphans and widows in their distress, *and* to keep oneself unstained by the world" (NASB). James 4:7–8 adds, "Submit therefore to God. Resist the devil and he will flee from you. Draw near to God and He will draw near to you. Cleanse your hands, you sinners; and purify your hearts, you double-minded." (NASB). In this first epistle of John we have the same thing.[8] "And everyone who has this hope in Him purifies himself, just as He is pure" (1 John 3:3, NKJV). First John 5:21: "Little children, guard yourselves from idols" (NASB). There is the divine side of guarding that we cannot do. But there is a responsibility Scripture puts on us that God will not do for us. Both sides of this are scriptural.[9] So, we cannot eliminate either interpretation as untrue.

There is also a textual variance in 1 John 5:18 that enters into the debate. One family of texts has the word *heauton* which is translated "himself." Another family of texts has the word *auton* which is usually translated "him" but is sometimes translated "himself." The evidence for each side is about equal.[10] If the original text is *heauton*, then, without question, this is referring to the Christian, not to Christ. It must be translated "himself." If the original is *auton*, then the more common translation would be "him." However, it could be translated "himself."[11]

I think it is referring to the Christian himself for this reason. Nowhere else in John's writings is Jesus referred to as the begotten, using the Greek word here, *gennaō*. In his gospel he refers to Jesus as *monogenēs*. That is also the Greek word John uses in 1 John 4:9 to refer to Christ. Those passages are translated "only begotten," but the emphasis in the Greek word is on the uniqueness of Christ.[12] If John wanted to refer to Jesus in 5:18, it would have made more sense for him to use *monogenēs,* rather than *gennaō.* Again, John never uses that term *gennaō* to refer to Jesus. Alternatively, since he has been referring to Jesus in the context as the Son of God, it would have made better sense for him to write, "But the Son of God keeps him."[13] Therefore, I think John is saying something very similar to what he has already said in 3:9. The Christian does not live a lifestyle of sin because his new nature motivates and empowers him to guard himself from the wiles of the devil.[14]

Having said all that, the other interpretation is possible and those who adapt it are not violating any scriptural principle. Either way, John is assuring believers that they do not have to be dominated by sin. They can live a victorious Christian life.

"We know that whoever is born of God does not sin; but he who has been born of God keeps himself, and the wicked one does not touch him" (1 John 5:18). Of course, the wicked one is referring to Satan. When we use the word touch we mean light contact. But the Greek word translated touch does not mean that. It means Satan cannot grab him or lay hold on him. He can touch him in the sense of troubling him, tempting him, opposing him. But he cannot take hold of him.[15] So, first in verse 18 we have assurance of victory over the power of sin. Then in verse 19, having processed the three tests of salvation, John brings another assurance.

## ASSURANCE OF BEING "OF GOD"

Verse 19 begins with the words, "We know." The Greek word carries the idea of certainty.[16] This is not a "hope so" position. We have examined ourselves with the three tests John presented in the epistle. We did not prove to be perfect, but we did prove to be genuine. We know we are Christians. No one has sound footing for his walk with God or his battle with Satan until he knows for certain he is born of God and belongs to the Lord. That is foundational. Do you know you are a child of God? This epistle is designed to bring us into that assurance.

John identifies two contrasting facts in verse 19. Let me deal with the second one first. "We know . . . the whole world lies under the sway of the wicked one." This is a profound truth that is denied by most of society. They want us to concede to a kind of "you're okay and I'm okay" position of non-confrontation. This biblical worldview that John sets forth in our text is quite disturbing to them. But we either accept the biblical worldview that John teaches here or we reject that and accept the world's position. John sees only one of two possibilities for every human being. You are either *of God* or you are under the sway and control of the evil one, Satan. There is no other position. A person either receives Christ and is translated from the kingdom of darkness into the kingdom of light or that person is part of Satan's anti-God system.

This worldview has two practical effects on the believer. First, it tells us that our connection with the world is superficial and temporary. John has already told us in chapter two to not love the world. He has told us that the desires of the world are passing away. This world is not our home; our citizenship is in heaven. We have to go into the world to work and shop. There is daily contact with the world. But we are not *of the world*. We are *of God*. Therefore, there is a certain separation from the world and its desires that we are to maintain.[17] This worldview means that we don't give ourselves to the same goals and values that the world embraces.

Secondly, this worldview motivates us to evangelize. If the world is lost and undone, if the world is under the control of God's archenemy Satan and destined for destruction, we want to rescue all of them we can. We were once blinded by the god of this world.[18] We were once under the sway and control of the wicked one. Someone declared to us the good news of Jesus. Someone pointed us to Christ, and we were saved. Now we want others to experience the same mercy. So, we tell them what God has done for us and what He will do for them. God is not willing that any of them perish, and neither are we! This world view has a profound effect on the way we live our lives.

When we pander to the world for favor, when we look to the world for better means and methods, I wonder how much we believe John's statement in this text. Why would we look to a world system under the sway of Satan for guidance? Surely the danger of deception in that is significant. We must continually look to God and the wisdom of His word for our guidance.[19] If we do it God's way, the world will probably not like it. John says in 3:13 of this epistle, "Marvel not, my brethren, if the world hate you" (KJV). There is an animosity between good and evil, between God and Satan. We are wise to recognize that. Jesus said,

> If the world hates you, you know that it has hated Me before *it hated* you. If you were of the world, the world would love its own; but because you are not of the world, but I chose you out of the world, because of this the world hates you (John 15:18–19, NASB).

That is the reality if we are really living for God. It doesn't mean we have to be obnoxious and unkind. No, it happens even when we act in love and compassion toward them. It is simply a fact of life.

The contrast made, and the word of assurance in verse 19 is that we are *of God*. We are born of His seed.[20] We are of a different kingdom. We have a different destiny. John wants us to take courage in that. The Gnostics were claiming to be the ones *of God*. They were claiming spiritual enlightenment. They were telling orthodox Christians to come over to their way of thinking. John is fortifying his spiritual children against that by reminding them of this simple truth: already, we are of God, and we know it without a doubt. If you're a Christian, as John defines it in this epistle, you are *of God* and need nothing from the Gnostics or from the world. Your sufficiency is in God.[21]

## ASSURANCE OF KNOWING THE TRUE GOD AND HAVING ETERNAL LIFE

The third word of assurance is in verse 20, the assurance that we know the one true God and have eternal life in Him. First John 5:20 says, "And we know that the Son of God has come and has given us an understanding, that we may know Him who is true; and we are in Him who is true, in His Son Jesus Christ. This is the true God and eternal life." There are four statements in that word of assurance that we want to consider: four facts we know for sure.

First, "We know that the Son of God has come." John began this epistle declaring the incarnation, and now he brings us back to that truth at the end of the letter. First John 1:1–3 says,

> What was from the beginning, what we have heard, what we have seen with our eyes, what we have looked at and touched with our hands, concerning the Word of Life— and the life was manifested, and we have seen and testify and proclaim to you the eternal life, which was with the Father and was manifested to us— what we have seen and heard we proclaim to you also, so that you too may have fellowship with us; and indeed our fellowship is with the Father, and with His Son Jesus Christ (NASB).

The Son of God has come out of heaven. He has taken upon Himself the form of a man. That positioned Him to offer His body on the cross for our salvation. You've got to know *the Son of God has come.* Without the incarnation there is no salvation. In various ways, the Gnostics have denied this truth. It is non-negotiable as far as John is concerned, and as far as we are concerned as well. John doesn't have time to say much in these last few verses. But one thing he does want to say is this: "We know that the Son of God has come."

Secondly, John adds, "And has given us an understanding, that we may know Him who is true." The Son of God has given us understanding that we may know the Father, "Him who is true." This word translated "understanding" is very interesting. *Dianoia* refers to the faculty of knowing, the ability to reason correctly.[22] It is not so much about the content as the capacity to know, the ability to find truth.[23] We could have never come to Christ in the first place if the Lord had not done this for us. Unbelievers are blinded by the god of this world. They do not have the capacity to see truth.[24] At Paul's conversion, Jesus told him that He was sending him to the gentiles "to open their eyes so that they may turn from darkness to light and from the dominion of Satan to God, that they may receive forgiveness of sins and an inheritance among those who have been sanctified by faith in Me" (Acts 26:18, NASB). Do you realize what God did for you when He opened your eyes to the truth of the gospel, when He gave you the capacity to "know

Him who is true"? Nobody figures it out on his own. He may ponder and consider the historical truth. He may hear the message and evaluate it which is part of the process. But salvation only comes to those who receive the *capacity* to know Him. "The natural man does not receive the things of the Spirit of God, for they are foolishness to him; nor can he know them, because they are spiritually discerned" (1 Cor. 2:14, NKJV). The Gnostics will tell you they know the one true God. But they reject the biblical Christ, and that is the only place you get the faculty for knowing the true God. Jesus has sent the Holy Spirit, and He alone can lead us into truth. So, don't think the Gnostics have it just because they tell you they do. We have it because the Son of God has come and given us *dianoia*, "understanding," the capacity to know God, spirit to Spirit.

Thirdly, "And we are in Him who is true, in His Son Jesus Christ." "We are in the God who is true by being in His Son who is true."[25] To know the Son is to have the Father. To reject the Son is to reject the Father. It is only through the Son that anyone can know the Father. First John 2:23 states that plainly. "Whoever denies the Son does not have the Father; the one who confesses the Son has the Father also" (NASB). So, John is assuring every true believer in Christ, you have the one true God. By receiving His Son, you receive Him.

Finally, "This is the true God and eternal life." The true God here is probably a reference to the Father.[26] Some very good scholars think it refers to the Son.[27] That is possible. Certainly, the New Testament teaches that Jesus is divine. But it seems more natural that John would consistently talk about us knowing the *true God*, the Father, through the revelation given by the Son. Either way John is emphasizing our relationship with the true God in contrast to the false gods that he will mention in verse 21. Stay with the true God! In Him is "eternal life." That has been a major theme in this epistle.

John opens this letter with a declaration of eternal life from the Father through Jesus Christ, and he closes with this theme as well.[28] Nothing is more important than eternal life. In this epistle, John has shown us the way to have that. Do you have eternal life? It is only available through Jesus Christ. It is available to all who will receive it. You receive it by putting your faith in Jesus Christ. "For God so loved the world, that He gave His only begotten Son, that whoever believes in Him shall not perish, but have eternal life" (John 3:16, NASB). First John 5:12 affirms, "He who has the Son has the life; he who does not have the Son of God does not have the life" (NASB). God offers that life to anyone who will humbly receive it.

# Endnotes: Chapter 29

1   Notice in 5:21 how he affectionately addresses his readers as *little children*, just as he has done throughout this letter.

2   Rick Goettsche, "Before You go. . . ." preached April 22, 2007, *Faithlife Sermons*. Retrieved Apr. 1, 2018 at https://sermons.faithlife.com/sermons/90488-1-john-5-18-21.

3   Lewis, *Mere Christianity*, 142.

4   The high standard of righteousness that Jesus proclaims in the Sermon on the Mount is designed to expose man's sinfulness and his need for salvation. No one can live in accordance with those standards without a new nature and the empowerment of the Holy Spirit.

5   Cf. Chapter 14 of this book. Also see Stott, 192.

6   The resolution of John's statements that Christians commit acts of sin, yet do not live a lifestyle of sin seems to be the best explanation of what John is communicating. Most scholars take this position based on the Greek tenses. However, it should be acknowledged that 1 John 5:16 uses the present tense in reference to a sinning brother. While present tense generally means ongoing action, that is not always the case. John is probably referring to repeated action in verse 16 and a more long-term activity in verse 18, but we cannot be absolutely sure of that. When we take biblical teaching on this subject as a whole, we must conclude that a lifestyle of sin for the Christian is inconsistent with the core desires as a child of God. The new nature is a powerful influence that is not present in the unbeliever. Additionally, God disrupts the pattern of sin in a believer by administering disciple according to Hebrews 12.

7   Cf. John 10:27–29; Rom. 8:35–39; Jude 24–25.

8   Also see 1 John 2:13–14. Many other New Testament passages attest to the human responsibility and many passages attest to the divine side. Neither can be dismissed.

9   To embrace the side of human responsibility and dismiss the divine side of protection would ultimately lead to legalism. To embrace the divine side and dismiss human choices and responsibility would ultimately lead to universalism. For a biblical understanding of this matter, the whole counsel of God must be received.

10  Yarbrough, 321; Law, 408; Painter, 320. Zodhiates, *The Epistles of John* (p. 407) prefers the *heauton* text. Contra; Brooke, 148–149.

11  Painter, 323. Cf. Raymond Brown, 621.

12  Burdick, 320–321. Cf. James Hope Moulton and George Milligan, *The Vocabulary of the Greek New Testament* (Grand Rapids: Eerdmans, 1930) 416–417; Painter, 323.

13   Law, 408–409; Raymond Brown, 620: "One would have expected 'the Son of God' if Jesus were meant. . . ." Burdick (p. 392) and Smalley (p. 303) see the shift in *gennaō* from the perfect participle to the aorist participle in 5:18 as an indication John has change from the Christian to a different person, namely Christ. However, Raymond Brown points out the weakness of that position writing, "Finally, as we have seen throughout this commentary, interpretations based on exact Johannine distinctions between the perf. and the aorist are very dubious."

14   Raymond Brown, 622.; Law, 229–230. Cf. Painter, 623–624; Marshall, 252; Smalley, 303; Yarbrough, 316; Burdick, 404–405; Eph. 6:10–18; Jude 21. The Greek word translated "keeps" in 1 John 5:18 is *tēreō* meaning "to be on one's guard" (Zodhiates, *The Epistles of John,* p. 408) or to "keep unharmed" (Bauer, et al., p. 1002).

15   Burdick, 393; Law, 410; Stott, 193; Brook, 149: "The word probably suggests the idea of laying hold of in order to harm."; Zodhiates, *The Epistles of John,* 409: "to touch with the purpose of attaching oneself to."

16   Stott, 191; Smalley, 302; Law, 366, 408: ". . . *eidenai* . . . expresses the fact of knowledge absolutely." Bauer, et al., s. v. "*oida*" (1e) p. 693: "The formula *oidamen 'oti* is freq. used to introduce a well-known fact that is generally accepted." Cf. Spurgeon, "Positivism," preached Sept. 9, 1909. Accessed at The C. H. Spurgeon Collection on CD-ROM (AGES Software, Inc., 1998).

17   Cf. 2 Cor. 6:14–18; Gal. 6:14; 1 Pet. 1:13–16; Lloyd-Jones, pp.691–701.

18   Eph. 2:1–5.

19   Responding to the suggestion that the preacher must catch the spirit of the age, G. Campbell Morgan said, "God forgive him if he does. Our business is never to catch, but by eternal truth to correct the spirit of the age." G. Campbell Morgan, "Preaching," *The G. Campbell Morgan Archive,* Retrieved April 5, 2018 at http://g42leadershipacademy.org/wp-content/uploads/2011/02/Preaching_GCampbellMorgan.pdf.

20   Burdick, 300: "The Greek prepositional phrase *ek tou theou* 'from God,' [source] is to be understood as a shortened form of *gegennēmenos ek tou theou* [3:9] 'born of God' (cf. pp. 224, 291)."

21   Cf. Col. 2:8–10.

22   Rogers and Rogers, 599; Brooke, 150–151; Stott, 194.

23   Colin Brown, ed., vol. 3, s. v. "Reason" by G. Harder, 127; Burdick, 394: "The word translated understanding (*dianoian*) should not be interpreted as designating knowledge or thought content. In light of its general New Testament usage, it can only refer to the capacity to understand. Behm explains that it means that Christ has 'awakened in us the mind and given our thinking the orientation to know God, to receive His revelation. . . .'" See Kittel, ed., Vol. 4, s.

v. "dianoia", by J. Behm. 967. Cf. Zodhiates, *The Epistles of John,* 421; Yarbrough, 318–319; Raymond Brown, 624; 1 John 2:20–21, 27; Jer. 31:33.

24  2 Cor. 4:4; Eph. 4:17–18.

25  Raymond Brown, 625; Yarbrough, 320.

26  Smalley, 308; Stott, 195–196; Law, 413; Painter, 326–327; Boice, *The Epistles of John,* 148–149.

27  Raymond Brown, 625–626. Cf. Wallace, 326–327.

28  Law, 184: "With this theme the Epistle begins (1:2) and ends (5:20), while the purpose of the whole expressly is, 'That ye may know that ye have Eternal Life' (5:13).

# CHAPTER 30

# Idolatry: A Very Real Danger
# 5:21

Dear children, keep yourselves from idols.
1 John 5:21, NIV.[1]

## Expository Message

In the previous three verses John has been assuring these believers in their relationship with *the true God*. In verse 20 he writes, "And we know that the Son of God has come and has given us an understanding, that we may know Him who is true; and we are in Him who is true, in His Son Jesus Christ. This is the true God and eternal life" (NKJV). As believers in Jesus Christ, we are standing on solid ground. We know the true God through Christ. But John has also reminded us in verse 19, "The whole world is under the control of the evil one" (NIV). The world is under the deception of false gods; John does not want us to be deceived by those influences. We are of God. Nevertheless, we must be on guard against the temptations that surround us in the world. Our text is a passionate warning from this father in the faith.

Notice the affection out of which John speaks, referring to them as *dear children*. This is the seventh time he has referred to them with that phrase. John is not speaking cold doctrine. He is speaking loving words of concern. "Be careful; there are dangers lurking all around you. Watch and pray so that you don't give into temptation."[2] At first glance, this last verse in the letter seems to come out of nowhere. But when we take a closer look, it seems perfectly natural that this loving pastor would issue this final warning.[3] "Dear children, keep yourselves from idols." To apply this exhortation to our own lives, we will explore three questions: (1) What is the idolatry John is warning us of? (2) What are the consequences of disobeying this warning? (3) What must we do to obey the passage?

## THE IDOLATRY IN JOHN'S WARNING

What is the idolatry John is warning us of? A good place to begin is with the ten commandments in Exodus 20. The first two commandments will help us understand what John has in mind.[4] Exodus 20:3 gives us the first commandment. There God simply says, "You shall have no other gods before Me (NIV)."[5] That is a prohibition against worshipping or serving false gods.

At times in Israel's history, they forsook the Lord and served false gods.[6] But at other times they violated this commandment by worshipping the true God *and* false gods. That was a subtler violation of this commandment. I would suggest, it is a subtler danger for you and me as well. It is easy to compartmentalize our lives. We come to church on Sunday morning and worship the Lord. Then during the week, do we give ourselves to some form of idolatry? Church on Sunday morning and the bar on Saturday night or perhaps some other violation of this commandment! Listen to what 2 Kings 17:41 says about the people living in Samaria. "Even while these people were worshipping the Lord, they were serving their idols. To this day their children and grandchildren continue to do as their fathers did" (NIV).

The first commandment is sometimes violated by people who turn away from the true God and serve false gods.[7] But that commandment is also broken when people serve God, yet also serve their idols.[8] Elijah confronted that mentality on Mount Carmel. In 1 Kings 18:21 he said to the people of God, "How long will you waver between two opinions? If the Lord is God, follow him; but if Baal is God, follow him" (NIV). God wants all our heart, not just part of it. He will not share His glory with another god or another affection.[9] Jesus said the greatest commandment is "Love the Lord your God with all your heart and with all your soul and with all your mind."[10]

In Exodus 20:4–6 we are given the second commandment.

> You shall not make for yourself an idol in the form of anything in heaven above or on the earth beneath or in the waters below. You shall not bow down to them or worship them; for I, the LORD your God, am a jealous God, punishing the children for the sin of the fathers to the third and fourth generation of those who hate me, but showing love to a thousand [generations] of those who love me and keep my commandments (NIV).

"After the first commandment rejects all other gods, so that only Yahweh remains, the second commandment rejects every wrong form whereby people desire to worship Yahweh."[11] Israel was forbidden to make any carved or molted images to represent the Lord because, as Moses put it in Deuteronomy 4:15, "You saw no form of any kind the day the Lord spoke to you at Horeb out of the fire" (NIV). The way God revealed Himself on Mount Sinai taught them not to equate Him with anything in creation. To depict the eternal, transcendental nature of God in any form seen in creation detracts from His glory.[12] A clear separation from the Creator and His creation must be maintained in worship. God cannot be properly reflected by any image created by man.[13]

Aaron violated this second commandment even while it was being given to Moses. Remember when he molded the golden calf and said to Israel in Exodus 32:4, "These are your gods, Israel, who brought you up out of Egypt" (NIV). That calf was intended as an image of the Lord. In Egypt, Israel was surrounded by idolatry that provided visuals to enhance the worship. "They were not intending to reject the Lord and go serve other gods. They just wanted to worship Him in a manner contrary to the second commandment."[14] So, here is an additional subtlety of idolatry: the idea that I am worshipping the true God, I just want to do it my way. The warning ought to be obvious for pastors. Israel was adapting their worship to the ways of Egypt. That seemed to be more appealing to the people. The people seemed to really enjoy the new "freedom" found in this new way of worshipping Yahweh.[15] You know the rest of the story. You know what God thought of it. We are not free to worship the true God any way we please. We are not free to adapt it to the world's liking. We are to do it according to the revealed will of God in Scripture.[16]

Jeroboam broke this second commandment using two gold calves in the Northern Kingdom. He provided the people a more convenient way of worship. In fact, he said to them in 1 Kings 12:28, "It is too much for you to go up to Jerusalem. Here are your gods, Israel, who brought you up out of Egypt" (NIV). It's almost the same language Aaron used. God had told His people to worship at the temple in Jerusalem. Jeroboam made it easier on the people by providing them two calves to represent the Lord, one in Bethel and one at Dan. That suited the majority of them quite well. Just because it's popular does not mean it's right. God is not nearly as concerned about making our lives comfortable as He is making them meaningful and aligned with His purposes. There is much more we could say about all this.[17] But we're just laying the foundation of what the first two commandments said about idolatry. Commandment one: only worship the Lord. Commandment two: don't make images that represent Him to facilitate the worship. Jesus put it this way in John 4:24, "God is spirit, and his worshipers must worship in the Spirit and in truth" (NIV).

With that background, we will define idolatry as anything that claims the loyalty and adoration that belongs to God alone. Luther said, "Whatever your heart clings to and relies upon, that is your God. . . ."[18] Idolatry "can refer to the worship of other gods besides the true God, or the reverence of images."[19]

At the most obvious level, John was warning his readers against the pagan worship of false gods that occupied the world in which they lived. His reminder to them in 5:19 was, "The whole world is under the control of the evil one." (NIV). There was widespread, blatant, pagan idolatry throughout the Roman Empire. Worship of Caesar himself was even required at times. It's relatively easy to identify that kind of danger.

But idolatry does not always take on such obvious forms. Sometimes it comes as a cute horoscope in the newspaper. Sometimes it is expressed by reliance on government aid instead of relying on the Lord. Sometimes it is a new car or new house. Like Jeroboam, the Gnostics presented an alternative to biblical worship. Some of them were very liberal in their attitude toward sin. Their line of reasoning might go something like this. "Your activities at the pagan festivals are just something done in the body. You're still okay in your spiritual being which is above all that. Go ahead, have some fun and don't worry about it."[20] We don't know all that John had in mind when he issued his warning. But we do know that idolatry can take on many forms and nuances.

Just as in John's day, we are seeing Christians led away from orthodox Christianity with the promise of something better. Like the Gnostics in the early church, there are people promising *secret* knowledge that supposedly liberates from the constraints of God's commandments and biblical beliefs—beliefs insisted on in 1 John. In his book, *The Great Spiritual Migration: How the World's Largest Religion is Seeking a Better Way to be Christian*, Brian McLaren writes,

> For centuries, Christianity has been presented as a system of beliefs. That system of beliefs has supported a wide range of unintended consequences, from colonialism to environmental destruction, subordination of women to stigmatization of LGBT people, anti-Semitism to Islamophobia, clergy pedophilia, to white privilege. What would it mean for Christians to rediscover their faith, not as a problematic system of beliefs. . . ."[21]

Then he goes on to suggest that Christianity ought to be instead a "beloved community for all." To begin with, I don't know how he blames environmental destruction, stigmatization of LGBT people, Islamophobia, and clergy pedophilia on the fact that the church has its system of beliefs. But his suggestion is that if we will abandon our Christians belief system and just be loving and accepting, all will be well.[22] His deception begins by blaming the world's problems on the church's system of beliefs. If we can just see all the evil that proceeds from the church's belief system, we will want to do away with all that teaching and replace it with a community that accepts pretty much any and everything.

Satan's strategy is to pull the foundations of Christian doctrine out from under the people.[23] Take away those solid beliefs. Then you can feed them whatever error you want to. That prepares the way for any variety of idolatrous behavior. This intense, sinister attack against Christian beliefs is going on right now.

In Colossians 3:5 Paul identifies covetousness as idolatry.[24] He writes, "Mortify therefore your members which are upon the earth; fornication, uncleanness, inordinate affection, evil concupiscence, and covetousness, which is idolatry" (KJV). In another place he says, "The love of money is a root of all evil."[25] The materialism in America is like the paganism in the first century. For many the "almighty dollar" is what they live for. They do whatever they can to get it, and once they get it they hold onto it with a tight fist. Why is this love of money their priority? It is their source of status; it buys them comfort and pleasure; it is also their source of security.

We make a serious mistake when we dismiss 1 John 5:21 as only a warning for first century Christians. It is a very real danger for you and me now. It may take a different form, but idolatry is alive and well today. It is obvious in the occult and false religions. But it is there in subtler forms too. Materialism, the love of pleasure, pornography, sports, drugs, gluttony, and a long list of other things that can steal our affections and lead us away from God. Religion can even become an idol. I recently had a lengthy discussion with a Jehovah's Witness. The woman was extremely devoted to her religion. The more I talked with her, the more I saw strong loyalty to that, and the less I saw love for the Lord. Her message was not "Jesus Christ and Him crucified." Her message was "join my religion." It shut her off from receiving truth. A religious spirit forbade her openness to anything other than her cult. She is following a Gnostic concept of God much like the antichrists John talks about in chapter two. Worshipping a false concept of God is a form of idolatry.[26] One person defined idolatry as "worship of a god that man creates instead of worshipping the God who created man."[27]

What draws people into idolatry? The core motivation is self.[28] In fact, self-worship is the foundation of it all. Eve chose her own desires over the revealed will of God. Her pursuit of the tree of the knowledge of good and evil was idolatry. In our society self-image, self-realization, self-promotion are idols being pursued all around us.[29] In biblical times people pursued Baal and other false gods for prosperity. The orientation was "what's in it for me?" In 2 Chronicles 28 King Ahaz sacrificed to the gods of Syria because he thought they could help him. They did not help him. Baal worship was focused on getting good crops and therefore prospering.[30] God has a way of prospering His people. But when people are loving and pursuing the prosperity, rather than loving and pursuing God, there is a problem.

When people are *using* God to get what they want, they're actually in idolatry. A vivid example of this is found in 1 Samuel 4. There the people of God turned the ark of the covenant into a magic idol in order to get what they wanted.[31] It did not work for them. Beware of preachers who teach you how to use God for your own purposes. Notice how the words *for yourselves* or *for themselves* are associated with idolatry. Exodus 20:4 says, "You shall not make *for yourself* an image" (emphasis mine, NIV). Second Kings 17:16: "And made *for themselves* two idols cast in the shape of calves, and an Asherah pole" (emphasis mine, NIV). Selfishness is the root of idolatry. God told Zechariah to ask the people, "When you fasted and mourned in the fifth and seventh months for the past seventy years, was it really for me that you fasted? And when you were eating and drinking, were you not just feasting for yourselves?" (Zech. 7:5–6, NIV).[32] This selfishness can get into our most religious activities if we don't keep our hearts right.

People pursue idolatry because it makes them feel alive. It excites their emotions. It gives them the feeling they want. The shopaholic wants that buzz. So does the gambler. People fall into sexual additions because they want their passions aroused. In Isaiah 57:5 God said the idolaters were enflaming themselves with idols under every green tree.[33] Idolatry is about getting legitimate needs met in illegitimate ways. Instead of looking to God, looking to something else to find fulfillment! Your idol, or at least your potential idol, is that thing you love to do, that person you want to please, that possession you worked hard to buy. Where are your affections? What excites you and motivates you? What do you love more than anything else? Those are the things we must watch out for.

## THE CONSEQUENCES OF IGNORING JOHN'S WARNING

What are the consequences of disobeying the warning in our text? Lessons on this subject motivate us to be on guard against idolatry. We don't have time to be thorough, but let me just touch on a few consequences of idolatry.

A loss of spiritual perception follows idolatry. Psalm 115:4–8 begins describing the blindness and dumbness of idols. But notice how this passage concludes by ascribing this same blindness to the idolaters as well.

> But their idols are silver and gold, made by the hands of men. They have mouths, but cannot speak, eyes, but they cannot see; they have ears, but cannot hear, noses, but they cannot smell; they have hands, but cannot feel, feet, but they cannot walk; nor can they utter a sound with their throats. Those who make them will be like them, and so will all who trust in them" (emphasis mine, NIV).[34]

They have rejected the word of the Lord; and what wisdom is in them?[35] Wisdom comes through the counsel of the Lord. But idolatry cuts us off from God's counsel. God told Ezekiel concerning the elders of Israel, "Son of man, these men have set up idols in their hearts and put wicked stumbling blocks before their faces. Should I let them inquire of me at all?" (Ezek. 14:3, NIV). The idols in the heart blocked their ability to successfully inquire of the Lord. Idolatry at its core is always a heart condition.[36]

Idolatry leads to captivity. We see that in the overall history of Israel. The principle remains the same today. In 2 Kings 17 the Lord gave the northern kingdom into captivity to Assyria. Verse 15–20 says,

> They rejected his decrees and the covenant he had made with their fathers and the warnings he had given them.[37] They followed worthless idols and themselves became worthless. They imitated the nations around them although the LORD had ordered them, 'Do not do as they do,' and they did the things the LORD had forbidden them to do. They forsook all the commands of the LORD their God and made for themselves two idols cast in the shape of calves, and an Asherah pole. They bowed down to all the starry hosts, and they worshiped Baal.

> They sacrificed their sons and daughters in the fire. They practiced divination and sorcery and sold themselves to do evil in the eyes of the LORD, provoking him to anger. So the LORD was very angry with Israel and removed them from his presence. Only the tribe of Judah was left, and even Judah did not keep the commands of the LORD their God. They followed the practices Israel had introduced. Therefore the LORD rejected all the people of Israel; he afflicted them and gave them into the hands of plunderers, until he thrust them from his presence (NIV).

Notice the phrase, "Gave them into the hands of plunderers." They went into bondage as a consequence of their idolatry.

God's people are destroyed because of a lack of knowledge.[38] They often find themselves in bondage and wonder what happened. Idolatry leads to bondage. Addictions and life-controlling habits are often developed in acts of idolatry. The alcohol becomes a substitute for the comfort of the Holy Spirit and leads to alcoholic captivity. Drug addictions follow the same pattern. Greed begins with the desire for more, but as it is pursued it becomes a life-controlling passion. Sexual addictions happen the same way. We are not designed to be self-sufficient. We need God in order to be fulfilled. Everything we need is in Him. But if our hearts draw back from God, we will find ourselves trying to fulfill those needs in some other way.[39] That is always idolatry. That always leads to captivity.

Idolatry leads to a loss of God's presence. Notice the statement in 2 Kings 17:18, "So the LORD was very angry with Israel *and removed them from his presence*" (emphasis mine, NIV). That last phrase is repeated in verse 20 and again in verse 23. It is a point that God does not want us to miss. The presence of the Lord is a precious thing.[40] It is something to be cherished and guarded. We don't want to ever grieve the Holy Spirit through idolatrous practices.[41]

When Adam pursued the forbidden fruit, he was driven from the Garden where he had enjoyed the manifest presence of God. He lost the intimacy he once had with the Lord.[42] In David's prayer of repentance he pleaded, "Do not cast me from your presence" (Ps. 51:11, NIV). I'm talking about the loss of intimacy with God because of idolatry.

God pronounced this sad judgment on Ephraim, the northern kingdom in Hosea 4:17: "Ephraim is joined to idols: let him alone" (KJV). One thing I don't want God to ever do to me is to leave me alone. I need Him every hour. I need His correction. I need His guidance. I need His encouragement and strength. "One thing have I desired of the Lord, that will I seek after; that I may dwell in the house of the Lord all the days of my life, to behold the beauty of the Lord, and to enquire in his temple."[43] One thing I don't want is for the Lord to leave me alone. Amen?

Idolatry also leads to shame. Isaiah 44:9–11 says,

> They that make a graven image are all of them vanity; and their delectable things shall not profit; and they are their own witnesses; they see not, nor know; that they may be ashamed. Who hath formed a god, or molten a graven image that is profitable for nothing? Behold, all his fellows shall be ashamed: and the workmen, they are of men: let them all be gathered together, let them stand up; yet they shall fear, and *they shall be ashamed together* (emphasis mine, KJV).

The idolatry of Achan brought shame on the whole nation of Israel at Ai.[44] The captivity of Israel was an experience filled with shame. It was a result of their idolatry. The shame can always be traced back to the thing worshipped or served. In Hosea 9:10 God said,

> I found Israel Like grapes in the wilderness; I saw your fathers As the firstfruits on the fig tree in its first season. *But* they went to Baal Peor, And separated themselves to that shame; They *became an abomination like the thing they loved* (emphasis mine, NKJV).

Notice the link between what they pursued and what they became. They became an abomination *like the thing they loved*. The covetous man becomes a miser. The lustful man becomes a pervert. The one who pursues vanity becomes superficial. The resentful become bitter. The idolatry carries in it its own judgment. So here is perhaps the most alarming consequence of idolatry.

Idolatry reproduces itself in the idolater. We become like the thing we worship. Look back with me at this statement in 2 Kings 17:15, "They followed worthless idols and themselves became worthless" (NIV). The horror of idolatry is that it changes who you are. It affects your character. Gregory Beale said it this way, "What you revere you resemble, either for ruin or for restoration."[45]

We see the positive side of this in 2 Corinthians 3:18. What happens to us when we love and serve the Lord? Paul writes, "But we all, with unveiled face, beholding as in a mirror the glory of the Lord, are being transformed into the same image from glory to glory, just as from the Lord, the Spirit" (NASB). Ponder the wonder of that statement. As we worship and serve the Lord, we are changed into His image from one level of glory to the next. That happens because we, as human beings, are designed to be reflectors of the glory of God.[46] The Lord showed me this principle years ago in a vision. It was later when I saw it in Scripture. God is His own source of light and glory.[47] He is not a reflector of glory; He is the eternal source of glory. We are not our own source of glory. As the moon reflects the glory of the sun, we are privileged to reflect the glory of God. And as we give ourselves to Him and worship Him, our capacity for that increases.

The problem with idolatry is that the principle works the same way. We become like that which we devote ourselves to. Jeremiah 2:4–5 says essentially the same thing we read in 2 Kings 17.

> Hear the word of the Lord, O house of Jacob, all you clans of the house of Israel. This is what the Lord says: "What fault did your fathers find in me, that they strayed so far from me? They followed worthless idols and became worthless themselves" (NIV).

There it is again. "They followed worthless idols and became worthless themselves" Could anything be more important than what you are becoming? You are becoming something. What you are at the end of life's process is of upmost importance. God's desire is that we would become like

Jesus.[48] That happens as we look to Him, worship Him, and serve Him. But those who follow worthless idols become like their idols.

Romans 1:18–21 provides insight on how this happens

> The wrath of God is being revealed from heaven against all the godlessness and wickedness of men who suppress the truth by their wickedness, since what may be known about God is plain to them, because God has made it plain to them. For since the creation of the world God's invisible qualities-his eternal power and divine nature-have been clearly seen, being understood from what has been made, so that men are without excuse. For although they knew God, they neither glorified him as God nor gave thanks to him, but their thinking became futile and their foolish hearts were darkened (NIV).

Now watch this process closely in verses 22–23. "Although they claimed to be wise, they became fools and exchanged the glory of the immortal God for images made to look like mortal man and birds and animals and reptiles" (NIV). In other words, they went into idolatry. We will see in what follows that this idolatry elevates and serves the creature rather than the Creator. Idolatry fails to give God His rightful place. Verses 24–25 says,

> Therefore God gave them over in the sinful desires of their hearts to sexual impurity for the degrading of their bodies with one another. They exchanged the truth of God for a lie, and worshiped and served created things rather than the Creator-who is forever praised. Amen (NIV).

The transformation is happening because God withdraws His restraint on their wickedness. Part of the judgment on idolatry is God letting the person pursue their own passion even into shameful perversions. Idolatry precedes homosexuality. According to this verse, that is not something people are born into, although the propensity toward it may be there. It is something they fall into through idolatry. This may not happen in a single generation; the pattern of decline described in this passage often occurs over multiple generations.[49]

> Because of this, God gave them over to shameful lusts. Even their women exchanged natural relations for unnatural ones. In the same way the men also abandoned natural relations with women and were inflamed with lust for one another. Men committed indecent acts with other men, and received in themselves the due penalty for their perversion (NIV).

They receive into their own personality and character the penalty for their sin. The sin changes who they are and conforms them into something base.

> Furthermore, since they did not think it worthwhile to retain the knowledge of God, he gave them over to a depraved mind, to do what ought not to be done. They have become filled with every kind of wickedness, evil, greed and depravity. They are full of envy, murder, strife, deceit and malice. They are gossips, slanderers, God-haters, insolent, arrogant and boastful; they invent ways of doing evil; they disobey their parents; they are senseless, faithless, heartless, ruthless. Although they know God's righteous decree that those who do such things deserve death, they not only continue to do these very things but also approve of those who practice them (Rom. 1:28–32, NIV).

We have seen enough of the consequences of idolatry to know that we don't what to go down that path.

## THE WAY TO OBEY JOHN'S WARNING

What do we need to do to obey John's exhortation? "Dear children, keep yourselves from idols." First, we must guard ourselves from the danger. We must be on the alert. "Watch and pray so that you will not fall into temptation."[50] The person that is not on guard is vulnerable. The person who pridefully thinks he is above failure is not thinking right. 1 Corinthians 10 reminds us of Israel's failure in the wilderness. Then it says to us in verse 12, "Therefore let him who thinks he stands take heed that he does not fall" (NASB). One way we stay on guard is to thoughtfully pray this every day: "And lead us not into temptation, but deliver us from the evil one."[51] By that prayer, we humbly recognize our dependence on the Lord and our confidence in His ability to keep us.

The temptation toward idolatry comes at us through "the lust of the flesh, and the lust of the eyes, and the pride of life."[52] John dealt with that in chapter two of this epistle. There we are told to watch out for these temptations and in 2:15 we are commanded, "Love not the world, neither the things that are in the world" (KJV). If we will set our affections on things above and not on the things of the world, we will be fine.[53] In Deuteronomy 12:30 God talks about the gentile nations in Canaan. Then He gives this warning to Israel: "And after they have been destroyed before you, be careful not to be ensnared by inquiring about their gods, saying, 'How do these nations serve their gods? We will do the same'" (NIV). Stay innocent concerning evil.[54] Don't inquire into the occult. Don't seek knowledge in the devil's playground. Stay in the word of God. Paul told Timothy, "Take heed to yourself and to the doctrine. Continue in them, for in doing this you will save both yourself and those who hear you." [55] The Lord told Joshua,

> This book of the law shall not depart from your mouth, but you shall meditate on it day and night, so that you may be careful to do according to all that is written in it; for then you will make your way prosperous, and then you will have success.[56]

Second, we must run from idolatry. Don't play around with it or it will play with you. I knew a man who had been clean and sober from alcohol for thirty years. One day he decided to just have one occasional beer to soothe his stomach pain. He became a raging alcoholic, drunk every day. Don't let the devil tell you that you can handle it. Don't think you can play with it and not get bitten.[57] Paul tells us to run from it!

"Therefore, my beloved, flee from idolatry" (1 Cor. 10:14, KJV). He then tells the Corinthians the sacrifices gentiles make to idols are being made to demons. The idol itself is nothing. But the demon inhabiting the idol is a false god. You cannot mess around with that stuff without invoking the Lord's judgment. First Corinthians 10:21 warns, "You cannot drink the cup of the Lord and the cup of demons too; you cannot have a part in both the Lord's table and the table of demons" (NIV). A clear separation must be maintained between us and the demonic activities of the world. "He who has been born of God keeps himself, and the wicked one does not touch him" (1 John 5:18, NKJV). Keep your guard up and stay away from all forms of idolatry.

Third, stay close to the Lord. "Draw near to God and He will draw near to you."[58] If we will feed off His presence, if we will delight ourselves in the Lord, we will enjoy an immunity from the temptations of the world around us. Our needs will be met by Him, and we will not be seeking other ways to meet those needs. Prayer, Bible study, and other disciplines are not always exciting. But the practice of these disciplines keeps our focus on the Lord as our source. "How," Hebrews 2:3 asks, "shall we escape if we neglect so great salvation?" (KJV). The danger comes when we begin to neglect the things of God. Guard your heart and stay close to Jesus. "Dear children, keep yourselves from idols."

# Endnotes: Chapter 30

1 The New King James Version includes the word amen at the end of the verse because the *Textus Receptus* has it in that family of manuscripts. The New International Version correctly excludes it. Cf. Yarborough, 325: "External support for the omission of *amēn* is decisive."

2 Cf. Matt. 26:41; 1 Thess. 5:6; 1 Peter 4:7.

3 Smalley, 309: "John's 'tender address' (Stott, 196), with which we are now familiar, replaces a formal farewell." Raymond Brown's interpretation (10) connects the idols in 5:21 to the "the secession from the Community, which has led former brothers to a different understanding of God reflected in Christ. . . ." (p. 628). He says, ". . . traditional Jewish usage would make 'idols' a perfect antithesis to 'the one true God' of 5:20. In my judgment Brown's interpretation (10) makes perfect sense of this antithesis, and it connects 5:21 tightly to the mention of sin, the Evil One, and the world in 5:18–19" (p. 629).

4 John was a Jew. Surely, the first two commandments would be somewhere in his thinking as he talks about idols. He was also familiar with Israel's history with idolatry which I will refer to later in this message.

5 Barker, ed., *The NIV Study Bible,* s. v. "Ex. 20:3, before" by R. Youngblood and W. C. Kaiser, Jr., p. 114: "The Hebrew for this word is translated 'in hostility toward' in Ge 16:12; 25:18. Something of that sense may be intended here."

6 For example, they did this in Judges 2:11–13; 10:6; 1 Kings 11:4–8; Jer. 11:9–10.

7 Manasseh brought his idolatry into the house of worship and profaned the sanctuary with it (2 Chron. 33:4–5). This strikes me as particularly heinous.

8 Solomon was led into this kind of compromise by his foreign wives (1 Kings 11:4–6 NIV).

9 Cf. Isa. 42:8; 48:11.

10 Matt. 22:37, NIV; Cf. Deut. 6:5; Matt. 10:37–39.

11 Jochem Douma, *The Ten Commandments: Manual for the Christian Life*, trans. by Nelson D. Kloosterman, 1931 (Phillipsburg, NJ: P & R Publishing, 1996) 35.

12 Ibid., 40: "An image attempts to make the Incomprehensible comprehensible. But in this way, the craftsman seeks to control God, when the reverse is in fact the case: Yahweh controls man and will not allow Himself to be controlled."

13 Cf. Gregory K. Beale, *We Become What We Worship: A Biblical Theology of Idolatry* (Downers Grove, IL: InterVarsity Press, 2008) 18–20.

14 Douma, 36.

15 Eugene Peterson, "Spirituality for All the Wrong Reasons," *Christianity Today*, March 2005, p. 45: "Do we realize how almost exactly the Baal culture of Canaan is reproduced in American Church culture? Baal religion is about what makes me feel good. Baal worship is a total immersion in what I get out of it.

And of course, it was incredibly successful. The Baal priests could gather crowds that outnumbered followers of Yahweh 20 to 1."

16  I am not saying we should not be relevant in the way we communicate our message to the culture. But we should remain cognizant of the fact that the Bible includes much more warning against compromise than exhortation to be relevant to the culture. Yes, Paul said in 1 Cor 9:22, "I have become all things to all people so that by all possible means I might save some" (NIV). But there are many, many passages that warn against adapting to the ways of the world. The 1 John 5:21 text is one of them. Tozier's astute observation is applicable, ". . . the sea is always trying to get into the ship, and the world is always trying to get into the church." A. W. Tozier, *The Tozier Pulpit: Selections from his Pulpit Ministry*, Vol. 1, compiled by Gerald B. Smith (Camp Hill, PA: Christian Publications, 1994) s. v. Book 3, Ten Sermons from the Gospel of John, p.159. Cf. Lev. 10:1–3.

17  The violation of the second commandment by Jeroboam paved the way for the widespread violation of the first commandment later in the history of the northern kingdom. With their worship more closely resembling pagan worship under Jeroboam, the transition into worshipping false gods in a similar fashion would not seems so dramatic. Perhaps there is a lesson in this for us today. Also, in Israel's history worship at the high places was worship of Yahweh according to their own liking, yet contrary to God's revealed will. Cf. 2 Kings 17:9–12; 18:22.

18  Martin Luther as quoted by Gregory. K. Beale, p. 17.

19  Beale, 17. Douma (p. 60) discusses how the Catholic Church, at the second Council of Nicaea in 787 A.D, justified images of Christ, Mary, angels, and saints by arbitrarily distinguishing veneration from worship. For the very interesting history of the second Council of Nicaea see Philip Schaff, *History of the Christian Church*, Vol. IV, pp. 459–463.

20  The alarming thing today is that this cavalier attitude toward sin is sometimes taught in the name of imputed righteousness. Without imputed righteousness we could not be righteous. But when it's on the inside, it will manifest in the external behavior (1 John 3:7).

21  Brian D. McLaren, *The Great Spiritual Migration: How the World's Largest Religion Is Seeking a Better Way to Be Christian* (London: Hodder & Stoughton, 2016), 3.

22  McLaren continues, "Could Christians migrate from defining their faith as a system of beliefs to expressing it as a loving way of life?" (p. 3). As loving as that sounds on the surface, it is not consistent with the New Testament. In this epistle John insists on a belief system as a test of authentic Christianity (1 John 5:1–3). In this epistle John insists on keeping the commandments of God as a test of really knowing God (1 John 2:3). The end result of unbiblical tolerance

can ultimately be very damaging. How wise would it be for a family with young children to accept a convicted pedophile to live in the home with no censure on that behavior. The result of that would not be loving at all. Cf. 1 Cor. 5:1-9; 15:33.

23 Cf. Ps. 11:3. The relativism in the American culture is making its way into the church. God has provided absolutes in His word that give footing for right living. Once those foundations are abandoned, people are vulnerable to dangerous error in both doctrine and lifestyle. The church can change its methods as long as they remain consistent with biblical principles. However, the mission (Matt. 28:18–20) and message (1 Cor. 2:2) of the church is firmly established in Scripture and must not be altered. Yet McLaren argues for fluidity in those as well. He writes, "We Christians have repeatedly adapted our message, methods and mission to the contours of our time" (p. 3).

24 Dietrich Bonhoeffer wrote, "Fornication and greed are idolatrous because in such cases a person's heart no longer belongs to God but rather the objects of desire of their own world." As quoted by Brian S. Rosner in *Greed as Idolatry: The Origin and Meaning of a Pauline Metaphor* (Grand Rapids: Eerdmans, 2007) 30.

25 1 Tim. 6:10, KJV; Cf. Eph. 5:5; Luke 16:13; 18:18–24.

26 The Pharisees of Jesus's day idolatrously served their religion yet rejected the living God. Cf. Matt. 23:14–15; Mark 7:8–13; John 5:39–42; Rom. 2:22; Beale, pp. 166–171.

27 Richardson, ed., s. v. "Idolatry" by William Hordern, p. 165.

28 Cf. Phil. 3:19, "Their destiny is destruction, their god is their stomach, and their glory is in their shame. Their mind is set on earthly things" (NIV). Characteristic of idolatry is setting the mind on earthly things. Rebellion and stubbornness, an insistence on having my own way is as witchcraft and idolatry (1 Sam. 15:23, KJV).

29 Caesar worship vividly illustrates man's desire for his own deification. Cf. Dan. 3; Rom. 1:25; Rev. 13:14–15.

30 Beale, 105.

31 Cf. Douma, p. 47. 1 Sam. 15:23 says, "For rebellion is as the sin of witchcraft, and stubbornness is as iniquity and idolatry" (KJV). The fundamental issue in witchcraft and idolatry is *control*. The correct relationship for us as redeemed creatures to our Creator is one of submission and obedience. When we are insisting on having our own way, we are in the wrong mindset before God (Luke 11:2). When we are trying to manipulate God to do what we want Him to do, we are dangerously close to witchcraft. Witchcraft is an attempt to maneuver spiritual powers for one's own purposes. Even when people are using legitimate Christian means, but operating out of a stubborn, unsubmitted will, they can function in idolatry. This is what Israel did in 1 Sam. 4. Rather

than submitting themselves to God in repentance, they turned the Ark of the Covenant, a legitimate symbol of God's presence, into an idol. The result was judgment, not blessing. Cf. My message preached April 23, 2018 from 1 Sam. 4 entitled, "Fetching the Ark," available at https://www.sermoncentral.com/ sermons/fetching-the-ark-richard-tow-sermon-on-231510?ref=SermonSerps.

32 Cf. Isa. 58.

33 NIV says, "You burn with lust among the oaks and under every spreading tree." Cf. Exod. 32:5–7, 25.

34 Cf. Ps. 135:15–18.

35 Jer. 8:9, KJV. Cf. Rom. 1:21–23; Hosea 4:11: "Harlotry, wine, and new wine enslave the heart" (NKJV).

36 Applying the second commandment can be challenging because the attitude and condition of the heart matters. For Moses and David, the ark of the covenant was not an idol at all. But Israel seemed to use it as one in 1 Sam. 4. God did not consider the brazen serpent an idol in Num. 21. But Israel later used it as an idol according to 2 Kings 18:4. Identifying an image as idolatrous is not as easy as it might first appear. Perhaps Paul's teachings in Rom. 14 and 1 Cor. 8 on issues of conscience are helpful in making the practical application.

37 In our text John is giving us this warning with emphasis on personal responsibility. "Dear children, keep yourselves from idols" (NIV).

38 Cf. Hos. 4:6–7, KJV.

39 Cf. Jer. 2:13; Isa. 55:2; Luke 15:16; John 7:37; Ps. 81:9–10.

40 Exod. 33:15.

41 Eph. 4:30. Cf. Heb. 3:10–17.

42 Beale, 133: "There is no explicit vocabulary describing Adam's sin as idol worship, but the idea appears to be inextricably bound up with his transgression."

43 Ps. 27:4, KJV.

44 Josh. 7; Cf. Isa. 1:29; 42:17.

45 Beale, 11.

46 Ibid., 22, 90, 110, 128–132.

47 Cf. 1 John 1:5; John 1:4; 8:12; Rev. 21:23; 22:5.

48 Cf. Rom. 8:29.

49 It is beyond the scope of this book to deal specifically with the complexities of propensities toward particular sins through Adam's fall, family line iniquities, and generational curses. Cf. Ex. 34:6–7.

50 Matt. 26:41, NIV. Cf. 1 Thess. 5:6.

51 Matt. 6:13, NIV.

52 1 John 2:16, KJV.

53 Cf. Col. 3:1–2; Rom. 8:5.

54 Cf. Rom. 16:19; Isa. 8:19.

55   1 Tim. 4:16, NKJV.
56   Josh. 1:8, NASB.
57   Cf. Prov. 6:27–29; 23:31–32.
58   Jas. 4:8, NASB.

# Conclusion

The purpose of this book is to call us, the church, back to the biblical criteria for assurance of salvation, as taught by the Apostle John in this epistle.[1] The church's departure from this revelation has been very costly. While there are pockets of spiritual fervency, much of the Western church is lukewarm and ineffective.[2] Many are unprepared for the challenges that lie ahead.[3] One reason for this condition is our failure to adhere to this biblical truth. We have substituted religious tradition for the word of God, and, in doing so, deprived ourselves of the benefits of God's instruction.[4]

By neglecting the tests of salvation given by John, we have drifted into what many call "easy believism." After quoting 1 John 5:12–14, Billy Graham wrote,

> It should not be surprising if people believe easily in a God who makes no demands, but this is not the God of the Bible. Satan has cleverly misled people by whispering that they can believe in Jesus Christ without being changed, but this is the devil's lie. The Bible teaches that belief in Him changes a person.[5]

In an interview on October 15, 2013 with *Christianity Today*, Graham said that before his conversion he thought he was a Christian. But his life changed on November 1, 1934 when he repented and turned his life over to God. Listen to the comment that he then makes in the interview. "If there is no change in a person's life, he or she must question whether or not they possess the salvation that the gospel proclaims. Many who go to church have not had a life-changing transformation in Christ."[6] Do *you* know that you have eternal life? If not, seek God until you know. You can have that assurance.

Other great men have warned against abandoning the rigors of discipleship taught by Jesus.[7] Before his death in 1912, William Booth issued an alarmingly prophetic warning. He said, "I consider that the chief dangers which confront the coming century will be religion without the Holy Ghost, Christianity without Christ, forgiveness without repentance, politics without God, and heaven without hell."[8] Dietrich Bonhoeffer's description of "cheap grace" follows a similar line of thought. He wrote, "Cheap grace is the grace we bestow on ourselves. Cheap grace is the preaching of forgiveness without requiring repentance, baptism without church discipline, Communion without confession. . . ."[9] One protection against this cheap grace is the teaching John has provided in his first epistle.

We evangelicals have often criticized other sections of the church for using external rituals as the criteria for assurance of salvation, such as baptismal formulas, church membership, participating in the denomination's administration of the Eucharist, etc. Have we not found our own ritual in "the sinner's prayer"? Instead of going to John's teaching in this epistle to help people find assurance, in many cases we assure people of salvation simply because they walked through some "ritual." I am not proposing we stop using the sinner's prayer. I am proposing we stop using it as *the* assurance of salvation. When used correctly it can help the seeker find words for his or her repentance and commitment to Christ.

Easy believism is attractive to leaders because it offers short-term, superficial signs of success. Evangelists can boast large numbers of converts, and pastors can celebrate large Sunday attendance. But we must make sure we're racing toward the right finish lines. The Great Commission is a call to make "disciples," not mere professors. Our safety is found in fidelity to the word of God. That will produce the right long-term results. We have revelation in 1 John concerning the assurance of salvation. It is there for our enlightenment.

What criteria for assurance of salvation have we learned from John in this letter? John recognizes the subjective test of internal assurance by the Holy Spirit. In 1 John 5:10 he writes, "He who believes in the Son of God has the witness in himself" (NKJV). This, of course, agrees with Paul's statement in Rom 8:16, "The Spirit Himself bears witness with our spirit that we are children of God" (NKJV). This subjective test should not be ignored. But John also gives three objective tests. These provide evidence that the supernatural, internal transformation has taken place. First, the test of practical righteousness should be considered. Those who genuinely have the imputed righteousness of Christ will demonstrate that by living in obedience to God.[10] Secondly, the person who is truly born again will demonstrate love for his or her brothers and sisters in Christ in practical ways. It will be more than an inner feeling. It will be expressed in observable, unselfish behavior.[11] Finally, authentic Christianity is based on belief in the truth, especially truth concerning who Christ is and the way of salvation He provides. Salvation is based on truth; it cannot be enjoyed through a lie. John points to specific beliefs about Jesus that must be addressed.[12] When a person is looking for assurance of salvation, these are the tests that should demonstrate the genuineness of his or her faith. We should use 1 John to help that person find eternal life and find assurance of eternal life. That is the main take away from John's epistle.[13] Failing to apply that revelation can be a matter of life and death. I don't just mean physical death; I am referring to eternal destinies! "These things" says John, "I have written to you who believe in the name of the Son of God, that you may know that you have eternal life, and that you may continue to believe in the name of the Son of God" (1 John 5:13, NKJV).

# Endnotes: Conclusion

1   When our congregation began this study, our purpose was simply to understand John's message more fully and apply that to our lives. As the Holy Spirit unveiled the central message in this epistle, the urgency to call the church back to this revelation emerged and this book was born.

2   In Rev. 3:14–22, Jesus called the Laodicean church to repent of her lukewarm condition. The Laodicean church probably represents the last period in church history, a time we may be living in now. W. A. Criswell points out the irony of the Laodicean's boasting in the light of their anemic spiritual condition. In their own eyes, their wealth and superficial success was evidence of their need for nothing. Criswell tells about the shock a Christian from a Communist country experienced when he saw the apathy and compromise of the American church. That man said he could not tell an American Christian from one who is not a Christian. We know that tares will be growing up with the wheat until the end of the age (Matt. 13:24–30). There will be professors of Christianity who are not genuinely born again mixing with true believers. However, as leaders in the church, we are responsible to preach biblical truth so that those mere professors have every opportunity to repent and have eternal life. If we substitute religious tradition for the word of God, their blood is on our hands! Criswell, *Expository Sermons on Revelation*, Vol. 2, pp. 167–176.

3   Cf. 2 Tim. 3:1; Luke 21:8.

4   In Mark 7:5–13 Jesus confronted the religious leaders of His day for substituting their own tradition for what the Bible plainly taught. In verse 13 He corrected them for "making the word of God of no effect through your tradition which you have handed down. . . ."

5   Billy Graham, *The Reason for My Hope: Salvation* (Nashville, TN: W Publishing of Thomas Nelson, 2013) 118.

6   "Q&A: Billy Graham's Warning Against an Epidemic of 'Easy Believism,'" *Christianity Today*, October 15, 2013, retrieved June 1, 2018 at http://www.christianitytoday.com/ct/2013/october-web-only/billy-graham-interview-my-hope-easy-believism.html?start=1.

7   Cf. Matt 16:24–25: "Then said Jesus unto his disciples, If any man will come after me, let him deny himself, and take up his cross, and follow me. For whosoever will save his life shall lose it: and whosoever will lose his life for my sake shall find it" (KJV).

8   William Booth, "William Booth Quotes," *Goodreads*. Retrieved June 1, 2018 at https://www.goodreads.com/author/quotes/151267.William_Booth. Cf. Paul Lee Tan, ed., *Encyclopedia of 7700 Illustrations: Signs of the Times*, 1128.

9   Dietrich Bonhoeffer, *Goodreads*. Retrieved June 1, 2006 at https://www.goodreads.com/quotes/83530-cheap-grace-is-the-grace-we-bestow-on-ourselves-cheap.

10  Cf. 1 John 1:8–2:6; 2:29–3:10; 5:3–5.

11  Cf. 1 John 2:7–17; 3:10–23; 4:7–5:3.

12  Cf. 1 John 2:18–28; 3:24–4:6; 5:3–21. There is a growing fad in the church to be "non-doctrinal." Some pastors boast that they avoid doctrinal matters and leave it up to the individual to decide what to believe. This is very different from the way the apostles operated. The New Testament is a doctrinal statement. Are the post-modern trends in our culture influencing our thinking on this? There are many non-essentials that we cannot be dogmatic about, and when we differ with one another we should do so humbly and respectfully. But the church is to be the pillar and ground of the truth (1 Tim. 3:15). Truth matters!

13  In the context of today's church environment, these tests may seem unduly demanding. But they are designed to bring real assurance of salvation, not false hope. We should have more confidence in God's wisdom revealed in Scripture than in our own reasoning power. We can trust His counsel!

# Selected Bibliography

Allen, David L. *1-3 John: Fellowship in God's Family*, Preaching the Word. R. K. Hughes, gen. ed. Wheaton, IL: Crossway, 2013.

Barclay, William. *The Letters of John and Jude*. The Daily Study Bible Series. 1958. rev. ed. Philadelphia, PA: Westminister Press, 1976.

Barker, Kenneth L., ed. *NIV Study Bible, 1985*. Grand Rapids: Zondervan, 1995.

Barna, George, and David Barton. *U Turn*. Lake Mary, FL: Frontline, 2014.

Bauer, Walter. *A Greek–English Lexicon of the New Testament and Other Christian Literature*. Translated and edited by W. F. Arndt, F. W. Gingrich, and F. W. Danker. 3rd ed. 1957. Chicago, IL. University Press of Chicago, 1979.

Beale, Gregory K. *We Become What We Worship: A Biblical Theology of Idolatry*. Downers Grove, IL: InterVarsity Press, 2008.

Boice, James M. *Genesis: An Expositional Commentary*. Grand Rapids: Zondervan, 1982.

—. *The Epistles of John: An Expositional Commentary* . Grand Rapids: Baker Books, 2004.

Bonhoeffer, Dietrich. *The Cost of Discipleship*. Trans. R. H. Fuller, rev. ed. New York: MacMillan Publishers, 1960.

Brooke, A. E. *A Critical and Exegetical Commentary on the Johannine Epistles*. The International Critical Commentary. Edinbrugh: T. & T. Clark, 1863, .

Brown, Colin, ed. *The New International Dictionary of New Testament Theology*, 4 vols., 1967. Grand Rapids: Zondervan, 1986.

Brown, Raymond E. *The Epistles of John.*, The Anchor Bible. Vol. 30. Garden City, NY: Doubleday & Co., 1982.

Bruce, F. F. *The Epistles of John: Introduction, Exposition and Notes* . Grand Rapids: Eerdmans, 1979.

439

Burdick, Donald W. *The Letters of John the Apostle: An In-depth Commentary.* Chicago: Moody Press, 1985.

Burge, Gary M. *The Letters of John.* Grand Rapids: Zondervan Publishing, 1996.

Cairns, Earle E. *Christianity Through the Centuries, 1954.* Grand Rapids: Academic Books Zondervan, 1981.

Carson, D. A. Exegetical Fallacies, 2nd. ed. Grand Rapids: Baker Books, 1996.

Cassuto, U. *A Commentary of the Book of Genesis.* Part 1. trans. by Israel Abrahams . Jerusalem: Magnes Press, 1978.

Chafer, Lewis Sperry. *Systematic Theology.* 1947. 7 vols. Dallas, TX: Dallas Seminary Press, 1974.

Chandler, Russell. *Understanding the New Age.* Dallas, TX: Word Publishing, 1988.

Colson, Charles with Ellen Santilli Vaughn. *The Body: Being Light in Darkness.* Dallas, TX: Word Publishers, 1992.

Criswell, W. A. *Expository Sermons on Revelation: Five Volumes Complete and Unabridged in One.* 1962. Grand Rapids: Zondervan, 1978.

—. *Expository Sermons on the Book of Daniel.* 4 vols. Grand Rapids: Zondervan, 1972.

Dodd, C. H. *The Johannine Epistles .* London: Hodder and Stoughton, 1946.

Douma, Jochem. *The Ten Commandments: Manual for the Christian Life.* Trans. by Nelson D., 1931. Phillipsburg, NJ: P & R Publishing, 1996.

Edgar, Brian. *The Message of the Trinity: Life in God.* Vol. in Bible Themes Series. Ed. Derek Tidball. Downers Grove, IL: InterVarsity, 2004.

Fettke, Tom, ed. *The Hymnal for Worship & Celebration.* Waco, TX: Word Music, 1986.

Fjordbak, Everitt M. *Hebrews.* Dallas, TX: Wisdom House Publishers, 1983.

Friberg, Timothy and Barbara Friberg and Neva F. Miller. *Analytical Lexicon to the Greek New Testament. Baker's Greek New Testament Library.* Grand Rapids: Baker Books, 2000. Accessed in Electronic Database: Bibleworks. v. 6.0. 2003.

Gonzalez, Justo L. *The Story of Christianity.* Vol. 1 & 2. New York: HarperCollins Publishers, 1984.

Graham, Billy. *The Reason for My Hope: Salvation.* Nashville, TN: W Publishing of Thomas Nelson, 2013.

Grant, R. M. *Gnosticism and Early Christianity.*1959. 2nd. ed. New York: Columbia University Press, 1984.

Guthrie, Donald. *New Testament Introduction.* rev. ed. Downers Grove, IL: InterVarsity Press, 1990.

Hart, Archibald D. *Unlocking the Mystery of Your Emotions.* Dallas, TX: Word Publishing, 1989.

Hayford, Jack W. *Prayer Is Invading the Impossible.* Great Britain: Bridge Publishing: Chepstow, Gwent, 1985.

—., ed. *The New Spirit Filled Life Bible.* Nashville, TN: Thomas Nelson, 2002.

Hoeller, Stephan A. *The Gnostic Jung and the Seven Sermons to the Dead.* Wheaton, IL: The Theosophical Publishing House, 1982.

Ironside, H. A. *Address on the Epistles of John and an Exposition of the Epistle of Jude.* 1931. Neptune, NJ: Loizeaux Brothers, 1979.

Jamieson, Robert, and A. R. Fausset, and David Brown. *Jamieson, Fausset, and Brown's Commentary On the Whole Bible.* 1871, Accessed in electronic data base: Biblsoft 2000.

Kaiser, Walter C. Jr., P. H. Davids, F. F. Bruce, and M. T. Brauch. *Hard Sayings of the Bible.* Downers Grove, IL: InterVarsity Press, 1996.

Keener, Craig S. *The IVP Bible Background Commentary: New Testament.* Downers Grove, IL: InterVarsity Press, 1993.

Kittel, G., and Friedrich, G. *Theological Dictionary of the New Testament.* Translated by G. W. Bromiley. 10 vols. Grand Rapids: Eerdmans, 1964–1979.

Knight, Walter B., ed. *Knight's Master Book of New Illustrations. 1956.* Grand Rapids: Eerdmans, 1979.

Ladd, George Eldon. *A Theology of the New Testament.* Grand Rapids: Eerdmans, 1974, rev. ed., 1993.

Law, Robert. *Tests of Life: A Study of the First Epistle of St. John.* Edinburgh: T. & T. Clark, 1909. 3rd ed. Grand Rapids: Baker Book House, 1968.

Lewis, C. S. *Mere Christianity.* London: C. S. Lewis Pre. Ltd., 1952, revised and amplified, New York: HarperCollins Publishers, 2001.

—. *The Great Divorce.* New York: HarperCollins Publishers, 1946.

Liardon, Roberts. *God's Generals: Why They Succeeded and Why Some Failed*. Tulsa, OK: Albury Publisher, 1966.

Lindell, H. G. and Robert Scott, H. S. Jones, and R. McKenzie. *Lindell–Scott Greek–English Lexicon*. Oxford: Oxford University Press, 1843. Accessed in Electronic Database: Bibleworks. v. 6.0. 2003.

Lockyer, Herbert. *All the Messianic Prophecies of the Bible*. Grand Rapids: Zondervan, 1973.

Lohse, Eduard. *The New Testament Environment*, trans. John Steely. Gottingen, Germany: Vandenhoeck & Ruprecht. 1971. Nashville, TN: Abington Press, 1989.

Loyd–Jones, Martyn. *Life in Christ: Studies in 1 John*. Wheaton, IL: Crossway, 2002.

Luther, Martin. *Commentary on the Epistles of Peter and Jude*. Oringinally published: *The Epistles of St. Peter and St. Jude*. Minneapolis, MN: Lutherans in All Lands Co. 1904. Reprint. Grand Rapids: Kregel Publications, 1982.

MacArthur, John. *The MacArthur New Testament Commentary, 1–3 John*. Chicao, IL: Moody Press, 2007.

—. *The MacArthur New Testament Commentary: Acts 1–12*. Chicago, IL: Moody Press, 1994.

Marshall, I. Howard. *The Epistles of John*. New International Commentary. Grand Rapids: Eerdmans, 1978.

McQuilkin, Robertson. *Understanding and Applying the Bible*. Chicago, IL: Moody Press, 1992.

Moulton, James H., and George Milligan. *The Vocabulary of the Greek New Testament*. Grand Rapids: Eerdmans, 1930.

Murray, Andrew. *The Ministry of Intercession*. Springdale, PA: Whitaker House, 1982.

Nee, Watchman. *The Spiritual Man: In Three Volumes*. New York: Christian Fellowship Publishers, 1968.

Packer, J. I. *Knowing God*. Downers Grove, IL: InterVarsity Press, 1973.

Painter, John. *1, 2, and 3 John,* Sacra Pagina Series. Vol. 18. D. J. Harrington, ed. Collegeville, MN: Liturgical Press, 2002.

Pink, Arthur W. *An Exposition of Hebrews*. Grand Rapids: Baker Book House, 1954.

Pinnock, Clark H. *Flame of Love: A Theology of the Holy Spirit.* Downers, IL: InterVarsity Press, 1996.

Richardson, Alan, ed. *A Dictionary of Christian Theology.* Philadelphia, PA: Westminster Press, 1969.

Robertson, A. T. *Robertson's New Testament Word Pictures.* 1930. Accessed in electronic data base: Biblesoft 2000.

Rogers, Cleon L. Jr., and Cleon L. Rogers III. *The New Linguistic and Exegetical Key to the Greek New Testament.* Grand Rapids: Zondervan, 1998.

Rosner, Brian S. *Greed as Idolatry: The Origin and Meaning of a Pauline Metaphor.* Grand Rapids: Eerdmans, 2007.

Roukema, Riemer. *Gnosis and Faith in Early Christianity.* Harrisburg, PA: Trinity Press, 1999.

Rowell, Edward, ed. *Fresh Illustrations for Preaching & Teaching from Leadership Journal.* Grand Rapids: Baker Books, 2000.

Rudolph, Kurt. *Gnosis: The Nature and History of Gnosticism.* 1977. Trans. by R. M. Wilson. San Francisco: Harper & Row, Publishers, 1984.

Schaeffer, Francis A. *Genesis in Space and Time: The Flow of Biblical History.* Downers Grove, IL: InterVarsity Press, 1972.

Schaff, Philip. *History of the Christian Church.* 8 vols. Grand Rapids: Eerdmans, 1910, reprint 1976–1977.

Scott, John R. W. *The Epistles of John: An Introduction and Commentary.* Grand Rapids: Eerdmans, 1971.

Smalley, Stephen S. *1, 2, 3 John,* Word Biblical Commentary, Vol. 51, David Hubbard, ed. Waco, TX: Word Books, 1984.

Spurgeon, Charles H. *The C. H. Spurgeon Collection.* Accessed on CD–ROM. AGES Software, Inc. 1998.

—. *The Gospel of the Kingdom: A Popular Exposition.* Pasadena, TX: Pilgrim Publishing, 1974.

Stedman, Ray C. *Expository Studies in 1 John: Life by the Son.* Waco: Word Books, 1980.

Stevens, Denny. *The Speaking God.* Blooming, IN: Westbow Press, 2015.

Strong, James. *New Exhaustive Strong's Numbers and Concordance with Expanded Greek–Hebrew Dictionary.* Originally published: The Exhausive Concordance of the Bible, Cincinnatit: Jennings & Graham. 1890. Accessed in electronic data base: Biblsoft 2000.

Stronstad, Roger. *The Prophethood of All Believers: A Study in Luke's Charismatic Theology.* London: Sheffield Academic Press, 2003.

Thayer, Joseph. *Thayer's Greek Lexicon.* 1896. Accessed in electronic data base: Biblesoft 2000.

Tozier, A. W. *The Tozier Pulpit: Selections from his Pulpit Ministry.* Compiled by Gerald B. Smith. 2 Vol. Camp Hill, PA: Christian Publications, 1994.

Vincent, Marvin R. *Vincent's New Testament Word Studies.* 1903. Accessed in electronic data base: Biblesoft 2000.

Wallace, Daniel B. *Greek Grammar Beyond the Basics : An Exegetical Syntax of the New Testament : with Scripture, Subject, and Greek Word Indexes.* Grand Rapids: Zondervan, 1996.

Wesley, John. *The Works of John Wesley.* 1774. Accessed in electronic data base: Biblesoft 2000.

Westcott, Brooke Foss. *The Epistles of St. John: The Greek Text with Notes,* 1883. Grand Rapids: Eerdmans, 1974.

Wiersbe, Warren W. *Be Real.* Wheaton, IL: Victor Books, 1984.

—., ed. *Treasury of the World's Great Sermons.* Grand Rapids: Kregel Publishers, 1993.

Willard, Dallas. *The Spirit of the Disciplines: Understanding How God Changes Lives.* San Francisco, CA: HarperSanFarancisco, 1988.

Yarbrough, Robert W. *1–3 John,* Baker Exegetical Commentary on the New Testament, R. W. Yarbrough and R. H. Stein, eds. Grand Rapids: Baker Academic, 2008.

Zodhiates, Spiros. *The Complete Word Study Dictionary: New Testament. 1992.* Iowa Falls, IA: World Bible Publishers, Inc., 1994.

—. *The Epistles of John: An Exegetical Commentary.* Chattanooga, TN: AMG Publishers, 1994.

# Scripture Index

447

# Subject Index

## A

Abide, 21, 26, 45, 54, 62, 76, 116, 121–122, 126, 134–135, 139–144, 165, 188, 191, 198–199, 206, 211–212, 221, 235, 238, 265–267, 274, 276, 280, 286, 290, 325, 330, 337, 375, 395, 425

Advocate. *See* ; *See* Jesus Christ

Anointing, 76, 121–136, 143, 199, 236, 243, 296, 375

Antichrist, 4, 111–118, 121, 133–134, 136, 138, 140–141, 233, 238, 241, 243, 271, 311, 391

Antinomianism, xix, 84, 171, 173, 319, 322

Apostasy. *See* ; *See* Sin leading to death

Assurance, xvii, 25, 33, 41, 45, 71, 78, 81, 84, 89, 134, 150, 166, 180, 189, 220–221, 223, 264–266, 268–269, 271–276, 278–286, 312, 316–318, 325, 333–334, 350, 356, 360–361, 368–371, 375–377, 388, 399–400, 403, 405, 433–435, 437

Atonement, 25, 28, 33, 36, 41, 46–48, 57, 71, 163, 179, 181, 194, 228, 239–240, 255–256, 270, 330, 340–342, 345, 347–348, 350, 359, 372, 390–391

## B

Baptism. *See* ; *See* Jesus Christ

Barna Research, 172

Beliefs. *See* ; *See* Tests of Salvation

Bible. *See* ; *See* Word of God

Blood. *See* ; *See* Atonement

Borden, William story, 166

Born again, xvii, 60, 132, 142, 152, 154, 159, 164, 170–173, 179–180, 182–188, 198, 206, 210, 248, 250, 266, 268, 279, 293, 296, 304, 311–312, 316–319, 321, 325, 339, 345, 359–360, 369, 386–388, 390, 435–436

## C

Cain, 76, 194–197, 201–202, 204, 217, 298

Call of Duty game, 236

Chldren of God. *See* ; *See* Born again & love

Church, xvii, 2–5, 8, 15, 18, 22, 24, 27, 38, 42, 44, 48, 55, 67, 72, 84, 95, 101–103, 109, 115–116, 125, 128–129, 134–141, 144, 152, 159, 171–172, 176, 194, 207, 214, 224, 235–236, 243, 264, 294–295, 305, 312, 319, 322, 330, 365, 368, 374, 383, 413, 428, 433–434, 436–437

Colson, Charles, 22

Commandments. *See* ; *See* Tests of
Salvation
Conscience, 12, 173, 197, 218–232,
370, 372
Continue. *See* ; *See* Abide
Cults
Ancient, 43, 55, 65, 129, 152,
342, 417
Modern, xix, 65, 90, 116, 127,
140, 161, 238, 241, 247,
250, 340, 417, 425

# D

Death, spiritual, 40, 77, 88, 118, 198,
237, 250, 335, 381–382, 384–
385, 387, 389, 393, 435
Deception, xvii, 14, 21–22, 44, 75,
86, 112, 115, 122, 134–135,
137–139, 143–144, 171–172,
177, 235, 245, 298, 307, 356,
392, 404, 412
Steve Hill warning, 44
Devil, 41, 45, 85, 92, 97, 99, 108, 113,
170, 175–178, 197–198, 235,
237, 285, 328, 344, 370, 398,
402, 404, 425
Divinity of Christ. *See* ; *See* Jesus
Christ
Doctrine
Apostles', 135, 191, 245
Christology, 117, 238, 247, 255,
271, 395
False, 26, 48, 56, 58, 88, 116,
129, 136, 182, 266,
271, 317
Minimizing importance of, 117,
137–138, 315
Sound, 4, 20, 118, 138, 140, 145,
248, 264, 316, 318, 425

# E

Easy believism, 312, 433
Eternal life, xvii, 1, 71, 77, 142, 197,
263, 270, 293, 317, 350, 355–
356, 359, 363, 384, 407, 435
Knowing God, 60, 143, 266, 368
Quality of, 5, 253, 256–257, 265,
318, 364

# F

Faith
Demonstrated by behavior, 64,
69–70, 115–117, 142–143,
191, 202, 212, 230, 234,
246, 282, 311–312, 322,
328–329
Evidence for, 357–361, 365
In Christ, 6, 11, 16, 48, 52, 87,
91–92, 94, 132, 134, 137–
138, 158, 163, 168, 181–
182, 201, 223, 229, 270,
274, 281, 284, 304, 315,
324–325, 328, 330–331,
335, 339–340, 355–356,
365, 377, 379, 387, 391–
392, 396, 407, 435
False teachers. *See* ; *See* Deception
& Test the spirits
Fear, 17, 19, 25, 150, 242, 267, 279–
281, 283–284, 286–289, 327,
390, 421
Reverence, 8, 163, 197, 287–288
Fellowship
Koinonia, 1–2, 8, 34, 38, 63, 70–
71, 77–78, 90, 94, 142–143,
165, 178, 207, 318, 364,
368, 395
Light, 12, 14–17, 19–21, 24–26,
33, 36, 43, 85, 104, 229,
238–239
Porcupine illustration, 2

Printed in the United States
By Bookmasters